A MANUAL OF HINDU LAW

Owing to the antiquity and rarity of this book, certain pages are regrettably absent, and readability is compromised due to the blurring of the original text. If you possess any insights regarding the availability of these missing sections, kindly inform us. Your assistance is crucial in ensuring the completion of this significant work for the benefit of future generations.

A MANUAL OF HINDU LAW

STANDISH GROVE GRADY

GYAN

Published by

GYAN

Gyan Publishing House
5, Ansari Road
Daryaganj, New Delhi-110002
Phone: 011-47034999, 9811692060
E-mail: books@gyanbooks.com

Distribution Network
gyanbooks.com
India, USA, Canada, UK, Australia

ISBN: 978-93-6920-031-3 (HB)

First Published, 1871

2nd Impression 2025

Printed at: Gyan Press, Delhi.

A MANUAL OF HINDU LAW
Arthur STANDISH GROVE GRADY

A MANUAL

OF

HINDU LAW.

A MANUAL OF HINDU LAW.

FOR THE USE OF

STUDENTS AND PRACTITIONERS.

BY

STANDISH GROVE GRADY,

BARRISTER-AT-LAW, RECORDER OF GRAVESEND,
READER ON HINDU AND MOHAMMEDAN LAW, AND THE LAWS IN FORCE IN BRITISH INDIA,
TO THE INNS OF COURT.

Author of the "Law of Fixtures and Dilapidations, Ecclesiastical and Lay," and Joint-Author of the "Law and Practice of the Crown side of the Court of Queen's Bench;" Author of the "Hindu Law of Inheritance," the "Mohammedan Law of Inheritance and Contract," and Editor of the "Institutes of Menu and of the Hedaya."

LONDON:
WILDY & SONS, LINCOLN'S INN ARCHWAY.
ADVERTISING AND PRINTING CO., LIMITED.
167 POPHAM'S BROADWAY, BLACKTOWN, MADRAS.
1871.

Dedicated,

WITH

KIND PERMISSION,

TO

THE RIGHT HONOURABLE

SIR EDWARD RYAN, KNT., C.B.,

LATE CHIEF JUSTICE OF THE SUPREME COURT OF CALCUTTA,
PRESIDENT OF THE CIVIL SERVICE COMMISSION,
AND VICE-CHAIRMAN OF THE COUNCIL OF LEGAL EDUCATION,

AS A

Tribute of Respect

FOR HIS

DISTINGUISHED SERVICES

IN

THE CAUSE OF EDUCATION,

BOTH

IN ENGLAND AND IN INDIA.

BY

THE AUTHOR.

PREFACE.

I HAD not been long engaged in discharging the duties attached to the readership in Hindu and Mohammedan law in the Inns of Court, until I became convinced that students in the Hindu law have to encounter serious difficulties, in consequence of the want of some simple elementary work to elucidate and unfold its principles. At one time I thought that those elementary principles might be found in Sir Thomas Strange's *Elements of Hindu Law*, or Sir William H. Macnaghten's *Principles;* but the inquiries of my pupils as to what alterations and changes time, the development of society, and intercourse with the outer world had wrought in that law, soon satisfied me that they could not trace, in works published upwards of forty years ago, the existing state of the law upon any given subject.

Admitting the reasonableness of the grounds of this objection, I felt that it would be unfair to students to require them to devote time and attention to works which conveyed *no idea of the existing law*, and which failed to point out those decisions which had been overruled by more recent declarations of the law, as laid down in the High Courts and in the Privy Council. I therefore determined to prepare a Manual on Hindu law, including the principles of the law of contract, as a companion work to my manual on *The*

Mohammedan Law of Inheritance and Contract, in the hope that it will be found useful to the student preparing either for the bar or the civil service. I have pointed out the divergence in the different schools, marking the distinction in each, and have as frequently as possible endeavoured to effect this by contrasting the law under the head of each school, and where I have omitted to do so, I have marked the school in which the particular doctrine prevails by a reference to the authority where it is to be found. The school where the authority cited prevails can always be ascertained by a glance at the chapter on "The Sources of the Law," with which the present volume opens; a reference to which I have endeavoured to facilitate by presenting it in a tabular form. In the present manual I have attempted to supply the want of new editions of Strange and Macnaghten by preserving all therein that is now law; and have pointed out those doctrines which are not supported by the authorities cited. I have added the principles of recent decisions without encumbering the work too much by reference to the names of cases, which often only tends to perplex and distract the student.

I have added a chapter on the principles of the Hindu law of contract, including all the recent decisions that are to be found in the High Court reports; and as connected with the law of contracts, I have given the Limitation Act *in extenso*.

A copious index will be found appended to the work.

The candidates who go up for the annual examinations, held by the Governments in India, for the offices of Moonsiffs, Sudder Ameens, and other judicial uncovenanted appointments, will, it is hoped, find in this volume *all* that they may require.

I may here take the opportunity of making my acknowledgments to my young friend and pupil, Mr C. P. Lutchmeepathy Naidoo (a caste Hindu), a student of the Inner Temple, for the assistance he has rendered in passing this work through the press, otherwise the publication of it must have been delayed.

STANDISH GROVE GRADY.

2 Plowden Buildings, Temple,
3d *January* 1871.

CONTENTS.

CHAPTER I.—On Marriage.

CHAPTER II.—On Adoption.

Section I.

Section II.—Who may Adopt.

Section III.—Who cannot Adopt.

Section IV.—Who may Give.

Section V.—Who may be Adopted.

Section VI.—Effect of Adoption.

SECTION VII.—MODE OF ADOPTION.

CHAPTER III.—MINORITY.

CHAPTER IV.—PROPERTY.

CHAPTER V.—CHARGES ON PROPERTY.

SECTION I.

CHAPTER VI.—DISQUALIFICATION FOR INHERITANCE.

CHAPTER VII.—Alienation.

Section I.

Section II.

CHAPTER VIII.—STRIDHANA.

SECTION I.—SUCCESSION TO WOMAN'S PROPERTY.

SECTION II.—ORDER OF DESCENT OF WOMAN'S PROPERTY.

CHAPTER IX.—INHERITANCE OR SUCCESSION.

SECTION IV.—PARENTS.

CHAPTER X.—Partition.

Section I.

Section II.—Who are objects of Partition.

SECTION III.—MODE OF PARTITION.

SECTION IV.—PERIOD OF PARTITION.

SECTION V.—PARTITION AGAINST FATHER'S CONSENT OF ANCESTRAL PROPERTY.

SECTION VI. — DISTRIBUTION OF SHARES.—1. BETWEEN FATHER AND SONS.—2. BETWEEN CO-HEIRS.

SECTION VII.—AS TO THE RIGHT TO DEMAND PARTITION AMONG CO-HEIRS.

SECTION IX.—EVIDENCE OF PARTITION.

BOOK II.

THE HINDU LAW OF CONTRACT.

LIST OF ABBREVIATIONS.

Bac. Abr.	Bacon's Abridgment.
Bengl. H. C. R.	Bengal High Court Reports.
Bengl. L. R.	Bengal Law Reports.
Ben. Reg.	Bengal Regulations.
B. S. D. A. R.	Bengal Sudder Dewany Adawlut Reports.
Borr.	Borrodaile Reports.
Bom. R.	Bombay Reports.
Cal.	Calcutta.
Cl. R.	Clarke's Reports.
Coleb.	Colebrooke.
Coleb. Dig.	Colebrooke's Digest.
	Colebrooke.
C. O. B. R.	Circular Orders of the Board of Revenue.
Co. Lit.	Coke upon Littleton.
Coleb. Oblig.	Colebrooke's Contracts and Obligations.
Datt. Chandrika.	Dattaka Chandrika.
Dat. Mimansa.	Dattaka Mimansa.
Dig.	Digest.
D.	Dorin.
Elements of Hindu Law.	Sir Thomas Strange's Hindu Law.
E.	Ellis.
Ex. Min. Cons.	Extracts of Minutes of Consultation.
Fulton.	Fulton's Reports.
F. Macn. Cons.	Sir Francis Macnaghten's Considerations.
Inst.	Institutes.
Jim. Vahana.	Jimuta Vahana.
Judgt. of Sudr. Court in S. A.	Judgment of Sudder Court in Special Appeal.
Knapp. P. C.	Knapp's Privy Council.
Koollooka Bhat.	Koollooka Bhatta.
M. D.	Madras Decrees.
Mad. H. C. R.	Madras High Court Reports.
Mad. N. of Cas.	Madras Notes of Cases.
Mad. Reg.	Madras Regulations.
Mad. Sel. Dec.	Madras Select Decrees.
Mad. Sudr. Judgts.	Madras Sudder Judgments.
M. S. D.	Madras Sudder Dewany.
Macn. P.H. L.	Macnaghten's Principles of Hindu Law.

Mitac.	Mitacshara.
Mitacsh. on Inh.	Mitacshara on Inheritance.
Moore's In. Ap.	Moore's Indian Appeals.
Morl. Dig.	Morley's Digest.
O. S.	Original Suit.
Pro. of Sudr. Court.	Proceedings of Sudder Court.
R. A.	Regular Appeal.
Reg.	Regulations.
Sel. Dec.	Madras Select Decrees.
Smriti Chand.	Smriti Chandrika.
Sp. N.	Special Number.
Sudr. Court.	Sudder Court.
S. A. R.	Sudder Adawlut Reports.
S. D.	Sudder Dewany.
S. D. A.	Sudder Dewany Adawlut.
Sud. Dec.	Sudder Decrees.
Sud. D. U.	Sudder Dewany Udawlut.
S. S. A. A.	Special Appeals.
Steele.	Steele's Synopsis of the Law of Hindu Castes.
Stra. H. L.	Strange's Hindu Law.
Stra. Man. H. L.	Strange's Manual of Hindu Law.
Stra. N. of C.	Strange's Notes of Cases.
Stoke's H. L. B.	Stoke's Hindu Law Books.
Sutherl. Synop.	Sutherland's Synopsis.
W. R.	Weekly Reporter, Calcutta.

The following Table has been taken from page 1 of the Chapter on the Sources of the Law, and a reference to which will facilitate the study of that Chapter.

1. Gauria, or Bengal School.

1. Dharma Ratna. (see p. 9, 13.)
2. Dya Bhaga and Commentaries. (see p. 9, 13.)
3. Dayakrama Sangraha. (see p. 10, 13.)
4. Smriti Tatwa. (see p. 10, 13.)
5. Vivadarnava Setu. (see p. 13.)
6. Vivada Sararnava. (see p. 13.)
7. Vivada Bhangarnava. (see p. 13.)
10. Dattaka Chandrika. (see p. 12.)

2. Mithila School.

1. Mitacshara. (see p. 13.)
2. Vivada Ratnakara. (see p. 13.)
3. Vivada Chintamana. (see p. 13.)
4. Vyavahara Chintamani. (see p. 13.)
5. Dvaita Parisishta. (see p. 13.)
6. Vivada Chandra. (see p. 13.)
7. Smritisara. (see p. 13.)
8. Smriti Samuchchaya. (see p. 13.)
9. Madana Parijata. (see p. 13.)

Dattaka Mimansa. (see p. 12.)

3. Benares School.

1. Mitacshara & Commentaries by Vireshwara Bhatta and Balam Bhatta. (see p. 13.)
2. Viramitrodaya. (see p. 13.)
3. Madhaviya. (see p. 13.)
4. Vivada Tandava. (see p. 13.)
5. Nirnaya Sindhu. (see p. 13.)
6. Dattaka Mimansa. (see p. 12, 13.)

4. Maharashtra School.

1. Mitacshara. (see p. 13.)
2. Mayukha. (see p. 13.)
3. Nirnaya Sindhu. (see p. 13.)
4. Hemadri. (see p. 13)
5. Smriti Kustubha. (see p. 13.)
6. Madhaviya. (see p. 13.)
7. Menu. (see p. 13.)

5. Dravida School.

(a.) *Dravida Division.* (see p. 13.)

1. Mitacshara. (see p. 13.)
2. Madhaviya. (see p. 13.)
3. Sarasvati Vilasa. (see p. 13.)
4. Varadarajya. (see p. (13.)
5. Dattaka Chandrika.

(b.) *Karnataka Division.* (see p. 13.)

1. Mitacshara. (see p. 13.)
2. Madhaviya. (see p. 13.)
3. Sarasvati. Vilasa. (see p. 13.)

(c.) *Andra Division.* (see p. 13.)

1. Mitacshara. (see p. 13.)
2. Madhaviya. (see p. 13.)
3. Smriti Chandrika. (see p. 13.)
4. Sarasvati Vilasa. (see p. 13.)

The *Bengal* School embraces the whole province of Bengal Proper.
The *Mithila* School prevails in *Tirhoot*, or North *Behar*, the ancient kingdom of *Mithila*.
The *Benares* School prevails throughout the North-west Provinces, the Punjaub, and is also current in Orissa.
The *Maharashtra*, or Bombay School, prevails wherever the language of that school is spoken.
The *Dravida*, or Madras School, prevails throughout the whole of the Southern portion of the Peninsula.

A

MANUAL

OF

HINDU LAW.

SOURCES OF THE LAW.

Sruti and Smriti.—The Hindus believe their laws, both civil and religious, to be founded on revelation, a portion of which has been preserved, as they believe, in the very words revealed, and constitutes the Vedas, and are esteemed by them as sacred writ. They concern religion chiefly, and are termed *Sruti*, that which is heard or revealed, or traditional law. Another portion is termed *Smriti*, recollection (remembered law), in contradistinction to *Sruti*.

The *Smritis* comprise forensic law, or the *Dharma Shastra*, and are believed to be recorded in the very words of Brahma. The Vedas contain but few passages directly applicable to jurisprudence.

The *Smritis* or *Dharma Shastra* are the original text-books of the law. The law, civil and criminal, is to be found in the *Smritis*. Although a portion relates to religious observances, yet when *Dharma Shastra* is spoken of, forensic law is more particularly understood.

Authorities of Hindu law.—The *Dharma Shastra* or forensic law is to be found primarily in the institutes or collections (sanhitas), *Smritis* or text-books attributed to holy sages under the assumed names of *Menu*, *Yajnavalchya*, *Vishnu*, *Parasara*, *Guatama*, &c., which are implicitly received by Hindus as authentic works of those personages. On these, glosses and commentaries and digests (jagannathas) have been written, embracing the whole system of law, or portions thereof, and are regarded as conclusive authorities (*Preface to Stra. H. L.*). These two latter sources of information are termed *Vyakhyana* and *Nibandhana Grandha*.

Of the institutes, those of *Menu* are of the highest authority, and earliest in date. The work has been translated by *Sir W. Jones*, and Mr, afterwards *Sir Graves Haughten*. The other *Smritis* resemble that of *Menu* in form and doctrine, but none are now entire save *Menu's* work. *Menu* is the authority for the earliest age, or the *Krita Yuga*, and each of the other *Yugas* has its appropriate *Smriti*. *Mr Strange* says, "Usage has, however, interfered with the precepts of the *Smritis*, and time has rendered their language obscure." Hence the commentaries and digests are now looked to as the true expositories of the law.

Five schools of law.—These commentaries have given rise to the five schools of law now prevalent in India, in consequence of the preference given to each. These schools are the Gauda or Bengal, the Midhila (Mithila) or that of North Behar, that of Benares administered in Calcutta, the Mahratta law (Bombay), the Dravada (Deccan or Madras), to which may be added that of Canara and Malabar.

Difference in the schools.—These schools differ but little from each other, with the exception of Bengal, where, upon inheritance the law varies from the other schools.

Mr J. Strange says, "The school of Benares is the foundation of the Midhila, Mahratta, and Dravada schools." Thus the interpreters of the law are ranged under two great divisions—that of Bengal and that of Benares. In the Bengal school the letter of the law is modified by inferential reasonings, while in the Benares school the text is more closely followed.

Mr Morley says, It would be almost impossible to define with accuracy the limits of these several schools, nor indeed is there that distinction between them which some suppose. The Bengal, it is true, stands nearly alone, particularly with regard to the law of inheritance, in which there is a wide difference in doctrine between the northern and other schools, the latter receiving some treatises in common which are totally rejected by the Gauriya lawyers. The Bengal school assimilates in some respects with that of Mithila—inheritance, however, being still excepted.

Looking to west and south of India, the main distinction between the Benares, Mahratta, and Dravada schools is in fact rather a preference shown by each respectively for some particular work as their authority of law, than any real or important difference of doctrine.

In all western and southern schools the prevailing authority is the almost universal *Mitacshara;* and although the Mahrattas may prefer the *Mayukha* to the *Madhaviya*, and the contrary may be the case in the Karnataka country, whilst in other districts other treatises are referred to; still the law itself, even in regard to inheritance, is essentially the same throughout Southern India.

The Gauriya or Bengal school of law prevails over the province of Bengal proper, and is co-extensive with the Bengali language.

The Mithila school includes North Behar or Tirhoot.

The Benares school prevails in the city and province of that name, and is the school of Middle India. The doctrine of this school is current in Orissa, and extends from Midnapore to the mouth of the Hooghly, and thence to Chicacole.

The Maharashtra school governs the law in the Mahratta country.

The south limit of that country passes from Goa through Kolapoore, and Bedre to Chandra; the eastern line follows the Warda river to the Injadri or Satpoora Hills south of the Nerbudda, and which form its northern limit as far west as Nandod. The western boundary may be marked by a line drawn from Nandod to Daman, and thence along the sea-coast to Goa. The Maharashtra school prevails wherever the Mahratta language is spoken by the natives.

The Dravada school consists of the whole of the southern portion of the Peninsula, but it may be subdivided into three districts, in each of which some particular law treatises have more weight than others; these districts are Dravada, Karnataka, Andhra. Dravada proper is the country where Tamil is spoken, and occupies the extreme south of the Peninsula; its boundaries may be traced by a line drawn from Pulicat to the Ghats, between Pulicat and Bangalore, and then following the Ghats westward, and along the boundary between Malabar and Kanara to the sea, including Malabar. The Karnataka is bounded on the west by the sea-coast as far as Goa, thence by the Western Ghats up to Kolapoore; to the north by a line from Kolapoore to Bedre, and on the east by a line from Bedre through Adoni, Anandpur, and Nandidrug, to the Ghats between Pulicat and Bangalore; here the Karnataka language is spoken. The third district, Andhra, where the Telinga or Telugu is spoken, extends from the boundary line last mentioned, and which, prolonged to Chandra, will form its western limit; on the north it is bounded indistinctly by a line running eastward to Sohunpur, or the Mahanaddi river, and on the east by a line drawn from Sohunpur to Chicacole, and thence to Pulicat, where the Tamil country begins.

These are the limits of the various schools of law, as far as they can be approximately defined. They are marked in a map in Grady's "Hindu Law" of inheritance.

Hindu law books.—The *Dharma Shastra* may be divided into three classes—

1. The *Smriti*, or text-books, which are the foundation of all Hindu law, and which are attributed to various rishis, or sages, who are supposed to have been inspired. They are all, with slight variations in form and doctrine, the same with the *Institutes of Menu.*

2. The *Vyakhyana*, or glosses and commentaries on these *Smritis*, many of which partake of the nature of digests.

3. The *Nibandhana Granda*, or digests properly so called, either of the whole body of the law, or of particular portions thereof collected from the text-books and their commentators.

Those works by European authors, may be added.

The *Smriti* text-books, institutes, or collections attributed to various rishis, are all divided into three kandas or sections; the first, *Achara*, treating of religious ceremonies and daily observances; the second, *Vyavahara*, of law and the administration of justice; and the third, *Prayaschitta*, relating to penance and expiation.

Those books are all venerated by the Hindus as next in sanctity to the Vedas themselves.*

The *Manava Dharma Shastra*, or *Institutes of Menu*, the highest authority of memorial law, is universally allowed by the Hindus, not only to be the oldest work, but also the most holy after the Vedas; and as in addition to this, the other text-books are, as it were, formed on the same model, it may be fairly considered as the basis of the whole present system of Hindu jurisprudence. The author has recently edited a new edition of it, with a copious index, in which the original work was wanting.

Atri, the second writer of a text-book, according to *Yainavalchya*, but who is not mentioned in the *Padma Purana*, composed a law treatise in verse, which is extant. *Vishnu* is also said to have written an excellent treatise in verse, and *Harita* one in prose. The *Yajnavalchya Dharma Shastra* (or *Institutes of Yajnavalchya*) comprises three books.

Colebrooke, Dig. Pref. xvi. &c., 2d Ed., enumerates other *Smritis*, viz.:—

The *Institutes of Usanas* in verse.

A short Treatise by *Angiras*.

A short tract by *Yama*.

A work in prose by *Apastamba*.

A metrical abridgment of the *Institutes of Samavarta*.

A Treatise by *Katyayana*.

An abridgment of the *Institutes of Vrihaspati*.

A work by *Parasara*.

Some works connected with law by *Vyasa*, the reputed author of the *Puranas*.

The joint work of *Sankha* and *Likhita*.

A Treatise in verse by *Daksha*.

A Treatise in prose by *Gautama*.

An abridgment in verse on penance and expiation by *Satatapa*.

A work in prose mixed with verse by *Vasishta*.

Mr Morley says, that the *Smritis* are mostly of small extent, relating to observances and ceremonies, and only incidentally touching upon law. The *Smritis* which are received in common by all the schools, are no longer *final* authorities. *Vrihaspati* says, "A decision must not be made by having recourse to the letter of written codes, since, if no decision were made according to the reason of the law (or immemorial usage), there might be a failure of justice. The *Manava Dharma Shastra* itself is indeed now regarded as a work to be respected rather than in modern times to be implicitly

* It must be observed that many *Smritis* are quoted by legal writers, which are no longer extant. It is said to be the opinion of the Brahmins that, with the exception of *Menu*, the entire work of no one of those sages has come down to the present time, *Col. Dig.* vol. i., p. 454, *Morl. Dig.* cxciv.

followed. For *final* authority, then, in deciding questions of law, recourse must be had to the commentaries and digests.

2. **Commentaries.**—The commentaries which form the second great authority of the Hindu law, some are merely explanatory of the text, while others are regarded as final authorities; and these latter, together with the Digests, the third class of law books, are the immediate authorities for the opinions of lawyers in the respective schools where the doctrines they uphold may prevail. Many of the commentaries on the *Smritis*, those for instance on *Menu's Institutes*, which are merely explanatory of the text—are not considered to be final authorities any more than the *Smritis* themselves; but others again, which by the introduction of quotations from other writers, and by interpreting and enlarging on the meaning of the author, partake so far of the nature of general Digests, are referred to for the *final* decision of questions. The *Mitacshara* is a remarkable instance of this, since, though professedly a commentary on the *Smriti* of *Yajnavalchya*, it is consulted as a final authority over the whole of India, Bengal alone excepted.

The *Manava Dharma Shastra* has been the subject of several commentaries. Amongst these the most celebrated are by *Midhatithi*, son of *Virasvami Bhatta;* the comment by *Govinda Raja;* another by *Dharanidhara;* the famous gloss of *Koolooka Bhatta*, entitled *Manavartha Mooktavali*. It is a commontary on *Menu*, and is held in the highest repute of any.

In addition to these, *M. Deslongchamps* mentions that in preparing his edition of the Institutes, he made use of one by *Raghavananda*, entitled *Manvarta Chandrika*, which he states to be, in many instances, more precise and clear than *Koolooka*. *Bhaguri* is also said to have written a commentary on the *Manava Dharma Shastra*. *Steele* mentions two other glosses on *Menu*, as known among the Mahrattas—the *Madhava*, by *Sayanacharya*, which is stated to be of general authority, especially in the *Carnatic;* and the *Nandarajkrit*, by *Nandaraja*. *Colebrooke* mentions another commentary on *Menu, Morl. Dig.* cciii. These are all merely explanatory of the text, and must not be considered as final authorities. The commentary on the *Institutes of Vishnu*, entitled *Vaijayanti*, written by *Nanda Pandita*. The copious gloss of *Aparaka* is supposed to be the most ancient commentary on the *Institutes of Yajnavalchya*, and to be therefore earlier than the more celebrated comment on the the same text. The *Mitacshara* of *Vignaneswara* is, as we have observed, a gloss on *Yajnavalchya Dharma Shastra*. It abounds with apposite quotations from other legislators, and expositions of those quotations, as well as of the text which it professes to illustrate. *Vignyaneswara* follows the arrangement of *Yajnavalchya Dharma Shastra*. It is divided into three parts, or kandas—viz., the *Achara Kanda*, which treats of social and religious duties; the *Vyavahara Kanda*, which treats of jurisprudence, or the laws of the people, that is, of private contests and administrative law; and the *Prayaschitta Kanda*, which treats of penance, devotion, and purification.

The *Mitacshara* is one of the greatest, and if we take into consideration the extent of its influence, the greatest of all the Hindu law authorities, for it is received, as *Colebrooke* observes, in all the schools of Hindu law, from Benares to the southern extremity of the Peninsula, as the chief groundwork of the doctrines which they follow, and as an authority from which they rarely dissent.

The works of other eminent writers have, concurrently with the *Mitacshara*, considerable weight in the schools of law, which have respectively adopted them, as the *Smriti Chandrika* in the south of India. This is a treatise on judicature, by *Davanna Bhut*, and is a work which *Colebrooke* considers of uncommon excellence. It is an especial authority in the Madras school, and stands next in estimation to the *Mitacshara*. It differs, however, in some few points from the doctrines of that work. *Mr T. Kristnasawmy Iyer* has recently published what professes to be a translation of it.*

The *Vivada Chintamani*, recently translated by the late *Hon. Prossonno Coomar Tagore*, member of the Asiatic Society and the Legislative Council of the Lieutenant-Governor of Bengal; the *Ratnacara* and *Vivada Chandra* are authorities in Mithila.

The *Viramitrodaya* and *Kamalakara* in Benares.

The *Vyavahara Mayukha* in the Mahratta country.

All, however, agree in deferring to the *Mitacshara*, in frequently appealing to its text; and in rarely, and at the same time, modestly dissenting, from its doctrines on particular questions.

The *Mitacshara* must then be considered as the main *authority for all the schools of law, with the sole exception of that of Bengal.*

As the *Mitacshara* is a commentary on *Yajnavalchya*, so the *Mitacshara* has in its turn been commented on by others. *Colebrooke* refers to four, and describes two; one the *Suboudhini*, by *Visvesvara Bhatta*, and the other by *Balaam Bhatta*. The former is a collection of notes illustrating the obscure passages concisely but perspicuously. The latter is a running comment expounding the original, word by word. The author follows the *Suboudhini* as far as it extends.

Nanda Pandita (*vai ja yanti*) is mentioned by *Mr Sutherland* as the author of a commentary on the *Mitacshara*, entitled *Pratitakshara.*

Various editions of the *Mitacshara* have been published. The sixth chapter, which treats of inheritance, has been translated by *Colebrooke*, with notes and glosses from his own pen.

* So little reliance can be placed upon this work that a translation of it will soon appear from the pen of one of the first Sanscrit scholars in Europe, Dr Goldstucker, Professor of Sanscrit in the University of Oxford.

In the case of the *Collector of Maduar* v. *Srimutu Muttu Vijuya Ragunnada Muttu Rumalinga Sethupati* (2 Mad. H.C.R. 206), the High Court of Madras* said, with reference to the authorities current in Madras :—

"In dealing with the authorities which have been presented, it is obviously necessary, as far as possible, to ascertain the titles of their authors to respect, either from the weight attached to them by the people for whom they wrote, or from the intrinsic weight of the reasoning upon which their conclusions are based. The following passage of the *Younger Macnaghten*, Pref. page 21, which follows his statement, that which all the schools follow the original *Smritis*, each of the five schools has particular commentators, to whom it attaches marked preference, says the *Mitacshara*, the *Smriti Chandrika*, the *Madhavyani*, and the *Saraswati Vilasa*, are the works of paramount authority in the territories dependent on the Government of Madras."

"How important, too, is the caution of the learned author: 'I do not mean to affirm that these are the only works of paramount importance recognised in the respective schools; but they are most frequently referred to; they are sufficient to solve the ordinary legal questions which arise, and suspicions may justly be excited where an exposition of law is supported by citations from more recondite authorities.' He then proceeds to show the general prevalence over all the schools of the *Dattaka Mimansa*, of *Nunda Pandita*, the *Dattaka Chandrica* of *Davanna Bhat*."

"*Nunda Pandita*, an author born in Southern India, is of course a distinct authority that the widow can neither give nor receive a son. . . . . We then come to the *Smriti Chandrica* and the *Dattaka Chandrika*—works of *Davanna Bhatta*. The *Smriti Chandrika* is a work next in authority to the *Mitacshara*, and the *Dattaka Chandrika* is the latest work of its author intended to dispel any doubts which the former celebrated treatise may have left. . . . The works of *Vidya Narainsamy* are admitted to have great weight in the Madras School. One of his works is a treatise on adoption, another is a work called *Madavyean*, a commentary upon *Parasara Smriti*. *Mr Ellis*, *Sir T. Strange*, and *Sir W. Macnaghten* testify to his authority in Southern India, and particularly in the district of Kanara. *Mr Ellis* says he may be called the legislator of the last Hindu dynasty, which is that of the Rajahs of Vijyanagar, who succeeded the Betal Rajahs. The territories of these Rajahs for a short time embraced nearly the whole of the south of India, so that the general authority of this jurist, who is said to have been the minister of the founder of the kingdom, would necessarily extend over the whole of the widely-extended empire. In one place in the *Literary Journal*, *Mr Ellis* states what is unquestionably the case, that where other treatises conflict with the *Mitacshara*,

* Frere & Holloway, J. J.

they are to give way, while in another he says there is difficulty in choosing between the *Mitacshara* and *Madhavyam*. Although this may be considered to put the case too strongly, there is no doubt but this writer is an authority of great weight. It has been said that with many others he has been overruled by the judicial committee in the *Vasureddy* case. He was, it is true, incidentally referred to in the very vague exposition of the *Pundits* who supported the legality of a second adoption, but no passage from his work was quoted, and it was only too likely that none was to be found there. Passing their judgment, as the judicial committee did upon the work of *Sir W. Macnaghten*, and upon the reasons for making an adoption, it is impossible to consider that the judgment has impaired the general weight of an authority because that author's name was thrown in by the pundits as a make-weight to their opinion, contrary to that at which the judicial committee finally arrived. . . . . *Sir Rama Pandita* is an authority very generally cited in Southern India. . . . These are all the authorities whom we are at all able to recognise as possessed of weight. . . . . If we are to assume that the authorities of the Benares and Mahratta schools are all equally binding upon us, that all the schools except those of Bengal and Mithila are governed by the same rule, then, feeling ourselves bound by the case reported in 2 Knapp., we should be compelled to say that this adoption is invalid. It is quite clear, however, that there are material differences between the several subordinate schools, and these differences have always been recognised. . . . . It seems to us that it would be trifling with the subject to quote as authorities the works of authors of whom we know nothing. They may be, and probably are, the speculative essays of law students upon jurisprudential subjects. The *Vyavahara Kaustubha*, the *Vyavahara Mayukha*, the *Vivahara Mitroduga*, the *Niernaga Sindhu* are authorities of other schools. The *Vaidhiza-Nisniam*, and other works of which we know nothing, brought from Tanjore, are of little weight, because the Mahratta dynasty, reigning in that country, would necessarily bring with them judicial notions derived from *Nila Kunta*, the author of the *Magukha*. The *Nirnaga Sindhu* also is clearly a Mahratta authority. The *Ratnamala*, a commentary upon this work, was supplied by an official in Tanjore, and it is subject to the remark made upon the *Vaidhiza-Nisniam*."

In addition to the commentaries already referred to, there are others by *Devabodha* and *Visvarupa*, and by *Sulapani*, entitled *Dipakalika*, in repute in the Gauriya school.

Yama's text-book in verse has been illustrated by *Koolooka Bhatta*, the author of the gloss on *Manava Dharma Shastra*.

Nanda Pandita wrote a comment on the *Parasara Smriti*.

The *Madhaviya* of *Vidjarayansvami*, named after *Madhava Acharya*, the brother of its author, and based on the text of *Parasara*, is an authority in the southern schools, but especially in the Karnataka. It is, in fact, a digest of the law prevalent in the southern portion of the Peninsula. *Vidjaraynasvami* was the virtual founder of the Vijyoanagara empire, and his work became the standard of its law. It is of some authority in the Benares school.

Gautama's text-book was commented on by *Haradattacharya*, who resided in Dravada. His work is called *Mitacshara*, but must not be confounded with *Vijnanesvara's*. The *Varadarajya* by *Varadaraja*, is a general digest, but it may be placed among the commentaries, since it is framed on the *Narada Smriti*. It is of authority in the southern schools, especially in Dravada.

There is another commentary entitled *Chatur Vimsati Smriti Vyakhya*.

The *Smriti Chandrika*, already referred to as a Mithila authority, is an authority in the Madras school, and has stood next in estimation to the *Mitacshara*. It differs, however, in doctrine from the *Mitacshara* in some few points.

The *Saraswattee Vilasa*, by *Pratapa Rudradeva*. The *Vyavahara Mayukha*, by *Neelakanta*, translated by *Mr Borrodaile*, is an especial authority among the Mahrattas. The *Madhaveum*, the *Mitacshara*, and the *Smriti Chandrika*, are five works which are accounted of paramount authority, and are referred to as *Puncha Grandhi*, or five books. *Maharaja*, a prince of *Telingana* country, is supplanted to some extent by the *Mitacshara*.

3. **Digests**, or *Nibandhana Grantha* are the third chief authority of Hindu law.

They are either general, or are confined to separate or distinct subjects of law, and consist of texts taken from the *Smritis* with explanatory glosses reconciling their apparent contradictions.

For the following summary of the digests, as indeed the preceding account of the original sources of the law, and the various commentaries upon them, the author is indebted to *Mr Morley*, who, in his Introduction to the first volume of his Digest, enters very fully into this branch of his subject.

Mr Morley adds, Several of them, in common with several of the glosses and commentaries above mentioned, are of less authority than others, and in many cases their names even may not often be heard in an Indian court of justice.

Bengal.—The *Dharma Ratna* of *Jimoota-Vahana* is a digest of the law according to the Guariya school. The chapter on inheritance, the celebrated *Daya Bhaga*, is the standard authority of the law in Bengal. It is on almost every disputed point opposed to the *Mitacshara*, and it is indeed on this very branch of the law—viz., inheritance—that we find the greatest difference in doctrine in the various schools.

Colebrooke translated *Jimoota-Vahana's* chapter on inheritance as well as that of the *Mitacshara*, with notes and comments.

The earliest commentary upon the *Daya Bhaga* is that of *Srinatha*

Acharya Chudamani. The next is that of *Achyuta Chakrvarti* (author also of a commentary of the *Stradha Viveka*): it cites frequently the gloss of *Chudamani*, and is quoted by *Mahesvara.*

The commentary by *Srikristna Tarkalankara* is the most celebrated of all the treatises on the text of *Daya Bhaga.* Another gloss bears the name of *Raghunandana. Ramanatha Vidya Vachespati* has also written a commentary on the *Daya Bhaga. Srikristna Tarkalanchara* has written an epitome of the law of inheritance, entitled *Daya Krama Sangraha.* This has been translated by *Mr Wynch.*

The *Smriti Tatwa* of *Raghunandana Vandyaghatiya*, the greatest authority of law in the Guariya school, is a complete digest of twenty-seven volumes. This great writer is often cited as *Smarta Bhattacharya.*

The *Daya Tatwa*, or that portion of the *Smriti Tatwa* of *Rhaghunandana* which relates to inheritance, is highly spoken of by *Colebrooke.*

Kasirama has written a commentary on the *Daya Tatwa.*

The *Daya Rahasya*, or *Smriti Ratnavali*, by *Ramatha Vidya*, is of considerable authority in some districts of Bengal. It differs from *Jimoota-Vahana* and *Raghunandana*, and this tends to create uncertainty.

Dvaita Nirnaya of *Vachespati Battacharya*, a treatise on general law, and the *Daya Nirnaya* of the same author, which treats of inheritance, being little more than an abridgment of the *Daya Bagha* and *Daya Tatwa*, are also Bengal authorities.

Mithila,—*Kesava Misra*, a native of Mithila, is the author of the *Chandoga Parisishta* and the *Dvaita Parisishta;* the former, together with its commentary, the *Parisishta Prakasa*, are works of great authority, and treat of the duties of priests; the latter is a more general treatise.

The *Vivida Ratnakara*, a general digest, compiled under the general superintendence of *Chandeswara*, Minister of Harasinhadeva, King of Mithila. The *Vivida Chintamani*, the *Vyavahara Chintamani*, and the other works of *Vachespati Misra*, are all considered of great authority in Mithila; as are also the *Vivada Chandra* and other treatises by the learned *Lady Lachimadevi*, who wrote under the name of her nephew, *Misaru Misra. Sri Karacharya* and his son, *Srinathacharya*, were also celebrated in the Mithila school of law; the former wrote a treatise on inheritance; the latter, the *Acharya Chandrika*, a text on the duties of the fourth class.

The *Smritisara*, or *Smrityarthasara*, by *Sridharacharya*, a treatise on religious duties, but mentioning civil matters incidentally, is according to the Mithila school; it quotes the *Pradipa, Kalpadruma*, and *Kalpalata*, works otherwise unknown.

There seem to be several *Smritisaras. Sir W. Macnaghten*

mentions one by *Harinathopadhyaya*, which is of authority in Mithila. There is another by *Yadavendra*. The *Smriti Samucharya*, or *Smriti Sara Samuchchaya*, is also a Mithila authority, and is known among the Mahrattas.

The *Madana Parijata*, a treatise on civil and religious duties, by *Visvesvara Bhatta*, but containing a chapter on inheritance, is a Mithila work, and prevails also among the Mahrattas; it quotes the *Sapararka*, the *Smriti Chandrika*, and the *Hemadri*. The work was composed by order of *Madana Pala*, and is sometimes cited in his name. *Sir W. Macnaghten* calls the author *Madano Padhyaya*. *Sulapani* wrote a treatise on penance and expiation, which is an authority in Bengal and Mithila.

Benares.—The *Viramitrodaya* of *Mitra Misra* is a treatise on *Vyavahara* in general, according to the doctrines of the Benares school, and systematically examines and refutes the opinion of *Jimoota-Vahana* and *Raghunandana*. The *Vivada Tandava* of *Kamalakara*, younger brother of *Dinakara Bhatta*, and son of *Ramakristna Bhatta*, defends the doctrines of *Vignyaneswara* in opposition to the writers of the Gauriya school.

The *Nirnaya Sindhu* is of authority at Benares and with the Mahrattas. It is by *Kamalakara*. It treats of rites and ceremonies, touching incidentally only on questions of a legal nature.

Neither *Mitra Misra* nor *Kamalakara* differ from the *Mitacshara* on any important point.

Mahratta.—The *Vyavahara Mayukha* of *Neelakanta* is the greatest authority, after the *Mitacshara* in this school, and is one of the twelve treatises by the same author, all bearing the title of *Mayukha*, and treating of religious duties, penance, and expiation. The *Mayukhas* are designated collectively the *Bhagavat Bhaskara*. The *Vyavahara Mayukha*, which is the sixth in the list, is devoted exclusively to law and justice, and is a general digest and collection of texts. *Mr Borrodaile*, as we before observed, has translated this work, to which he has added notes referring to passages on other works on Hindu law.

The *Smriti Koustubha*, by *Anandee Deva Kasikar*. It is one of twelve works bearing the title of *Koustubha*, all of which are to be met with at Benares; it is known at Poonah, and treats of *Achara*, *Vyavahara*, and *Prayaschitta*.

The *Hemadri*, by *Hemadri Bhatta Kasikar*, is of authority in Bombay.

So is the *Dyot*, by *Gaga Bhatta Kasikar*. It consists of twelve divisions, and treats of all subjects.

The *Pursuram Pratap* is a general digest.

The *Prithi Chandroa* is also a general digest of *Achara*, *Vyavahara*, and *Prayaschitta*. The *Vyavahara Sakar*, by *Nagojee Bhatta*, is a work of general authority.

The *Sara Sangraha* is a work treating of *Prayaschitta Smarta, Vyvahara*, &c.

The *Madana Rutna*, by *Madana Singh*, is a treatise on *Achara, Vyavahara*, and *Prayaschitta*, of notoriety.

The *Achararcha*, by *Sunkur Bhatta Kasikar*, is a work on *Achara* and *Vyavahara*, of general notoriety.

Andhra.—The *Sarasvati Vilasi*, a general digest, is one of the chief authorities, after the *Mitacshara*, in the whole of the southern portion of India. It was the standard law-book in the entire Andhra country, and is still of authority to the northward of the Pennar, where many customs exist, especially regarding land, which are derived from it. But even there the *Mitacshara* is of paramount authority.

Dravada.—The *Smriti Chandrika* we have already referred to. It is an authority in the Dravada school, and is, as well as the preceding work, of authority in the Andhra country.

The *Dharesvariya* is a general digest, and is an authority in the south.

Adoption.—The *Dattaka Mimansa* of *Nanda Pandita* (whose other works we have already alluded to) is upon the subject of adoption.

The *Dattaka Chandrika* is also on adoption. It is of great and general authority, and is supposed to be the basis of *Nanda Pandita's* work. The *Mimamsa* and *Chandrika* have been translated by *Mr Sutherland. M. Orianne* has translated the latter into French.

Mr Ellis, on the Law Books of India, mentions works bearing the same names by other authors, as well as works bearing different titles, as general digests of the law of adoption.

On the law of adoption there is little difference in the several schools. The *Mimamsa* and *Chandrika* are greatly respected all over India. Where they differ, the doctrine of the latter is adhered to in Bengal and in Southern India, while the former is relied on in the Mithila and Benares schools. *Sir C. Scotland, C. J.* says, nearly all the schools follow the latter in preference to the former, where they differ.

Helayudha composed the *Nyaya Sarveswa*, the *Brahmana Sarvaswa* and *Pandita Sarvaswa*, and other tracts on the administration of justice and duties of caste.

Lakshmidhara wrote a treatise on the administration of justice, and also a digest called *Kalpataru. Narasimha*, son of *Ramachandra*, wrote the *Govindarnava* and other law tracts.

Jitendriya is cited in *Mitacshara* and by *Jagannatha Tarkapanchanana.*

The *Vivadarnava Setu*, the *Vivada Sararnava*, and the *Vivada Bhangarnava* of *Jagannatha Tarkapanchanana*, translated by *Colebrooke*, and commonly cited as the Digest, have been compiled since the establishment of the British in India, under the auspices of *Warren Hastings* and *Sir William Jones.*

These three digests are commented upon and described by *Mr Morley.*

We may refer to the *Vyavestharatnamala* by *Sri Lakshmi Narayana Nyayalankara.* It is a catechism in the vernacular of Bengal. The principles advanced are supported by quotations in Sanscrit from works of authority. It contains a succinct view of the law of inheritance according to the doctrines of *Jim. Vahana* contrasted with those of the *Mitacshara,* together with a short treatise on Adoption.

Mr Morley recapitulates the works that are received as final authorities in the different schools, excluding text books and explanatory comments—viz.,

Bengal, or Gauriya.—Dharma, Ratna, Daya Bhaga (by *Jemuta Vahana*), and its commentators; Srikrishna Tarkalankara; Daya Krama Sangraha, by the same author; and Srinatha Acharya Chindamani; Smriti Tatwa; Daya Tatwa; Vivadarnava Setu; Vivada Sararnava; Vivada Bhangarnava.

Mithila.—Mitacshara, Vivada Ratnakara, Vivada Chintamani; Vyavahara Chintamani; Dwaita Parisishta; Vivada Chandra; Smriti Sara Samuchchaya Madana Parijata.

Benares.—To which the Madras school belongs, Mitacshara; Viramitrodaya Madhaviya; Vivada Tandava; Nirnaya Sindhu.

Maharashtra.—Mitacashara, Mayukha, Nirnaya Sindhu; Hemadri; Smriti Koustubha; Madhavya; Menu.

Dravada (including the division of that name, that of the Karnataka and Andhra).—Mitacshara, Madhaviya, Sarasvati Vilasa; Varadarajya, Smriti Chandrika.

The *Dattaka Mimansa* is preferred in Bengal and in the south. The *Dattaka Chandrika* in Mithila and Benares, *ante* p. 12.

The above works are quoted most frequently, but they do not include all that are cited by lawyers in the several schools. Nor are they *all* constantly referred to. In Bombay *Chief Justice Sausse,* in *Pranjeevandas Toolseydas* v. *Dewcooverbaee,* 1 Bombay, *H.C.R.* p. 131, *post,* p. 273, says that *Menu Mitacshara* and *Mayukha* are the authorities in that presidency (see *Bor. Bomb. Rep. Pref.* iii.), and in Benares the Pundits were required to consult the *Mitacshara,* and report the exposition of law there found applicable to the case. With the exception of the law of adoption, the works of the Bengal school are of no authority out of the limits where Bengali is the language of the people. But with this exception, there seems to be no reason why in the other schools the authorities should not be received indiscriminately, and particularly where a case does not rest upon any peculiarities of a particular school, but depends more upon the general principles of Hindu law. In such case the judge may safely decide by analogy to other authors, and not be guided by the doctrine of any particular test.

Malabar.—"The rule of nephews," or the Marumak Katayam law, prevails as to inheritance.

Canara.—The law of Aliya Santana exists in Canara (see *post*). This law more consistently carries out the Malabar doctrine, that all rights of property are derived from females.

The law has undergone some changes in late years by decision and by the Act of the legislature. Thus in *Abraham* v. *Abraham*, 9 *Moore's In. Ap.* 195, it has been decided that upon the conversion of a Hindu to Christianity, the Hindu law ceases to have any continuing obligatory force upon the convert; that he may renounce the old law, by which he was bound, as he had renounced his old religion, or if he thinks fit, that he may abide by the old law, notwithstanding he has renounced the old religion. That the convert, though not bound as to his rights and interest in property either by the Hindu law or by any other positive law, may by his course of conduct after his conversion have shown by what law he intended his rights to be governed; that the *Lexloci* Act of 1850 does not apply where the parties have ceased to be Hindus in religion, and that the conversion of a Hindu to Christianity amounts by Hindu law to a severance of parcenership. By legislative enactment, Act v. of 1843, slavery has been abolished, and by Act xv. of 1856, the remarriage of widows is authorised. But they are deprived of all right to maintenance out of their deceased husband's property, as well as to the right of inheritance from them. Reg. i. of 1830 abolishes suttee. By Act xxi. of 1850 apostasy and exclusion from caste have no effect upon the right of inheritance. By Reg. v. of 1820, and Act xxvii. of 1860, the wills of Hindus are recognised. In 1870, a Wills Act was passed which is in operation in Bengal. It only remains to mention *Steele's* "Summary of the Law of Caste," printed by order of the Governor in Council of Bombay.

It remains to mention the names of Europeans who have written works of authority on Hindu Law. In Bengal, *Sir Francis Macnaghten* published in 1824, his *Considerations on Hindu Law*. It may, however, be regarded more as essays and notes, than as a complete treatise. Then afterwards, *Sir W. H. Macnaghten*, of the Civil Service, in 1828 published a treatise entitled *Principles and Precedents of Hindu Law*. This is a production of deserved celebrity. It distinguishes to some extent between the Bengal, Benares, and Mahratta schools. *Mr Sutherland*, translator of the *Dattaka Memamsa* and the *Dattaka Chandrika*, published a synopsis on Adoption.

Mr Elberling, of the Danish Civil Service, published a succinct and comprehensive treatise on Hindu, Mohammedan, and other laws administered in India. In the first, he distinguishes the Benares and Bengal law. In 1825, *Sir Thomas Strange* published his "Elements of Hindu Law," the clearness and perspicuity of which are conspicuous. *Mr Justice Strange*, late of the High Court of Madras, has published a Manual of Hindu law. *Mr Reginald Thompson* has also published a Manual of Hindu Law, based on *Sir Thomas Strange's* work. On these several works, the author has commented in the introduction to his "Hindu Law" of inheritance, and these observations it is unnecessary to repeat here. This epitome would be defective if I neglected to notice the very able work on Hindu Wills, published this year by Mr W. A. Montriou, barrister-at-law of the High Court of Calcutta, and which displays great learning and research.

INTRODUCTORY REMARKS.

The law of property and "family relation"—Reserved by charters of justice for India—Collateral subjects where necessary discussed—The Hindu law of inheritance hinges on the "family relation"—Subjects discussed.

The law of property and "family relation."—This treatise, as its title imports, embraces the Hindu law affecting "Property and Family Relation," as administered in the "High Courts" at our presidencies in Madras, Bombay, Calcutta, and in the Privy Council.

Reserved by charters of justice for India.—This is one of the two great legal subjects of Hindu law, which the Charters of Justice for India and local regulations have expressly reserved in extending the authority of English law over the natives; the law of contract being the other: as *Sir Thomas Strange* observes, in his *Introduction to Hindu Law*, p. 7, imposing on the courts so created, whilst administering these subjects, the duty of adjudicating upon them, not, as in other cases, according to our law, but according to the law of the parties, as they happen to be Hindu or Mohammedan.

By *Beng. Regulation*, 17th April 1780, sec. 27, it is enacted, "That in all suits regarding inheritance, marriage, and caste, and other religious usages or institutions, the laws of the Koran with respect to Mohammedans, and those of the Shaster with respect to Gentoos, shall be invariably adhered to." This section was re-enacted in the following year in the revised code, with the addition of the word "succession." It has been superseded by Reg. iv. of 1793, Bengal Reg. viii. of 1795, Benares iii. of 1803, S. 16 Agra.

In 1781, the declaratory act of 21 Geo. III., c. 70, sec. 17, enacted with reference to the powers and jurisdiction of the Supreme Court at Fort-William in Bengal, that respecting disputes between the native inhabitants of Calcutta, their inheritance and succession to lands, rents, and goods, and all matters of contract and dealing between party and party, shall be determined in case of Mohammedans by their laws and usages, and in the case of Gentoos by their laws and usages, and where only one of the parties shall be Mohammedan or Gentoo, by the laws and usages of the defendant. In 1797 this was extended to Madras and Bombay, with the addition of the words, or by such laws and usages, as the same would have been determined by, if the suit had been brought and the action commenced, in a native court. This applies to natives not by birth only, but by religion, *Abraham* v. *Abraham*.

Whenever in any civil suit the parties to such suit may be of different persuasions, when one shall be Hindu and the other Mohammedan, or where one or more shall not be either, the laws of those religions shall not be permitted to operate to deprive such party or parties of any property to which, but for the operation of such laws, they would have been entitled; in all such cases the decision shall be governed by the principles of justice, equity, and good conscience, it being clearly understood that this provision shall not be considered as justifying the introduction of the English or any foreign law, or the application to such cases of any rules not sanctioned by these principles, *Bengal Reg.* of 1832.*

Collateral subjects where necessary discussed.—The discussion of these subjects will necessarily require a divergence from the main point into other collateral questions. Where a clearer elucidation necessitates such a course, we have found it convenient to follow the consideration of the incidental question, for the charters already referred to require, in administering their powers, a special regard to the constitution and usages of the natives of India.

The Hindu law of inheritance hinges on the "family relation."—The Hindu law of inheritance turns on the relative principle. The family relation is continually and prominently kept before our eyes. It is the connecting link in every branch of the Hindu law of inheritance.

Questions on marriage seldom form the subject of litigation in Madras, owing probably to their submission to the head man of the village or caste. The placita cited in *Morley's Digest*, with one exception, relate to Bombay.

Subjects discussed.—In this treatise we shall discuss the subject under its natural divisions, viz.—

I. Marriage.
II. Adoption.
III. Minority.
IV. Property, ancestral and self-acquired.
V. Charges on property.
VI. Disqualification for inheritance.
VII. Alienation *inter vivos*, and by will.
VIII. Succession.
IX. Partition.

* See "Introduction" to *Grady's Hindu Law of Inheritance*, where the regulations applicable to Bombay and Madras are referred to.

CHAPTER I.

ON MARRIAGE.

Marriage forms the substratum of the whole order of civil life—Barrenness of parents—Marriage is compulsory—Eight species of marriage—Wedding rites accompany all marriages—Different rites where wife not a virgin—At the nubile age husband may claim wife—Period of marriage of males—Period of marriage of females—Father bound to select husband for daughter—If he fail to do so, selection devolves upon her paternal relations, or mother, or the girl herself—Return of presents on annulling the engagement—Stridhana—Marriage consists of two ceremonies—Betrothal, and Consummation—Betrothal is absolute marriage—Mode of contracting marriage—Contract fixes the connubial relation—Rights thus created—Duration of union—Severance of—Infidelity—Husband not entitled to damages—Before betrothal—With whom the contract may be entered into—Caste or class—Sudra need not marry in the same caste—Woman cannot marry in lower caste—Illegitimacy is not an absolute disqualification for caste—Marriage with daughter of bastard—Loss of caste—If by a sonless female—If she have a son—Prohibited degrees—Marriage of younger brother or sister before an elder—Adopted son—Causes of separation—Supersession or polygamy—Justifying circumstances—1st, Consent—2d, Legal causes—Present on second marriage—Illegal supersession—Residence of first wife—Entitled to inherit—Residence of several wives—Personal chastisement of wife—Withdrawal of conjugal rights—Divorce according to Hindu law—Re-marriage.

Marriage forms the substratum of the whole order of civil life.—The subject of marriage is of the first importance with reference to its bearing on property. It forms the *substratum* of the whole order of civil life amongst Hindus. It is primarily a religious ceremony entered into for religious objects and ends, and affecting the religious state of the man both here and hereafter. If his marriage should prove unproductive—a result that frequently happens, he is obliged to resort to "Adoption."

With Hindus it is indispensably necessary that there should be a son to perform obsequies or religious funeral rites, and to discharge ancestors' debts, spiritual and temporal.

Barrenness of parents.—These objects may be frustrated by the barrenness of the parents. In that case adoption is resorted to, which is a ceremony of especial import as regards inheritance, although that is merely a secondary consideration with Hindus; the primary object being to save the soul from Put, or Hell, or a place of torment.

Marriage is compulsory.—As marriage affects the religious state of the man, it is compulsory, not by judicial process, but in accordance with their own customs and usages. It is contracted at an immature age on the part of the woman, or rather infant. Its consummation, however, is postponed until the nubile age. But consummation is not necessary, as with us, to make the marriage valid, or to confer upon the wife all the rights and obligations of widowhood, should her husband die before her nubile age, and he has taken her to his own home. If the wife die, the husband is bound to marry immediately, whereas a widow was not permitted to contract a second marriage until the passing of Act xv. of 1856.

Eight species of marriage.—There are eight species of marriage, viz. :—The *Brahma*, the *Daiva*, the *Arsha*, the *Prajapatya*, which are appropriate for Brahmins, or the sacerdotal order, and are based upon disinterested motives.

The *Gandharva*, or love marriages.

The *Racshasa*, or forcible connection, which were peculiar to the shetriyas or the military class.

The *Asoora*, which is appropriate for vysyas, or the mercantile body, and for

Sudras, or the servile class, wherein the consent of the person giving away the girl is obtained by pecuniary consideration, forbidden because of its sordid character.

And the *Paishacha*, which is reprobated by all classes.

Menu enjoins that the two latter, *Asoora* and *Paishacha*, should never be observed, and *Sir Thomas Strange* cites the *Digest* to show that "at present the Brahma nuptials only are practised by good men, though it is admitted that the *Asoora* and the rest are sometimes resorted to by others, and it is questionable whether any other form is now observed in Southern India. At all events, it is clear that the several castes are not confined to the form applicable to themselves, for a *Brahmin* may contract an *Asoora* marriage, and a Sudra a Brahmin. Sudr. Court in *S. A.* 193 of 1858, and these two seem to be the most usual form of marriage. Custom, too, will regulate the form.

Wedding rites accompany all marriages.—Nuptial or wedding rites accompanying all classes of marriage, have the effect of distinguishing even the less approved from commerce purely illicit, to which otherwise the Gandharva and Racshasa might be assimilated.*

* Probably the Gandharva, the Racshasa, and Paishacha forms were originally considered as marriages, with a view to save the character of the woman and legitimate the offspring.

Different rites where wife not a virgin.—Should, however, the bride be known not to be a virgin, the rite is a distinct one. Marriage is celebrated with the ceremonies described, *post*, p. 21. The essence of the rite consists in the consent of the man on the one hand, and the father of the bride, or whoever gives her away, on the other.

The consent of both parents to the contract must be first had.

At the nubile age husband may claim wife.—A girl when married continues to reside with her own family until she reaches maturity, of which it is the duty of the mother to give notice, when her husband can claim her and remove her to his home.

Period of marriage of males.—There are certain rules laid down in *Menu* with regard to the respective ages at which men and women may marry, but which are seldom followed. *Mr Justice Strange* says, the Brahmins, Shetriyas, and the Vysyas may not contract marriage until they have completed the age of studentship, the opening of which period is marked by the performance of Oopanayana or investiture with the sacred thread, and the close by a ceremony *Samavurthana*. For the Sudras or servile class, who have no stage of studentship, there is no limitation of the time for marriage.

Period of marriage of females.—The proper time for betrothment of females precedes puberty. *Menu* enjoins the betrothment, although the girl may not have attained the age of eight years. Girls are given in marriage at the age of two and upwards until maturity. A Brahmin girl attaining maturity without having contracted marriage forfeits caste. The rule is not observed by Sudras.

Father bound to select husband for daughter.—Every Hindu father is expressly bound to select a suitable husband for his daughter at an age when she can have no idea of the object for which the contract has been entered into.

If the father fail to make the selection the duty devolves upon a succession of paternal relatives, viz., the grandfather, brother, uncle, male cousins.

Or mother.—And ultimately upon the mother. Practically she has the right of choosing after the death of the father.

Or the girl herself.—If a husband be not selected for the girl for three years from the time when she becomes marriageable, that is the attainment of eight years, she may choose for herself. Though the law be so, it may be a question whether, according to modern practice, the right does not in this case continue to attach to the substitutes for the father instead of vesting in the girl.

Return of presents on annulling the engagement.—If from any legal impediment, viz., incurable disease or other legal defect or consanguinity within the prohibited degrees, or from the death of the young woman, the marriage is not consummated, presents made to her *bonâ fide* as tokens of courtesy and pledges of affection, not as paid to her kinsmen for their own use by way of sale of her, which is forbidden, are to be returned, and in the latter case the expenses of both parties are defrayed by the gentleman. If the breach be on the girl's side without discovery of legal impediment, *her* family must bear the expenses.

Stridhana.—Those presents where the marriage has been completed constitute part of the woman's *stridhana*, or her peculiar property. See *post*, STRIDHANA.

Marriage consists of two ceremonies.—Marriage consists of two ceremonies. 1. Betrothal; 2. Consummation. Between each there may be a long interval of years. The betrothal, as it is termed, is in fact, as well as in law, the marriage. Although the execution of the contract, or consummation, necessarily follows it, it is not essential to the validity of the marriage.

Betrothal is absolute marriage.—Betrothal, as commonly understood, is merely a promise of marriage to be carried out at some future period. But as the word is understood in English works on Hindu law, it is, more properly speaking, an absolute marriage, so much so, that if a man dies before consummation the girl is entitled to all the rights, and incurs all the duties of widowhood, so that the death of the husband will not annul the contract. Formerly, she was debarred from contracting a second marriage with a different man, the Hindu law prohibiting a girl from being more than once married. But see now Act xv. of 1856, *post*, p. 28. English writers, treating on Hindu law, do not sufficiently mark the distinction between the betrothal as a step preceding a marriage, and the ceremony of marriage.

Mode of contracting marriage.—For legal purposes the ceremonies legally prescribed and followed are almost, if not altogether, immaterial. In a civil point of view the only thing necessary is mere gift and acceptance. *Mr Strange* says, that the only binding circumstance essential to the completion of a marriage are gift and acceptance of the girl, and the ceremony termed Sapthapathi, or the seven steps. The betrothment is effected by the bride and bridegroom walking seven steps, hand and hand, during a particular recital, and *Mr Strange* says, sacrifices by fire (Homam) are of minor importance. The tying the Taly, or nuptial token, round the neck of the bride is a practice sanctioned by usage, but not prescribed in the Shasters or sacred books, so that the many ceremonies imposed by ancient law in these matters would seem to have been observed merely with a view of obtaining satisfactory evidence of the contract, and much less is now required, since the object of these many ceremonies is more easily attained; and if it can be shown that the contract was made, all the other ceremonies subside into very secondary importance. The contract, being perfected, may be enforced by the husband at the maturity of the girl.

Contract fixes the connubial relation.—The matrimonial contract in itself fixes the relation of the contracting parties as married, without the requirement of consummation, which does not take place until the girl arrives at the nubile age, when her husband takes her from her home to his. The *contract* draws the girl, in the event of her husband's death, into widowhood, with its attendant consequences, and gives her the right of inheritance, or maintenance in her husband's family. But if her husband were divided, she, of course, would inherit as his heir, he leaving no male issue.

Rights thus created—duration of union—severance of—infidelity.—The only circumstance which the Court would consider a justification of the absolute severance of the contract of marriage is the adultery of the wife. The husband in such cases has the option either of absolute separation from his wife, or of superseding her by another, she still continuing to be legally connected with him. But in this latter case the adulterous wife is entitled in law only to a *starving maintenance;* the barest and smallest amount possible; and not even that where she has been divorced for adultery, and has continued in her crime during her husband's lifetime, and in unchastity after his death, *Muttammal* v. *Kamakshy Ammal, 2 Mad. H. C. R.*, 337; 1 *Mad. H. C. R.*, 372. A wife living in adultery apart from her husband, cannot recover maintenance from him so long as the adultery is uncondoned, *Teata Shavatri* v. *Teata Narayana Nambudiri*, 1 *Mad. H. C. R.*, 372. Her title to maintenance and also to inheritance on her husband's death therefore depends upon her preserving her chastity, unless the adultery has been condoned, in which case she is entitled to maintenance, *Teata Shavatri* v. *Teata Narayana Nambudiri.*

Sir Thomas Strange expresses an opinion that a wife cannot be divorced for adultery. But the better opinion seems to be that she can. *Sutherland's Synopsis: 2 Mad. H. C. R.*, 337.

Husband not entitled to damages.—The husband is not entitled to damages from the adulterer; the Hindu law not providing for discretionary damages upon any account. But this is doubtful. The exemption is placed on the ground that adultery is a crime punishable as such. This offence is now punishable under the Penal Code.

Before betrothal.—Previously, and up to betrothal, the contract rests legally in promise, which may be broken, subject to consequences as the breach can or cannot be justified. Breach of promise of marriage does not entail any special consequences. According to Hindu usage an agreement for marriage would be lawfully determined on the part of the man by the occurrence of unfavourable auspices, as the meeting of a single Brahmin, or a cat, or a flight of birds, or the chirping of a lizard, when seeking a prosperous hour for the wedding. These events may prevent the completion of betrothment, and *Sir Thomas Strange* adds, many causes are enumerated, warranting, as they respectively apply, retraction on either side.

With whom the contract may be entered into.—Another peculiar result of the religious character essential to the ceremony is, that a marriage may take place with a lunatic or an idiot, *a nativitate.* However immoral it may seem, the marriage with such a person, if made with the consent of his parents, is valid, and becomes binding. The reason would seem to be that a marriage is not a civil contract, but a sacrament. See *Macn. H. D.*, 2d ed., 57. But if the lunacy come on after his birth, and the marriage take place during the lunacy, the marriage is good even though without family consent. This case is based on the opinion of the Pundits who cite no authority. See *Tirumamagal Ammal* v. *Ramasvami Ayyangar*, 1 *Mad. H. C. R.*, p. 214, where an idiot was held incapable of inheriting.

Caste or class.—As to the necessity for an equality of caste to constitute a good marriage, *Sir Thomas Strange* says, that in the present era both parties must belong to the same caste, but of distinct and unconnected families, but the authorities quoted by him allowed the three higher castes to intermarry with the caste next below their own.

Sudra need not marry in the same caste.—It seems a Sudra need not marry a wife of the same sect or caste with himself.

Woman cannot marry in lower caste.—No woman can marry a man of a lower caste; such a contract is altogether illegal, the children are absolutely illegitimate, and consequently debarred from inheriting.

Illegitimacy is not an absolute disqualification for caste.—Hindu law does not discountenance illegitimacy. It has been held therefore by the High Court of Madras, that, independently of special usage or custom, the law does not make illegitimacy an absolute disqualification for caste, so as to affect in the relations of life not only the bastard but his legitimate children.

Marriage with daughter of bastard.—A Hindu of a caste governed by the Shasters may contract a valid marriage with the daughter of a bastard, *Pandaiva Telaver* v. *Puli Telaver*, 1 *Mad. H. C. R.*, p. 478. The general law applicable to all the classes or tribes does not seem opposed to marriage between individuals of different sects or divisions of the same class or tribe; and even as regards the marriage between individuals of a different class or tribe, the law appears to be no more than directory. Although it recommends and inculcates a marriage with a woman of equal class as a preferable description, yet the marriage of a man with a woman of a lower class or tribe than himself appears not to be an invalid marriage rendering the issue illegitimate. According to this view of the law, there being no proof of special custom or usage, the marriage would be valid even though the parties had been of different sects or caste-division of the fourth or Sudra class. This case came upon appeal to the Privy Council, when their lordships, in delivering judgment, said, all the parties being of the Sudra caste, it is said that because it is shown by a decree that the father of the mother of the present plaintiff respondent was illegitimate, therefore the child of that father could not contract a valid marriage, and was in substance of no caste at all. This contention is based upon the opinions of the Pundits, by whom no authority is cited; and where they refer to authority, it is to authority which applies to persons of two different but higher castes, not to the Sudra caste at all, and still less to what may be called different classes or divisions of one and the same Sudra caste. Their lordships are satisfied that in the Sudra caste illegitimate children may inherit and have a right to maintenance; and that in this very instance the illegitimate father of the mother of the plaintiff, as well as his daughter, were treated as members of the family, and that on the whole, seeing that these parties are both of the Sudra caste, and that the utmost that has been alleged really is that the zimindar was of one part of the Sudra caste, and the lady to whom he was married was of another part, or of a subcaste, their lordships hold the marriage to have been valid.—Privy Council, 14 July 1869.

It has been held that an agreement between two brothers for dividing their self-acquired property after their death equally between their wives and the sons born in concubinage was valid, *Sri Gajapathi Radhika Patta Maha Devi* v. *Sri Gajapathi Nilamani Patta Maha Devi*, 2 *Mad. H. C. R.*, 369. But the case coming up on appeal to the Privy Council, the Lords Commissioners held that, in their opinion, the High Court erred in making the illegitimate sons sharers with the widows.—*Ib.* 29 July 1870.

Loss of caste.—When forfeiture of caste is incurred by either, intercourse between husband and wife ceases.*

If by a sonless female.—Should the loss of caste be on the side of the female, and she be sonless, she is accounted dead, and funeral rites are performed for her.

If she have a son.—He is bound to maintain her, and by this means her existence is recognised.

Prohibited degrees.—But though the caste may be the same, the prohibited degrees of relationship are not to be infringed. Amongst the higher castes, a woman must not be descended from the paternal or maternal ancestors of her proposed husband within the sixth degree. But these rules, like those of caste, have greatly relaxed, and in all castes only uncles, brothers, and sisters, and their descendants are prohibited as being too nearly allied.

Marriage of younger brother or sister before an elder.—

* Degradation as a disqualification for inheritance is removed by Act xxi. of 1850.

It is said that the marriage of a younger brother or sister before an elder is discountenanced.

Adopted son.—An adopted son is considered as a natural child in all matters regarding marriage and degrees of affinity, but though he loses the rights of property derived from the family to which by birth he belongs, yet in respect of marriage and affinity he is still a member of that family, so that he is under a double disadvantage as regards marriage. He can neither marry within the prohibited degrees into the family who has adopted him, nor can he marry within the same degrees into the family from which he has come. See "Adoption."

Causes of separation.—There are other causes of separation besides infidelity, not absolute indeed, or a severance of the marriage tie, but entitling the wife to maintenance. These are mainly caused by disappointment of the object of marriage, and arise from impotence in the man, confirmed barrenness in the woman, loathsome incurable disease in either, or production of only daughters, and the like.

Supersession * or polygamy.—Supersession is that right by which a man claims to have a plurality of wives. According to Hindu law and usage, polygamy is permitted, and it is competent to the Hindus to have several wives. How many, *Sir Thomas Strange* observes, it is competent to him to have at one and the same time does not distinctly appear.† The prohibition which is found to be directed against a plurality of wives, save under certain justifying circumstances, such as the first wife's infidelity, bad temper, barrenness, or production only of daughters, appears to be treated alike, as many other rules of Hindu law, as merely directory and not imperative. It is a practice, however, which is objected to by a majority of Hindus in Bengal, who have petitioned the Governor-General of India in council to suppress it by enactment.

But the husband cannot supersede his wife at his mere pleasure. In some instances it is justifiable, in others it is only admissible; and where it can neither be justified nor tolerated, it is illegal.

Justifying circumstances.—Such circumstances may be classified under two heads—viz., 1st, Consent; 2d, Legal causes.

1*st*, *Consent.*—The consent of the wife without any disqualifying causes on her part of itself warrants re-marriage. Many devices are resorted to for the purpose of obtaining her consent and reconciling her to her altered position, such as a suitable settlement, a compensation, amounting, with her *stridhana*, or

* The word "supersession" has been retained in deference to the earlier writers on Hindu Law. It is not accurate to say that because a man takes a second wife he supersedes the first. Both live together if possible in harmony.—Polygamy is more correct.

† In one case the husband had seven wives.

woman's property, to a value equivalent to the expenses of the second marriage. But the measure of gratuity for supersession seems not to be settled. In estimating it, however, account is to be taken of what she already possesses, and the difference only is to be given her, and if the difference is the other way, then a trifle only for form's sake.

2*d, Legal causes.* When the first wife is addicted to habits of intoxication, has been long diseased, bears daughters for ten years, exhibits want of chastity, is habitually disobedient or disrespectful towards her lord, is bad-tempered, barren, expensive, mischievous, abusive.

It has, however, been said that cheerful acquiescence on her part entitles her to proportionable liberality, while contumacious resistance subjects her to coercion, public exposure, and correction.

The second marriage will not be invalidated by reason of the absence of these justifying causes.

Present on second marriage.—We have seen that when the wife has consented to the second marriage, the husband is bound to make her a suitable present equal, with her *stridhana*, to the expenses of the second marriage. We may observe, however, that for this the wife may sue the husband, although her misconduct would be an answer to the action.

Illegal supersession is the abandonment for another, of a blameless and efficient wife who has given neither cause nor assent, for which the husband may be brought to his senses by the king, by severe chastisement.

The respondent betrothed his daughter to the appellant, who having afterwards contracted a second marriage (by the Natra rite), the respondent sought to compel the appellant either to consent to a divorce, or to dissolve the second marriage, and admit his daughter to her rights. It was urged, in defence, that the appellant was full grown, and the respondent's daughter not arrived at years of puberty, and under these circumstances a second marriage was permitted by the rules of their caste (*Lewa Koonbi*); it was held that the appellant's conduct was justified by the rules of the caste, and by the laws of the Shaster, and the divorce, or annulment, was refused.

A wife is entitled to a divorce for ill treatment according to the rules of the Kunsara caste.

A divorce will be granted on account of a husband's dissolute life and bad character if the caste permits it, though the *Shaster* does not admit of divorce under any circumstances. A man of the Gandharva caste married a second wife; the court held that unless there was good cause, *natra* was not permitted amongst them. The court granted a divorce to the first wife, as they both did not agree.

A wife leaving her husband for a justifying cause is entitled to maintenance; but not if there is no such cause. But the second marriage of the wife is not a justifying cause, *Virasvami Chetti* v. *Appasvami Chetti*, 1 *Mad. H. C. R.*, 375; and if in such a case the first wife leaves him, she has no implied authority to pledge his credit for her support, *ib.*

But adultery is not a sufficient cause for the wife to desert her husband, although insanity, impotence, and degradation might perhaps be considered so.

Residence of first wife.—A wife who has been thus superseded, whether justifiably or not, must be provided for. She should continue to reside with her husband, or if he oblige her to leave him, with his relatives; or failing them, her own, and he is bound to maintain her.

Entitled to inherit.—Abandoning an innocent wife under circumstances other than those named is immoral and punishable. In such a case the first wife is in nowise to suffer in position. She will, for instance, inherit just as if no second wife had been taken, and her debts would be binding on her husband.

Residence of several wives.—Where there were several wives, according to the old rule, of different castes, they ranked according to their castes. But precedence is now given according to seniority of marriage, as all must be of the same caste. The one first married is therefore the one who is to be still honoured, not having been superseded for any fault, and she it is, the elder, not necessarily in years, but according to priority of nuptials, who succeeds eventually to her husband as heir, maintaining the others, who inherit in their turn on her death, or even during her life, in the event of her degradation, or on her marriage, forfeiture of inheritance having in that case been ordained (Act xvi., 1856), possessing as they do a capacity for the performance of religious ceremonies being the consideration upon which the widow as well as the son is preferred in inheritance. See *post*. Mr Justice Strange observes, it has been held that where there may be a plurality of wives the one first married succeeds to the exclusion of the others, *judgment of Sudr. Court in R. A.* 5 of 1824, and i. of 1835. This, he remarks, is not the law in Southern India, where the wives are viewed as on an equality, and inherit jointly. Mr Strange refers to *Smiriti Chand.* p. 178, § 57, by which he is supported.

Personal chastisement of wife.—According to Menu the husband occupied the place of a father to his wife, and was permitted therefore to exact absolute obedience by personal chastisement. But such a law would receive no sanction in a British court.

Withdrawal of conjugal rights.—The denial or withdrawal of conjugal rights by either party is denounced with heavy penalties, and the relative duty of maintaining each other is enjoined.

Divorce according to Hindu law.—This right would seem to be confined to the husband. Amongst some of the lowest castes divorce is obtainable by each, and the woman may marry again. Such marriage is called *Natra,* and is familiar in Bombay.

Re-marriage.—The doctrine that a Hindu widow cannot re-marry, has been abolished by Act xv. of 1856. Section 1 provides that no marriage contracted with Hindus shall be invalid, and the issue of no such marriage shall be illegitimate by reason of the woman having been previously married, or betrothed to another person, who was dead at the time of such marriage, any custom and any interpretation of Hindu law to the contrary notwithstanding. Section 2 annuls upon a marriage all rights and interests which any widow may have in her deceased husband's property by way of maintenance, by way of inheritance to her husband, or to his lineal successors, or by way of any will or testamentary disposition conferring upon her without express permission to re-marry, only a limited interest in such property with no power of alienating the same. Section 4 provides that, nothing in this Act shall be construed to render any widow who, at the time of the death of any person leaving any property, is a childless widow, capable of inheriting the whole or any share of such property; if before the passing of this Act, she would have been incapable of inheriting the same by reason of her being a childless widow. Except as in the preceding sections is provided, a widow shall not by reason of her re-marriage forfeit any property or any right to which she would otherwise be entitled, and any widow who has re-married shall have the same right of inheritance as she would have had, had such marriage been her first marriage, *sect.* 5.

Where a Hindu died leaving a widow, a minor son, and daughter, the estate vested in the son, but the widow re-married. The son died, and the mother claimed to succeed by inheritance to him, but his step-mother took possession of the property. Both the superior courts decided in favour of the mother, and on the final appeal the High Court confirmed the decision of the court below. The Chief-Justice, Sir Barnes Peacock, held that the right of the mother to inherit to her deceased son accrued, after her re-marriage, and was not taken away by the operation of sect. 2, and Mr Justice Jackson, concurring with the Chief-Justice, intimated an opinion that, although the decision was in accordance with the words of the Act, it was not in accordance with the intention of the legislature. But it is not, said the learned judge, our province to set aside the clear meaning of the words of the legislature for the purpose of getting rid of apparent inconsistencies.

Suttee or wife-burning or burying alive is abolished, *Reg.* 1 of 1830, § 4, cl. 2, and § 5.

All persons convicted of aiding and abetting in the sacrifice of a Hindu widow by burning or burying her alive, whether the sacrifice be voluntary or not, shall be guilty of culpable homicide, and shall be liable to be punished by fine, imprisonment, or both, nor shall it be held to be any plea of justification that he or she was desired by the person sacrificed to assist in putting her to death, *ib.*

When husband and wife live together, the presumption is that the wife is the husband's agent for contracting debts for the necessities of the family. But by Hindu law this presumption is perhaps not so strong as it is by English law, 1 *Mad. H. C. R.*, 375.

CHAPTER II.

ON ADOPTION.

Sections.

I. General observations.
II. Who may adopt.
III. Who cannot adopt.
IV. Who may give.
V. Who may be adopted.
VI. Effect of adoption.
VII. Mode of adoption.

Section I.—*General observations.*

Hindu law of adoption based on spiritual necessities—Marriage directed to sonship—Adoption put in force in failure of male issue—Etymology of Puttra—Some difference in the several schools on adoption—By Hindu law adopted son becomes as a natural born son—Exception to rule—Failing son, widow may perform obsequies—Presumption in favour of adoption—Evidence of adoption—Natural born sons—Failure of—It is not the son's performance of obsequial rites that saves from Put—The father may adopt whom he will.

Hindu law of adoption based on spiritual necessities.—The Hindu law of adoption, like that of inheritance, is based upon the spiritual necessities of a Hindu.

Marriage directed to sonship.—Sonship being indispensable to him, his marriage is mainly directed to that object, with a view to the procreation of a fitting person to perform exequial rites and discharge his ancestor's debts, or spiritual obligations; and so important are these held to be by Hindus, that if marriage should fail in its object, they must have recourse to the expedient of adoption, by which a substitute for a natural born son is obtained.

Adoption, on failure of a son, as a substitute for one, is regarded as the means of redemption from an instant state of suffering after death. The dread is of a place called Put, or Hell, a place of horror to which the *manes* of the childless are supposed to be doomed, there to be tormented with hunger and thirst, for want of those oblations of food and libations of water, at prescribed periods, which it is the pious, and indeed indispensable, duty of a son to offer. By this means he is supposed to save his parent from Put, and is consequently called *puttra*, or son.

Etymology of Puttra.—The etymology of *Puttra*, the Sanscrit word for "son," shows the necessity that compels every Hindu to perpetuate his name. *Menu* says, "Since the son (trayate) delivers his father from the hell named Put, he was therefore called *puttra* by Brahma himself." Again, "A son of any description should be anxiously adopted by one who has no male issue, for the funeral cake, water, and solemn rites, and for the celebrity of his name," *Smriti*, quoted in *Ratnakara*.

The ancient law recognised eleven kinds of adopted sons, but now the one or two recognised are *dattaka*, or the son *given*, and the *kritrima*, or son made, which are, generally speaking, the only subsisting adoptions allowed to be capable of answering the purpose of sons, though in some of the northern provinces forms of adoption other than that of the Dattaka still prevail. The *Kritrima* form of adoption prevails in the province of Mithila. In strictness, perhaps, this form should be held to be abrogated. But the practice of adopting in the *Dattaka* form should not vitiate a *Kritrima* form, unless that mode was prohibited by works on law of paramount local authority. But immemorial usage legalises any practice.

Some difference in the several schools on adoption.—On the subject of adoption there is some difference in the several schools. The *Dattaka Chandrika* and *Dattaka Mimamsa* are the two chief authorities, and equally respected by all the schools. Nearly all schools follow the Dattaka Chandrika in preference to the Dattaka Mimamsa, where these celebrated treatises differ, *The Ramnad case*, 21 May 1868.

By Hindu law adopted son becomes as a natural born son.—To all intents and purposes the adopted becomes as the natural born son of the adoptive family, and loses all rights in his native family, since he is introduced for religious purposes and benefits, to rescue the father from Put or everlasting misery. If the adoption be invalid, his natural rights would remain unaffected, or unless in a *dwyamushyayana* adoption.

Exception to Rule.—There is, however, only one exception to this rule, and this is the case of an after-born son. And in this case, the natural born son supersedes the adopted son, who, however, receives one-fourth of the share of the after-born son as a consideration for the injury done him by removal from his own family. Should the natural born son die without male issue, the adopted child will succeed to the whole of the property of his adoptive father, subject to charges elsewhere noticed. See *post*, "Charges on Property."

Failing son, widow may perform obsequies.—Failing a son, a Hindu's obsequies may be performed by his widow, or, in default of her, by a whole brother or other heirs, but not with the same benefit as by a son. That a son, therefore, of some description, is with him, in a spiritual sense, next to indispensable, is abundantly certain. But exacted as adoption is, whenever the want exists, in terms sufficiently peremptory, it is a right, and not a duty to be enforced by the civil power, succession to his property being in all events provided for, whether he have a son to inherit it or not.*

Presumption in favour of adoption.—The presumption in favour of adoption is strong, for the spiritual welfare of the husband depends upon his being represented by a son.

Evidence of adoption.—Where there is conflicting evidence upon the fact of an adoption, much will depend upon the probabilities of the case, to be collected from facts as to which both parties are agreed: as, in the case of a childless Hindu advanced in years, where it was in the highest degree improbable that he could have any children by his wives, and he adopted a boy, in despair of having issue, who died in his adoptive father's lifetime, the fact of his religious tenets, by which his salvation depended upon his leaving a son to perform his funeral oblation, was held to be strong probability in favour of such adoption.

The evidence of witnesses to the fact of a parol adoption, without deed, was contradictory. The provincial law courts in India held that a claimant to the succession as adopted son had not established, by credible testimony, the fact of such adoption. Upon appeal, such decrees were reversed, the court holding that the presumption in the circumstances was in favour of adoption, and that the evidence was sufficient to establish the claimant's title.

Natural born sons.—Of course, if there are natural born sons, or sons born in wedlock, no difficulties as to heirship can possibly present themselves in performance of exequial rites.

Failure of.—But should male issue fail, or, in consequence of their disqualification for inheritance where they exist, they should be incompetent to the performance of funeral rites, then very important questions arise as to the rights of adoption amongst Hindus.

It is not the son's performance of obsequial rights that saves from Put.—Mr Strange maintains that the mere birth of a son, who may die immediately after, saves from Put, but adds he may nevertheless adopt a son to perform his funeral rites, and keep up his line.

In *Chinna Gaundan* v. *Kumara Guaundan*, 1 *Mad. H. C. R.*, 57,

* It is on this ground that wills are said to be unknown to Hindu law. See *post*, "Alienation by Will."

Sir Colley Scotland, C.J., says, Mr Strange's argument rests on the assumption that it is the birth, or adoption of the son that delivers the natural, or adoptive, father from Put. Surely this is erroneous. It is the son's performance of the father's exequial rites, not his birth or adoption, that relieves the father from Put. Adoption takes place, according to *Atri* (*Dattaka Chandrika*), for the sake of the funeral cake, water, and solemn rites. According to *Menu* (and *Dattaka Miman.*) for these objects, and also for the celebrity of the adoptive father's name, but not for the sake of the supposed efficacy of the mere act of adoption. If, then, the saving virtue lies solely in the performance of exequial rites, Mr Justice Strange's doctrine of the total expenditure on the natural father of the efficacy of the son's birth does not seem to warrant his conclusion. The adoptive son may well perform his adoptive father's rites, and in certain cases it appears, when he is dwyamuchyayana (*i.e.*, the son of two fathers), those of his natural father also. See observations on this case, *post*.

The Father may adopt whom he will.—We shall consider the subject under the following heads:—

1. Who may adopt.
2. Who cannot adopt.
3. Who may give.
4. Who may be adopted.
5. The effect of adoption.
6. The mode of adoption.

SECTION II.

WHO MAY ADOPT.

Sonless man—Consent of wife—Whether a father, having given away an only son, may adopt another—Who included in legitimate issue, son, grandson, and great-grandson—Grandson by daughter—Two individuals cannot adopt the same son—Uncle cannot adopt a nephew already given in adoption to another—The adoption must be valid when made—Where male issue incompetent to the performance of funeral rites—Successive adoptions—Undivided brothers.

Sonless man.—Any Hindu may adopt, who is destitute of male issue competent to the performance of his funeral rites, or, as it is expressed, for the sake of the funeral cake, water, and solemn rites, and celebrity of his name, and redemption from debt to his progenitors. A man is destitute of male issue, to whom no son has been born, or whose son has died. None can adopt, therefore, who have male issue competent to the performance of funeral rites, *infra*. At the moment of birth a man becomes father of male issue, and is absolved from debt to his progenitors.

Consent of wife.—The consent of a wife to the adoption of a son by her husband (a childless Hindu) is not essential to the validity of the adoption. Adoption is an act of the husband alone, although the wife may join in it, and although it may inure for the benefit of both.

Whether a father, having given away an only son, may adopt another.—The benefit of the son may form a consideration with a father for giving him in adoption. Thus, he may be himself without the means of providing for his son, and may consequently, for the lad's interests, be induced to give him in adoption to one who is sonless, but possessed of property. Being thus deprived of the most fitting person to perform his exequial rites, there seems to be no objection to his adopting a son for that purpose.

Who included in legitimate issue, son, grandson, and great-grandson.—"Male issue" comprises three generations—viz., the son, the grandson, and the great-grandson, *i.e.*, the son's grandson. All stand in the relation of sons for the purposes of inheritance and religious ceremonies. Where there is, therefore, a son's son or grandson, adoption is not necessary; and not only is it not necessary, but the son being dead, adoption would operate prejudicially to their rights of inheritance.

It therefore results, that one only destitute of a grandson or great-grandson may adopt.

Grandson by daughter.—It has been doubted, says *Macn.* in his *Principles of H. L.*, note, by the author of the *Considerations*, whether a grandson by a daughter is within the above rule; but there is no solid foundation on which such a doubt can rest. It must have arisen from the indiscriminate use of the word ("grandson") in the English translations, as applicable to the daughter's son, as well as to the son's son. *Mr Sutherland*, in his *Synopsis*, infers, and justly, that if male issue exist who are disqualified by any legal impediment (such as loss of caste) from the performance of exequial rights, the affiliation may legally take place. In the *Summary of Hindu Law*, it is laid down as a rule that the insanity of a begotten son would not justify adoption by a parent; but to this and other general positions laid down in that work, I cannot altogether accede. For instance, it is stated that the *Púna Shastris* do not recognise the necessity that adoption should precede marriage; that a younger brother may be adopted by an elder one; that the youngest son of a family cannot be adopted, &c., &c.; for none of which can I find authority, though undoubtedly the whole of these positions may be just when applied to that side of India, as founded on the *lex loci* or immemorial custom.

Two individuals cannot adopt the same son.—The same person must not be adopted by two individuals, except in the case of one nephew by several uncles, the whole brothers of his natural father, *Suther. Synop.*

Uncle cannot adopt a nephew already given in adoption to another.—It may be inferred that a legal impediment would exist to the affiliation by an uncle of a nephew, whom his father had given away in adoption as a *Sudha Dattaka,* who retains no filial relation to his natural father, *Suther. Synop.* Head 2d.

The adoption must be valid when made.—The adoption must be valid when made, for its inherent defects cannot be cured.

Where male issue incompetent to the performance of funeral rites.—If a man have male issue, who, however, from any reason, such as degradation from caste, insanity, disease, &c., are incompetent to the performance of funeral rites, to all intents and religious purposes he is without issue, and may therefore adopt.

Successive adoptions.—Whatever reasons require the adoption of one, also allow succeeding adoptions to be made when the purposes of the first fail, as when the first dies without issue or adoption. But only one adopted son can be taken at a time, and he succeeds to all the property of his adoptive father.

In *Rungama* v. *Atchama* and *Atchama* v. *Ramanadha,* 4 *Moore's In. Ap.* 1, the Privy Council held that a second adoption of a son, the first living, was illegal and void.

This case has been acted on *Sudanund Mohapattur* v. *Bonomallee,* 1 *Beng. H. C. R.,* 317. Although no second adoption can be made during the life of the son first adopted; and though no adoption can be cancelled or annulled for any purpose whatsoever which would not justify a disinheritance; yet in case of death, disinheritance, or the like, another may be adopted, because in such case the very objects of adoption would be frustrated.

Undivided brothers.—Adoption is made quite regardless of the rights which may be injuriously affected by it as by one of two undivided brothers.

Section III.

WHO CANNOT ADOPT.

Unmarried men—Wife or Widow—When to be adopted—Verbal authority—Widow under authority granted by minor ward without authority of Court of Wards—Dancing girls—Disqualifying circumstances—Minor—Lunatic—Out-caste.

Unmarried men.—*Sir Thomas Strange* says, the necessity of the thing applies whether a man be single, married, or a widower, since to all equally his future state, according to his conception of it, is of the last importance. If with the Hindus the competency of a single man to adopt do not appear to rest upon much authority, it is probably owing to the universality of early marriages between both sexes, which makes celibacy exceptional, *Sutherland's Synopsis*. *Mr Justice Strange* in his *Manual*, takes a different view. He says, an unmarried man cannot make an adoption; but for this he cites only a Pundit's opinion. Again he says, unmarried males, of whatever age, and females, whether married or unmarried, are not in danger of Put. No adoption on their account is hence necessary, neither would such adoption be valid; but for this no authority is cited. It has been held by the High Court of Madras, that an adoption by a widower is valid according to Hindu law. See observations on this case in *Grady's Hindu Law*, p. 31.

Wife or widow.—A wife or widow may adopt on behalf of her husband, but on the authority of the husband only, given during his life and for his benefit; the child being adopted to him, and not to herself. The adoption having taken place, the adopted becomes son to both, and is capable of performing funeral rites to both. But in *Anandayí* alias *Kunjara Natchiar* v. *Rani Parvatavardani Natchiar*, 2 *Mad. H. C. R.*, 206 (the Ramnad case), it was held that a widow can adopt a son without the consent of her husband, according to Hindu law; and that where a widow adopted a son, with assent of the majority of the surviving kindred of her husband, the adoption was valid. But if the requirements of the consent of the sapindas is anything more than a moral precept, the assent of any one of them will suffice.

This decision came upon appeal before the Privy Council on the 21st of May 1868, when their Lordships, in delivering judgment, said :—

"The principal contest has been upon the broad and general question, whether by the Hindu law, as current in what is known as the Dravada country (wherein Ramnad is situate), a widow can adopt a son to her husband without his express authority; and if so, by whose assent that defect of authority must be supplied.

"Their Lordships think it will be convenient to consider in the first place how this question really stands upon the authority of *Mr Colebrooke* and *Sir Thomas Strange*.

"*Mr Colebrooke's* note on the *Mitacshára* (chap. i., sect. 2, art. 9), which has been much discussed, clearly involves three propositions :—1. That the widow's power to receive a son in adoption, subject to some conditions, is now admitted by all the schools of Hindu law, except that of Mithila. 2. That the Bengal (or Gaura) School insists that the widow must have the formal permission of her husband in his lifetime. 3. That some at least of the other schools admit the adoption to be valid, if made by the widow with the assent of her husband's kindred. The two first propositions are admitted; but it has been argued for the appellants, that on the true construction of this note, *Mr Colebrooke's* authority for the last proposition is limited to the Mahratta School, in which the treatise called the *Mayucha* is the predominant authority. *Balambhatta*, however, whom he cites as an authority for a power of adoption in the widow, wider even than that expressed in the third proposition, was a commentator of the Benares School. And the several notes of *Mr Colebrooke*, at pp. 92, 96, and 115 of the 2d volume of *Strange's Hindu Law*, seem to their Lordships to show conclusively that he considered the doctrine embodied in the third proposition to be common 'to the followers of the *Mitacshára* in the Benares as well as in the Mahratta School,' and as such to be receivable as the law current in the Zilla Vizagapatam, which lies within the northern or Andhra division of the Dravada country.

"Again, *Sir Thomas Strange's* statement of the law is clear and unambiguous. He says, 'Equally loose is the reason alleged against adoption by a widow, since the assent of the husband may be given to take effect, like a will, after his death; and according to the doctrine of the Benares and Mahratta Schools prevailing in the Peninsula, it may be supplied by that of his kindred, her natural guardians; but it is otherwise by the law that governs the Bengal provinces.'

"Their Lordships entertain no doubt that the term, 'the Peninsula,' as used here, and other passages by the same author, denotes that part of India which is south of the line drawn from Ganjam to the Gulf of Cambay, and includes the whole of the Dravada district. The learned counsel for the appellants, however, appeal from *Sir Thomas Strange* as a text writer, to *Sir Thomas Strange* as a judge, and cite his dictum in *Pillai* v. *Pillai* (2 *Strange's Notes of Cases*, p. 103), as opposed to this passage. In that case, *Sir Thomas Strange*, after citing the text of *Vasishta*, says: 'Hence it may be inferred, what appears confirmed by opinions of living Hindu lawyers, and by every case of the kind we are acquainted with, that the consent of the husband is indispensable to adoption into his family.' But this passage does not alter the view which their Lordships have already expressed as to the effect of the matured authority of *Sir Thomas Strange.* The precise question which is now under consideration was not in issue in that case, where there was a written authority from the husband, and where the real issue was, whether the widow could adopt a boy not designated in that written authority. Again, the case was decided in 1801, at a time when the ancient authorities of Hindu law were far less accessible to a European judge than they have since become. And *Sir Thomas Strange*, in his work composed twenty years later, says of this very case of *Pillai* v. *Pillai*, that it was discussed on comparatively imperfect materials; that the public was not then possessed of the extensive information contained in *Mr Colebrooke's* translation on the law of inheritance, and the treatises on adoption since translated by

Mr Sutherland, to say nothing of the MS. materials that came subsequently to his own hands, and which had contributed largely to every chapter of his work. There can, therefore, be no doubt but that the passage in his book contains the matured opinion of *Sir Thomas Strange*, and that it must be treated as an authoritative declaration of that opinion controlling his dictum in *Pillai* v. *Pillai*.

"Having thus ascertained what was the opinion of two of the highest European authorities upon this question of the Hindu law current in the south of India, their Lordships have next to consider whether any sufficient reason has been assigned for treating that opinion as unfounded.

"The remoter sources of the Hindu law are common to all the different schools. The process by which those schools have been developed seems to have been of this kind. Works universally, or very generally received became the subject of subsequent commentaries. The commentator put his own gloss on the ancient text; and his authority having been received in one and rejected in another part of India, schools with conflicting doctrines arose. Thus the *Mitacshára*, which is universally accepted by all the schools except that of Bengal as of the highest authority, and which in Bengal is received also as of high authority, yielding only to the *Daya Bhága* in those points where they differ, was a commentary on the *Institutes of Yajnavalchya*; and the *Daya Bhága*, which, wherever it differs from the *Mitacshára*, prevails in Bengal, and is the foundation of the principal divergencies between that and the other schools, equally admits and relies on the authority of *Yajnavalchya*. In like manner there are glosses and commentaries upon the *Mitacshára*, which are received by some of the schools that acknowledge the supreme authority of that treatise, but are not received by all. This very point of the widow's right to adopt is an instance of the process in question. All the schools accept as authoritative the text of *Vasishta*, which says, 'Nor let a woman give or accept a son unless with the assent of her lord.' But the Mithila School apparently takes this to mean that the assent of the husband must be given at the time of the adoption, and, therefore, that a widow cannot receive a son in adoption, according to the Dattaka form, at all. The Bengal School interprets the text as requiring an express permission given by the husband in his lifetime, but capable of taking effect after his death; whilst the *Mayucha* and *Koustubha* treatises which govern the Mahratta School, explain the text away by saying that it applies only to an adoption made in the husband's lifetime, and is not to be taken to restrict the widow's power to do that which the general law prescribes as beneficial to her husband's soul. Thus upon a careful review of all these writers, it appears that the difference relates rather to what shall be taken to constitute, in cases of necessity, evidence of authority from the husband, than to the authority to adopt being independent of the husband.

"The duty, therefore, of a European judge, who is under the obligation to administer Hindu law, is not so much to inquire whether a disputed doctrine is fairly deducible from the earliest authorities, as to ascertain whether it has been received by the particular school which governs the district with which he has to deal, and has there been sanctioned by usage. For under the Hindu system of law, clear proof of usage will outweigh the written text of the law. The respondent *Ramalinga* insists that, tried by either test, the proposition for which he contends will be found to be correct.

"The industry and research of the counsel in the courts below have brought together a *catena* of texts, of which many have been taken from works little known and of doubtful authority. Their Lordships concur with the Judges of the High Court in declining to allow any weight to these. But the highest European authorities, *Mr Colebrooke, Sir Thomas Strange, Sir William Macnaghten*, all concur in treating as works of unquestionable authority in the south of India, the *Mitacshára*, the *Smriti Chandrika*, and the *Madhavyam*, the two latter being, as it were, the peculiar treatises of the southern or Dravada school. Again, of the *Dattaka Mimansa* of *Nanda Pandita*, and the *Dattaka Chandrika*, two treatises on the particular subject of adoption, *Sir William Macnaghten* says that they are respected all over India; but that when they differ the doctrine of the latter is adhered to in Bengal and by the southern jurists, while the former is held to be the infallible guide in the provinces of Mithila and Benares. The *Dattaka Mimansa*, by the author of the *Madhavyam*, is also recognized as of high authority in the south of India by *Mr Ellis*, in his note at page 168 of the 2d volume of *Strange*.

"Of these treatises, the *Mitacshára* is silent on the point in question. The *Dattaka Mimansa* of *Nanda Pandita* (sec. 1, arts. 15 to 18, and arts. 27 and 28) is opposed to the respondent's view of it; but it seems equally opposed to an adoption by a widow under any circumstances. The *Dattaka Chandrika* (sec. 1, arts. 31 and 32) allows a widow to give a son in adoption where her husband has not forbidden her to do so, implying his assent from the absence of prohibition. The *Smriti Chandrika* also permits a mother to give her son, if she be authorised to do so by an independent male. And it is argued that what these two last authorities lay down concerning a widow's right to give, must, by parity of reasoning, be taken to be laid down concerning her right to receive a son in adoption. The *Madhavyam* (if that term is confined to the *Parasara Madhaviya*, and does not embrace all the works of *Vidya Narainsamy*) seems also to contain no direct determination of the point in question; but the *Dattaka Mimansa* of that author clearly and explicitly declares the right of the widow to adopt with the authority of her father-in-law, and whatever other kinsmen of her husband may be comprehended under the *et cætera*. It cannot, therefore, be said that the proposition laid down by *Mr Colebrooke*, and adopted by *Sir Thomas Strange*, is not supported by at least one of the original treatises of undoubted authority in Dravada. The *Dattaka Mimansa* of *Sri Rama Pandita*, who is stated by the Judges of the High Court to be an authority very generally cited in the south of India, also confirms the proposition.

"Their Lordships have excluded from their consideration of what is the positive law of Dravada, the peculiarly Mahratta treatises (the *Mayucha* and *Koustubha*): and also the *Viro Mitrodaya*, which is a treatise of especial authority at Benares. It must, however, be admitted, that the fact of the reception of the doctrine in question by schools so closely allied to that of Dravada, is in favour of the hypothesis that it also obtains in the latter, and strengthens the authorities which directly support that hypothesis.

"The evidence that the doctrine for which the respondents contend has been sanctioned by usage in the south of India, consists partly of the opinions of Pundits, partly of decided cases. Their Lordships cannot but think that the former have been too summarily dealt with by the Judges of the High Court. These opinions, at one time enjoined to be followed, and long directed to be taken by the courts, were official, and could not be shaken without weakening the foundation of much that is now received as the Hindu law in various parts of British India. Upon such materials the earlier works of European writers on the Hindu law, and the earlier decisions of our courts, were mainly founded. The opinion of a Pundit, which is found to be in conflict with the translated works of authority, may reasonably be rejected; but those which are consistent with such works should be accepted as evidence that the doctrine which they embody has not become obsolete, but is still received as part of the customary law of the country. A considerable body of these futwahs or opinions is collected in the third part of what has been called throughout the argument in this case the 'green book.' It is not necessary to consider whether they can all of them be supported to the full extent of what they affirm. But they show a considerable concurrence of opinion to the effect that where the authority of her husband is wanting, a widow may adopt a son with the assent of his kindred in the Dravada country.

"The decided cases, exclusive of those in the Bombay Presidency, which may be taken to be governed by the *Mayucha*, are certainly not many. But there is at least the case G, decided by the late Sudder Court of Madras, and there are the French cases, which ought not, their Lordships think, to be wholly disregarded as recognitions of the law prevailing in the south of India. They are to be relied on in this case as affording evidence of a long-continued series of opinions officially given, and judicially received, which were adopted as the ground of decision, showing a continued and recognised existence of a doctrine, which suffices to remove from the opinions of the Pundits in this case every suspicion of being opinions given to support the interests or judgments of others. Against these authorities the appellants have invoked that of the case in 2 *Knapp*, p. 203. But what was, in fact, decided by the very guarded judgment delivered by the late *Lord Wensleydale* in that case? It was that, according to the native text-writers —including probably *Vasishta*, certainly including the *Dattaka Mimansa* of *Nanda Pandita*—the authority of the husband was a requisite to a valid adoption; that the strictness of the law had been in many districts, and particularly in the Mahratta States, relaxed or modified by local usage, but that it had not been established to their Lordships' satisfaction that that relaxation had extended to the particular district of Etawah, in Upper India. Disclaiming, therefore, the intention to decide what was the law in other parts of India, their Lordships held that they could not say that the law in that district did not require the direction of the husband in order to the validity of an adoption, which it was necessary for them to do in order to reverse the judgment of the court below. It is clear that that decision was not intended to govern, and cannot be taken to govern, a case arising in the south of India.

"Upon the whole, then, their Lordships are of opinion that there is enough of positive authority to warrant the proposition that according to the law prevalent in the Dravada country, and particularly in that part of it wherein this Ramnad zemindary is situate, a Hindu widow, not having her husband's permission, may, if duly authorised by his kindred, adopt a son to him. And they think that that positive authority affords a foundation for the doctrine safer than any built upon speculations touching the natural development of the Hindu law, or upon analogies, real or supposed, between adoptions according to the Dattaka form, and the obsolete practice, with which that form of adoption co-existed, of raising up issue to the deceased husband by carnal intercourse with the widow. It may be admitted that the arguments founded on this supposed analogy are in some measure confirmed by passages in several of the ancient treatises above referred to, and in particular by the *Dattaka Mimansa* of *Vidya Narainsamy*, the author of the *Madhavyam*; but as a ground for judicial decision these speculations are inadmissible, though as explanatory arguments to account for an actual practice they may be deserving of attention.

"It must, however, be admitted that the doctrine is stated in the old treatises, and even by *Mr Colebrooke*, with a degree of vagueness that may occasion considerable difficulties and inconveniences in its practical application. The question who are the kinsmen whose assent will supply the want of positive authority from the deceased husband, is the first to suggest itself. Where the husband's family is in the normal condition of a Hindu family—*i.e.*, undivided—that question is of comparatively easy solution. In such a case the widow, under the law of all the schools which admit this disputed power of adoption, takes no interest in her husband's share of the joint estate, except a right to maintenance. And though the father of the husband, if alive, might, as the head of the family and the natural guardian of the widow, be competent by his sole assent to authorise an adoption by her, yet, if there be no father, the consent of all the brothers, who, in default of adoption, would take the husband's share, would probably be required, since it would be unjust to allow the widow to defeat their interest by introducing a new co-parcener against their will. Where, however, as in the present case, the widow has taken by inheritance the separate estate of her husband, there is greater difficulty in laying down a rule. The power to adopt, when not actually given by the husband, can only be exercised when a foundation for it is laid in the otherwise neglected observance of religious duty, as understood by Hindus. Their Lordships do not think there is any ground for saying that the consent of every kinsman, however remote, is essential. The assent of kinsmen seems to be required by reason of the presumed incapacity of women for independence, rather than the necessity of procuring the consent of all those whose possible and reversionary interest in the estate would be defeated by the adoption. In such a case, therefore, their Lordships think that the consent of the father-in-law, to whom the law points as the natural guardian and 'venerable protector' of the widow, would be sufficient. It is not easy to lay down an inflexible rule for the case in which no father-in-law is in existence. Every such case must depend upon the circumstances of the family. All that can be said is, that there should be such evidence of the assent of kinsmen as suffices to show that the act is done by the widow in the proper and *bonâ fide* performance of a religious duty, and neither capriciously nor from a corrupt motive. In this case no issue raises the question that the consents were purchased, and not *bonâ fide* attained. The rights of an adopted son are not prejudiced by any unauthorised alienation by the widow which precedes the adoption which she makes; and though gifts improperly made to procure assent might be powerful evidence to show no adoption needed, they do not in themselves go to the root of the legality of an adoption.

"Again, it appears to their Lordships that inasmuch as the authorities in favour of the widow's power to adopt with the assent of her husband's kinsmen, proceed in a great measure upon the assumption that his assent to this meritorious act is to be implied wherever he has not forbidden it, so the power cannot be inferred when a prohibition by the husband either has been directly expressed by him, or can be reasonably deduced from his disposition of his property, or the existence of a direct line competent to the full performance of religious duties, or from other circumstances of his family which afford no plea for a supersession of heirs on the ground of religious obligation to adopt a son in order to complete or fulfil defective religious rites.

"Their Lordships having thus stated the conclusions to which they have come upon the general question of law involved in these appeals, will now consider whether the High Court of Madras has correctly applied that law to the facts of the present case.

"They are of opinion that both the courts below were right in holding that the collateral kinsmen of Ramasami were to be found in the Taver family, of which the printed pedigree forms part of the record. According to Hindu law Ramasami was the son, though by adoption, of Annasami; and he again was the son, though by adoption, of the first Ramasami, who was a Taver; and the heirs of Ramasami, in the absence of descendants, were traceable upwards through these two persons, as if they had been his natural father and grandfather. There is no ground for saying that this, the legal consequence of the successive adoptions, was affected by the assumption of the name of Satoopati, the family name of the ancient Zemindars of Ramnad and of Mangalaswari, the grantee of the Zemindary. It is to be observed, however, that this line affords none but very remote kinsmen, if their relationship to Ramasami be calculated on the principle just stated. The nearest of them, Motoosamy, would on that principle stand in a degree of relationship to Ramasami which, according to the rule of the *Mitacshára* (cap. 2, sec. 5, art. 6), would exclude him from the category of Sapindas, and place him in that of Samánódacas, or those connected only by a libation of water, and a common family name. He was, however, the natural brother of Annasami, and that circumstance might strengthen his title to be considered, in the absence of nearer connections, the natural male protector of Ramasami's widow. Again, the person who really filled the office of protector, and that by the express appointment of Ramasami, was, up to the time of her quarrel with her daughter-in-law, Mootoo Verayee. Nor is it by any means unusual in a Hindu family to find the mother-in-law occupying a position of considerable power and importance. Moreover, she was unquestionably the heir to the property next in succession to Purvata, after the failure of Ramasami's descendants. It therefore appears to their Lordships that in this state of the family the assent of Mootoo Verayee, of Motoosamy, and of the other persons who are proved beyond all question to have assented, was sufficient to legitimate the adoption, even if the evidence has failed to prove the consent of the yet remoter kinsman Ramrajah Taver.

"It has been argued, however, that even if this adoption would have been regular had Ramasami died childless and intestate, his arzi relating to the management and descent of the Zemindary contains an indication of his intention that his daughters and their descendants should be his successors and representatives, which ought to be taken to imply a virtual prohibition of the act of adoption by his widow. Their Lordships cannot accede to this argument. Ramasami, no doubt, intended to be represented by his daughters' line, should that line continue. But he made no express provision for its failure, and the same reasons which justify a presumption of authority to adopt in the absence of express permission, are powerful to exclude a presumptive prohibition to adopt when on a new and unforeseen occasion the religious duty arises. His widow has not claimed a power to adopt, except on the happening of the contingency for which her husband omitted to provide. And her power so limited, not having been qualified by his disposition, must be determined by the general law.

"Another argument for the appellants was founded on the attempted adoption of a son, Annasami, by Dorarajah. That person is not a party to either of these suits; he has not impeached the adoption of the respondent Ramalinga; he has, on the contrary, supported it as a witness. Nothing decided by the decrees under appeal can prejudice his rights, if he has any, under an adoption which the revenue authorities at the date of it seem to have treated as illegal. Their Lordships have not before them the necessary materials for determining whether that adoption was, in fact, valid or invalid; or whether, if valid, it would have any, and what effect, on the title of the respondent Ramalinga. In that state of things neither of the present appellants can be allowed to insist on this supposed *jus tertii* as an objection to the decrees which they impeach.

"Their Lordships have therefore come to the conclusion that these decrees and the judgment on which they proceed are substantially right in so far as they affirm, as between the parties to this litigation, the validity of the adoption by Purvata of the respondent Ramalinga.

"They also think that there is no foundation for the other and minor objection taken by the collector to the decree of the 18th of March 1861, on the ground that it asserts a power in Purvata to alienate or affect the Zemindary beyond her life-interest. Her power of alienation is expressly stated to be 'subject to the provisions of Hindu law;' and the only object of that part of the decree was to affirm her right to exercise that power within the limits prescribed by the Hindu law, free from the control of the Government or its revenue officers.

"Their Lordships are further of opinion that there are no grounds for impeaching the decree of the 12th of April 1861, in so far as it found that the appellant Kunjara stood in the relation only of stepmother to Ramasami, and therefore could have no right to inherit his estate. They think that this conclusion is supported by the Document No. 36, at page 55, which expressly states that Ramasami was adopted by Annasami and Mootoo Verayee unanimously.

"Upon the cross appeal their Lordships have only to observe that the *quantum* of maintenance is a question with which the Courts of

India, having local knowledge, and being conversant with the habits of native families, are peculiarly competent to deal; and that strong grounds shonld be shown to justify any interference by this committee with their discretion in that matter. And their Lordships see no reason for questioning the soundness of the discretion exercised by the High Court of Madras in the present case."

In Madras the Pundits have expressed an opinion that the widow may adopt with the consent of the husband's relatives.

In Bengal the husband's assent seems indispensable; so likewise in Benares. See the judgment of the Privy Council in the *Ramnad* case, *supra*, p. 36.

In Behar permission of the husband is necessary, and leave from the husband's kindred is not sufficient. See judgment of the Privy Council in the *Ramnad* case, *supra*.

In the Mahratta School the *Mayucha* and *Koustubha* treatises explain the texts away by saying that it applies only to an adoption made in the husband's lifetime, and is not to be taken to restrict the widow's power to do that which the general law prescribes as beneficial to her husband's soul. See the judgment of Privy Council in the *Ramnad* case, *supra*. If the husband specify any one child, she can only adopt that one.

It is doubtful whether she may adopt a second in the event of the death of the first.

If a particular child be named by the husband, and he dies before, or after the appointment, there would be reason for contending that her authority has been exhausted, and that she had not the power to adopt another; but if she can adopt without his consent, there seems no reason why she should not on the death of the first adopted son make a second adoption.

If a general authority be given, she may adopt whom she pleases and whenever she pleases, although the boy be not in existence at her husband's death.

When to be adopted.—In the *Ramnad Zemindary* case, the adoption did not take place for a period of twenty years after the husband's death; but decorum and propriety require it to be done immediately after his death. If no authority be given, *Sir Thomas Strange* says, that by the law of the Benares and Maharashtra Schools, the assent of the kinsmen after any lapse of time is sufficient and necessary.

Verbal authority.—The authority may be given in words in any form whatever.

Widow under authority granted by minor ward without authority of court of wards.—A Hindu minor, and ward of court, authorised his widow, without obtaining the consent of the Court of Wards, to adopt a son,—held that the adoption was invalid.

Dancing girls.—Dancing girls are permitttd to adopt females only. See *post*.

Disqualifying circumstances.—A doubt might be entertained as to the validity of adoption by a blind, impotent, or other person disqualified from inheriting. The more correct opinion, however, appears to be that such adoption would be good, though it seems reasonable that one excluded from the inheritance should confer no right of inheritance on the adopted, of which the adopter is debarred by law, *Sutherland's Synop.*, Head iv.

Minor.—For the most part a minor being married may adopt. See 9 *Moore's In. Ap.* 295, where the adoption by a minor was held invalid for want of permission of the Court of Wards.

A lunatic.—A lunatic cannot adopt, because an act of assent is necessary, there being a formal contract between the two fathers.

An out-caste.—An out-caste cannot adopt—1. Because he is in so helpless a state as to the future that no adoption would benefit him; 2. Because he cannot inherit; 3. Because the principles of Hindu law affect those only who are Hindus. But now under the Emancipation Act, xxi. of 1850, these rules do not apply. That Act declares, that so much of the law and usages now in force within the territories, subject to the E. I. Co., as inflicts on any person forfeiture of rights or property, or may be held in any way to impair, or affect any right of inheritance by reason of his or her renouncing, or having been excluded from the communion of any religion, or being deprived of caste, shall cease to be enforced as law in the courts of the E. I. Co., and in the courts established by royal charter within the said territories.

Section IV.

Who may Give.

The Father—Mother—Brother—Uncle.

The father.—Any one who has absolute authority over the child, *e.g.*, the father, may give him in adoption. "He whom his father or mother with her husband's assent gives to another as his son, provided that the donee have no issue, if the boy be of the same class and affectionately disposed, is considered as a son given, the gift being confirmed by pouring water."

The mother.—The consent of the mother is not necessary. She cannot give her child in adoption without the consent of her husband, unless he be dead or otherwise incapable of giving his sanction; but in cases of urgent distress and necessity, the assent of the husband may be presumed; or, when he is *civiliter mortuus*, as by permanent emigration, entering a monastery, &c., the mother may make the gift. *Sir Wiliam. H. Macnaghten*, says, the only exception to the above rule of Menu that has been propounded by the commentators is contained in the *Dattaka Mimansa*, sec. 4, § 12, which refers to the gift of her son by a widow during a season of calamity. But in the *Ramnad* case (*P. C.* 21 May 1868), it has been held that in the Dravada country the widow may adopt with the consent of her venerable preceptor, &c., *ante* p. 36.

According to *Madana* the disjunctive "or," in *Menu's* text, means that if the mother be not present, the father alone may give him away, and if the father be dead, the mother; but if both be alive, then both.

The brother.—Though *Mr Morley* mentions a case where an elder brother was allowed to give a younger one in adoption after the death of the father, *Strange, J.*, denies this to be law, and with some reason, for the rights of both are co-ordinate; and further, it is necessary that the rights of the child should be protected against the attacks of a designing brother. See *Orphan, post.*

When both parents are dead, the elder brother cannot give his brother in adoption. See *Orphan, post.*

The uncle.—For the same reason an uncle cannot give a nephew away.

SECTION V.

WHO MAY BE ADOPTED.

Must be the son of a woman whom the adopter might have married—Reflection of a son—Brother's son—Sister's son—Daughter's son—Exceptions to the rule—Only son—The result of the authorities—Dwyamuchyayana—Orphan—Illegitimate son—Whether an adopted son may be given in adoption—Same caste as adopter—Same gotra or family—Natural brother—A girl—Age bars adoption—Tonsure, removal of—Oopanayana—Whether illegal adoption curable—Marriage—Sudras.

He must be the son of a woman whom the adopter might have married.—The ruling canon here is, that no boy can be adopted with whose mother the adopter could not have married. The reason assigned being that the son must, by physical possibility, be as like the natural child as may be managed. A male child alone can be adopted, not a female, except by dancing girls, *post.*

Reflection of a son.—He must be "the reflection of a son," and that is interpreted to mean the son of a woman upon whom, if he were begotten by the adoptive father, he would not be the production of an incestuous intercourse. It is explained in *Datt. Miman.* to be "the capacity to have sprung from the adopter himself, through an appointment to raise issue on another's wife, as in the case of a son of a brother, a near or distant kinsman, and so forth."

Accordingly, the brother, paternal and maternal uncles, the daughter's son, and that of the sister, are excluded, except amongst Sudras (see *post*), for the adopter could not be the father of any of them without committing incest.

Brother's son.—It is true that a brother's son inherits, and performs obsequies to his uncle dying without preferable heirs; but then it is as his nephew, not as his son, and the spiritual efficacy in the one case and in the other is considered to be different. To render him a substitute for a son, he must have been filiated.

The spiritual efficacy does not appear to differ; for if we look at the texts upon the subject, we shall find that "if one among brothers of the whole blood be possessed of male issue, *Menu* pronounces that they are all fathers of the same by means of that son." See this subject discussed in *Grady's Hindu Law of Inheritance.*

Sister's son.—"The daughter's son and the sister's son are declared to be the sons of Sudras, and may be affiliated by Sudras. In Madras a daughter's or sister's son may be adopted. Such adoptions are allowed to all classes, at all events when no others are procurable. For the three superior tribes the sister's son is nowhere mentioned as a son. Here even the term "sister's son" is illustrative, including all not resembling a son, for prohibited connection is common to them all. Now, prohibited connection is the unfitness of the son proposed to be adopted, to have been begotten by the individual himself, through appointment to raise issue on the wife of another.

The mutual relation between a couple being analogous to one, being the father, or mother of another connection, is forbidden; as, for instance, the daughter of the wife's sister and the sister of the paternal uncle's wife. The meaning of the text is this: where the relation of the couple, that is, of the bride and bridegroom, bears analogy to that of father or mother, if the bridegroom be as it were the father of the bride, or the bride stand in the light of mother to the bridegroom, such a marriage is a prohibited connection. The conclusion is, that one, with whose mother the adopter could not have legally married, must not be adopted. On examination of the texts (§ 74, sec. ii.; § 19, sec. v.), and other passages, it will be seen that the author entertained such contempt for the Sudra that he looked upon him as a slave, unworthy of any civil rights, but still laid down the broad principle that adoption can only be made of one with whose mother the adopter might have legally intermarried. He does not except the Sudra, nor does he show that a Sudra is at liberty to marry his sister. The decision of the High Court, presently quoted, draws no such distinction, notwithstanding the authority of the *Dattaka Mimansa*, inconsistent as that work is, in this respect, with the governing principle. We consider that it remains to be decided whether a Sudra can make a legal adoption of his sister's or daughter's son.

In the Andhra country, as in Bengal, a Brahmin cannot adopt his sister's son, *Narasammal* v. *Balarama Charlu*, 1 *Mad. H. C. R.*, 420.

In delivering the judgment of the court in that case, Mr Justice Halloway said, In Bengal a Hindu (a Brahmin) cannot adopt his sister's son, as it imports incest. Nor in the north-west provinces. So a Brahmin widow cannot adopt her uncle's son, as she could not be his mother. In Madras it has been held there can be no adoption where there is such blood relationship between the adopter and adopted son's mother as would have prohibited marriage with her in her maiden state.

By the law and usage of Mithila such an adoption, even by persons of high caste, according to the *Kritrima* form of adoption, is valid. Mr Morley, in a note to this case, says :—"The Datt. Mimam. must be considered to refer only to the Datt. adoption, and not to the Kritrima form. The same point as in the above case was ruled by the Sudr. Court of Allahabad, 16th July 1833, in *Mt. Bala* v. *Mt. Botola*, in which the parties were Mithila Brahmins. It is presumable, from a part of the decree (which generally upheld the validity of the Kritrima adoption of a sister's son), that the parties were governed by the Mithila law ; but this is not clear."

Adoption by a childless Hindu Vysya, or a man of the third class of Hindus, of his sister's son is valid, *Ramalinga Pillai* v. *Sadasiva Pillai*, 9 *Moore's In. Ap.* 506.

A Sudra may adopt the son of a sister, or even a daughter's son. But *vide* p. 36.

Daughter's son.—A Brahmin, having a daughter and daughter-in-law living, cannot adopt the son of a daughter predeceased ; nor can such person if so illegally adopted adopt his wife's sister's child, and make him heir to the grandfather's property, which would pass to the daughter-in-law on the Brahmin's death, and subsequently to the daughter, the daughter-in-law not being allowed to alienate the property during the daughter's life, *Baee Gunga* v. *Bayee Sheosunkur*, *Sel. Rep.* 73 ; 1 *Morl. Dig.* 18. A daughter's son and a sister's son are affiliated by Sudras.

Exceptions to the rule.—There are, however, some strong exceptions in Madras, where usage permits a daughter's or sister's son to be adopted. The rule does not apply to Sudras, it being confined to the three superior classes, *Narada* cited in *Datt. Nir.* This is in accordance with the texts of *Datt. Mimam.*, which have already been observed upon.

Only son.—It is said, *Suther. Synop.* 2d Head : "An only son cannot become an absolutely adopted son (*Sudha Dattaka*), but he may be affiliated as a Dwyamuchyayana, or son of two fathers. In this case the reason of the prohibition—viz., extinction of lineage to the natural father—would not apply. An only son of the whole brother assuredly, if no other nephew exist for selection, must be adopted by his uncle requiring male issue, and is son of two fathers. . . . . It may, however, be inferred that a legal impediment would exist to the affiliation by an uncle of a nephew whom his father had given away in adoption, as a Sudha Dattaka who retains no filial relation to his natural father."

The adoption of an only son is, when made valid according to Hindu law.

The result of the authorities.—The result of all the authorities, says *Sir Thomas Strange*, is that the selection is finally a matter of conscience and discretion with the adopter, not of absolute prescription, rendering invalid an adoption of one, not being precisely him who on spiritual considerations ought to have been preferred.

The decision in the case of *Chinna Goundan* v. *Kumara Goundan*, 1 *Mad. H. C. R.*, 54, is discussed at length in *Grady's Hindu Law*, p. 43.*

Dwyamuchyayana.—*Sir Thomas Strange* says that the son of a brother adopted by his uncle becomes a Dwyamuchyayana; and he applies the same term to the son of a different family when at the time of the adoption a special agreement may have been entered into that the adopted son should not cease to belong to his natural parent's father. He cites *Mitacshara*, chap. 1, sec. x. § 1, 13; sec. xi. § 9; vol. ii. pp. 118, 202, of his own work; and *Sutherland's Synopsis*, title, Qualification and Right to be Adopted, in the fourth paragraph of which the word Dwyamuchyayana, or son of two fathers occurs, and is apparently used in reference to the authorities there cited. *Macnaghten*, i., pp. 70–76 concurs generally in the view taken by *Sir Thomas Strange*. The meaning of the term "Dwyamuchyayana," is discussed in *Grady's Hindu Law*, p. 47.

Orphan.—An orphan cannot be adopted. It was held that where both parents were dead a child might be given in adoption by his elder brother. But this position is contested by Sir F. Macnaghten, in his *Considerations on Hindu Law;* and his citations, p. 210, from *Coollooca Bhattu*, *Vachespati Misra*, and the *Aditya Purana*, certainly seem to show that an orphan cannot be adopted. To constitute a valid adoption there must be a *giving* as well as a *receiving*. Here there seems to have been no one to give the child. No amount of ratification can supply the absolute essentials of a transaction like the present.

Illegitimate son.—An illegitimate son cannot be adopted.

Whether an adopted son may be given in adoption.—This is

* As to the validity of the adoption of an eldest son, see *R. A.* 49 of 1853; *M. S. D.*, 1854, p. 31; *Abajee Dinkur* v. *Gungadhur Wasdeo Gosavee*, 3 *Morris Bomb. R.*; *S. D. A. R.*, 420, 424.

a question which has not, so far as our researches extend, come under judicial decision. There appears to be objection to such an adoption, for the performance of the religious ceremonies might operate as an obstacle. There might, moreover, be fraud upon the lad himself; and as the virtue to deliver from Put was expended on his first adoption, he could confer none by his second adoption.

Same caste as adoptor.—The canon requires that the adopted son should be of the same caste as the adoptor, *Menu*, because the religious purposes of the adoption would fail as to the performance of ceremonies, the inheritance of property, &c.

Same gotra or family.—It is said, moreover, that he should be of the same gotra, or family, but this is not imperative. Amongst the Sudras, a childless Hindu may adopt a son from a gotra or family different from his own. And, as usual, the relaxation has affected the Brahmins, so that now it is merely a matter of conscience that a near relation should be adopted. No court of law would annul the adoption of a stranger merely on that ground, if he were not otherwise excluded, as by caste.

Natural brother—adopted son cannot adopt his natural born brother.—A boy after adoption cannot adopt his natural brother, such an adoption would be invalid under the first canon, see *Sud. Dec.* of 1858, p. 117; nor can the natural born brother inherit property from his brother acquired by the adoption, see *post*; nor can a widow adopt the natural brother of her deceased husband.

A girl.—Dancing girls, or professional prostitutes, may adopt, but only girls. *Morley* doubts whether such adoption is valid.

Mr Justice Strange says:—Dancing girls form an exception in Hindu community. They do not marry, but live in professional concubinage, which does not degrade them from caste if not carried on with an out-caste. Having no husbands, adoption cannot be made in that channel; they are consequently allowed to make adoption themselves for transmission of their property; and this must be of daughters, for descent from females is in the female line. To adopt, the dancing girl must accordingly be daughterless. It is immaterial whether she have a son or not.

If this adoption is made for the transmission of property only, there may be some reason for Mr Morley's doubts, for this object may now be attained by testamentary disposition. In *Chalakonda Alasani* v. *Chalakonda Ratnachalam*, 2 *Mad. H. C. R.*, 56, the adoption of the defendant by the appellant, a dancing girl, was alleged and admitted, and the suit proceeded to trial on the assumption that the family was undivided. Such adoptions are not compulsory for the devolution of their property, for sons may inherit as well as daughters. For the devolution of a prostitute's property, see Inheritance, *post*.

Age bars adoption.—The age in this case is determined generally by the religious ceremonies performed at different periods among different castes. *Mr Thomas Strange* says, that the ceremonies performed by the family, and in the name of the father, constitute the act of affiliation; the fewer of them that have been performed previous to adoption the better, the more nearly does he come into the position of a natural son.

Two ceremonies, chudavarana, tonsure or shaving the head, and the Oopanayana, or investiture with the thread, in general prevent adoption. But here the authorities differ: *Sir Thomas Strange* holds that Oopanayana can be annulled, and the effect of this is that a re-investiture can be góne through; while *Mr Strange* in his *Manual*, holds a contrary opinion. This subject is discussed in *Grady's Hindu Law*, p. 50. The weight of authority is against the validity of the adoption of one upon whom the rite of Oopanayana has been already performed. There is no authority on the other side.

Tonsure, removal of.—According to Morley the effects of tonsure may be removed for the purposes of adoption. *Mr Justice Strange* thinks tonsure would not prevent adoption, since it can be performed in the adoptive family.

Oopanayana should be performed among the Brahmins at the age of eight; among Shetriyas at eleven; among Vysyas at twelve, *Reg. Ap.* 18 of 1814, Sudder Court. This does not apply to Sudras.

The difficulty, or rather impossibility, of laying down any unvarying principles which would be universally decisive on these subjects, is obvious. The most general and consistent rule which presents itself is this:—Any person on whom the adoptor may legally perform the Oopanayana rite is capable of being affiliated as a Dattaka son, while one not so qualified may be lawfully adopted as a Kritrima son.

Sir Thomas Strange says:—"But if in the classes to which they apply they (*Tonsure* and *Oopanayana*) have been performed for the adopted in his own family, a remedy is found in the *putreshti*, or sacrifice by fire, by recourse to which they may be annulled, so as to admit of their re-performance with effect in the family of the adoptor, who is thus enabled to perfect the test upon which he relies for the continuance of his name, and the solemnisation of his obsequies.

Whether illegal adoption curable.—An adoption originally illegal, it is said, may be cured by lapse of time and the acquiescence of the parties concerned. But this will evidently be overruled, as it is very questionable law, *Mad. Dec.* of 1854, p. 36; of 1858, pp. 84, 89. Undisputed possession by the defendant, an illegally adopted son, will protect him only under the statute of limitations. If he were plaintiff, for the same reason, he could not recover rights enjoyed by others. Nor in any case if he held his property for a time shorter than that required by the statute, could he deprive others of property.

Marriage.—All castes agree that marriage is an absolute bar.

Sudras.—With Sudras marriage is the only obstacle.

Semble.—In Bombay a man of mature age, married, and having a family, is admissible to be adopted, he being a Sagotra.

SECTION VI.

EFFECT OF ADOPTION.

The relationship with natural family ceases—The adopted son becomes as a natural born one—Rights and duties in adoptive family—Exception—Adopted son loses his natural rights—Succession to property of childless adopted son—Invalid adoption—Right to maintenance—Cannot intermarry with either family—Second adoption—Disinheritance on adoption of second son—Cancellation—Limitation—Whether one member of a family can inherit property of one taken out of that family—Adoption by widow—Sale of property by widow previous to adoption—Adoption by widow under power—Death of adopted son—Widow his heir—Effect of Kritrima form of adoption—Need not be in writing—Intention—Right of one excluded from inheritance to adopt—Maintenance—Gotra of adopted son—Rights of Dwyamuchyayana.

The relationship with natural family ceases.—According to *Sir Thomas Strange*, when a father gives away his son after the rites of initiation, his relationship with his own or natural family ceases, and a relation to the adoptor commences. His relationship with his own family is replaced by the new relationship with that family into which, in effect, he is transferred. He is completely regarded as a natural son, and not only so, but he is taken into the family. He becomes connected with it both lineally and collaterally. Thus he inherits from any lineal and collateral branch the property to which he would have succeeded if he had been a natural born son. He acquires the rights of a son in the hereditary immovable property of the adoptive father, of which he cannot be deprived by assuming to adopt a second son, and settling the hereditary property upon him, with a declaration that the first was disinherited.

The adopted son becomes as a natural born one.—The theory of adoption being a complete change of paternity, the son is to be considered as one actually begotten by his adoptive father, and he is so in all respects save one, an incapacity to contract marriage in the family from which he was taken.

Rights and duties in adoptive family.—His position is therefore that of a son begotten. Being transferred from his own family, he becomes as the natural son of the adoptor, and enjoys the right of succession in his new family, with the duty of performing for his adoptive father his exequial rites and ceremonies, and his rights of succession attaches to the entire property of the adoptor, real and personal, and self-acquisitions undisposed of by the father. In the Dwyamuchyayana form he performs the funeral rites of his natural father as well.

Of course if the father of the adoptor is disabled from inheriting, by reason of any of the established causes of disqualification, the son can have nothing to inherit through his adoptive father; in that case he is only entitled to maintenance.

This rule must be taken with a qualification which a fair construction of the Hindu law authorises. On birth, a son becomes partner with his father in the family property. At the instant of birth he confers a benefit on his father by delivering him from Put, and being in existence to perform exequial rites; at the same time, he inflicts a correlative injury on his father by becoming a sharer in the family property, and he cannot be deprived of his share without his consent. A son therefore possesses two rights—one as partner in his own share of the family property; and one as heir, entitled to succeed to his father's share on his father's death. Consequently, if his father is disqualified from inheriting from his ancestors, or relatives, the adopted son cannot be placed in a better position than himself. It is, however, but reasonable to conclude that the son is entitled to succeed to the property to which his adoptive father, on the principle explained, was entitled.

Exception.—The right of inheriting by the adopted son is subject to the rights of a natural born son after the adoption, in which case he is entitled in compensation to one-fifth and the natural son to four-fifths of the property, Jagannatha gives them one-third and two-thirds. *Sir W. H. Macn.* says, the adopted son takes one-third according to the law of Bengal. In *Ayyavu Muppanar* v. *Miladatchi Ammal*, 1 *Mad. H. C. R.*, 45, it was held that in Southern India he was entitled to one-fourth of the other's share of the property. *Sir Thomas Strange* says, that amongst Sudras both share equally the parental estate.

Adopted son loses his natural rights.--And so on the other hand the adopted son is transplanted out of his own family, and consequently loses his rights therein.

The adoption once completed, the son adopted loses all claims to the property of his natural family; but the estrangement does not extend to the social relations. Thus he cannot marry within the prohibited degrees in his natural family. With regard to mourning, &c., the family connexion still subsists.

Succession to property of childless adopted son.—When an adopted son dies without issue, property which he has inherited from his adoptive father goes to the natural heirs of the latter, *S. A.* No. 71 of 1858; *M. S. D.* 1859, p. 265. His own father cannot claim to inherit from him, but the widow of the adopting father will succeed to the property, if he himself leaves no widow.

Invalid adoption—Right to maintenance.—So complete has this severance from his natural family been supposed to be, that it has been said he cannot inherit their property, even should the adoption be altogether illegal, and that he can claim maintenance only from the new family into which he has been supposed to have been engrafted. But this unreasonable and illogical doctrine has been overruled in the case of *Bawani Sankara Pandit* v. *Ambabay Ammal*, 1 *Mad. H. C. R.*, 363, where it was held that the adopted son of one whose alleged adoption has been invalid, has no claim to be maintained by the alleged adoptor, and that an invalid adoption does not sever the person so adopted from his natural rights.

Cannot intermarry with either family.—He is, however, connected in only one case with both families, for he cannot marry within the prohibited degrees in either family, being by birth and a fiction of law related to both, and can therefore neither marry nor adopt within the circle of prohibition, *Mad. Dec.* 1858, p. 117; *Narasammal* v. *Balaramacharlu*, 1 *Mad. H. C. R.*, 420. In this case it is laid down that the theory of adoption is a complete change of paternity. The son is to be considered as one actually begotten by the adoptive father, and he is so in all respects save an incapacity to contract marriage in the family from which he was taken. Nor can the son of two fathers marry into either.

Second adoption.—We have seen that no second adoption can be made during the life of the one first adopted.

Disinheritance on adoption of second son.—When a Hindu has adopted a son, the adopted acquires the rights of a son in the hereditary immovable property of the adoptive father, and he cannot be deprived of those rights by the adoptive father afterwards assuming to adopt a second son, and settling the hereditary property upon such second adopted son, coupled with the declaration that the first son was disinherited, *Sudauund Mohapattur* v. *Bonomallee*, 1 *Beng. H. C. R.*, 317.

A childless Hindu adopted A. as his son. Afterwards he adopted B. as his son, and made a will, dividing his property, ancestral as well as acquired, between A. and B. A. filed a petition denying the right of his adoptive father to adopt B., and protesting against the will; but afterwards he signed a consent to the will:—held that as the father afterwards endeavoured to deprive A. of all his rights, as well those under the will as by the adoption, the consent did not bind A., since it was given on the basis of a family arrangement, from which the father afterwards departed. *Ib.* It seems, that if the consent were given by A. in ignorance of his rights, it would not be binding on him. *Ib.*

Cancellation.—Adoption cannot be annulled for any purpose whatsoever, which would not justify a disinheritance. There is no express text declaring illegal a renunciation of adoption; but at the same time there is not any which can be construed as approaching to a justification of it. In this respect it differs from adoption as practised by the Greeks.

Although under no circumstances can an adoption be revoked or cancelled, yet in case of death, loss of caste, or the like, another may be adopted.

Limitation.—In a suit to set aside an adoption of a son, the period of limitation is not to be reckoned from the date of the adoption, if the members of the family who seek to set it aside have not known of it; it should be reckoned from the time when there was distinct knowledge of the adoption, *Sooburnomonee Dabea* v. *Petumber-Dobey*, 1 *Beng. H. C. R.*, 221.

As against an adopted son suing for his share of the ancestral estate, the law of limitations does not begin to run until the allotment of such share has been demanded and refused, *Ayyàvu Muppanar* v. *Niladatchi Ammal*, 1 *Mad. H. C. R.*, 45.

Whether one member of a family can inherit property of one taken out of that family.—A member of the adoptor's natural family cannot inherit the property acquired by the adoptor in consequence of his adoption. The severance of an adopted son from his natural family is so complete that no mutual rights as to succession to property can arise between them, *Rayan Krishnamachariyar* v. *Kuppanayyangar*, 1 *Mad. H. C. R.*, 180.

Adoption by widow.—Upon adoption taking place by the widow, the child becomes heir of the deceased husband, and the widow's title to his estate merges into that of the guardian of the child.

A childless Hindu by deed directed a widow to adopt a son; after his death the widow brought a suit for partition, and the possession of her husband's share in the joint undivided estate. Pending the suit, she adopted a son. By the Hindu law the act of adoption divested the property from the widow, and vested it in the adopted son, subject to the maintenance of the widow. Notwithstanding the adoption, the suit was prosecuted in the widow's name, and a decree made directing her to be put into possession. Held that under the circumstances she prosecuted the suit as the guardian of the adopted son, and was put into possession as his trustee, and was accountable to him for the profits of the property so decreed to her.

Lord Campbell, in *Dhurm Das Panday* v. *Mussumat Shama, Soondri*, *supra*, in delivering the judgment of the lords of the Judicial Committee, said the widow of a childless husband succeeds as his heir, and his property real and personal vests in her. But if in the exercise of a power conferred upon her husband, she adopts a son, the property is divested from her, and vested in her adopted son. Now upon the authorities there seems to be no doubt that this is the result of an act of adoption, because the property is in the widow from the death of her husband, till the power of adoption is exercised. Then that adoption divests it from the widow and vests it in the adopted son.

Sale of property by widow previous to adoption.—The question whether a retrospective right could be claimed by a son, after he had been adopted, so as to bar a sale made by his adoptive mother previous to his adoption, to the injury of rights at that time contingent and eventual, but which actually accrued to him upon his adoption, was raised in *Ranee Kishanamee* v. *Rajah Oodwaut Singh*, 3 *Sud. Dew. Adaw.*, p. 228. There the son, when adopted, became the undoubted heir, and it was of course the correct doctrine that no sale made by a widow who possesses only a very restricted life-interest in the estate, could have been good against any ultimate heir, whether an adopted son, or otherwise, unless made under circumstances of strict necessity. Besides, by the terms of the will of her deceased husband, the widow was only the appointed manager of the estate, the right of property vested in the son, subsequently appointed from the time of the rajah's death, and the widow had no authority but that of intermediate management under her husband's will.

Adoption by widow under power—Death of adopted son—Widow his heir.—A childless Hindu, a member of a divided family in Bengal, by an Unomuttee Potta, authorised a widow to adopt a son for him after his death, and by that instrument made her his heir. His widow exercised the power, and adopted a son who died in his minority. Held that the widow was entitled to a life-estate in her husband's property after the death of the adopted son, either under the deed, or as heir of the adopted son, *Soondur Koomaree Debbea* v. *Gudadhur Pershad Tewarree et é contra*, 7 *Moore's In. Ap.*, 54.

Effect of Kritrima form of adoption.—The Kritrima son, as usually affiliated in the Mithila country, would indeed take the estate both of his own and of his adoptive father. He continues a member of his natural father, and is not considered as prolonging the line of his adoptor.

The person adopted in this form by the widow does not thereby become the adopted son of the husband, even though he sanctioned the adoption, and the express consent of the person nominated for the adoption must be obtained during the lifetime of the adopting party. The relation of Kritrima son extends to the contracting parties only, and the son so adopted will not be considered the grandson of the adopting father's father, nor will the son of the adopted be considered the grandson of his adopting father. He does not inherit collaterally, being ninth in the enumeration according to Yajnavalchya. In Mithila the husband and wife may adopt each a Kritrima son. The sanction of the husband is not necessary in this form, and the son appointed by the woman will perform her obsequies, and succeed to her peculiar property though not to that of the husband. See the Crita form of adoption referred to in 2 *Stra. H. L.*, 107, and *Macn. Prins. H. L.*, 101. In Mithila there is no limit as to age, and no condition as to performance of ceremonies. A man may adopt his own brother, or even his own father, and he and his issue remain members of his natural family, and he inherits in both.

Need not be in writing.—Adoption need not be in writing any more than authority to a widow to adopt.

Intention.—Mere intention to adopt is as insufficient as a mere agreement to do so. There must be actual adoption, gift, and acceptance, manifested by some overt act.

An adopted son is not liable for a debt contracted by his natural father, whether contracted by the father in person or by the adopted as his father's agent.

Right of one excluded from inheritance to adopt.—A person excluded from inheritance may nevertheless adopt, but the adopted will be subject to the same disqualification, and cannot inherit where the claim to inheritance can only be made through the adopted. He will be entitled to maintenance only.

Maintenance.—A son, whether adopted or begotten, can claim maintenance of his father until put into possession of his share of the ancestral estate, *Ayyavu Muppanar* v. *Niladatchi Ammal*, 1 *Mad. H. C. R.*, 45.

Gotra of adopted son.—The adopted son belongs to the gotra, or family, of his adoptive father, while he disowns that of his natural parent. His relation too as sapinda in the family of his adoptive father commences from the date of his adoption, unless where a Dwyamuchyayana.

The ceremony of *Datta-Homam* converts the adopted son from the gotra of his natural to that of his adoptive father.

Rights of Dwyamuchyayana.—The Dwyamuchyayana inherits the estate and performs the exequial rights of both fathers, but the relation of his issue is confined exclusively to his adoptive father's family. But if a son is born to the adoptor after adoption in that form, such adopted son would take only one half the share to which under the Dattaka form he would be entitled in participating with a son subsequently born ; and where a son is born to the natural father, the Dwyamuchyayana takes in the estate of such father the half of the share of a legitimate son.

SECTION VII.

MODE OF ADOPTION.

Absence of ceremonies does not make adoption invalid—Kritrima—Malabar.

Absence of ceremonies does not make adoption invalid.—The ceremonies, both religious and civil, were formerly numerous, and many *directions* have been given advising the proper mode, but nothing more, such as sacrifices, the invitation of relatives, &c., but the absence of these does not make the adoption invalid. Amongst the three higher classes the only essential ceremony is *Datta-homam*, or sacrifice by fire. Mr Ellis considers that in Southern India this ceremony is confined to Brahmins; and in Bengal also. All classes require a common assent of both parties with reference to the purpose of adoption, or if a minor, the assent should be given by a competent authority. In 2 *Knapps P. C.*, 290, the Privy Council ruled that neither *any* religious ceremony nor any written acknowledgments were essential to the validity of an adoption, however advisable their presence may be. All that is required for civil purposes is the consent of the necessary parties, the adoptor having no male issue, the child being within legal age and not ineligible.

Whatever benefit the Hindus may think, in a spiritual point of view, they derive from the observance of these ceremonies, for civil purposes they can have no efficacy; all that a court of law would be bound to inquire into is, whether there was a giving and receiving by proper parties of a proper child, the prescribed forms not being essential. Not as *Sir T. Strange* says, that an unlawful adoption is to be maintained, but that a lawful one actually made is not to be set aside for any informality that may have attended its solemnisation.

Kritrima—The adoption of a Kritrima son is valid, without the performance of any particular form or solemnities.

This form of adoption is prevalent in the Mithila country, and is rarely practised in other parts of India.

Malabar—On failure of the sister's progeny, male and female, the head of the family may make adoption. The descent being in the female line, the adoption must be of a female. In view of the probable minority of her offspring at the period when the management may fall in, a male, her brother, may be taken in adoption at the same time with herself, in order to afford provision for the administration of the affairs of the family, and for the conduct of the religious rites to be observed therein.

CHAPTER III.

MINORITY.

Benares and Mithila schools—Bengal school—Regulation period—Father proper guardian—Mother—Elder brother—Paternal relations—Maternal kindred—Ruling power—Females—Assets make heir liable pro tanto—*The grounds of the liability of the heir discussed—If manager contract debt not within scope of his authority, his own undivided share is liable—General rule laid down by Coleb. refers to divided families—Minors may now be sued by their guardians—Suits instituted in favour of and against minors—Share of minor in joint property—Acts of minor in regard to property—Tutelage of women.*

Benares and Mithila schools.—In the Benares and Mithila schools minority lasts until the completion of sixteen years, with respect to females as well as males. In the Bengal school the end of fifteen years is the limit of minority. *Raghunandana*, the great authority of Bengal, says—"One who has not arrived at years of discretion is one whose age is less than sixteen years." *Sir Thomas Strange*, vol. i., p. 72, says—"Belonging to any one of the three superior classes, the youth ceases to be in ward upon ending his studentship and returning from his preceptor; if a Sudra, upon his completing his sixteenth year. A Hindu father may postpone his son's majority by will beyond sixteen years.

Regulation period.—Minority is extended to the eighteenth year, with respect to minors under the guardianship of the Court of Wards, *Bengal Regulation* 26, sec. 2, 1793; *Madras Regulation* 5, sec. 4, 1804.

Father proper guardian.—When the father is alive he is the legal guardian of his children.

Mother.—If the father be dead, or incompetent from idiotcy, the mother may assume the guardianship, and in Bombay this has been held to include the stepmother, whose right of guardianship is declared to be superior to that of the minor's paternal uncle.

Elder brother.—In default of the mother the elder brother of a minor is competent to assume the guardianship of him.

Paternal relations.—In default of an elder brother the paternal relations generally are entitled to hold the office of guardian.

Maternal kindred.—Failing them the office devolves upon the maternal kinsmen, according to their degree of proximity.

Ruling power.—But the appointment of guardians universally rests with the ruling power, who, whether natural or legal guardians be living or dead, is recognised to be the legitimate or supreme guardian of the property of all minors, whether male or female. Thus property of a woman and the goods of a minor falling into the king's power should not be taken by him as owner. . . . But it may be here remarked that the property of a minor should be intrusted to heirs and the rest, appointed with his concurrence; or if the infant be absolutely incapable of discretion, with the consent of a near and unimpeachable friend, such as his mother and the rest.

Strange says, the king is the universal superintendent of those who cannot take care of themselves, and in this capacity it rests with him, *i.e.*, the judicial power exercising for him this branch of his prerogative, to select for the office the fittest amongst the infant's relations, preferring always the paternal male kindred to a maternal ancestor or female. It is stated that in practice the mother is the guardian. But *Sir Thomas Strange* adds, as a Hindu widow is herself liable to the same sort of tutelage, it is more correct to regard her as proper, if capable, to be consulted on the appointment of one. *Macn.* says, where the duties of manager and guardian are united, the mother is, in the exercise of the former capacity, necessarily subject to the control of her husband's relations; and with respect to the minor's person likewise there are some acts to which she is incompetent, such as the performance of the several initiatory rites, the management of which rests with the paternal kindred.

The concurrence of a minor in the appointment of a guardian should not be disregarded if he is of competent understanding.

Persons authorised by law to make such appointment may, by will, appoint guardians to minors succeeding to landed property, liable to the jurisdiction of the Court of Wards, sec. xviii. Reg. v. of 1802, and cl. 5, sec. xix. In the event of no guardian having been appointed by will, the collector may recommend a person to be appointed. The next and legal heir or person having a direct or indirect advantage in the death, or continued incapacity of the minor, are ineligible, cls. 2 and 3, sec. xix. Females can only be appointed guardians to female minors. Act ix. of 1861 of the Legislative Council of India empowers the Mofussil courts to dispose of claims to the guardianship of minors, but does not interfere with the powers of the Court of Wards, nor with the powers of the late Supreme Courts of India exercised under the English law.

Females.—The guardianship of a female, whether she be a minor or adult, rests with her father until she is married. In his default, with her nearest paternal relations.

When married the woman becomes a member of her husband's family, and is under their control, her husband being her natural guardian. In his default, his sons, grandsons, and great-grandsons. In their default, the husband's heirs generally, or those who will inherit his property after her death. In default of them, her paternal relations. In their failure, her maternal kindred, so that the dependence of women is strictly maintained.

Day and night must women be held by their protectors in a state of dependence; their fathers protect them in childhood, their husbands protect them in youth, their sons protect them in age: a woman is never fit for independence. *Grady's Menu.*

In disposing of any property she may have inherited from her husband, she is subject to the control of her legal guardians and advisers, as well as of her husband's heirs. A parent is bound to protect (maintain) his illegitimate children and their mothers, as also outcasts of his family, and those excluded from the inheritance through their fault or their misfortune.

Assets make heir liable pro tanto.—*Macnaghten* discusses the question of the power of the guardian over the property of his ward, and says,—"As I understand the provisions on the subject, minors are, under the protection of the law, favoured in all things which are for their benefit, and not prejudiced by anything to their disadvantage." It has been laid down by Sir W. Jones, that assets may be followed in the hands of any representative, *Coleb. On Obligations and Contracts.* Admitting the rule, he denies that latitude which has been given to it, and adds,—"It has been held, I believe, for this purpose, a guardian may be considered as the representative of the deceased; whereas, it is obvious that, *quoad hoc*, he is only the representative of his successor." I understand the expression to mean, that whoever takes the assets, whether near or remote in the order of inheritance, is liable for the debts of the deceased, so far as these assets go, provided such heir have attained his majority, and that, when the heir is a minor, the creditor must wait until the minority expires before he can recover his debt out of the assets. Subject to this condition the son must pay his father's debts, as well as all necessary debts contracted on his account during his minority; and, according to the Benares school, the debts of the father are binding upon the son whether the former left property or not, as well as those of the grandfather, but he need not pay interest on the latter.

If there are no assets the obligation is only a moral, not a legal one. *Mr Colebrooke*, in his *Obligations and Contracts*, chap. 2, § 51, lays it down as a principle, that heirs succeed to the obligations of ancestors without any reference to the adequacy of the property, and the rights of inheritance must be relinquished when its obligations are repudiated (see *post*, Charges on Property).

In Bombay an Act was passed to limit the liability of a son, grandson, or heir of a deceased Hindu for the debts of his ancestor, and the liability of a second husband for the debts of a Hindu widow by her deceased husband, and otherwise amend the law of debtor and creditor, *Bomb. Act* vii. of 1866; 2 *H. C. R. Bomb.*, 440. It provides that a Hindu son or grandson shall not be liable as such for the debt of a deceased ancestor (*ib.* § 1). That the heir is to be liable as repesentative of deceased ancestor to the extent of assets received, and personally to the extent of assets received and not duly applied (*ib.* 3). That the Act does not apply to pending suits in which judgment has not been pronounced saving as to costs (sec. 3). The husband of a Hindu widow is not to be liable for the debt of a deceased former husband, the section is to apply to pending suits in which judgment has not been pronounced, saving as to costs (sec. 4). A member of an undivided Hindu family is liable for the family debts contracted when he was less than twenty years old (sec. 5). But nothing in the Act shall affect the liability of a surviving member for a debt for which he would have been liable (sec. 6).*

The grounds of the liability of the heir discussed.—The grounds of the liability of the heir are discussed in *Grady's Hindu Law*, p. 65.

If manager contract debt not within scope of his authority, his own undivided share is liable.—If the manager contract a debt not within the scope of his authority as the agent of the family to contract, that is a debt not for a necessary purpose, or for the common weal. So far from that debt being obligatory on his parceners, his own undivided and unascertained share of the estate alone would be liable; and if that share were insufficient, the creditor could not, it would seem, come upon the other shares for reimbursement.

General rule laid down by Coleb. refers to divided families.—The general rule laid down by *Coleb.* in his *Treatise on Obligations*, is applicable in cases other than of an associated family; for instance, if after division a son should succeed by inheritance to his father's estate, or a brother to a brother's, a nephew to an uncle's; here no joint liability having been contracted with the deceased, it would be unjust to hold the heir responsible if the liabilities exceed the

* The presumption of Hindu law is, that a debt incurred by the head of a Hindu family residing together, is under ordinary circumstances a family debt; but when one of the members is a minor, the creditor seeking to enforce his claim against the family property must show that the debt was contracted *bonâ fide* for the benefit of the family, *Tandavaraya Mudali* v. *Valliammal*, 1 *Mad. H. C. R.*, 398; vide also *Huniomanpersaud Panday* v. *Must. Babooee Munraj Koonweree*, 6 *Moore's In. Ap.*, 393. A minor on coming of age must not only pay the debts of him whose property he has inherited, but also all necessary debts contracted on his account during his minority.

value of the assets. So in case of a wife or daughter succeeding to a husband or father, no joint liability with him having been contracted, they ought not to be held liable beyond the assets.

Minors may now be sued by their guardians.—How far this may have been the law at the time *Macnaghten* wrote, it certainly would not be acted upon now. There is scarcely an instance in which a guardian does not exist against whom a suit can be brought.

Suits instituted in favour of and against minors.—With regard to suits instituted in favour of or against minors, there is much obsolete law in the books; but as this subject is regulated at present by the practice of the existing courts, we have not considered it necessary to trouble the reader with that which can only be interesting to the antiquarian.

Share of minor in joint property.—The guardian of a minor may sue on his behalf for allotment to him of his share in family property, provided there may have been malversation of the estate to the prejudice of the minor's interests, but not otherwise.

Acts of minor in regard to property.—The acts of a minor in regard to property are not valid.

No act in regard to the property or liability of a minor is valid but such as may be clearly one of necessity, or for the benefit of the minor. All acts of the guardian of an infant which the minor if of age might reasonably and prudently do for himself, must be upheld when done for him by his guardian. A minor through his legal guardian may sue to establish his rights; but any friend of the minor may sue the legal guardian when he has invaded the minor's rights. The minor's consent is not necessary to the institution of an action on his behalf, so a minor in the same way may defend a suit.

An idiot or lunatic may also sue or be sued through a manager, guardians, or *prochain ami*. Where a purchaser of immovable property treats with a guardian, it lies upon the purchaser to give some reasonable account of the need which actually existed, or was alleged to exist, for the sale. Gifts by a minor are void, *Mayukha*.

Tutelage of women.—Women are considered unfit for independence. There is an exception to this rule in certain of the labouring classes, as washerwomen, cow-keepers, toddy-drawers, musicians, oil-mongers, &c.; the woman who contributes to the maintenance of the family may contract obligations if for the uses of the family, and render their husbands liable for the same. In *Virasvami Chetti* v. *Appasvami Chetti*, *Sir A. Bittlestone* says—By the law of England, in the case of husband and wife living together, the presumption is that the wife is the husband's agent for contracting debts for the necessities of the family; and, according to Hindu law also, a wife has authority to bind her husband by contracting for necessaries, in proportion as the management of the family is confided to her. By Hindu law, perhaps, the presumption of authority is not so strong as it is by English law. In a note upon the same case the learned reporter, observes *Katyayana,* says, debts incurred for domestic uses by the slave, wife, mother, or disciple, or one gone to a far country, or deceased, and also by a son, and also by his son, must be paid: so says *Bhrugu;* and *Yajnavalchya* holds a woman shall not pay debts incurred by her husband or son, neither a father those of his son; nor a husband those of his wife, unless contracted for the benefit of the family, *Vyavahara Mayukha.*

CHAPTER IV.

PROPERTY.

Property is fourfold—Modes of acquisition—Creation of right of inheritance—Absence for twelve years—Ancestral and self-acquired property—Joint-property—Self-acquired property—Stridhana.

Property is fourfold.—Property, according to Hindu law, is of four descriptions—viz., real, personal, ancestral, and self-acquired. The more correct expression in the original law books is movable and immovable; the former includes anything personal, the latter, lands and buildings; amongst these Hindu law writers class slaves* and corrodies †—that is, assignments on lands. Property is either ancestral or self-acquired, and with regard to its possession it is either joint or separate. But although, like ours, the Hindu law divided property into real and personal, yet it does not descend in the same way. With us real property descends to the heir, whilst personal property goes to the executors or administrators for distribution under the will, or under the statute of distributions; but amongst the Hindus they both descend alike to the same persons, and are subject to the same incumbrances. See "Charges on Property."

Modes of acquisition.—The various modes of acquisition, as occupancy, birth, gift, purchase, &c., have been detailed and discussed with all the *minutiæ*, elaborateness, and subtlety peculiar to Hindu jurists, in their various legal works, and not being considered appropriate to a purely elementary work like the present, further reference to them is deemed unnecesary.

Creation of right of inheritance.—Our inquiries here will be directed mainly to the nature of that property, the right to which is created by birth. To sonship must be traced all the impediments existing on alienation, a man without heirs having an absolute and uncontrolled dominion over his property by whatever means acquired. Macnaghten observes, that an indefeasible inchoate right is created by birth, seems to be universally admitted, though

* Slavery is abolished.

† Corrody (nibandha) is defined in the *Daya Bhaga* to be what is fixed by a promise in this form, "I will give that in every month of Kartiki." *Sri kristna* defines it as signifying anything which has been promised deliverable annually or monthly, or at any other fixed periods; and *Raghunandana*, in the *Daya-talva*, defines it to be, "A fixed amount granted by the king or other authority receivable from a mine or similar fund."

much argumentative discussion has been used to establish that this alone is not sufficient to create proprietary right. The most appropriate conclusion appears to be that the inchoate right arising from birth, and the relinquishment by the occupant (whether effected by death or otherwise), conjointly create this right, the inchoate right which previously existed becoming perfected by the removal of the obstacle, *i.e.*, by the death of the owner (natural or civil, or his voluntary abandonment). *Sir Thomas Strange* says, according to the doctrine of the *Mitacshara*, as prevalent in the Peninsula and North India, the sons of a man are considered as having with their father by birth so far a co-ordinate concern in that part of it which is ancestral, that if he thinks proper to come to a partition of it in his lifetime, he must divide as directed by law, *i.e.*, give them and himself equal shares, nor is it in his power to alienate any considerable portion of it without their concurrence. It is, according to this school, so far as regards the interest of parceners, inalienable. The Bengal school follows the same rule with respect to partition, admitting to the father otherwise an unreserved power of alienation over all that he possesses, however in particular instances its exercise may be liable to censure.

Absence for twelve years.—The absence of the ancestor for a period exceeding twelve years constitutes a legal title to the succession on the part of the heirs, his death after that period being presumed, 3 *S. D. A. R.*, 28 (25th April 1820). Some authorities, however, maintain that the period varies with reference to the age of the missing person.

Ancestral and self-acquired property.—Another division of property recognised in Hindu law is into ancestral and self-acquired.

Ancestral or inherited property is that which, as its name imports, is derived from ancestors, or which has descended from father to son, and includes whatever is obtained through its instrumentality, as by accumulations or exchange, &c. It may be either real or personal. In ancestral real property the right is always limited, and the sons, grandsons, and great-grandsons of the occupant, supposing them to be free from those defects, mental or corporeal, which are held to defeat the right of inheritance (see "Disqualifications for Inheritance"), are declared to possess an interest in such property equal to that of the occupant himself, so much so that he is not at liberty to alienate it, except under special and urgent circumstances, or to assign a larger share of it to one of his descendants than to another. If any property lost by the ancestor be recovered by the heir, it is no longer considered as ancestral, but classes as self-acquired, unless, indeed, it has been recovered by the use of the patrimony. See *post*, "Inheritance—Partition."

Self-acquired property includes everything that has been obtained without the aid of the family property. It may be obtained by gift, purchase, or by adverse and undisturbed possession. An indefeasible title is acquired after three generations—that is, after ninety years, if the possession has been adverse and undisturbed, that is, against the will of the proprietor; for, if he hold, under an agreement with the proprietor, it is not adverse. So the possession is not adverse if the holding be under his sapinda, his daughter's husband, a priest, or the sovereign. Ordinary gifts, if not made in return for something previously given; nuptial gifts, which a man receives with his wife; and presents made to the father or kinsman of the bride; lost ancestral property, recovered without the aid of the family bonds and property of the co-heirs, and other acquisitions enumerated under the head of Inheritance, are all ranked as self-acquired property.

Joint-property—Is that species of estate which is known as family property, or enjoyed in common by an undivided family, and includes ancestral property.

Self-acquired property—Is what a person enjoys independently of any co-sharer, and is acquired by his own personal exertions without any assistance from the joint-estate, by gift, by superior skill in intellectual pursuits, the professions, arts, or sciences.*

Stridhana.—With regard to woman's property, see *post,* "Stridhana;" and with regard to the power of alienation, see "Alienation."

* A Hindu's property is presumed to be ancestral, and not self-acquired.

CHAPTER V.

CHARGES ON PROPERTY.

SECTION I.

The estate descends charged with encumbrances—Payment of the debts—Order of payment—Where no assets—Priority amongst classes—Where creditor has taken a pledge for his debt—Capital contributing to gains—Creditor may follow assets—Liability during father's life—Liability of widow—Liability of managing members—The power of manager to charge ancestral estate by loan, &c., is limited—Debt incurred by head of family—Minors—Debts incurred for domestic use by a slave, wife, &c.—Liability for wife's debts for necessaries—Debts contracted by wife living apart from her husband—Liability of family property—Debts contracted by brother for support of family—But in trade consent necessary—Diminution of share on account of profuse expenditure—If debt exceed surplus—Separate acquisitions liable—Liability of widows' heirs.

The estate descends charged with encumbrances.—According to Hindu law, the estate descends to the heir charged with certain encumbrances. *Sir Thomas Strange* says, these are of three kinds :—

1. Debts and other obligations in the nature of legacies.
2. Certain specific duties to be provided for out of the estate where it has descended to a single heir, and out of the common fund where it has vested by survivorship in undivided co-heirs.
3. Maintenance of all requiring and entitled to it.

Mr J. Strange says,—The charges on the estate are the just debts; the obsequial monthly, half-yearly, and yearly ceremonies of ancestors; initiatory ceremonies terminating in the oopanayana, marriages, and maintenance.

Payment of the debts.—The primary obligation on the heir is the payment of the debts of the ancestor. Formerly a son was bound to pay his father's debts whether he had assets or not; but this was a moral rather than a civil obligation, and could be evaded by a relinquishment of the paternal estate. As this obligation was not civilly binding on the heir, our courts, considering it inequitable to enforce it, have held that the liability extends only to the amount of assets descending to the heirs, *Sudr. Court in S. A.* 12 of 1851. The reason assigned for the debts following the assets is a religious one, "for the peace of the father's soul." This is unsatisfactory, but it is as good as most reasons given for a rule of law. See *Blackstone, passim,* who certainly has detracted very much from the value of his work by the reasons he has given in many places for the law which he has enunciated. We have, in our opinion, given the true reason at pp. 65-67 of *Grady's Hindu Law* of Inheritance.

Order of payment.—The father's debt must be first paid, and next, a debt contracted by the man himself; but the debt of the paternal grandfather must even be paid before either of these, *Vrishaspati.*

The sons must pay the debt of their father when proved as if it were their own; *or with interest,* the son's son must pay the debt of his grandfather, and his son, or the great-grandson, shall not be compelled to discharge it unless he be heir and have assets, *ante,* title "Minority." First the debt of the grandfather should be discharged; next the debt of the father; and, lastly, the debt contracted by the man himself, with interest. But the debt of a grandfather may be paid without interest, and the great grandson shall not be compelled against his will to discharge the debt of his great-grandfather; but if the great-grandson be willing, it may be discharged by him. Debts being a charge upon property, all of which are not barred by the statute of limitation, ought to be paid by the successors to the property.

Where no assets.—It seems settled at Bengal that the obligation of the son to pay the debts of the ancestor has no legal force independent of assets, without which a son and grandson are under a moral and religious, not a civil obligation to pay the debt, but assets may be followed in the hands of any representative. *Sir Thomas Strange* says, To the southward the doctrine of the *Mitacshara,* supported by *Madhavya* and *Chandrika,* is said to render the payment of the father's debts with interest, and the grandfather's without interest, independent of assets, a legal as well as a sacred obligation.

Priority amongst classes.—With regard to the priority amongst classes, the old law has become obsolete; it is now mere matter of procedure, which is governed by the practice of the courts.

Where creditor has taken a pledge for his debt.—The creditor who has received a pledge to be used shall not receive a share of the dividend, for he trusted to the chattel possessed by him for the recovery of his debt. But he may demand a sale of the pledge, and he is not bound to share it with the other creditors. Those debts which are due at the time of distribution shall receive a dividend. The subject is further discussed by *Jagannatha.*

Capital contributing to gains.—*Katyayana* suggests an exception to those rules, viz., that capital on which it is proved that the assets were gained, and no other debt must be repaid by the debtor out of these assets, so that a debtor would have *a lien* upon the assets produced by his particular loan, out of which he is entitled to be paid in preferenee to any other creditor. *Jagannatha* says,—If there be at once many creditors of the sacerdotal and other classes, he through whose loan the assets were gained must be paid out of these assets, not any other creditor; should a surplus remain, it shall be paid to the other creditors by a dividend, or in the order of classes. For example, borrowing a sum from one man, and therewith paying the revenue which is due to the king by the custom of the country, or supporting his own dependants and the like—the debtor conducts agriculture, the produce of that culture is applicable to the payment of the debt due to that creditor alone, *ib.* 380.

Creditor may follow assets.—The assets of the debtor may be pursued by a creditor into whosoever hands they may come, *Yaina-valchya*, as property descends on the death, whether natural, presumed, or civil, so the liability then arises, *Vishnu.*

Liability during father's life.—During his father's life his son is not liable for his debts, they being payable from the family property, if incurred for the benefit of the family, or from his own share, if purely personal. But after death the son is liable for *all* the debts, to the amount of the assets, if he once receive them, even though they are then lost, stolen, or destroyed. But probably equity would interfere if the loss was through no fault of his own.

Liability of widow.—The widow is not liable for her husband's debts, unless she possess assets of the debtor. The debts must be paid, whether enough remain for her maintenance or not. The principle is applicable in the case of all other surviving relatives. If a wife possessing separate property render it by special agreement liable for a debt contracted by her husband, she must, in his default, pay it, or if she have possessed herself of her husband's property, she is liable to that extent for his debts. A widow is liable in these two cases only. The Sastrie (Pundit) considers the claim of the widow to subsistence from the husband's estate as preferable to the claim of his creditors; and as he is confessedly one of the most respectable of those whose names are found in these papers, the presumption is that he is right, though for this part of his opinion I know not whence he derives his authority, *Ellis.* It is doubtful, however, whether the Pundit's opinion would now be considered worthy of the respect paid to it by Mr Ellis.

Liability of managing members.—Where property is held in common, the managing member is answerable for all claims on the family. Of course he should be answerable jointly with the other members. No family debt affects self-acquired property, except perhaps to the extent of the acquirer's own share, in the event of the joint-property being insufficient to satisfy the debt. A junior member may bind his own share of the property, but only to the extent of that share.

The power of manager to charge ancestral estate by loan, etc., is limited.—The power of a manager for an infant heir to charge ancestral estate by loan or mortgage is, by the Hindu law, a limited or qualified power, which can only be exercised rightly by the manager in a case of need, or for the benefit of the estate. But where the charge is one that a prudent owner would make, in order to benefit the estate, a *bonâ fide* lender is not affected by the precedent management of the estate. The actual pressure on the estate, the danger to be averted, or the benefit to be conferred, in the particular instance, are the *criteria* to be regarded. If that danger arises from any misconduct to which the lender has been a party, he cannot take advantage of his own wrong to support a charge in his favour against the heir, grounded on a necessity which his own wrong had helped to produce. The lender, however, in such circumstances is bound to inquire into the necessity for the loan, and to satisfy himself as well as he can with reference to the parties with whom he is dealing, that the manager is acting in the particular instance for the benefit of the estate. If he inquire, and act honestly, the real existence of an alleged and reasonably credited necessity is not a condition precedent to the validity of the charge which renders him bound to see to the application of the money.

A *bonâ fide* creditor who has been deceived, but who has acted honestly, and with due caution, is not to suffer. The mere creation of a charge by a manager of an infant's estate, securing a proper debt, is not to be viewed as an improper act.

No general rule can be laid down upon whom the *onus* lies as to the allegation and proof of *bonâ fides* of a manager, whose title to alienate is qualified in contracting debts and resorting to loans. The presumption proper to be made varies with the circumstances, and is regarded by and dependent upon them. The mortgagee, however, in enforcing his security against the heir, must allege and prove the facts which embody the representations made to him of the alleged needs of the estate, and the motives influencing the loan.

A mortgage bond to secure a sum of money lent to a party deceased, in substitution of a previous deed, executed by a former proprietor, by way of further security for a sum advanced by the mortgagee to the widow of the deceased, charging part of the ancestral estate described, the widow, as having a beneficial proprietary right in the mortgaged estates, although in fact she was only the curator of her son, a minor, the heir of the deceased—held that the description, though inaccurate, was not such an assumption of ownership as was derogative to the rights of the heir, but was to be viewed as an act done by her, as director, in behalf of the heir; and as the mortgage was beneficial to the estate, it was binding upon the heir, *Hunoomanpersaud Panday* v. *Mussumat Babooee Munraj Koonweree*, 6 *Moore's In. Ap.*, 393.

Debt incurred by head of family—Minors.—A debt incurred by the head of a Hindu family residing together is, under ordinary circumstances, presumed to be a family debt. But where one of the members is a minor, the creditor seeking to enforce his claim against the family property must show that the debt was contracted *bonâ fide*, and for the benefit of the family, *Hunoomanpersaud Panday* v. *Mussumat Babooee Munraj Koonweree*, *supra*; *Tandavaraya Mudali* v. *Vali Ammal*, 1 *Mad. H. C. R.*, 398.

A Hindu testator by his will empowered his executor and guardian of his infant children, who was also manager of his zemindary, to charge the same for payment of debts and advances during his children's minority, and directed that when the children came of age they should repay the amount raised. The executor borrowed of a banking firm money for payment of government revenue, and gave bonds charging the zemindary with the sums so borrowed. On the children coming of age, they executed a *kistbandy*, or instalment bond, for repayment of the amount then due. This instrument they afterwards repudiated, and on a suit being brought against them by the lender, upon the *kistbandy*, they in defence not only denied the existence of the bond, but alleged fraudulent collusion between the lender and executor, in obtaining the loan and granting a lease to the nominee of the lender at an inadequate rent. Held that the executor had power under the will to charge the zemindary with advances made for the purposes of the zemindary, *Golaub Koonwurree Bebee* v. *Eshan Chunder Chowdhooree*, 8 *Moore's In. Ap.*, 447.

Debts incurred for domestic use by a slave, wife, etc.—*Katyayana* says, "Debts incurred for domestic uses by the slave, *wife*, mother, or disciple of one gone to a far country, or deceased, and also by his son, must be paid: so says *Bhrugu;* and *Yajnavalchya* holds a woman shall not pay debts incurred by her husband or son, nor a father those of his son; nor a husband those of his wife, unless contracted for the benefit of the family."

Liability for wife's debts for necessaries.—By Hindu law a wife has authority to bind her husband, by contracting for necessaries in proportion as the management of the family is confided to her. By Hindu law, perhaps, the presumption of authority is not so strong as it is by the English law, per *Bittlestone, J.*, in *Virasvami Chetti* v. *Appasvami Chetti*, 1 *Mad. H. C. R.*, 375.

Debts contracted by wife living apart from her husband.—If it were permitted by the Hindu law for a husband to supersede his first wife by taking another to live with him, and this was her sole reason for refusing to live with him, his doing so would not, according to Hindu law, justify his first wife in separating herself and remaining apart from him of her own free will, and could not without more, give her implied authority as his agent to bind him for debts incurred for necessaries, per *Scotland, C.-J., ib.*, 375.

Liability of family property.—The family property is not liable for the debt of an individual member, not even if by his death the family property is augmented.

Debts contracted by brother for support of family.—A debt contracted by one brother living in family partnership for the support of the family, is binding upon all in every case.

The debtor's share in the property will, however, be liable. The creditor would have to sue to have the share set out by partition, in order to make it thus available to him. Allowance would first have to be made out of the share for the share of the debtor's male issue, the residue only being available to meet the debt.

But in trade consent necessary.—But consent, express or implied, is requisite in the case of one contracted in the course of trade or for charitable purposes. Supposing the elder brother to be manager for the family, this might exonerate the person of the younger one,* but not the property, 1 *Dig.* clxxx., clxxxiii.

A Hindu possessed of landed and other property died leaving two sons, the younger a minor. The elder took possession and borrowed money (exceeding his share of the property), for which he gave his note, mortgaging for the payment of it the family property. The younger son was not privy to the contracting of the debt, nor had he ever recognised its validity, so far as his interest was concerned, nor did it appear that it was incurred on account of the family. The question raised was, Is the debt chargeable on the family property beyond the share of the elder brother? *Mr Colebrooke* remarks :—"On the subject of the question which you had lately before you, I entirely agree with you that a mortgage, sale, or gift by one of several joint-owners without the consent of the others is invalid for others' shares. In Bengal law it is clear that it is good for his own share, and for that only. In other provinces it is as clear that the act is invalid, as it concerns others' shares, and the only doubt which the subtlety of Hindu reasoning might raise, would be whether it would be maintainable even for his own share of undivided property. On the other two points, as stated by you, the law is undoubtedly as you have viewed it. On the third point I take the law to be, that the consent of the sharers, express or implied, is indispensable to a valid alienation of joint property beyond the share of the actual alienor, and that an unauthorised alienation by one of the sharers is invalid beyond the alienor's share as against the alienee. But consent is implied, and may be presumed in many cases, and under a variety of circumstances, especially where the management of the joint-property intrusted to the part-owner who disposes of it implies a power of disposal; or

* Whether the person of the younger brother would be exempted or not would depend on the existing procedure of the Court.

where he was the only ostensible or avowed owner, or generally when the acts or even the silence of the other sharers had given him a credit, and the alienee had not notice. . . . I rather consider it to be a point of evidence what shall suffice to raise the presumption of consent or acquiescence, 2 *Stra. H. L.* (*vide Peddamuthulaty* v. *N. Timma Reddy*, 2 *Mad H. C. R.*, 270), than a matter on which the Hindu law has pronounced specifically, and I do not recollect any passages more express than those to which you have referred, showing that the alienation is invalid against the alienee. The case of *Prannath* v. *Calispunker*, *Beng. S. D. A. Rep. ante* 1805, to which you refer, was, I conceive, determined on the ground of implied consent, the land being answerable for the revenue for which the managing owner had engaged on the part of himself and sharers, besides other peculiar circumstances in the case."

Diminution of share on account of profuse expenditure—If debt exceed surplus—Separate acquisitions liable.—A co-heir who may have been guilty of profuse expenditure, or who may have dissipated the property by unauthorised alienations, is to have his share diminished by the amount wasted or alienated by him, but should this exceed the value of his share, the surplus is not to be made a debt against him, for the other heirs should have checked his guilty waste in time, and must suffer for their neglect. This might be done by a court declaring his acts null, or compelling a division, or removing him from the management. His separate acquisitions would, however, be liable.

Liability of widows' heirs.—When property passes to a widow, those succeeding to her are not liable for debts contracted by her, unless they are of such a nature as would have warranted her alienating the property to discharge them, such as payment of husband's debts, Government Kist, debts, &c. Hers is only a life-interest interposed between her husband and successor, who is not so much her heir as her husband's.

SECTION II.

The debt must have been for a good consideration—Debts due for fines or tolls—Suretyship—Nuptial debts—Borrowed for use of family —The course of payment of debts on partition—Friendly gifts —Performance of obsequies—Expenses of initiation and marriage —Escheated property—Persons under disability—Daughters.

In actions against the heir three things are to be considered :— 1. The debt must have been for a good consideration, otherwise it will not bind. 2. It must not have been a ready-money transaction, as a toll or fine ; if it is, the heir is not liable. 3. The debt, when incurred for ceremonies, marriage, &c., in order to make it binding on the son, must have been reasonable in amount.

1st, It must have been for a good consideration—so that if the consideration for the debt be gaming, or the purchase of spirituous liquors, or debauchery, or other improper objects, the son is not liable, unless at those festivals where gaming and drinking are authorised, or where the use of spirituous liquors is allowed by custom; so, a debt due for a cause repugnant to good morals, *Vyasa.*

Because the ancestral property has been encumbered, it by no means follows that a sum borrowed has been a wasteful expenditure; it may well be that a father has obtained by it something much more valuable than the original estate, *Tara Chund* v. *Reeb Ram*, 3 *Mad. H. C. R.*, 179.

If the managing member should enter into speculations with the *bonâ fide* hope and reasonable expectation of increasing the property for those who are to come after him, his co-parceners will be liable for the losses he may sustain, *ib.*

Where self-acquired property has descended burthened with debts, the estate in the hands of the heirs is liable for these debts, and the propriety of discharging it on the ground that the managing member ought to have discharged it cannot be recognised, *ib.*

The passage in the *Mitacshara* stating the right of the sons to prohibit excessive expenditure, by no means involves the logical consequence that if that right of prohibition has not been, or from nonage of the sons could not have been, exercised, there would be after the lapse of any period, how long so ever, a right of restitution. It may be said that the case of a minor requires a different consideration: the law counterbalances his liabilities with many privileges; and it may well be that he might be entitled to restitution, although a son of full age would not be. It may also be that the absence of the power of interposition would be a loss attendant upon his disability, from which no law could relieve him, *ib.*

Debts due for fines or tolls.—A fine due to the king for some offence is not a debt for which the son is liable.* So, a debt due for a toll, *i.e.*, a duty of custom payable at a wharf, or the like. *Sir Thomas Strange* says, The reason of which may be that they are to be regarded as ready-money payments, for which credit will have been given at the risk of him by whom they ought to have been received.

Suretyship.—So debts originating in suretyship, commerce, and the rest, shall not involve the sons, they shall not be paid by the sons of the debtor, *Gautama.*

Nuptial debts.—Where the debt attaches upon the common property, as for instance, where it has been incurred for the nuptials of any of the family, the expenses attending the ceremony must have been reasonable, according to the usage and means of

* The Indian Criminal Procedure Code (1860) empowers magistrates to levy fines.

the family. If the expenses have been extravagant or excessive, the member incurring them will alone be liable unless the family has adopted them.

Borrowed for use of family.—If the money borrowed was expended for the use of the family it must be paid by that family, divided or undivided, out of their own estate, *Menu;* contracted fairly for the use of the family by any member, whether uncle, brother, son, wife, servant, pupil, or dependants, it binds the whole.

The course of payment of debts on partition.—This subject has been discussed under the title "Partition."

Sir Thomas Strange says, Modified as the details of Hindu law are everywhere by local usage and practice, how far the whole of the ancient provisions for the payment of debts are at present applicable must be left to the discretion of the courts exercising jurisdiction within particular limits.

Friendly gifts.—*Sir Thomas Strange* says, Connected with the duty of paying the debts of ancestors, is the discharge of obligations resting on the intention of the deceased sufficiently manifested; since, though nothing occurs in the Hindu law expressly in favour of the testamentary power as exercised under other codes, it provides distinctly for the performance of promises by the ancestor in his lifetime to take effect after his death, and to this extent a friendly gift, as it is called, not being an *idle* one, far less one founded on an *immoral* consideration, being available in law as a charge upon heirs, may be assimilated to a legacy.

In support of this he refers to cases, vol. ii., p. 426, which are cited in *Grady's Hindu Law*, p. 85.

Sir Thomas Strange adds, But according to the doctrine of the *Mitacshara,* such a gift referring to property held in common, in order to be good must have had the consent of the deceased coparceners, *Mitac.* ch. i. s. i., § 30; as if made by a widow, it must have had that of her guardian and next heirs. What was promised shall be received by the descendants of the donee down to the fourth in descent, if not vested; if vested in the donee, it is partible amongst the co-heirs if he have any. According to Davala, that which a husband has promised to his wife for separate property must be made good by his sons even as a debt.

2d, Performance of obsequies (sraadhas).—Of property which descends by inheritance, half should be carefully set apart for the benefit of the deceased owner, to defray the charges of his monthly, six monthly, and annual obsequies, on the ground that wealth is useful for alms and enjoyment, *Vrihaspati, Apastamba.*

Expenses of initiation and marriage.—The expenses incurred for the initiation of the uninitiated and for the marriage of the unmarried members of the family are also charges upon the estate. *Yajnavalchya* says, Uninitiated brothers should be initiated by those for whom the ceremonies have been already completed. Upon which the *Mitac.* ch. i. s. vii., § 4, has the following exposition, By the brethren who make a partition after the decease of their father the uninitiated brothers should be initiated at the expense of the whole estate. *Yajnavalchya* says, Unmarried sisters should be disposed of in marriage, giving them a quarter of a share, *Mitac.* ch. i. s. vii., § 5, *et seq.* But the *Chandrika* and *Madhavya* countenance the opinion that the specified allotment intends only a sufficiency for the charges of the sister's nuptials.

Initiation involves a succession of religious rites attended with more or less expense, commencing with purification and terminating in marriage. They are ten in number, of which marriage is the only one competent to females and Sudras; the rest being confined to males of the three superior classes.

We have seen, *supra*, that the duty of initiation attaches to those who themselves have been initiated, and the provision for it is like that for the payment of debts, to be made before partition out of the common stock; and, as we have before seen, the expenses must be reasonable.

This obligation does not extend beyond brothers and sisters, consequently not to collaterals, such as nephews. In *Mitac.* ch. i. s. iv., § 19, s. v., § 2, s. vii., § 4, no mention is made of nephews.

Escheated property.—An estate taken by escheat is subject to the same trusts and charges, if any, previously affecting the estate, *The Collector of Masulipatam* v. *Cavaly Vencata Narrainapah*, 8 *Moore's In. Ap.*, 500.

When the crown takes by escheat for want of heirs, it has the same power to impeach an unauthorised alienation by the widow which the heirs of the widow (had there been any) would have had, *ib.* 529.

The question was raised in *Bawani Sankara Pandit* v. *Ambabay Ammal*, 1 *Mad. H. C. R.*, 363, whether if the right to maintenance had existed in a son whose adoption was held to be invalid, that right would as an estate descend to his sons natural or adopted, but was not decided, and under the view taken by the court in respect of the right of a person whose adoption is not valid, it is not likely to arise again.

Persons under disability.—We have already said in chapter vi., that all those who are excluded from the inheritance for the reasons there referred to, are entitled to maintenance, except the out-caste and his issue subsequently born. With regard to the out-caste, the *Mitac.* ch. ii. s. x., § 1, says, he must be maintained, citing *Yajnavalchya*; whilst *Jim. Vahana*, ch. v., § 11, 12, citing *Devala* and *Baudhayana*, excludes the out-caste, and the latter, his issue also. *Menu*, however, does not except them. Under Act xxi. of 1850 out-castes are entitled to maintenance. *Sir Thomas Strange*, arguing by analogy, says, Admitting the right of the out-caste to food and raiment, it must be difficult to exclude the adulterer's widow.

Daughters.—The daughters of persons labouring under disability must be maintained until married, and the expenses of their nuptials defrayed, *Yajnavalchya ; Mitac. ;* and their childless widows must be supported for life, *Jim. Vahana ; Mitac.*

SECTION III.

Maintenance—How estimated—Whether stridhana is to be included —Where property unproductive—Widow and only son—Where one of united brothers dies leaving a widow and a son—A mother's right as between herself and her sons—There is no distinction in the different tribes—Half-brothers and childless widow—The rights of a brother's widow having a son—Rights of father's wives on partition among the brothers—How maintenance is to be provided for—Want of Chastity—Desertion of husband by his wife—Implied agency—Polygamy—Widow's right to recover arrears of maintenance—Where husband's property proves deficient—Grandmother—Stepmothers—Sisters—Daughter—Illegitimate children —Illegitimate son—Shatra caste.

Maintenance.—The maintenance of dependent members of the family is also a charge upon the common fund. The widow, where she does not take as heir, is the first who is entitled to maintenance, and her maintenance is the first charge upon the estate, after payment of the debts.

How estimated.—*Sir Thomas Strange* says, In awarding it to her, what she possesses as stridhana, or her peculiar property, is to be matter of account, the utmost that she can claim being to have it made up to her equal to what would be a son's share in the event of partition ; and again, an opinion that her maintenance should be independent of her peculiar property is unsupported ; again, whether in estimating her stridhana on the occasion, her clothes, ornaments, and the like are to be taken into account, or only such articles of her property as are productive of income to her or conducive to her subsistence, does not distinctly appear, though the restricting this account to the latter would seem to be reasonable, considering the object.

We cannot think that this is the correct view of the law. It is in right of her husband that she is entitled to maintenance, and her claim to it is irrespective of her stridhana. See opinion, *Mr Ellis*, 2 *H. L.*, 291 ; *Mr Colebrooke's* 2 *Stra. H. L.*, 294 ; and *Grady's Hindu Law* of Inheritance, 88, 89.

Whether stridhana is to be included.—See *Grady's Hindu Law* of Inheritance, 89.

Where property unproductive.—*Mr Ellis* says, If she have property of her own, not consisting merely of pearls, clothes, ornaments, and the like, but from which an income is derivable, in this case it is to be made up equal to a share without reference to any fanciful division of halves and quarters, of which the Pundits (mistaking the explanatory language of the law, as "she shall otherwise receive a half or a quarter," for positive injunction) are so fond. I say above, "from which an income is derivable." I cannot just now refer to my authority for this, as I have not my books at hand; but it is the sense of the law. The law says, she shall have a maintenance, but it is not required that either the family stock, or her own, shall be reduced to afford it. It is clearly meant that it shall be a maintenance by income; if, therefore, she have no property from which she can derive an income, without destroying the property, she is entitled to a full share.

Widow and only son.—The father being dead, leaving a widow and infant son with property, the son and estate being in the hands of the brother of the deceased, the widow demanded the custody of each. The Pundit said the estate is the son's, out of which the widow is only entitled to be maintained. The son is not compellable to live with his mother; it is rather her duty to live with him. Upon which *Mr Colebrooke* remarks, The sovereign is the guardian of minors. The mother cannot claim a share, but a maintenance merely, from an only son, her right to a specific allotment arising only when a partition is made.

Where one of united brothers dies leaving a widow and a son.—If there be undivided brothers, and one die, leaving a widow and son, they succeed to his share of the joint property, is the answer given by a Pundit to a case submitted to him; upon which *Mr Ellis* remarks, As long as the family continues undivided, all the parceners, their wives and families, are entitled to a joint maintenance. On division, widows, wives, and children can claim only on the partition of their respective husbands and fathers. In the present case, if the son were alive at the time of division, his mother would have to look to him alone for maintenance; if he were dead, she would be entitled in right at once both of her husband and son to succeed to a full share of the estate—that is to say, a full share should be the *maximum* allowed her. If litigation take place, it is the measure to be adopted by the court; not that the dividing parties are bound to give her so much, if they can prevail on her to take less, nor any share at all if they can provide among themselves for her maintenance. Such, at least, I believe to be the correct doctrine; whether her dominion over the property be limited or otherwise is another question.

A mother's right as between herself and her sons.—A case illustrating this is cited in *Grady's Hindu Law*, p. 90.

There is no distinction in the different tribes.—Two brothers of the *Shetriya* tribe, being about to divide, after his death, the estate of their father, the question is as to the rights of the mother, who claims to share with them. To what in this tribe is she entitled? The Pundit's answer was, that the mother has by law no right to share with her sons. She is entitled to her *stridhana*, and if there be land yielding an annual produce, to as much of it as will suffice to be settled upon her for a maintenance. *Mr Colebrooke* remarks, The law provides, that when a partition takes place among brothers, the mother shall have an allotment made up to her, equal to a full share. There is no distinction in this respect amongst the different tribes.

Half-brothers and childless widow.—In a question between a childless widow and the half-brothers (by the same father) of her deceased husband as to her rights, the Pundit replied, That she is entitled to demand of them as much as will provide her food and raiment with sufficient for the *shradum*, or annual ceremony of her husband; and *Mr Colebrooke* remarks, They are bound to maintain her, see *Narada cited Mitacshara*, ch. ii. s. 1. § 7. But *Mr Ellis* denies that this is the law of the *Smritis*. He says, it is the convenient law of more modern commentators, endeavoured to be supported by proposing alterations in the original texts, for which there is no foundation. In recent times, however, when the operation of the Hindu law had been interrupted, and none other established in its stead, the nefarious practice of the males of the family seizing all the property of it, and reducing the females to a state little short of slavery, came gradually to prevail, which practice, as appears throughout these papers, the present race of Pundits are sufficiently inclined to support. The correct doctrine is, that a widow succeeds to the "entire share" (*christnam unsam**) of her husband immediately, if partition have taken place; eventually, if it have not. What, then, is the situation of a widow of a coparcener during the time the family continues undivided? Is she merely entitled to a maintenance? No; she is in the situation of her deceased husband, and is entitled to the use of the joint-property to the full extent that he was entitled to it, remembering always that as a female she is under the protection of her natural guardians.

The rights of a brother's widow having a son.—The plaintiff's husband and the defendants were brothers. The plaintiff had a son aged four years by her husband, and she instituted a suit for a share of the undivided property for herself, and another for her son; and the Pundit was asked his opinion as to her rights under the general law of inheritance and partition, she being, moreover, charged

* "*Christnam ansam*"—the entire share. This expression is read by some, *christnam artham*, the "entire estate;" and on this reading, it is maintained that the widow takes the estate of her deceased husband in the event only of previous partition. But this is confuted by the better jurists.

with adultery;* and he replied, "There is no ground for the claim of separate shares for herself and her son. The share that is given to the son must maintain his mother. Though she should not conduct herself to the entire satisfaction of her caste people, still she must be supported out of the share allotted to her son, who, in the meantime, is to continue under her care till he attain his age. Nor though she should prove an adulteress, can he refuse to supply her with the necessaries of life." *Mr Colebrooke* remarks, The son is entitled to the share of his father, who was one of four brothers, *Mitac.* ch. i. s. v. § 2, and his mother must be maintained out of his allotment; but the sovereign, or a person selected by his authority, is the guardian of the widow. Brethren are not bound to maintain the unchaste widow of their childless brothers, *Mitac.* ch. ii. s. i. § 7. Nor has any authority been found for imposing it as a civil obligation on the son to maintain his mother if she be an adulteress (query, unchaste); and *Mr Ellis* says, Correct as to the exclusive right and consequent obligation of the son; I do not think, however, and probably the Pundit does not intend, that the defendants could be compelled to a division of the estate until the majority of the child.

Rights of father's wives on partition among the brothers.— In cases of partition among the brethren, to each of the father's wives, who is a mother, must be assigned a share equal to that of a son, and to the childless wives a sufficient maintenance; but, according to the *Mitacshara* and other works current in Benares and the southern provinces, childless wives are also entitled to shares, the term *matha* being interpreted to signify both mother and step-mother. The *Smitri Chandrica* is the only authority which altogether excludes a mother from the right of participation. A step-mother has no right of succession according to the law of Bengal, and the property of her step-son will rather go to her uncle's adopted son. If, after the death of R, the first widow of K, her adopted son N died without issue, his share goes to the adopted son of K's full brother—*i.e.*, to the cousin-german by adoption, not to the second widow of K (step-mother by adoption), nor to the heirs of the half-brothers of the adopting father. If, however, the adoption by the appellant (the second widow) of K be good, which was made on the death of N, then her adopted son is heir to N.† The reason why the appellant, the step-mother of N, cannot succeed to his share is, that in the *Daya Bhaga* and other authorities current in Bengal, wherever the word *matha*, or mother, occurs, it is explained to intend *jananee*, or actual mother. These books do not authorise the step-mother's succession; but she receives a maintenance out of

* She could not be charged with adultery after the husband's death.

† In the *Shastras* there is no express prohibition, or sanction of two adoptions. If it be the usage in Bengal to make two adoptions, the adoption of R is valid, and he succeeds, *ib.*

the estate. In the books of the *Dekkan*—viz., the *Mitacshara*, &c.—the word *matha* implies both mother and step-mother; according to these, the step-mother would share, *Menu*, *Baudhayana*, *Gautama*.

How maintenance is to be provided for.—There seems to be three modes of providing for the payment of the allowance. One is to estimate the value of the maintenance to be allowed, and to give the widow a sum; a second is, by assignment of land revertible to the estate after the death of the widow—in both these cases in proportion to the amount of the property of the husband, and to her support as well as those dependent upon her, including the performance of charities and the discharge of religious duties; a third, is to invest a sum at interest for the payment of the maintenance, or to deposit company's paper.

Want of chastity.—*Sir Thomas Strange* says, "As chastity is a condition of her inheriting on failure of male issue, so it would seem that by a want of it she forfeits her right to maintenance, leaving it a question, however, in the case of the Hindu, whether, notwithstanding, she be not entitled (as out-castes generally are) to food and raiment.

Mr Ellis remarks, *Menu* nowhere says that a woman divorced is not entitled to a maintenance. She is to be "abandoned," deprived of nuptial rights; she is to be divested of her ornaments and separate property; but she must be maintained, as must an out-caste be, by his family.

Mr Colebrooke remarks, "Brethren are not bound to maintain the unchaste widow of their childless brothers (*Mitac.* ch. ii. s. 1, § 7), nor has any authority been found for imposing it as a civil obligation on the son to maintain his mother if she be an adulteress.* If she be unchaste, a woman must be turned out of doors, and without a maintenance, *R. A.* No. 2 of 1863.

Adultery uncondoned bars a suit against a husband for maintenance. A Hindu adulteress, therefore, living apart from her husband, has no claim upon him for maintenance so long as the adultery is uncondoned, *Ilata Shavatri* v. *Ilata, Narayanan Nambudiri*, 1 *Mad. H. C. R.* 372. A claim by a Hindu widow for an allowance from her husband's family was dismissed on proof of such impropriety of conduct on her part as, in the opinion of the Court, deprived her of all legal claim, according to the Hindu law, to a maintenance from them.

A woman divorced for adultery, who continued in adultery during her husband's life, and in unchastity after his death, is not entitled to maintenance out of the property of her husband, *Muttammal* v. *Kamakshyammal*, 2 *Mad. H. C. R.* 337.

Harita says, If a woman, becoming a widow in her youth, be headstrong (suspected of incontinency), a maintenance must in that

* Query, unchaste?

case be given to her for the support of life (see *Nevada Chintamani*), upon which there is this commentary in the *Mitac.*, "This passage is intended for a denial of the right of a widow suspected of incontinency to take the whole estate."

Where a widow succeeds as heir, she takes, subject, among other things, to defray the expenses of the education and of the nuptials of unmarried daughters—in the latter case, to the extent of a fourth part out of the husband's estate. Since sons are required to give that allotment, much more should the wife or any other successor give a like portion. *Sir Thomas Strange* adds, that she is bound also to maintain those whom the deceased was bound to support.

Desertion of husband by his wife—Implied agency—Polygamy.—A Hindu wife is not entitled to maintenance if she leave her husband without a justifying cause. Polygamy does not afford such a cause. If, therefore, a Hindu husband marry a second wife, and his wife thereupon leave him, the first wife has no implied authority to borrow money for her support, *Virasvami Chetti* v. *Appasvami Chetti*, 1 *Mad. H. C. R.* 375.

It seems the prohibition against a plurality of wives, save under certain circumstances, is merely directory and not imperative, *ib.*

Widow's right to recover arrears of maintenance.—No rule of Hindu law precludes the recovery of arrears of maintenance. The only bar to the enforcement of a purely legal right is the lapse of the time required by the law of limitations to bar the remedy, and the statute does not operate when there is a constantly accruing right, and there is no authority for saying that a woman who is entitled to maintenance must, to obtain that to which she is entitled, bring annual actions.

Where husband's property proves deficient.—Where the husband's property proves deficient, the duty of providing for her is cast upon his relatives; and failing them, upon her own,—an obligation that attaches, though she should have wasted what was assigned her for the purpose, 1 *Stra. H. L.* 172. A Hindu died possessed of no property, but leaving a widow on his death, she left the house of her father-in-law, and went to reside with her father. Her father-in-law was not possessed of any ancestral property. Held that she could not sue her father-in-law for a sum of money on account of maintenance, *Khetramani Dasi* v. *Kashonath Das*, *Bengl. L. Rep.* vol. 3, pt. 1, p. 15.

Grandmother.—The grandmother as a member of the family is also entitled.

Step-mothers.—Step-mothers must be maintained with food and raiment, *Daya Krama Sangraha*, ch. vii. § 3.

A son, on succeeding to his father's estate, must maintain his step-mother and her daughters.

Sisters.—The married sisters are considered as provided for.

Mr Colebrooke says, The law gives nothing to a married daughter where male issue is left. The claim of an unmarried daughter only is noticed, *Mitac.*

To unmarried sisters *Vijnyaneswara* allots a quarter of a share, *Mitac., Yajnavalchya.* But the *Chandrika* and *Madhavya* countenance the opinion that the specified allotment intends only a sufficiency for the charges of the sister's nuptials. This does not mean a fourth to each sister, to be deducted from the share of each brother, but a participation out of the whole, equivalent to a fourth of a brother's share, irrespective of the number of brothers. The meaning is not that a fourth part shall be deducted out of the portions allotted to each brother, but that the girl shall be allowed to participate for a quarter of such a share as would be assignable to a brother of the same rank with herself.

A widowed sister, not otherwise provided for, is entitled to maintenance. *Sir Thomas Strange* is not supported by the authority he cites.

Daughter.—A daughter living apart from her father without any sufficient cause has no legal claim upon him for maintenance, *Ilata Shavatri* v. *Ilata Narayanan Nambudiri*, 1 *Mad. H. C. R.* 372.

Illegitimate children.—With the exception of illegitimate children of the Sudra class, who take by inheritance, all others are entitled to a maintenance, *Mitac.* An illegitimate son of a Sudra by a concubine, not being a female slave, is entitled to maintenance according to Hindu law, *Muttasamy Jagavire Zettapa Naikar* v. *Vankatasubha Yellain*, 2 *Mad. H. C. R.* 293. It would seem that the mothers of such children have also a claim for maintenance out of the property of their father, even where the property escheats to the king for want of heirs, *Mitac.*

Illegitimate son—Shatria caste.—In the case of a disputed succession to the *Raidom* and *Zemindary of Ramnugger* in Bengal, it was held that an illegitimate son of a *Shatria*, one of the three regenerate castes, by a Sudra woman, cannot by the Hindu law succeed to the inheritance of his putative father, but is entitled to maintenance out of his estate. In the case of the Sudra class, illegitimate children are qualified to inherit, *Chuoturya Run. Murdun Syn.* v. *Sahab Purhulal Syn*, 7 *Moore's In. Ap.* 18 ; see *Telavar* v. *Telavar*, *ante*, page 9.

CHAPTER VI.

DISQUALIFICATION FOR INHERITANCE.

Mental and corporeal defects disqualify—Who are disqualified—The defect must have preceded partition—Qualified sons of a disinherited man may inherit with certain exceptions—Special rule for their wives and daughters—Religious orders—Enemy to his father—Disease—Vicious son—Dissipation—Dissipation of the family estate by gaming, &c.—Women—Barrenness—Defect removed—Illegitimacy—Sons of a woman married in irregular order—Sons of a woman of a higher class—Maintenance—Adoption—Religious institutions.

Mental and corporeal defects disqualify.—There are certain defects, mental or corporeal, which according to Hindu law defeat the right of inheritance. *Macn.* says, "Various diseases and various offences have been declared by the Hindu legislators to be of such a nature as to disqualify for inheritance. It is problematical how far our courts would go in support of objections which must in some instances be deemed irrational prejudices."

But as no judicial opinions have been expressed upon many of the causes of disqualification for inheritance propounded by the old authorities on Hindu law, we are compelled to take a cursory view of the ancient law; a more detailed notice of it being rendered unnecessary, partly for the above reason, and partly because of the elaborate enumeration of the disqualifying causes which is contained in 3 *Dig.*

Sir Thomas Strange says, Like succession, exclusion from inheritance is connected with the obsequies of the deceased, from the incapacity to perform which the excluded are incompetent as co-heirs, *Jim. Vahana.*

Who are disqualified.—An impotent person, whether naturally so or by castration, an out-caste,* or his issue, one lame, born blind or deaf, or who has lost the use of a limb, a madman, an idiot, one incurably diseased, as well as others similarly disqualified, *Yajnavalchya.*

An out-caste is one guilty of sacrilege or other heinous crime—"his issue," the offspring of an out-caste, *Jim. Vahana.*

* The loss of caste is a ground of exclusion, but this part of the law has been abrogated by the Indian Legislature, Act xxii. of 1850.

Lame—is one deprived of the use of his feet; one who cannot walk is lame, *Jim. Vahana.* But this would hardly be held now to be a disqualification.

A madman—affected by any of the various sorts of insanity, from whatever cause, *Mitac.*

An idiot—a person deprived of the internal faculty, meaning one incapable of discriminating right from wrong. A person not susceptible of instruction, *Jim. Vahana*, ch. v. § 9. The mental incapacity which deprives a Hindu from inheriting on the ground of idiocy is not necessarily utter mental darkness; a person of unsound mind, who has been so from birth, is in point of law an idiot. The reason for disqualifying a Hindu idiot is his unfitness for the ordinary intercourse of life. Such unsoundness is to be determined upon tangible and unmistakable facts, not upon fine-drawn speculations. *Tirumamgal Ammal* v. *Ramasvami Ayangar*, 1 *Mad. H. C. R.* 214.

Blind—destitute of the visual organ. A blind daughter could not be considered disqualified, because her right to inherit is placed on the ground of having male issue to perform her ancestor's obsequies; and blindness is no impediment to her having such issue.

Afflicted with incurable disease—affected by an irremediable distemper, such as erasmus, or the like, *Mitac.*

Narada also declares, an enemy to his father, an out-caste, an impotent person, and one formally expelled, take no share of the inheritance, even though they be legitimate, much less if they be sons of a wife by an appointed kinsman.

One afflicted with an obstinate or a grievous disease, and one insane, blind, or lame from his birth, must be maintained by the family. But their sons may take the shares of their parents.

"Formally expelled" has reference to degradation from caste, and it means a person excluded from drinking water in company, *Jim. Vahana*, ch. v. § 3; 3 *Dig. Sankha* and *Lakhita.* The heritable right of him who has been formally degraded, and his competence to offer oblations of food and libations of water, are extinct. But the Emancipation Act xxi. of 1850 would prevent the operation of this law.

The doctrine of Hindu law that out-castes are incapable of inheritance has no bearing upon the case of the members of new families which have sprung from persons so degraded, *Tarachand* v. *Reed Ram.*, 3 *Mad. H. C. R.* 51.

The consequences of degradation, or being out-caste, are enumerated by *Sir Thomas Strange*, 1 vol. 160. *Vide* also *Abraham* v. *Abraham*, 9 *Moore's In. Ap.* 195.

The power to degrade is in the first instance with the caste themselves, assembled for the purpose, from whose sentence, if not acquiesced in, there lay an appeal to the King's Courts.

The main feature in which degradation differs from other causes of disqualification, is that it extends its effects to the son if born subsequently, though if born before he is entitled to inherit as if his father were dead, *Devala, Vishnu, Daya Krama Sangraha, Jim. Vahana.* In all other instances of exclusion the son who is free from similar defects shall obtain his father's share of the inheritance, supporting with food and raiment him who is excluded, *Jim. Vahana, Mitac.*—*Sir Thomas Strange* adds, "The same right extending as far as the great-grandson."

The defect must have preceded partition.—When the disqualification of the out-caste and the rest who are not excluded from natural defects arises before the division or descent of the property, they are debarred of their shares. But one already separated from his co-heirs is not deprived of his allotment, *Mitac.* Hence adultery in the wife bars her right of inheritance, for by loss of caste, unexpiated by penance and unredeemed by atonement, it is forfeited. It has been decided that a woman guilty of adultery is not entitled to maintenance while the adultery is uncondoned by the husband, *ante.* But it does not appear to be yet decided whether, with reference to Act xxi. of 1850, loss of caste in consequence of adultery would bar a widow from inheritance. If condoned, it might be argued from the above decision that all rights to which she would have been entitled had she not committed adultery would be secured to her; it is doubtful, therefore, whether adultery, *per se*, is, under the existing change in the law, sufficient to exclude.

The law with reference to the loss of caste has been abrogated by the British Legislature, Act xxi. of 1850.

Dumb—one who is incapable of articulating sounds, *Jim. Vahana*, ch. v. § 9.

Deaf, blind, and dumb, are excluded on the ground of the absence of the rights of initiation and investiture, owing to their being unable to master the necessary ceremonies.

The qualified sons of a disinherited man may inherit with certain exceptions.—But the blameless sons, even of one from these causes disinherited, shall take a share according to the text of *Vishnu.* The legitimate sons even of these are sharers of the patrimony, but not the sons born to a degraded man after the commission of the act which caused the degradation, nor those who are procreated on a woman of a higher class; that is, in the inverse order of the classes, their sons do not participate even in the property left by the paternal grandfather. "But their sons, whether legitimate or the offspring of the wife by a kinsman (*shetrya*), are entitled to allotments if free from similar defects," *Yajnavalchya, Mayukha, Mitac.*

Special rule for their wives and daughters.—*Yajnavalchya* delivers a special rule concerning the daughters and wives of these: "Their daughters must be maintained likewise until they are provided with husbands. Their childless wives, conducting themselves aright, must be supported, but such as are unchaste should be expelled, and so, indeed, should those who are perverse." If she be *unchaste*, a woman must be turned out of doors, and without a maintenance, *Mayukha, Mitac.* But the commentator says, "Maintenance must not be refused solely on account of perverseness," *Mitac.*

Religious orders.—They who have entered into another order (perpetual student, hermit, ascetic) are debarred from shares, *Vasishtha, Mayukha,* and the next heir succeeds as though the devotee were naturally dead, *Menu, Vasishtha, Mitac.*

So the religious pretender, and apostate from a religious order, *Jim. Vahana.*

Enemy to his father.—One who hates his father is a professed enemy to him. Enmity is manifested by attempting his life, and so forth; but after the death of the father, by withholding the libations of water, and the like, which should be offered for his sake.

Disease.—As to the nature of disqualifying diseases, and the grounds upon which the disqualification proceeds: disease is made a cause of disability from the idea that it is the mark and consequence of sin committed in a former birth. Nothing but the removal of the disease will take away the disability.

A vicious son does not inherit if other sons exist. All those sons who are addicted to vice lose their title to the inheritance.

Addicted to vice—that is, adhering to a contrary or improper course, such as drinking, gaming, &c. This rule appears to be more directory than mandatory.

Dissipation.—There would be great difficulty in applying this rule in consequence of the impossibility of ascertaining the amount of guilt that would disqualify, as well as the nature of the crime; and English judges would be slow to recognise it; moreover, there is no case in which, according to Hindu law, disability may not be expiated.

Mr Strange says, "The perpetration of crime in general is not to disqualify for inheritance. This alteration in the Hindu law on the subject arises from the Hindu criminal, having been superseded by British criminal, law, and the offence of the criminal having been adequately provided for by the latter law, his sentence cannot be enhanced by the application to him also of the Hindu law, *Judgt. of the Sudder Court in Sp. Ap.* 40 of 1858. Act xxi. of 1850 removes the disability arising from exclusion from caste. A case, however, may arise which might be thought so heinous as to be considered a cause of disability, independently of the exclusion from caste, which would not be relieved by that Act. Thus when a party has stolen a portion of the common inheritance, he is civilly disabled from claiming a share in the inheritance.

Dissipation of the family estate by gaming, &c.—We have discussed this subject under the head of "Partition."

Sir Thomas Strange cites the following observations of *Mr Colebrooke* :—" In regard to the cases of disinheritance discussed in the *Digest*, b. v. ch. v. § 1, corresponding with fifth chapter of *Jimuta Vahana* and the tenth sec. ch. ii. of *Mitac.*, I am not aware that any can be said to have been abrogated, or to be obsolete. At the same time, I do not think any of our courts would go into proof of one of the brethren being addicted to vice,* or profusion, or of being guilty of neglect of obsequies and duty towards ancestors. But expulsion from caste, leprosy, and similar diseases, natural deformity from birth, neutral sex, unlawful birth resulting from an uncanonical marriage, would doubtlessly now exclude, and I apprehend it would be so adjudged in our Adawluts. That the causes of disinheritance, most foreign to our ideas, are still operative, according to the notions of the law among the natives, I conclude from some cases that came before me when I presided in the Zillah Court. I will mention but one, which occurred at Benares, at the suit of a nephew against his uncle to exclude him from inherited property, on the ground of his having neglected his grandmother's obsequies. He defended himself by pleading a pilgrimage to Gaya, where he alleged that he had performed them. His plea, joined with assurances of his attending to his filial duty in this respect in future, was admitted, and the claim to disinherit him disallowed."

Amongst a people with whom community of interest is the ordinary form of enjoyment of property, it is expedient that some security likely to be efficient should exist to protect families against the consequences in any of their members of vicious extravagance. The extravagant member does not dissipate his own wealth alone; the other members of the community have an interest in it in common with himself. Many authors exclude a man addicted to gaming and other similar vices, while others do not deprive them of their shares. But by whatever means they dissipate that wealth, their allotment on partition is diminished by so much as they have squandered and wasted; the difference, if against them, constituting a debt, leaving it to the pursuit of courses more distinctly criminal to work at once an entire forfeiture, 3 *Dig.* 298, 300 ; but see *post*, " Partition."

Women.—A woman is excluded for like defects, and therefore the wife, daughter, mother, or any other female may be disqualified for the like defects, *Mitac.* 8.

Barrenness does not disqualify.

Defect Removed.—If the defect be removed by mendicaments, penance, and atonement, at a period subsequent to partition, the right of partition takes effect by analogy to the case of a son born after separation. When a son has been separated, one who is afterwards born of a woman equal in class shares the distribution, *Mitac.*

* See 1 *Beng. Rep.* 144, where a will by a father partially disinheriting one of his sons on the ground of vicious conduct was sustained on appeal.

If after division, virility, or the other absent qualification, be regained by medicines or other means, the person will then receive his share as a son born after partition does, *Mayukha.*

Illegitimacy.—Illegitimate offspring, save among Sudras, cannot inherit. Among Sudras the bastard gets a smaller share than the others, *Jim. Vahana.*

Sons of a woman married in irregular order.—The sons of a woman married in irregular order, as well as he who is produced through a kinsman (sagotra), and an apostate from a religious order, never obtain the inheritance, *Katyayana, Mayukha, Jim. Vahana.* For an explanation of the expression, "produced through a kinsman," see *Mayukha.*

Sons of a woman of a higher class.—If sons be begotten by a husband on a wife sprung from a higher class, they shall not take the inheritance, *Mayukha, Jim. Vahana.*

But the son of a woman màrried in irregular order may be heir, provided he belong to the same tribe with his father, and so may the son of a man of a different but superior tribe by a woman espoused in the regular gradation. The son of a woman married to a man of an inferior tribe is not heir to the estate. Food and raiment only are due to him by his kinsman ; but on failure of them he may take the paternal wealth, *Jim. Vahana.*

Maintenance.—An impotent person, an out-caste and his issue, one lame, a madman, an idiot, a blind man, and a person afflicted with incurable disease, as well as others similarly disqualified, must be maintained, *Yajnavalchya* citing *Mayukha, Menu,* All those excluded from participation must be maintained during the rest of their lives by those who get the estate, *Mayukha, Jim. Vahana, Mitac.,* except those entering another order, out-castes and their sons, *Mayukha, Jim Vahana, Daya Krama Sangraha.* The penalty of degradation is incurred if they be not maintained, *Mitac., Menu.*

The incompetency of the wives of disqualified persons to inherit has also been declared by *Yajnavalchya.* Their childless wives, conducting themselves aright, must be supported, but such as are unchaste should be expelled ; and so, indeed, should those who are perverse. Their daughters also should be maintained until provided with husbands.

If those labouring under disqualification should marry, the offspring of such as have issue shall be capable of inheriting, *Menu, Jim. Vahana.* If they be free from similar defects, their daughters must be maintained until married, and their childless wives must be supported during life.

Adoption.—Of these (two descriptions of offspring, legitimate offspring, and issue of the wife) the impotent man may have that termed issue of the wife, the rest may have legitimate progeny likewise. The specific mention of "legitimate issue" and "offspring of the wife" is intended to forbid the adoption of other sons, *Mitac.,* so that no adoption can take place; such a son, if adopted, could not get anything which his father was disqualified to inherit. See "Adoption." An adopted son may be disinherited for like reasons as the legitimate son, but he cannot perfect the relation of son. 2 *Stra. H. L.* 126, *Coleb.*

Religious Institutions.—This is another description of property which is referred to in other portions of this work, and will be found under this head in the Index.

CHAPTER VII.

ALIENATION.

SECTION I.

Gifts inter vivos—*Gift binding as against alienee—Manasaputra—For payment of a debt of an undivided Hindu by widow—Childless widow where collateral heirs of husband—In default of male issue widow succeeds to her husband's estate without the power of alienating what devolves upon his heirs after her death—The question discussed and authorities cited—Stridhana—No restrictions on alienation except land, the gift of husband—Saudaiyaca—Katyayana—Shotriyam conferred for life—Each holder can only alienate his own interest—Sunnud, or maintenance-deed—Construction of "from generation to generation"—Subject to allowance for certain classes of the family—Toras Garas—Zemindar cannot alienate his zemindari—Zemindar's estate and powers to encumber and alienate—Alienability of share of undivided family property—Partition—The validity of a sale of such share under a fi. fa.—Malabar law—Sale by consent of all the members of the tarawad—The consent of the anandravar is necessary—Personal property, whether ancestral or self-acquired—Property acquired or recovered is alienable—Restrictions on alienation.*

Gift inter vivos.—It is competent to a Hindu to make a gift of his property by deed *inter vivos* (which is the nature of a will), *Grady's Hindu Law of Inheritance*, p. 107. It would not perhaps be good if given to one son in exclusion of the others.

Gift binding as against alienee—Manasaputra.—By the Hindu law a man may make a gift of any of his property binding as against himself. Where a Hindu made a gift to a person, whom he said he had taken as his *manasaputra*,* he cannot set it aside on the ground that he made a mistake in supposing that the donee could perform his funeral rites. *Per curiam*, nothing is clearer than the proposition, that by Hindu, as by English law, any man may make a gift of any of his property binding as against himself.

For payment of a debt of an undivided Hindu by widow.—

* From *Can. Manasu* (borrowed from Sanskrit *Manas*, μενος,) *and Putra*, *son.—Stokes.*

The widow of an undivided Hindu has no right to sell his property for payment of his debts, even if self-acquired. Her husband's brothers were living; consequently they succeeded to her husband's property, and were bound to pay his debts.

A father-in-law, although of the Reddi caste, cannot disinherit his heir in favour of his son-in-law, *Grady's Hindu Law of Inheritance*, p. 10.

Childless widow where collateral heirs of husband.—If there be collateral heirs of the husband, the widow cannot alienate the property except for special purposes. For religious or charitable purposes, or those which are supposed to conduce to the spiritual welfare of the husband, she has a larger power of disposition than that which she possesses for purely worldly purposes. To support an alienation for the latter she must show necessity. On the other hand, it may be taken as established that an alienation by her, which would not otherwise be legitimate, may become so if made with the consent of her husband's kindred. But it surely is not the necessary or logical consequence of this latter proposition that in the absence of collateral heirs to the husband, or on their failure, the fetter on the widow's power of alienation altogether drops. The exception in favour of alienation with consent may be due to a presumption of law, that where that consent is given the purpose for which the alienation is made must be proper. Nor does it appear to their lordships that the construction of Hindu law which is now contended for can be put upon the principle "*cessante ratione cessat ipsa lex.*" It is not merely for the protection of the material interests of her husband's relations that the fetter on the widow's power is imposed. Nevertheless, authorities from *Menu* downwards may be cited to show that, according to the principles of Hindu law, the proper state of every woman is one of tutelage, that they always require protection, and are never fit for independence. *Sir Thomas Strange* cites the authority of *Menu* for the proposition that if a woman has no other controller or protector, the king shall control or protect her. Again, all the authorities concur in showing that, according to the principles of Hindu law, the life of a widow is to be one of ascetic privation, 2 *Coleb. Dig.* 459. Hence, probably, it gives her a power of disposition for religious, which it denied her for other purposes. These principles do not seem to be consistent with the doctrine, that on the failure of heirs a widow becomes completely emancipated, perfectly uncontrolled in the disposition of her property, and free to squander her entailed wealth for the purpose of selfish enjoyment.

Their lordships are of opinion that the restrictions on a Hindu widow's power of alienation are inseparable from her estate, and that their existence does not depend on that of heirs capable of taking on her death. It follows that if, for want of heirs, the right to the property, so far as it has not lawfully been disposed of by her, passes to the crown, the crown must have the same power which an heir would have of protecting its interests by impeaching any unauthorised alienation by the widow, 8 *Moore's In. Ap.* 553.

In default of male issue widow succeeds to husband's estate without power of alienating what devolves upon his heirs after her death.—According to Hindu law the widow, in default of male issue, is entitled to succeed to the whole of her deceased husband's estate. But her title to such estate is only as tenant for life, and she has no power to alienate or devise any portion of her husband's estate, which on her death devolves on his legal heirs, 2 *Moore's In. Ap.* 331. See *Rajunder Narain Rae* v. *Bijai Govind Sing*, 2 *Moore's In. Ap.* 181, 191.

The question discussed and authorities cited.—In *Cossinaut Bysack* v. *Hurroosoondry Dosse* and *Cummolemoney Dosse*, 2 *Morl. Dig.* p. 198 (1819), a very important judgment was delivered in Bengal by Chief-Justice East, bearing upon the question as to the rights of a childless widow to the property of her deceased husband, and in which all the authorities in Bengal and Tirhoot are reviewed. The case is set out in *Grady's Hindu Law of Inheritance*, p. 110, and three questions are discussed in the judgment: 1st, What right the husband had over his real and personal estate; 2d, What interest the widow has in either by devolution on his death without male issue according to best writers on Hindu law, and other Hindu authorities, either native or British; and 3d, How far the decisions which have taken place have decided the question. The case is well worthy of the perusal of the student. The Chief-Justice concludes his judgment thus (see *ib.* p. 125).

The result of the whole is this, that unless the authority of the *Ratnacara* and *Chintamani* are to give the rule on the point in judgment in Bengal, the decree in its present form is erroneous: and it appears by the general opinion of the Pundits of the *Sudder Dewanny Adawlut*, and of our own, supported by the authority of *Mr Colebrooke*, and in effect by the decisions in the *Sudder Dewanny Adawlut* in *Bhya Jha's* case, and other cases, when the doctrine of those books has been applied to cases, on the specific ground of their arising in Tirhoot, that the same doctrine does not apply to Bengal, being in opposition to the doctrine of the *Daya Bhaga*, which is the ruling authority in this province. And it seems that, by the *Daya Bhaga*, no distinction is taken between the realty and personalty as to the *quantum* of the widow's estate; but the whole appears to be given to her absolutely for some purposes, though restricted in her disposition as to others, and therefore she takes more than a life-estate in the realty for these allowed purposes, and less than an absolute estate in the personalty for other and different purposes; and if this be so, the decree cannot be supported in its present form. The decision was affirmed on appeal by the judicial committee of the Privy Council on the 24th July 1826. See *Cl. R.* 1834, 91.

Stridhana—No restrictions on alienation, except land, the gift of husband.—Land, or any other property, may be possessed by a woman as *stridhana*, *Mitac.*, and the law with respect to that kind of property (except perhaps land, the gift of her husband) is, that a widow is not subject to the restrictions against alienation which apply to property that she succeeds to upon her husband's death.

According to the Bengal school of law, it seems clear that, whether as wife or widow, a woman has an absolute power of alienation over her stridhana, with the exception of *immovable* property bestowed upon her by her husband, see *Daya Bhaga*. But, as is observed by *Mr Sutherland*, in his remarks at p. 430 of the 2d vol. of *Sir Thomas Strange's* work on Hindu law: "The *Mitacshara* is wholly silent on the power of women to alienate their peculiar property, though explicit in disavowing all authority in the husband to appropriate the same." And the language used by *Sir Thomas Strange*, as well as the remark of *Mr Sutherland*, when looked at, alone tend to raise a doubt whether, according to the Benares school of law, there is not a general restriction against alienation by a wife or a widow of immovable property held by her under whatever title; when, however, we find it stated in the same work, and by numerous other authorities in broad and general terms, that a woman's stridhana is her absolute property, at her independent disposal (with perhaps the exception of land, the gift of her husband), and there being no ground that we can see for any distinction in this respect between movable and immovable property held by a woman, we are of opinion that the Hindu law recognises the power of alienation to the extent we have laid down, *Scotland*. See *Grady's Hindu Law of Inheritance*, p. 127.

Saudaiyaca.—With regard to the capability of a Hindu widow to alienate her *saudaiyaca*,* *i.e.*, the property given her by her kindred, or husband before or after her marriage, the following texts may be quoted, and which are collected by the former learned editor of the *Madras H. C. Reports*, *Mr W. Stokes*, vol. i., p. 90.

Katyayana.†—What a woman, either after marriage or before it, either in the mansion of her husband or of her father, receives

* *Mr Strange*, in the first edition of his *Manual*, observes: In that which constitutes woman's property, a distinction obtains of what has been given to the woman, whether it be immovable or movable, by her father, mother, or brothers; this is termed *saudaiyaca*; over such she has exclusive control, without regard to her husband or heirs. *Mitac.*, *Saraswatee Vilasa*, *Veyavahara Mayukha*. But it would appear that in holding dealings with regard to her *saudaiyaca*, the wife must, however, act through her husband; and she is bound to fulfil his wishes, she being empowered to dispose of this species of property at will, *Smriti Chandrika*, and *Saraswatee Vilasa*, *Stra. Man.*

† Unless *Katyayana* contradicts himself, we must hold that the words, "*the estate*," in the following text, refer solely to the property which a widow inherits as such. "The childless widow, preserving inviolate the bed of her lord, and strictly obedient to her spiritual parents, may frugally enjoy the whole estate until she die, and after her the legal heir shall take it."

from her lord or her parents, is called "a gift from affectionate kindred."

And such a gift having by them been presented through kindness, that the women possessing it may live well, is declared by law to be their absolute property.

"The absolute exclusive dominion of women over such a gift is perpetually celebrated, and they have power to sell or give it away as they please, even though it consists of lands and houses, 3 *Coleb. Dig.* 573, 574. The last clause is thus rendered in the *Daya Krama Sangraha,* ch. ii. s. ii. § 26. The power of woman, *lege,* women over the gifts of their affectionate kindred is ever celebrated both in respect of donation and of sale, according to their pleasure, even in the case of immovables. So also in the *Daya Bhaga,* ch. iv. s. i. § 21, and the *Vyavahara Mayukha,* ch. iv. s. x. § 8."

"Texts restricting the power of a widow to alienate immovables given to her by her husband are these :—*Narada*—Property given to her by her husband, through pure affection, she may enjoy at her pleasure after his death, or may give it away, except land or houses, 3 *Dig.* 575."

Vishnu (or *Narada*)—What has been given by an affectionate husband to his wife, she may consume as she pleases when he is dead, or may give it away, excepting immovable property, *Mitac.* ch. i. s. i. § 20.

The Ratnakara. A woman has absolute exclusive dominion over such gifts (scil., gifts to her separate use) consisting of lands and houses, except such immovables as her husband gave her, 3 *Dig.* 575.

The Daya Krama Sangraha, ch. ii. s. ii. § 31, "Even in the case of immovables," relates to immovable property other than that which has been bestowed upon her by her husband; for a prohibition exists against the gift or sale by a woman in regard to immovable property given to her by her husband. So *Narada* what has been given to her, &c., *ut supra.*

The Daya Bhaga, ch. iv. s. i. § 23. But in the case of immovables bestowed upon her by her husband, a woman has no power of alienation by gift or the like; so *Narada* declares. What has been given, &c., *ut supra.* It follows, from the specific mention of "given by a husband," that any other immovable property, except such as has been given to her by him, may be alienated by her, else (if this text forbid donation in the case of immovables in general *Sri Krishna*), the preceding passage concerning the power of women in respect of donation and of sale, "according to their pleasure, even in the case of "immovables," would be contradicted.

The Vyavahara Mayukha, ch. iv. s. x. § 9. "But over immovable property given them by their husbands they do not possess full power from this text of *Narada.* What has been given, &c., *ut supra.**

The right of wife to sue for the fee given her by her husband on her second marriage, is discussed in *Grady's Hindu Law,* p. 128.

Shrotriyam conferred for life—Each holder can only alienate his own interest.—Each holder of a Shrotriyam conferred for life can only alienate his own life-interest.

The right of an adopted son to succeed to a Shrotriyam was recognised by the Court of Directors, 30th May 1843; *C. O. B. R. I.*: 406, and by Government; *ib. I.* 407, 408; so the right of a widow to succeed to a Shrotriyam during life has been recognised, *Ex. Min. Cons.* 14th August 1847; *ib. I.* 281; *Sloan's Jud. and Land Revenue Code, I.* 559; see 1 *Stra. H. L.* 209; 2 *ib.* 365, 366.† See Index "Shrotriyam."

Sunnud, or maintenance-deed—Construction of, from generation to generation—Subject to allowance for certain classes of the family.—The zemindar in possession by a sunnud, conveyed to A., as the head of a branch of the grantor's family, an estate, part of the zemindari in lieu of maintenance, to which A. was entitled out of the zemindary "to hold and enjoy possession from generation to generation," subject to an allowance for maintenance to a certain class of the family described as Lowahokans and Matalokams' descendants, and relations. A.'s heirs afterwards alienated a part of the estate for a valuable consideration, held, first, In the absence of evidence of any class of persons answering the description of Lowahokans and Matalokams (which might have created a trust), A. took an absolute estate in the lands assigned to him.

2dly, That the limitation in the sunnud, "from generation to generation," did not create such an estate as to operate as a bar to alienation by sale, *Rajah Nursing Deb.* v. *Roy Kylasnath,* 9 *Moore's In. Ap.* 55. See *post.*

Toras garas.—Toras garas, an annual fixed money payment in nature of black mail, is alienable, and subject to sale or mortgage like other property, *Sumbhoolall Girdhurlall* v. *The Collector of Surat,* 8 *Moore's In. Ap.* 1.

Zemindar cannot alienate his zemindari.—A zemindar has no more power to charge a perpetual annuity in favour of a stranger on the income of the zemindari than he has to alienate the corpus. See *Grady's Hindu Law of Inheritance.*

Zemindar's estate and powers to encumber and alienate.—A zemindar's estate is analogous to an estate in tail as it originally stood upon the statute *de donis.*

* *Vide,* also *Vivada Chintamani,* pp. 260, 261, "Consequently a woman can dispose of movable property which has been given her by her husband, but she can never dispose of immovable property. The same rule holds good in the case of Saudaiyaca, or the gifts of affectionate kindred," p. 261.

† This subject is not connected with Hindu law, but has been noticed here as connected with property.

A zemindar is the owner of the zemindari, but can neither encumber nor alienate beyond the period of his own life.

Alienability of share of undivided family property—Partition.—By the Hindu law, as applied in Madras, a member of an undivided family may alienate the share of the family property to which, if a division took place, he would be individually entitled.

The validity of a sale of such share under a fi. fa.—There may be a valid sale of such share under an execution in an action for damages for a tort.

Malabar law—Sale by consent of all the members of the tarawad.—According to the Malabar law, a sale of family property is valid when made with the assent, express or implied, of all the members of the tarawad, and when the deed of sale is signed by the karanavan and the senior anandravar if *sui juris.*

Such signature is *primâ facie* evidence of the assent of the family, and the burden of proof of their dissent lies on those who allege it.

The consent of the anandravar is necessary.—The assent of the anandravars is necessary to a sale of tarawad land by a karanavan. The chief anandravar's signature to the instrument of sale is sufficient, but not indispensable evidence of such assent.

Personal Property, whether ancestral or self-acquired—Property acquired or recovered is alienable—Restrictions on alienation.—With respect to personal property of every description, whether ancestral, or self-acquired, and with respect to real property acquired, or recovered by the occupant, he is at liberty to make any alienation or distribution which he may think fit, subject only to spiritual responsibility, *Vrihaspati.*

Whatever may have been the soundness of the grounds for doubting the power of a Hindu to alienate his property by will, it is now well established by authority that he enjoys that right. The learning upon this subject is collected in *Grady's Hindu Law*, page 141.

SECTION II.

Ancestral real property cannot be alienated at pleasure—Validity of nuncupative will—No transaction by Hindu law requires to be in writing—Childless zemindar may alienate by deed or will such portion of his estate as would not vest in his wife without his consent—Provision in partition deed against alienation—Testamentary disposition regulated by Hindu law—Direction that property shall go in male line—Rights of widow of one of heirs—Division of accumulations does not constitute a divided family—Rules for construction of Hindus' wills—Accumulations of joint-family—Right of wife of co-sharer—Testamentary power in North Western provinces—Construction—Devise of self-acquired property by way of remainder or executory devise—Income—Accumulation—Hindu widow—Rights of maintenance—Ancestral property—Adoption—Construction of Hindus' will from generation to generation—Descendants—Rule against perpetuity.

Ancestral real property cannot be alienated at pleasure.—Thus in Bengal a man may make an unequal distribution among his sons of his personally-acquired property, or of the ancestral movable property, because, though it has been enjoined (*Katyayana*, 2 *Dig.* 540) upon a father not to distinguish one son at a partition made in his lifetime, nor on any account to exclude one from participation without sufficient cause, yet as it has been declared in another place that the father is master of all movable property and of his own acquisitions (*Yajnavalchya*, 2 *Dig.* 159), the maxim that a fact cannot be altered by a hundred texts (*factum valet*), here applies to legalise a disregard of the injunction, there being texts declaratory of unlimited discretion of equal authority with those which condemn the practice.* In other parts of India, where the maxim in question does not obtain, the injunction applies in its full force, and any prohibited alienation would be considered illegal, see "Partition;" see 1 *Stra. H. L.* 123; 1 *Bomb. R.* 154, 372, 380; 2 *ib.* 6, 471; 1 *Macn. Prins. H. L.* 15.

Validity of Nuncupative will—No transaction by Hindu law requires to be in writing.—A Hindu may make a nuncupative will of property, whether movable or immovable. Gapaluchariyar, previous to his death, directed, in the presence of witnesses, that his property should be equally divided between the appellant, the first defendant, and the second defendant, the son of the first. He left surviving him two daughters. The plaintiff, one of the daughters, brought the suit to recover half of his property. The district munsiff upheld the disposition of the property, and decreed one-third of it to the plaintiff. The civil judge modified the decree, by according one-half to the plaintiff, because he thought the transaction amounted to a will, and could not therefore be enforced, referring to *Strange's Man.*

This decree was appealed from, and it was admitted that *Valliarayagum Pillai* v. *Pachche*, 1 *Mad. H. C. R.* 326, established the legality of a Hindu will. But it was argued that, as wills were introduced into the Hindu from the English law, the testamentary disposition was governed by the English law, and therefore must be in writing.

Childless zemindar may alienate by deed or will such portion of his estate as would not vest in his wife without his consent.—By the Hindu law a zemindar having no issue is capable

* By this construction the maxim is made to mean that one text (or fact of that kind) cannot be repealed by other texts, but such an interpretation must be found as will reconcile them all.

of alienating by deed or will a portion of his estate, which, in default of lineal male issue and intestacy, would not vest in his wife without his consent,* *Mulraz Lachmia, widow*, v. *Chalekany Vencata Rama Jagganadha Row*, 2 *Moore's In. Ap.* 54.

The question involved in this case, was the validity by the Hindu law of a devise made in confirmation of a previous gift by a man having no lineal male heirs in prejudice of his wife, in whom the succession vested in case of no alienation and of intestacy.

Mr Baron Parke, in delivering the judgment of the Judicial Committee of the Privy Council, said the only question is, whether the late Rajah was capable of alienating the property in question, it being part of his zemindary; or whether his wife, the appellant, was entitled by the Hindu law to the whole of the zemindary for her provision. The Sudder Court examined the Hindu law officers on that point, and their opinion was clearly in favour of the Rajah's right to make such alienation. That Court thought the will sufficiently proved in the former suit, and upon the authority of the Hindu law dismissed the appeal. Their lordships agree in such decision.

Provision in partition deed against alienation.—H., an Englishman, the father of five illegitimate children by two Madras Hindu women, who lived together in co-parcenery as Hindus, their rights being governed by that law, bequeathed to his said children an estate in equal shares. A suit was instituted by one of the children against his brother for partition of the estate. The parties entered into a deed of razeenamah, by which the shares and amounts to be paid to each were ascertained, and provision made against alienation by sale, mortgage, lease, or security, of any separate share. Held that this deed did not affect the right which each co-sharer had to alienate by will, *Myna Boyee* v. *Ootaram*, 8 *Moore's In. Ap.* 400.

Testamentary disposition regulated by Hindu law.—Direction that property shall go in male line—Rights of widow of one of heirs—Division of accumulations does not constitute a divided family.—Although the power of a Hindu to make a will is recognised, yet the extent of the power of disposition by a testator is to be regulated by the Hindu law, and cannot interfere with a widow's right to succeed to her husband's estate.

A Bengalee Hindu bequeathed all his movable and immovable property to his family idol, and directed that his (four) sons, their sons or grandsons in succession, should enjoy "the surplus proceeds only;" and the will after appointing one of the sons manager to the estate to attend to the festival and ceremonies of the idol, and maintain the family also, directed whatever might be the surplus, after deducting the whole of the expenditure, the same should be

* *Semble.*—A will established in a former suit cannot be impeached in a subsequent suit brought by the same parties, *ib.*

added to the corpus; and in the event of a disagreement between the sons and family, directed that after the expenses attending the estate, the idol, and maintenance of the family, whatever net produce and surplus there might be, should be divided annually in certain proportions among the members of the family. At the date of the will the family were joint in the estate, food, and worship, and the accumulations of the will were divided as directed. Held first, that the gift to the idol was not an absolute gift, but was to be construed as a gift to the testator's four sons and their offspring, in the male line, as a joint family, so long as the family remained joint, and that the four sons were entitled to the surplus of the property after providing for the performance of the ceremonies and festivals of the idol, and the provisions in the will for maintenance.

2. That the division of the accumulations of the income amongst the members of the family did not constitute them a divided family.

One of the sons of the testator died, leaving three sons, one of whom also died without issue, leaving a widow. Held that the direction contained in the will, that the property should go in the male line, did not exclude the widow of the grandson of the testator, and that the widow was entitled to a third share of a fourth part of the property and accumulations, without prejudice to her rights as a Hindu widow, when the property should be divided, *Sonatun Bysack* v. *Sreemutty Juggutsoondree Dossee*, 8. *Moore's In. Ap.* 66.

Rules for construction of Hindus' wills.—In the case of *Sreemuttee Soorjeemoney Dossee* v. *Denobundoo Mullick*, 6 *Moore's In. Ap.* 526, the following rules for construing wills of Hindus were laid down by the Lords of the Committee of the P. C. In determining the construction of a will, what we must look to is the intention of the testator. The Hindu law, no less than the English law, points to the intention as the element by which we are to be guided in determining the effect of a testamentary disposition, nor, so far as we are aware, is there any difference between one law and the other as to the materials from which the intention is to be collected. Primarily, the words of the will are to be considered. They convey the intention of the testator's wishes, but the meaning to be attached to them may be affected by surrounding circumstances, among which is the law of the country in which the will is made, and its dispositions are to be carried out. If that law has attached to particular words a particular meaning, or to a particular disposition a particular effect, it must be assumed that the testator in the dispositions he has made had regard to that meaning or to that effect, unless the language of the will or the surrounding circumstances displace that assumption.

Accumulations of joint family—Right of wife of co-sharer.—

A testator by his will made an absolute gift of his real and personal estate to his five sons, (an undivided Hindu family) in equal shares, and in a subsequent part of his will, in the event of any of his sons dying without a son or son's son, there was a gift over to such of his sons or son's sons as should be alive. After the death of the testator the sons lived together, and no partition of the estate was made, the surplus income and increment being kept with the common stock. Upon the death of one of the sons without leaving male issue, his widow, who was entitled to a life-interest in her husband's estate, claimed her husband's share of the accumulations of income, and the increment thereon. Held that in the absence of any direction of the testator that his sons should continue a joint family,* such intention could not be imported into the will, and that the testator's intention was that his sons should enjoy during their lives their interest in the respective shares of the property, and therefore, that although the deceased co-sharer's share went over to the survivors, the widow of the deceased was entitled to one-fifth of the surplus income which had accumulated since the testator's death and during her husband's lifetime, and the increment arising from such accumulations.

Testamentary power in North-Western Provinces.—By the Hindu law, as administered in the North-West Provinces, a Hindu has power to make a testamentary disposition in the nature of a will.

A disputed will made by a Hindu disposing of self-acquired estate amongst his family established.

It is perfectly competent by the Hindu law, as at present prevailing, for a Hindu to make a will. See *Grady's Hindu Law of Inheritance*, p. 160.

The foundation of the testamentary restriction rests upon the Hindu law of an undivided family: kinsmen and co-parceners having a right which cannot be divested without their consent, *Mitac.*

Where the *Mitacshara* governs, a father cannot by will exclude his son.

In Bengal a Hindu may leave by will, or bestow by deed or gift, his possessions, whether inherited or acquired. The only restriction, according to *Colebrooke, 2 Stra. H. L.* 435, 436, is, if the testator has sons.

Construction—Devise of self-acquired property by way of remainder, or executory devise—Income—Accumulation—Hindu widow—Rights of Maintenance.—There is nothing in the general principles of Hindu law, or public convenience, to prevent a Hindu testator from devising self-acquired property, by way of remainder,

* We think it is immaterial what were the testator's intentions. The question is one of fact—did the sons live in union?

or executory devise, upon an event which is to happen on the close of a life in being.

A Hindu testator, in the Presidency of Bengal, by the first clause of his will mentioning his five sons, one of whom since died, and whose share of the property is now in dispute, gave them in effect all his property in such a way, as, if there were no more in his will, would make them absolute owners of it. But in a subsequent clause (eleven) the testator says, " But should, peradventure, any among my said five sons die, not leaving any sons from his loins, nor any son's son, in that event neither his widow, nor his daughter, nor his daughter's son, nor any of them, will get any shares out of the share that he has obtained of the immovables and movables of my said estate. In that event of my said property, such of my sons and my son's sons as shall then be alive, they will receive that wealth according to their respective shares. If any one acts repugnant to this it is inadmissible. However, if any sonless son shall leave a widow, in that event she will only receive 10,000 Company's rupees for her food and raiment." The family remained joint. Surroopchunder, one of the sons, died after the testator's death without issue male, but leaving a widow, his heiress-at-law. It was held by the Judicial Committee of the P. C. that by the words "not leaving any sons from his loins, nor any son's son," the testator meant, not an indefinite failure of male issue, but a failure of male issue of any one of his sons at the time of the death of that son.

Lord J. Knight Bruce said, in giving judgment, this happened in the case of Surroopchunder, who died without leaving male issue, living at the time. Accordingly, an event has happened which the testator pointed out. The testamentary power of Hindus over their property has long been recognised, and is completely established. Is there, then, anything against public convenience, anything generally mischievous, or anything against the general principles of Hindu law, in allowing a testator to give property, whether by way of remainder, or by way of executory bequest (to borrow terms from the law of England), upon an event which is to happen, if at all, immediately on the close of a life in being? Their Lordships think that there is not; that there would be a great general inconvenience and public mischief in denying such a power, and their Lordships, therefore, being of opinion that, according to the true meaning of this will, the property was given over, upon an event which was to take place, if at all, immediately on the close of a life in being at the time when the will was made, and seeing that that event has happened, consider that the testator, in making this provision, did not infringe, or exceed the powers given him by the Hindu law, and that the clause effectually gives the corpus of the property to the surviving sons immediately on the death of that son who died without leaving male issue. Held, that upon the death of Surroopchunder without male issue, his interest in the capital of the estate determined, and that the appellant became entitled, as his widow, heiress, and representative, to a fifth part of the accumulations which arose from the testator's estate, from the time of his death to the death of his son Surroopchunder, the part to which she is so entitled, to be held by her as a Hindu widow, in the manner prescribed by Hindu law, and that she was also entitled absolutely in her own right to the interest and accumulations which had since Surroopchunder's death arisen from such fifth part of the accumulations. By the decree Surroopchunder's widow was declared entitled to 10,000 rupees, given by the will, with the benefit of a residence in the family dwelling-house, and participation in the means of worship. The question as to the amount of her maintenance as a Hindu widow was left open by the Judicial Committee, as that point could be raised on further directions after taking the accounts. *Sreemuttee Soorjeemoney Dossee* v. *Denobundoo Mullick*, 9 *Moore's In. Ap.* 123.

Ancestral property — Adoption.—A will by a Hindu without male issue, kinsman, or co-parceners, after providing for the maintenance of his widow, daughter, and female relations, devised ancestral and other real and personal estate to trustees upon certain charitable trusts. The will was impeached on the ground that the testator had authorised his widow, if the child of which she was pregnant happened to be a daughter, to appoint a son, such act rendering him incompetent to exercise a testamentary power, and that the testator, being a Hindu, had no power by law of devising ancestral estate by will. Held that, although in the absence of male issue of the deceased, there was a strong presumption, arising from religious considerations, in favour of a delegation by the deceased to his widow of authority to adopt a son for him, yet that the evidence entirely failed to prove that fact.

And that, by the Hindu law prevailing in Madras, a Hindu in possession without issue male, kinsman, or co-parcener, had power to make a will disposing of ancestral as well as acquired estate, *Nagalutchmee Ummal* v. *Gopoo Nadaraja Chetty*, 6 *Moore's In. Ap.* 309.

By will, construction of Hindus' will "from generation to generation"—Descendants—Rule against perpetuity.—A bequest of ten rupees a month was followed by a direction; "in this manner continue to pay in the legatee's name so long as he shall be alive; after his death continue to pay the same to his descendants from generation to generation." Held, that the legatee took only a life-interest under the bequest.

That the words, "from generation to generation" were synonymous with "absolutely" and "for ever" in an English instrument; that the descendants in existence at the time of the death of the tenant for life took absolutely as a class. Descendants of A. in a

Hindu's will would include children and grandchildren living at his decease, but does not include A.'s brother or widow.

There is no rule of Hindu law imposing any restriction in point of time on the operation of a bequest creating a series of successive life-interests in each generation of a legatee's descendants.

But *semble.* The grounds of the rule against perpetuities are applicable to the property of Hindus, and the Court will be very reluctant to construe a Hindu will so as to tie up property for an indefinite period, *Arumugam Mudali* v. *Ammi Ammal*, 1 *Mad. H. C. R.* 400.

This case decides some very important points in Hindu Law :—

1. That the legatee took a life-interest, not an estate, in the sense of the term according to English law.

2. "Generation to generation" means in Hindu wills absolutely and for ever ; they are not technical in their import.

3. Descendants means lineal descendants—children and grandchildren.

4. The English doctrine of *cypres* with respect to personal estate is not applicable to Hindu wills.

5. The rule against perpetuity on the ground of public convenience and as a rule of construction, ought to be upheld in Hindu cases, more especially as the Hindu authorities are silent on the subject, *i.e.*, non-prohibition does not imply permission.

6. Successive life-estates or interests in each generation of a Hindu's descendants is opposed to the policy of Hindu law.

7. In construing the intention of the testator, where there is no provision to meet the case of the failure of the descendants of the legatee, he must have meant the estate to be absolute and not limited, and, therefore, that the descendants at the time of the death of the tenant for life should take absolutely as a class.

8. In Hindu will cases, where an estate is bequeathed to A. and his children, or descendants, the interest of the first legatee is limited to life and the children, or descendants existing at the time of his death, taken as a class.

9. Where the testator reserves to himself and his heirs the reversion, the construction of the will must be in favour of the heirs, as the whole of the estate did not pass under the bequest.

10. The principal question before the court was, whether the whole of the interest of the donee was parted with or not ; and it was sufficient to hold that the widow of the testator took no share in the property under the term "descendants." It was not necessary to decide whether the children of the legatee not living at the time of the testator's death took jointly with the children born in the testator's lifetime.

Gifts or devises of inheritance under the Hindu law take the character of endowments for the donee and his children, *i.e.*, gift to A. and his children is not for the exclusive benefit of A., but also for his family; the children, according to the familiar idea of the East, being in co-parcenery with their father. Hence the English doctrine of *cypres* with respect to personal property, when it is attempted to be entailed, is inapplicable to Hindu and oriental cases.

CHAPTER VIII.

STRIDHANA.

SECTION I.

SUCCESSION TO WOMAN'S PROPERTY.

Definition and explanation of stridhana, or woman's property—Derivation—Stridhana not governed by ordinary rules of inheritance —What constitutes—Different descriptions of.

SCHOOLS GOVERNED BY THE MITACSHARA.—*Nature of the separate property of women—Gifts subsequent—Property devolving by inheritance—Right of husband to succeed to wife's property depends on nature of wife's title,* viz., *whether stridhanum, or peculiar property—Wife or widow may alienate.*

BENGAL SCHOOL.—*Different kinds of stridhana—Gift subsequent—Wealth earned by mechanical arts—In case of immovables bestowed on her by her husband—Where taken by husband in case of distress.*

What gifts from strangers—Self-acquisitions—Ornaments worn by the wife.

BOMBAY SCHOOL.—*Different kinds of stridhana—The nature and amount of a woman's separate property—Women have no absolute property in their earnings, or in anything but stridhana—In some kinds they possess absolute property—But not in immovable property given by their husbands—Husbands and others do not possess absolute power over women's property—A husband in such case may be compelled to return it.*

MITHILA SCHOOL.—*Different kinds of stridhana—How it is to be used—Ornamental apparel—Ornaments worn with consent of the husband—What property enjoyed by women after their husband's death—How a woman on the death of her husband may enjoy his estate, and where she is to live—Chastity of childless widow—How a widow shall enjoy immovable property—The property protected during life of husband—Alienation of immovable property—Immovable property inherited from son.*

Definition, or explanation of stridhana, or woman's property.— The property of females is the object of the care and protection of the Hindu law, as well as that of males.

Derivation.—This species of property is termed *stridhana*, or *stridhun*. The word is derived from *sri*, female, and *dhana*, wealth. It does not necessarily mean money; it may consist of anything else of value, as of land (or formerly slaves), or jewels, or other ornaments. It is chiefly with reference to wives or widows that the law concerning it comes in question; few women among the Hindus from the time that they are marriageable remaining single. We may here, however, observe that, according to the *Mitacshara*, whatever a woman may have acquired, whether by way of inheritance, purchase, partition, seizure, or finding, is denominated woman's property; but it does not constitute her *peculium*.

Stridhana not governed by ordinary rules of inheritance.—This description of property is not governed by the ordinary rules of inheritance. It is peculiar and distinct, and the succession to it varies according to circumstances. It varies according to the condition of the woman, and the means by which she became possessed of the property. *Menu* defines woman's *peculium* thus:—"What was given before the nuptial fire, what was given at the bridal procession, what was given in token of love, and what was received from a mother, a brother, or a father, are considered as the sixfold property of a married woman."

What constitutes.—To constitute stridhana, it must have been the gift not of a stranger, but of a husband or some of the owner's near relations. If derived from a stranger, or earned by herself, it seems that it vests in the husband, if she have one, and is at his disposal. Stridhana of a married woman is hers, except in Bengal in the case of land given to her by her husband, of which the dominion remains with him. The husband may use his wife's stridhana in any exigency for which he has not otherwise the means of providing without being accountable for what he has so applied, viz., general want during a famine, any distress preventing performance of religious duty, sickness, imprisonment, and even the distress of a son. It is not, however, liable to be seized in execution for a debt of a husband, though, had he been arrested, he might have applied the ornament on her neck to his discharge, having no other means of obtaining his liberation. It seems that any gross abuse of her property by herself will be controlled while single by her father, while married by her husband, and by her guardians after his death, under the control, however, of the judicial power, *Narada, Katyayana*. In the Bombay reports there are numerous instances where the courts refused to exact security from her against misapplication, or to restrict her in the enjoyment or disposal of what she has.

Different descriptions of.—There is a difference of opinion as to the number of descriptions of women's property. Some authors confine the number to eight, some to six, some to five, some to three. The number of six is not restrictive. Whatever is at her sole disposal, is a woman's peculiar property, *Jim. Vahana*, iv. 31 § 18.

Schools governed by the Mitacshara.—Nature of the separate property of women.—The author of the *Mitac*, cites *Yajnavalchya*, in describing the nature of the separate property of women, viz. :—"What has been given to a woman by the father, the mother, the husband, or a brother, or received by her at the nuptial fire, or presented to her on her husband's marriage with another wife, as also any other (separate acquisition) is denominated a woman's property."

That which was given by the father, by the mother, by the husband, or by a brother, and that which was presented (to the bride) by her maternal uncles, and the rest (as paternal uncles, maternal aunts, &c.), at the time of the wedding before the nuptial fire, and a gift on a second marriage, or gratuity on account of supersession, "to a woman whose husband marries a second wife, let him give an equal sum as a compensation for supersession," and also property which may have been acquired by inheritance,* purchase, partition, seizure, or finding, are denominated by *Menu*, and the rest, woman's property.

Woman's property is not a technical expression.

What is given to women at the time of their marriage, near the nuptial fire, is celebrated by the wise as woman's property bestowed before the nuptial fire. That, again, which a woman receives while she is conducted from her father's house to her husband's dwelling is instanced as the property of a woman under the name of gift in the bridal procession. Whatever has been given to her through affection by her mother-in-law, or by her father-in-law, or has been offered to her as a token of respect, is denominated an affectionate present. That which is received by a married woman, or by a maiden in the house of her husband or of her father, from her brother, or from her parents, is termed a kind gift, *Mitac.*

That which has been given to her by her kindred, as well as her fee, or gratuity, or anything bestowed after marriage, *Yajnavalchya;* what is given to a damsel by her kindred, by the relations of her mother or those of her father, the gratuity for the receipt of which a girl is given in marriage; what is bestowed or given after marriage or subsequently to the nuptials.

Gifts subsequent.—It is said by *Katyayana*, What has been received by a woman from the family of her husband at a time posterior to her marriage is called a gift subsequent, and so is that similarly received from the family of her father. It is celebrated as woman's property.

Property devolving by inheritance.—It would appear from the whole of the chapter in the *Smriti Chandrika*, in which the different kinds of *stridhana* are defined, that property devolving on a woman by inheritance is not classed as stridhana. According to the *Mitac.*,

* See *Sengamalattammal*, appellant, v. *Valayuda Mudali*, respondent, 2 *Mad. Jur.* 202.

however, property acquired by inheritance ranks as *stridhana*. This doctrine is questioned, see 2 *Mad. H. C. R.* 402; in which the court observes that property devolving on a woman by inheritance is not stridhana, and does not follow the law of succession peculiar to properties of that description.

Right of husband to succeed to wife's property depends on nature of wife's title, viz., whether strichanum, or peculiar property.—Property inherited by a woman is not her stridhanum—dictum of *Mitacshara*, contrary to all other schools, and not supported by the *Smriti Chandrika.*

Even although the property inherited by a woman was her mother's stridhanum, once it has devolved, its further devolution is governed by the ordinary rules of inheritance.

Hnsband can only be heir to his wife if the property be strictly her peculiar property, *Sengamalattammal*, special appellant (fourth defendant), *Valayuda Mudali*, special respondent (plaintiff). 2 *Mad. Jur.* 202. The judgment on this case and observations upon it, will be found in *Grady's Hindu Law*, p. 176.

Wife or widow may alienate.—In *Kullammal* v. *Kuppu Pillai*, 1 *Mad. H. C. R.*, p. 85, the High Court of Madras has held that a Hindu wife or widow may alienate her *stridhana*, whether it be movable or immovable, with the exception perhaps of land given her by her husband. In a subsequent case, *Dantuluri Rayapparas* v. *Mallapudi Rayudu*, 2 *Mad. H. C. R.*, p. 360, the same court observes that they could not, without the greatest consideration, conclude that a woman can, without the consent of her husband during connexion, absolutely alienate even her own landed property.

Strange has the following enumeration, viz. :—

I. What is given to a young woman, or to her husband in trust for her at the time of her marriage, *i.e.*, during the space between the beginning and close of the nuptial ceremony, but not to be confined rigorously to the day, if given on account of the marriage.

II. Her fee, or what is given to her in the bridal procession upon the final ceremony, when the marriage is about to be consummated, as a bribe to induce her to repair more cheerfully to the mansion of her lord.

III. What is given to her on her arrival at her husband's house when she makes prostration to her parents.

IV. Gifts subsequent, by her parents or brothers.

V. Upon her husband proposing to take another wife, the gratuities given by him to reconcile the first to the supersession, the measure of which seems not to be settled, but supposed to be equal to the sum spent on the ceremony.

VI. What a woman receives from the bridegroom on the marriage of her daughter.

VII. What she owes at any time to the good graces of her husband, as, for instance, a reward for performing well the business of the house in her department, called her perquisite.

VIII. Anything given her at any time by any of her relations, being specially given, which includes gifts made to her before marriage, while yet an unbetrothed member of her own family.

IX. The earnings of her industry, as by sewing, spinning, painting, and the like. These are the enumeration in the *Smriti Chandrika*. The 9th does not occur in the *Mitac.*, nor in *Menu;* and *Jim. Vahana* and others exclude it, observing that the husband has a right to it independently of distress. Yet it seems admitted that her heirs, and not his, succeed to them after her death, she having survived him. The reason for the doubt as to their constituting *stridhana*, being, that it was sent by strangers, not a gift from her husband or any of her relatives, a circumstance belonging to the description of property in question.

X. What is given to a wife for sending, or to induce her to send, her husband to perform particular work, which by some is included, by others excluded.

XI. Property which a woman may acquire by inheritance, purchase, or finding. What has been inherited by her being so classed by *Vijnyaneswara*, whose authority prevails in the peninsula, while it is otherwise considered by writers of the Eastern school.

XII. The savings of her maintenance.

Bengal school.—Different Descriptions of Stridhana.—In the Bengal school *Jim. Vahana* cites *Vishnu*, who says, "What has been given to a woman by her father, her mother, her son, or her brother, what has been received by her before the nuptial fire, what has been presented to her on her husband's espousal of another wife, what has been given to her by kindred, as well as her perquisite, and a gift subsequent, are a woman's separate property."

Gift subsequent.—*Katyayana* describes a gift subsequent—what has been received by a woman from her husband's family at a time posterior to her marriage, and so is that which has been similarly received after her nuptials either from her husband or from her parents through the affection of the giver, *Bhruyu*.

By the word "kindred" her father and mother are denoted. Hence anything received subsequently to the marriage from paternal or maternal uncles, or other persons who are related through the father or the mother, or from the two parents themselves, or from the husband or his family, viz., father-in-law, and the rest. But the term "kindred" in the text of *Vishnu* intends maternal uncles, and others; for the father and the rest are specified by the appropriate terms, either the husband or the parents inherit that which was received at the time of the nuptials according to the difference between marriages denominated Brahma, &c., and those called Asoora, and so forth.

Menu and *Katyayana* describe her separate property thus :—

"What was given before the nuptial fire, what was presented in the bridal procession, what has been conferred on the woman through affection, and what has been received from her brother, her mother, or father, are denominated the sixfold property of a woman." So *Narada* says, what was given before the nuptial fire, what was presented in the bridal procession, her husband's donation, and what has been given her by her brother or by either of her parents.

Katyayana defines "gift before the nuptial fire," and "gift presented in the bridal procession," and her husband's donation.

Wealth given her by her husband she may dispose of as she pleases when he is dead; but while he is alive she should carefully preserve it. This is intended as a caution against profusion.

That wealth which is given to gratify a first wife, by a man desirous of marrying a second, is a gift on second marriage, for its object is to obtain another wife with the assent of the first.

Devala says, Her subsistence, her ornaments, her perquisite, and her gains, are the separate property of a woman. She herself exclusively enjoys it, and her husband has no right to use it except in distress.

Vyasa says, Whatever is presented at the time of the nuptials to the bridegroom, intending the benefit of the bride, belongs entirely to her, and shall not be shared by kinsmen.

The number of six sorts is not restrictive, whatever is at her sole disposal is a woman's peculiar property.

Wealth earned by mechanical arts.—*Katyayana* expresses this rather concisely, "The wealth which is earned by mechanical arts, or which is received through affection from any other (but the kindred), is always subject to her husband's dominion. The rest is pronounced to be the woman's property."

And wealth received in presents from any other but father, mother, or husband, and wealth earned by the wife in the practice of a mechanical art, as spinning, or weaving, her husband has control over. He has a right to take it even though no distress exist. Hence, though the goods be hers, they do not constitute woman's property, because she has not independent power over them.

But in other descriptions of property, excepting those two, the woman has the sole power of gift, sale, or other alienation. So *Katyayana* declares, That which is received by a married woman, or a maiden in the house of her husband, or of her father, from her husband, or from her parents, is termed the gift of affectionate kindred. The independence of women who have received such gifts is recognised in regard to that property, for it was given by their kinsmen to soothe them, and for their maintenance. The power of women over gifts of their affectionate kindred is ever celebrated both in respect of donation and of sale according to their pleasure, even in the case of immovables. See 1 *Mad. H. C. R.*, 87, p. 126, 182; *Grady's Hindu Law of Inheritance*, 186.

But in the case of immovables bestowed on her by her husband.—So *Naradà* declares, What has been given by an affectionate husband to his wife she may consume as she pleases when he is dead, or may give it away, excepting immovable property.* It follows, from the specific mention of "given by a husband," that any other immovable property, except such as has been given to her by him, may be aliened by her ; else (if this text forbid donation in the case of immovables in general) the preceding passage concerning the power of women in respect of donation and of sale according to their pleasure, even in the case of immovables, would be contradicted, *ib.* § 23.

Where taken by husband in case of distress.—*Yajnavalchya*, declares a husband is not bound to make good the property of his wife taken by him in a famine, or for the performance of a duty, or during illness, or while under restraint.

Katyayana denies the right of the husband to do so in any other circumstances : Neither the husband, nor the son, nor the father, nor the brothers can assume the power over a woman's property, to take it, or bestow it. If any one of these persons consume by force the woman's property, he shall be compelled to make it good with interest, and shall also incur a fine. If such person, having obtained her consent, use the property amicably, he shall be required to pay the principal when he becomes rich. But if the husband have a second wife, and do not show honour to his first wife, he shall be compelled by force to restore her property, though amicably lent to him. If food, raiment, and dwelling be withheld from the woman, she may exact her due supply, and take a share (of the estate) with the coheirs.

If the husband, having taken the property of his wife, live with another wife and neglect her, he shall be compelled to restore the property taken by him. If he do not give her food, raiment, and the like, that also may be exacted from him by the woman.

Thus a definition of women's property has been propounded, *Jim Vahana.*

Stridhana—What gifts from strangers—Self-acquisitions.—The different acquisitions included in *stridhana* may for all practical purposes be included in gifts or the like from her husband or kindred before, during, or after her marriage, Gifts to a married woman from a *stranger*, that is to say, from other persons than her husband and kindred, and *not* made at the time of her marriage, belong to the husband's estate, and are considered as *his* property, and so are all her acquisitions by the practice of any mechanical art, as spinning, weaving, or the like ; but what she acquires by her own exertions in a state of widowhood belongs of course to her own property.

Ornaments worn by the wife during her husband's lifetime, and not distinctly given to her by her husband, are not considered her

* Not found in *Narada's Institutes*, but cited in *Mitacshara* and *Ratnakara*,

property as long as he lives, but become so at his death if she survives him, and are afterwards inherited as *stridhana.*

Bombay school—Different kinds of stridhana.—The sources of a woman's property are six. *Menu,* " What was given before the nuptial fire; what was presented in the bridal procession; what was given in token of love; what was received by her from her brother, her mother, or her father, are denominated the sixfold property of a woman."

What has been given to women at the time of their marriage, near the nuptial fire, is celebrated by the wise as woman's property bestowed before the nuptial fire. That again which a woman receives whilst she is conducted from her father's house to her husband's dwelling, is instanced as the property of a woman under the name of a gift presented in the bridal procession. What has been given to her through affection by her mother-in-law, or by her father-in-law, or has been offered to her as a token of respect, is denominated an affectionate present. What has been received at a time subsequent to her marriage, from the family of her husband, is called a gift subsequent, and so is that which has been similarly received from her own family. What has been received as the value of household utensils, of beasts of burden, of milch cattle, or ornaments of dress, or for work, is called her perquisite. The meaning is, when the bride does not (as usual) obtain household utensils and the rest, then whatsoever is given to her at the time of her marriage, as the price of them, is termed her perquisite. What she receives on her supersession is explained, *ante.*

That which a husband has promised for separate property (stridhana), must be made good by his sons as a debt, *Devala.*

The nature and amount of a woman's separate property.—On the subject of giving property to women, *Katyayana* declares separate property, except immovables, is to be given to women by their father, mother, husband, brother, according to their means, as far as 2000. " The wealth to be given excludes immovable property, and must not exceed 2000 panas," *Madana. Vyasa.* If they are able, even immovable property may be given, *Madana.*

But in property given to a woman with a view of cheating the heirs out of it, as well as ornaments, or the like, given to her merely for the purpose of wearing, a woman has no ownership or property, for thus says *Katyayana,* " But whatever has been given to a woman with a fraudulent design, as well as intrusted to her for use by her father, brother, or husband, is declared not to be woman's property" (*stridhana*).

Women have no absolute property in their earnings, or in anything but stridhana.—In what they have earned by the arts, or obtained from friends, or those distinct from parents, or the rest, women have no property; for thus says the same author, "The wealth which is earned by mechanical arts, or which is received through affection, from any other but the kindred, is always subject to her husband's dominion. The rest is pronounced to be woman's property." However, though a text, *Menu* says, "A wife, a son, and a slave are in general incapable of property, the wealth which they may earn is regularly acquired for the man to whom they belong," it also relates only to wealth earned by mechanical arts and the like. It is, moreover, agreeable to reason, to refer this also to their not having absolute dominion in wealth, received on their supersession and the like, *Mayukha.*

In some kinds they possess absolute property.—Again, *Menu* says, "A woman should never make expenditure from the goods of her kindred (which are) common to (her and) many; or even from the property of her lord without his consent," ch. ix. § 190. (Expenditure is disbursement); yet, in some kinds of wealth, they are declared to possess sole property by *Katyayana:* "That which is received by a married woman, or a maiden, in the house of her husband or of her father, from her brother or from her parents, is termed the gift of affectionate kindred. The independence of women who have received such gifts is recognised in regard to that property, for it was given by their kindred to soothe them and for their maintenance. The power of women over the gift of their affectionate kindred is ever celebrated in respect of donation, and of sale according to their pleasure, even in case of immovables," *Mayukha.*

But not in immovable property given by their husbands.—But over immovable property given them by their husbands, they do not possess full power from this text of *Narada:* "What has been given by an affectionate husband to his wife, she may consume as she pleases when he is dead, or may give it away, excepting immovable property," *Mayukha.*

Husbands and others do not possess absolute power over women's property.—The non-existence of absolute power in husbands and the rest over women's property is declared by the same author: "Neither the husband, nor the son, nor the father, nor the brothers, can assume the power over a woman's property, to take it or bestow it. If any of these persons by force consume the woman's property, he shall be compelled to make it good with interest, and shall also incur a fine. If such person, having obtained her consent, use the property amicably, he shall be required to pay the principal when he becomes rich." *Menu:* "Such kinsmen (as by any pretence) appropriate the fortunes of women during their lives, a just king must punish with the severity due to thieves," ch. viii § 29, ch. ix. § 200. Such ornamental apparel as women wear during the lives of their husbands, the heirs of the husband shall not divide amongst themselves; they who do so are degraded from their tribe: "*Wear*, meaning things worn by them which have been given to them for the purpose by their husbands or the others,"

Devala. "Her maintenance, ornaments, perquisite, and gain, are the separate property of a woman; she herself exclusively enjoys it and her husband has no right to it, except in distress. If he let it, go on a false consideration or consume it, he must repay the value to the woman with interest; but he may use the property of his wife to relieve a distressed son." *Maintenance* is wealth given her by her father or the others for the purpose of subsistence. *Gain* is interest (or profit). "To let go, get rid of, and give away," have all the same meaning in this place. The word "son" is here used in its general sense for any member of the family. "A husband is not liable to make good the property of his wife taken by him in a famine or for the performance of some religious duty, or during illness, or while under restraint." Here, by using the husband alone, it is virtually declared that woman's private property must not be taken by any other but him, even when distressed by famine or other calamity; "religious duties," such as are indispensable; "under restraint," in prison, *Mayukha.*

A husband in such case may be compelled to restore it.—In some cases a husband, though unwilling, may be compelled to restore it; for, says *Devala,* But if the husband have a second wife, and do not show honour to his first wife, he shall be compelled by force to restore her property though amicably lent to him. If suitable food, raiment, and dwelling be withheld from the woman, she may exact her own property and take a share (of the estate) with the co-heirs "that is at their hands," *Mayukha.*

This, however, relates to a virtuous wife, for a wicked one should receive no portion.—Accordingly, the same author says, "But a wife who does malicious acts injurious to her husband, who acts improperly, who destroys his effects or who takes delight in being faithless to his bed, is held unworthy of separate property;" and again, "Wealth was conferred for the purpose of defraying sacrifices, therefore distribute wealth amongst honest persons, not amongst women, ignorant men, or such as neglect their duties," *Mayukha.*

Mithila school—Different kinds of stridhana.—*Menu* and *Katyayana,* "There are six kinds of property of a woman," the same as those described in the Bengal, Madras, and Bombay schools. There cannot be a less number, *Vivada Chintamani.*

Katyayana explains what is property given before the nuptial fire. Property of a woman given at her nuptial procession: wealth gained by amiability.

What a woman receives for her consolation when her husband takes a second wife is the seventh kind of peculiar property.

Yajnavalchya: A woman whose husband takes a second wife, shall have compensation for the supersession if no property have been bestowed upon her; but if any have been given they shall get so much as will make her share equal to that of the new bride.

Vishnu says:—The property of a female is what her father, mother, son, or brother has given her; what she received before the nuptial fire, *or at the bridal procession;* or when her husband took a second wife; what her husband agrees should be regarded as her perquisites; what is received from his or her kinsmen as a gift subsequent to the marriage.

The latter *Katyayana* explains as the small sums which are received by a woman as the price or rewards of household duties; using household utensils, tending beasts of burden, looking after milch cattle, taking care of ornaments of dress, or superintending servants, are called her perquisites.

Explanation.—What the master of the house, pleased with the performance of the household duties, gives to a woman, is her perquisite. What is a gift subsequent is also explained.

The peculiar property of women is thus explained:—

Saudayaka is the name by which the different kinds of the peculiar property of women are known.

Katyayana says:—"That which is received by a married woman or a maiden in the house of her husband or her father, from her brothers or from her parents, is termed the gift of affectionate kindred." By the words "her husband," are to be also understood his kindred.

Hence the meaning is, what a married woman or maiden receives from her parents or their kindred is called the gift of affectionate kindred. The means of subsistence and other kinds of women's property will be described hereafter.

How it is to be used.—*Katyayana* says, "The independence of women who have received such gifts is recognised in regard to that property," for it was received through the kindness of the donors. "The power of women over the gifts of affectionate kindred is ever celebrated, both in respect of donation and sale at their pleasure, even in the case of immovables." Women are competent to make gifts and so forth of the immovables given by their husband's kindred.

Apastamba thus speaks of the gifts of affectionate kindred:— "Ornaments are the exclusive property of a wife, and so is wealth given her by kinsmen or friends; according to some legislators, "given by kinsmen," means that which is given at the time of marriage and so forth, by kinsmen and the kinsmen of her parents, or those of her husband.

Ornamental apparel worn by women during the lives of their husbands cannot be taken by the heirs of the latter. They who divide it among themselves fall into deep sin, *Menu, Vishnu, Chintamani.*

Ornaments worn with consent of the husband.—Any ornament worn with consent of the husband shall be the woman's peculiar property, even if it have not been given to her. *Madhatithi* declares that, according to the foregoing text of *Katyayana*, a woman is competent to give away or sell any immovable or movable property which she has received from her husband's kindred.

What property may be enjoyed by a woman at pleasure after her husband's death.—*Narada* says, Property given to her by her husband, through pure affection, she may enjoy at her pleasure after his death, or give away, with the exception of lands or houses.

Explanation.—Consequently a woman can dispose of movable property which has been given her by her husband, but she can never dispose of immovable property. The same rule holds good in the case of *Saudayaca*, or the gifts of affectionate kindred.

How a woman, on the death of her husband, may enjoy his estate, and where she is to live.—*Katyayana* says, "That a woman, on the death of her husband, may enjoy his estate according to her pleasure; but in his lifetime she should carefully preserve it. If he leave no estate, let her remain with his family."

A childless chaste widow shall, during her life, enjoy her husband's property.—A childless widow, preserving her chastity, shall enjoy her husband's property with moderation as long as she lives. After her death the heirs shall take it.

This admits of two meanings. The one is, that on the death of the husband, his property devolves on his wife, and becomes her own in default of other heirs.

The other is, that the property, which she enjoys with the consent of her husband in his lifetime, is to be regarded as her peculiar property. *Katyayana* says, as to the first of these, "Let a woman, on the death of her husband, enjoy her husband's property at her discretion." This refers to property other than immovable, *Chintamani.*

How a woman shall enjoy immovable property.—The following provision is made for immovable property. Let a woman enjoy it as long as she lives. After her death let the heirs take it.

Explanation.—"Moderation" means without much expenditure. "Childless widow" means who has no heir of her own.

The property protected in the lifetime of her husband.—On the second, it is said that, "while he lives she should carefully preserve it;" or, in other words, the property should be protected in the lifetime of the husband. If her husband have left no wealth, the widow shall live with his family.

Alienation—Immovable property cannot be disposed of by the widow at her pleasure.—Hence the immovable property which a woman gets after the death of her husband, cannot be disposed of at her pleasure.

Explanation.—The meaning of this is consonant with that of the husband's donation (which can only be enjoyed, but not spent).

The texts of *Katyayana* do not refer to the peculiar property of a woman. The inconsistency owing to this is removed by the similarity of meaning.

As a woman cannot make a present of or at pleasure dispose of immovable property given to her by her husband in his lifetime, so she cannot dispose of any immovable property which she inherits on his death. The same opinion is maintained in the *Ratnakara* and the *Prakasakara.*

Nor the immovable property inherited from her son.—If the mother on the death of her son get his immovable property, she cannot make a gift of it or dispose of it at her pleasure. *Devala* says, as to the property in question:—"Food and vesture, ornaments and perquisites, and wealth, received by a woman *from a kinsman*, are her own property; she may enjoy it herself, and her husband has no right to it except in extreme distress."

Explanation.—"Food and vesture" mean, "funds appropriated to her support;" "ornaments" mean, "ornamental apparel;" "perquisites" mean, "wealth given to a damsel on demanding her in marriage;" "wealth received" means, "that which is received from kinsmen."

These are the several kinds of the peculiar property of women.

As to texts showing that the property of a woman should not be used, but for the relief of a distressed son.

When the husband shall pay the principal only.

If the wife give the property to her husband in distress.

When the husband is not liable to make good the property taken from his wife.

When money taken from his wife is not to be repaid by a man.

When a wife can forcibly take her own property.

That a bad wife is unworthy of peculiar property. See *Grady's Hindu Law of Inheritance*, 193.

Section II.

ORDER OF DESCENT OF WOMAN'S PROPERTY.

Order of succession to stridhana varies in Bengal, Benares, and Mithila—Madras and Benares schools—Property not given at the time of nuptials—Property inherited by a daughter as her mother's stridhun—Property acquired as her own stridhun—Distribution of woman's property—The heirs differ according to form of marriage ceremony.

In Bengal.—*Descent of stridhana—Where deceased was unmarried—Succession to the peculiar property of a maiden—Order of descent—When given to her by her father—If not given to her by her father.*

Bombay School.—*Successors to married woman's property—Argument against the reciprocal rights of sons and daughters—Amongst* *daughters the unmarried are first, sharing with sons—All property acquired by marriage the daughter, not the son, takes—All property, except two kinds, goes to daughters unmarried or unprovided—A distinction when wives of different classes exist—In default of daughters, their issue succeed—Among daughters and among their sons, is according to mothers—Issue of daughters succeed on their default—On failure of daughters and their issue—The right of daughters and their issue confined to the six kinds of property—Woman's property is an exception to the general right of sons—On default of offspring, kinsmen succeed—The right of kinsmen depends on the form of marriage—The effect of these rights is different in the various classes—Heirs of a woman on failure of her husband and parents defined—The son in that case inherits presents from kindred—And the brother gets the perquisite—Gifts to be restored to the bridegroom when bride dies before marriage, deducting charges—Presents by maternal kindred belong to the brothers of the deceased damsel.*

Mithila School.—*Succession to a woman's separate property—How a woman's property is to be divided—Who receive a woman's separate property—Daughter shall receive a share from the maternal estate—Unmarried daughter inherits nuptial gifts—Who receives residue of mother's property after payment of the debts—Where the rule is applicable—Who succeed on failure of daughters—Married sisters share with kinsmen—On failure of daughters, &c.—Married sister shall receive something from the estate given to her by her kindred—The property of woman married according to certain ceremonies shall go to her husband on failure of issue—When her property goes to her parents—Where this text applies—Who shall take the wealth of a deceased damsel—Order of succession to the peculiar property of women—Stridhana, how far heritable—Who may inherit—Daughters' daughters represent their mothers—Unmarried exclude married—Co-wife's children—Sister's son—Heirs of the separate property of the deceased proprietress.*

Order of succession to stridhana varies.—The succession to *stridhana* varies according to the condition of the woman, and the means by which she became possessed of the property, *Elberling* (Elberling is a Bengal authority). If deceased is a maiden, the heirs are—

Her brother.

Her mother.

Her father.

Her nearest kindred, but that which has been given by a bridegroom to her is to be returned to him, *Daya Krama Sangraha*, on paying the charges on both sides, *Mitac.*

If married, and the property was given to her at the time of her nuptials, her heirs are—

Daughters.
Maiden.
Betrothed.
Married, who has, or is likely to have male issue.
Barren and
Widowed collectively.

After the death of a maiden, a betrothed daughter on whom the inheritance *had devolved*, and who proved barren, or on the death of a widow who has not given birth to a son, the succession to the property which they had so inherited will devolve next on the sisters having, and likely to have, male issue, and in their default, on the barren and widowed daughters. The daughter of a contemporary wife is also admitted, *Mitac.*

The son.
The grandson's son.
The son's grandson.
The son of a contemporary wife.
Her grandson and
Great grandson.

In default of those descendants, supposing the marriage to have been celebrated according to any of the five first forms, *Brahma*, &c., the succession goes to

The husband.
The brother.
The mother.
The father.

If according to the *Asoora*, &c., the succession goes to

The mother.
The father.
The brother.
The husband.

In default of those the heirs are successively as follows:—

The husband's younger brother.
The husband's brother's son.
The sister's son.
The husband's sister's son.
The brother's son.
The son-in-law.
The father-in-law.
The husband's elder brother.
Sapinda.

Saculyas, failing them the property of a Brahmini will go to learned Brahmans of the same village, and of other castes to the ruling power.

According to the Benares and Mithila schools, the unmarried daughter is preferred to the married, the indigent to the wealthy, *Mitac.*; so, according to the same schools, the daughter's daughter succeeds on failure of daughters, *Mitac.*, and takes by representation. See also *Menu;* then the daughter's son, then the son. The daughter's daughter gets no share, according to the Bengal school. But it is fit, says *Menu*, that something should be given to her, *Elberling*.

If Married, and the property was not given at the time of nuptials.—When the deceased was married, and the property was not given to her at the time of her nuptials. If given by her father, the order is the same as in the case of property received at nuptials, *Daya Krama Sangraha*, *Daya Bhaga*. If not given by her father, the order is the following:—The son and unmarried daughter together, on the death of either of them, the property goes to the other (as with daughters).

The married daughters who have, or are likely to have, male issue.
The son's son.
The daughter's son.
The son's grandson.
The son of a contemporary wife; failing her,
Her grandson and
Son's grandson.
The barren and widowed daughters together.
Failing them the succession continues in the order as above, viz.,
The husband.
The brother.
The mother.
The father.

Raghunundana holds that the husband alone has a right to the property of his wife dying without issue, bestowed on her by him after marriage, and that the brother has in such case the prior right to the property which may have been given to her by her father and mother.

Having given this concise general outline of the order of succession, we shall now proceed to treat of the law of each school separately, and at greater length.

Madras and Benares Schools.—Property inherited by a daughter as her mother's stridhun—Goes to her heirs in the same order of succession as for males, because this acquisition is not by law included in what is termed *stridhun*. The sons will thus inherit this property in preference to daughters, and a brother in preference to a childless widowed daughter. According to Benares and Mithila schools, such property is considered as *stridhun*, and inherited as such, *Mitac.*

Property acquired as her own stridhun.—Property received as gifts or the like from her husband or kindred before, during, or after her marriage, and termed by the law stridhun, goes to her heirs, in an order which differs from the order of succession to other property.

Distribution of woman's property.—Her kinsmen take it if she die without issue. If a woman die without issue—*i.e.*, leaving no progeny—in other words, leaving no daughter nor daughter's son, nor son, nor son's son—the woman's property as above described shall be taken by her kinsmen, namely, her husband and the rest, *Mitac.*

The heirs are different according to the form of marriage ceremony, as shown by Yajnavalchya.—The kinsmen have been declared generally to be competent to succeed to a woman's property. That of a childless woman married in the form denominated Brahma, or in any of the four unblamed modes of marriage, goes to her husband; but if she leave progeny, it will go to her (daughter's) daughters; and in other forms of marriage, as the Asoora, &c., it goes to her father and mother on failure of her own issue, *Mitac.*

Of a woman dying without issue, and who had become a wife by any of the four forms of marriage denominated Brahma, &c., the whole property as before described belongs in the first place to her husband. On failure of him, it goes to his nearest kinsmen, sapinda, allied by funeral oblations. But in the other forms of marriage called Asoora, the property of a childless woman goes to her parents—that is, to her father and mother. The succession devolves first on the mother; after her, on the father; failing them, their next of kin, *Mitac.*

In all forms of marriage if the woman leave progeny, *i.e.*, if she have issue, her property devolves on her daughters, including granddaughters; the daughters share the residue of the mother's property after payment of her debts, *Yajnavalchya.*

Hence, if the mother be dead, the succession devolves upon the Daughters.

But this rule for the daughter's succession to the mother's goods, is exclusive of the fee, or gratuity, for that goes to brothers of the whole blood conformably with the text of *Goutama.* The sister's fee belongs to the uterine brothers after the death of the mother, *Mitac.*

On failure of all the daughters,

Granddaughters in the female line.

Daughters' sons.

Sons.

Step-daughter.

Grandsons.

Husband and other heirs. Should a damsel, anyhow affianced, die before the completion of the marriage, let the bridegroom take back the gifts which he had presented, paying, however, the charges on both sides. The circumstances under which each of these heirs succeeds are treated at length in *Grady's Hindu Law.*

The property of a woman must not be taken in her lifetime by any other kinsman or heir but her husband.

Bengal school—Descent of stridhana.—Stridhana which has once devolved according to the law of succession, which governs the descent of this peculiar species of property, ceases to be ranked as such, and is ever afterwards governed by the ordinary rules of inheritance. Thus the property given to a woman on her marriage is *stridhana*, and at her death passes to her daughter; upon the daughter's death it passes to the heir of the daughter like other property, and the brother of her mother would be heir in preference to her own daughter if she were a widow without issue.

Where deceased was unmarried.—So property left to an unmarried woman is inherited by her brother, her father, and her mother successively, and failing these, her paternal kinsmen in due order.

Succession to the peculiar property of a maiden.—In regard to the property of a maiden—the uterine brother, the mother, the father. *Narada* says, "The wealth of a deceased damsel, let the uterine brethren themselves take; on failure of them, it shall belong to the mother, or if she be dead, to the father, *excepting the gifts bestowed by a bridegroom, which he is entitled to receive back.*

Order of descent.—If the property were given to the woman at the time of her nuptials—

Daughters.
  The maiden.
    betrothed.*
    married, who has or likely to have male issue.
    barren.
    widowed.
Son.
Daughter's son, whom *Jim. Vahana* postpones to contemporary wife, an opinion which is refuted by *Srikristna* and other commentators.
Son's son.
Great-grandson in the male line.

In default of all these descendants, if the marriage has been celebrated in any of the approved forms—

Husband.
Brother.
Mother.
Father.

But if celebrated after any of the disapproved forms, the brother

* At the death of a maiden or betrothed daughter, on whom the inheritance had devolved, and who proved barren, or on the death of a widow who had not given birth to a son, the succession of the property which they had so inherited will devolve next on the sisters having, and likely to have, male issue, and in their default, on the barren and widowed daughters.

is preferred to the husband, and both are postponed to the mother and father.

In default of these the succession devolves according to the following table, as given by *Macnaghten* :—

Husband's younger brother.
His younger brother's son.
His elder brother's son.
Sister's son.
Husband's sister's son.
Brother's sons.
Son-in-law.
Father-in-law.
Elder brother-in-law.
Sapindas.
Saculyas.
Samanodacas.

When given to her by her father.—If the property be given to her by her father, but not at the time of her nuptials, the heirs are thus successively enumerated, viz. :—

A maiden daughter.
A son.
A daughter who has, or is likely to have, male issue.
Daughter's son.
Son's son.
Son's grandson.
The great-grandson in the male line.
The son of a contemporary wife.
Her grandson.
Her great-grandson in the male line.

In default of these, the barren and the widowed daughters succeed as co-heirs, and then the succession goes on as in the approved forms of marriage.

If not given her by her father.—If the property has not been given her by her father, and not given to her at the time of her nuptials, the heirs are in the same order as above, with the exception that the son and unmarried daughter inherit together, and not successively, and that the son's son is preferred to the daughter's son.

The right of succession to the separate property of a childless widow, the order of its succession, and the grounds upon which it is based, are discussed in *Grady's Hindu Law*, p. 205, *et seq.*

Bombay school—The successors to a married woman's property are her children.—The right of succession after a woman's decease, that (part of her), private property, which is entitled a gift subsequent, is thus settled by *Menu*, "What she received, after marriage, from the family of her husband, and what her lord may have given her through affection, shall be inherited, even if she die in his lifetime, by her children." The term "children" is thus explained by *Menu*, "On the death of the mother let all the uterine brothers and uterine sisters equally divide the maternal estate," *Mayukha.*

Argument against the reciprocal rights of the sons and the daughters.—When from non-existence of daughters and the rest, the right of inheritance devolves even to the sons from their connection, that it becomes reciprocal. When this right is taken up by unmarried daughters, then the son's succession arising from that connection is at an end; but according to the *Mitacshara*, it is not declared that the succession pertains (equally or) reciprocally to the brothers and unmarried sisters. Yet it has been said by others, "It is declared that there is no original connection of sons and daughters in property received by their mother after marriage, or given by her husband through affection," *Mayukha.*

Amongst daughters the unmarried are first, sharing with sons.—The distinctions in succession among daughters are pointed out by *Menu* :*—"A woman's property goes to her children, and the daughter is a sharer with them, provided she be not given away; but if married, she receives a mere token of respect." *Is a sharer;* shares equally with the sons. *Not given away;* unmarried. It means that, if there be one (unmarried), then the married (daughter) receives a mere token of respect—that is, only something very small. If there be no unmarried daughter, the share of the married daughter is equal to that of the brothers, according to the text of *Katyayana.* "Married sisters shall share with (brothers or) kinsmen, *Mayukha.*

The daughters' daughters get some trifle.

All property acquired by marriage, the daughter, and not the son, takes.—But all property acquired by marriage, *Yautaka*, goes to the unmarried daughter alone, not to the son. So a prior text of *Menu*, "Property given to the mother on her marriage, *Yautaka*, is inherited by her (unmarried) daughter." *Property given on her marriage*—whatever is received by her at the time of marriage, or other (ceremony), whilst seated together with her husband; for, according to *Madana*, "The word 'Yautaka' is, in the *Nighantu*, derived from their being then joined together, *Yuta.*

All the property, except two kinds, goes to daughters unmarried or unprovided.—In respect to woman's property before enumerated in the texts of other sages, distinct from that acquired subsequent to marriage, or through their husbands' affection, these distinctions are declared by *Goutama* : "A woman's property goes to her daughters unmarried or unprovided." *Unprovided;* such as are destitute of wealth, *Mayukha.*

A distinction when wives of different classes exist.—The daughter of a Brahmini wife, however, shall take the wealth of her stepmother. Thus *Menu*, "The wealth of a woman which has

* It is not a text of *Menu*, but of *Brihaspati*, note 6; *Mayukha*, § 15.

been in any manner given to her by her father, let the Brahmini damsel take, or let it belong to her offspring." By giving the particle *or* the sense of *and*, we have it, 'and shall be shared by (her issue'). Some say that the word Brahmini is used to denote any girl of equal or superior caste; but the proof of this must be well examined.

In default of daughters, their issue succeed.—If there be no daughters, then the issue of those daughters succeed, according to the text of *Narada*. "Let daughters divide their mother's wealth, or, on failure of daughters, their male issue, *Mayukha.*

Distribution among daughters and among their sons, is according to mothers.—A distribution among daughters by different mothers, as well as amongst the different daughters' sons, to be just, must be apportioned after the example of that prescribed for the sons of different fathers, where the partition is according to their father's shares (not to the number of the sons of each father), *Mayukha.*

Issue of the daughters succeed on their default.—*Yajnavalchya* says, "The daughters share the residue of the mother's property after payment of her debts, and the issue succeed in their default." Some say the word issue (*Anvaya*) has reference to the offspring of the daughters; whilst others hold, that if she leave no daughter, even her sons may take it, since the word *tad*, in the text of *Narada* above, distinctly points out the mother alone, and this (first) doctrine agrees with custom. *The residue after payment of her debts*—on this subject, those acquainted with the ancient law have declared that the sons alone must take the property (if only) equal, to or less than the amount of debt, *Mayukha.*

On failure of daughters and their issue.—If daughters or the rest do not exist, the sons, grandsons, and the rest must take it; for thus it is declared by *Katyayana*. But on failure of daughters the inheritance belongs to the sons.

The right of daughters and their issue confined to the six kinds of property.—This right of inheritance of daughters and the rest in the mother's property exists only in wealth given before the nuptial fire, and in the bridal procession, and the other (kinds) above recorded in the texts, specifying woman's property; for if relating to all wealth in which their mother has any property, it would go to set aside these texts (limiting it to six).

Woman's property is an exception to the general right of sons. —*Yajnavalchya*: "Let sons divide equally both the effects and the debts after (the demise of) their two parents," relates to (what is) acquired by the act of partition and the like, with the exception of that declared in the above texts as woman's property. From this it is clear that if there be daughters, the sons, or other heirs even, succeed to the mother's estate, distinct from that part before described (as woman's property.)

On default of offspring, the kinsmen succeed.—Her kinsmen take it if she die without issue, *Yajnavalchya*, *Mayukha*.

The right of kindred depends upon the particular form by which the woman was married.—The same author expounds the succession of kindred to be according to the different kinds of marriage. "The property of a childless woman, married in the form denominated Brahma, or in any of the other four (unblamed modes of marriage), goes to her husband; but if she leave progeny, it will go to her daughters; and in the other forms of marriage, as the Asoora, &c., it goes to her father and mother, on failure of her own issue." In the one case, if there be no husband, then the nearest to her in his own family takes it; and in the other case, if her father do not exist, the nearest to her in her father's family succeeds (for the law that), "to nearest sapinda the inheritance next belongs," as declared by *Menu*, denotes, that the right of inheriting her wealth is even derived from the nearness of kin to the deceased (female) under discussion—and though the *Mitacshara* holds that on failure of the husband it goes to his nearest kinsman (sapinda) allied by funeral oblations, and on failure of the father then to his nearest sapinda; yet from the context it may be demonstrated that her nearest relations are his nearest relations, and (the pronoun *tat* being used in the common gender) it allows of our expounding the passage "those nearest to him through her, in his own family," for the expressions are of similar import.

The effect of these rights is different in the various classes.—In the Brahma, or in any of the other four, relates to the Brahmanical class, on account of those rights being the only ones lawful in respect to them. But as the Gandharva right is also lawful to the Shetriya class and the rest, so also the wealth of her who has been married according to that form, devolves to her husband alone; and so *Menu*, ch. ix. § 106, 107, it is ordained that the property of a woman married by the ceremonies called Brahma, &c., shall go to her husband if she die without issue. But her wealth given on the marriage called Asoora, &c., is ordained on her death without issue to become the property of her mother and father, *Mayukha*.

Heirs of a woman on failure of her husband and parents defined.—On failure of the husband of a deceased woman, if married according to the Brahma or other four forms, or of her parents, if married according to the Asoora, or other two forms, the heirs to the woman's property, as expounded above, are thus pointed out by *Vrihaspati*—*

The mother's sister.
The maternal uncle's wife.
The paternal uncle's wife.

* In the translation of *Jim. Vahana*, the maternal uncle is put for his wife, and the paternal uncle's wife is not noticed. The present version will be found in the *Digest* 3, 618, except that his son is there explained the son's son.

The father's sister.
The mother-in-law.
The wife of the elder brother are pronounced similar to mothers.

If they leave no son born in lawful wedlock, nor daughter's son, nor his son, then

The sister's son and the rest shall take their property. Here must be understood, "on failure both of the daughter and also of her daughter," because only on failure of them does the right of inheritance pertain to the son born in wedlock, or to the daughter's son.

The son in that case inherits presents from kindred.—In respect of property given by the kindred (Bundhu) at an Asoora marriage, or the like, *Katyayana* says, "That which has been given to her by her kindred, goes, on failure of kindred, to her son.*

And the brother gets the perquisite.—But on the subject of the perquisite *Goutama* holds, "The sister's perquisite belongs to the uterine brothers after the death of the mother."

Gifts to be restored to the bridegroom when the bride dies before marriage, deducting charges.—But what *Sankha* says, "The lover may take back his nuptial present on the death of his betrothed mistress," must be understood of one dying previous to the celebration of the marriage. Here it is further remarked by *Yajnavalchya*, "If she die after troth plighted, let the bridegroom take back the gifts which he had presented, paying, however, the charges on both sides." The meaning is, that the husband may take back, if his bride is dead, what remains of the perquisite previously given, after calculating the expenses incurred by himself and by her father.

Presents by the maternal kindred belong to the brothers of the deceased damsel.—*Baudhayana* records a distinction on some points: "The wealth of a deceased damsel, let the uterine brothers themselves take. On failure of them, it shall belong to the mother, or if she be dead, to the father. Those skilled in the ancient law have declared that this relates to ornaments or the like presented by the maternal grandfather and the rest, at the time of betrothal to a girl, who afterwards dies before completion of the marriage."

Mithila school—Succession to a woman's separate property—How a woman's property is to be divided.—*Menu* says, "On the death of a mother, let all the uterine brothers of the same father and mother, and (if unmarried) the uterine sisters, divide the maternal estate in equal shares. It is fit that to the daughters of these daughters something should be given from the estate of their maternal grandmother, on the ground of natural affection."

Who receive a woman's separate property.—*Goutama* says that a woman's property goes to her daughters, unmarried and unprovided for.

"Unprovided" indicates misfortune, such as the want of a son,

* *Jim. Vahana*, 6 *Dig.* 593, 615, it is husband instead of son.

husband, or wealth. This opinion is held in the *Ratnakara*, and by some other writers.

The daughter shall receive a share from the maternal estate.—Even if the daughter, as above described, be destitute of a son, she shall receive a share from the maternal estate like the sons.

The unmarried daughter inherits the property given to the mother on her marriage.—*Menu* says, "Property given to the mother on her marriage (*Yautaka*) is the portion of her unmarried daughter."

"Yautaka" means the property received at the time of marriage from parents, and such like. *Nuptial gifts.*—*Vasishta* says, "Let the females share the nuptial gifts (*parinayya*) of their mother." "A nuptial gift (*parinayya*) that is, furniture, such as a mirror, combs, and so forth," *Chintamani*.

Who receives the residue of the mother's property after payment of the debts?—"Let the daughters divide the mother's effects remaining over and above the debts. On failure of such the (male) issue, that is, the sons (in other words), their brothers and their (daughters') sons, shall inherit, according to *Menu*."

Where the rule is applicable.—The foregoing rule refers to the property received by the woman at the time of her marriage in the form denominated Brahma, and her (nuptial gifts; that is) furniture, combs, and so forth.

Who succeed on failure of daughters.—*Katyayana* says, "But on failure of daughters the inheritance belongs to the son. That which has been given to her by her kindred goes, on failure of kindred, to her husband."

Married sisters share with kinsmen.—Married sisters shall share with kinsmen. This law concerning the separate property of "women is ordained in the case of partition."

On failure of daughters, and so forth.—The meaning of this is, that the mother's estate, which consists in her furniture, nuptial gifts, as well as the gifts of parents, goes to her son, provided there be no daughters.

The property, except the above-mentioned articles, goes to the son and daughter after the death of the owner. This has been ordained before, *Chintamani*.

Married sister shall receive something from the estate given to her by her kindred.—What is given by any one, except the father, goes to both the brother and sister; but the latter, if unmarried, becomes an equal sharer. The sisters, if married, shall receive something from the estate. This is the signification of the text regarding married sisters.

Explanation.—*On failure of kindred*, that is, in default of daughter's son, and the like, the woman's property devolves on her husband, *Chintamani*.

The property of a woman married according to certain cere-

monies shall go to her husband on failure of issue—When her property goes to her parents.—*Menu* says, "It is admitted that the property of a woman married according to any of the ceremonies called Brahma, Daiva, Arsha, Gandharva, and Prajapatya, shall go to her husband if she die without issue. But her wealth given to her on her marriage in the form called Asoora, or either of the other two (Rakshasa and Paishacha) is ordained, on her death without issue, to become the property of her mother and father." *Goutama* says, "The sister's fee belongs to the uterine brothers; after them it goes to the mother, and then to the father." Some say that it goes to him before her.

Where this text applies.—This text alludes to property received at the time of marriage (in the form) called *Asoora*, and the other two, *Chintamani.*

Who shall take the wealth of a deceased damsel.—*Baudayana* says, "The wealth of a deceased damsel, let the uterine brothers themselves take; on failure of them, it shall belong to the mother; or, if she be dead, to the father."

Appended to the *Vivada Chintamani*, following the preface, is the annexed summary:—

Order of succession to the peculiar property of women—Stridhana, how far heritable.—Any wealth, movable or immovable, which women receive or inherit, is their stridhana, that is, peculiar property, which they have the power to give away, sell, or dispose of at their pleasure. But they have no right to dispose of the immovable property from their husbands or other relations.

Who may inherit stridhana.—According to the *Mitac.*, and other works, the son of a woman cannot inherit her peculiar property during the lifetime of her *daughter*. But according to the *Vivada Ratnakara*, her daughter and son have an equal right to her whole property, excepting nuptial gifts (*parinayya*), *Yautaka*, &c., received from the father.

Daughters' daughters represent their mothers.—In the case of the succession of daughters' daughters, their shares shall be determined according to the number of mothers; in other words, if a daughter leave one daughter, and a second two, the grandmother's property shall be divided into two parts, according to the number of the mothers. They who are not married have precedence over those who are.

The unmarried exclude the married.—To the property of a woman, if married, according to the forms called Brahma, &c., in default of her sons and grandsons, her husband, and in his default, his sapinda (kinsmen) have right; but if married according to the forms called Asoora, &c., her mother and father, and in their default, her sapinda (kinsmen).

Co-wife's children.—According to the *Madana Parijata*, a co-wife's daughter, or daughter's son, is entitled to the wealth of a woman who dies leaving no children.

Sister's son, &c.—In the *Vivada Ratnakara* mention is made of the right of the sister's son, husband's sister's son, &c.

Heirs of the separate property of the deceased proprietress.—

	Order of Succession.
Unmarried daughter,	1
Barren widowed daughter,	2
Married daughter,	3
Daughter's daughter,	4
Daughter's son,	5
Son,	6
Grandson,	7
Co-wife's son (or stepmother's),	*nil.*
Co-wife's daughter,	*nil.*
„ grandson,	*nil.*
„ daughter's son,	*nil.*
„ great-grandson,	*nil.*
Husband,	*
Husband's sapinda,	*
„ sister's son,	*nil.*
Father,	*
Mother,	*
Mother's sapinda,	*
Brother,	*nil.*
Brother's son, &c.,	*nil.*
If she die unmarried her heirs are—	
Uterine brother,	1
Mother,	2
Father,	3

—*Chintamani, ib.*

CHAPTER IX.

INHERITANCE OR SUCCESSION.

SECTION I.—*Introductory Remarks.*

The law of inheritance complicated—Founded on consent rather than reason—Difficult to reduce rules to general principles—Comparison between English and Hindu law favourable to latter—Hindus are a patriarchal people—Co-proprietors—Line of descent—Meaning of heritage—Wealth not reunited—Right of the natural family to inherit property acquired by adoption—When adopted son dies without issue—Whether a mother succeeding to estate of her son, takes by way of inheritance—Death opens up the inheritance—Natural death—Presumption of death—Civil death—Loss of caste—Three classes of heirs—Limit of Sapindas—They extend to the sixth in descent—Limit of Samonadacas—Bundhus.

The law of inheritance complicated.—In all codes of law in all countries, the law of inheritance forms a most important branch of jurisprudence, and at the same time the most complicated and intricate. The real property law of all European states is complex and complicated in the extreme. It will not be matter of surprise, then, to find that the Hindu law of inheritance is equally so; nevertheless, compared with other codes, it certainly has the advantage in point of simplicity.

Founded on consent rather than reason.—This is accounted for on the principle that that law is founded more upon consent than on reason.

The rule that a son succeeds to the property of his parent is a natural and almost an universal law, yet nothing would be more difficult than to support this proposition by a process of reasoning. It is therefore founded more upon consent, and has consequently been modified by the customs of different nations. Hence we find one nation basing the rights of inheritance upon those of primogeniture, another dividing the inheritance, some equally, others unequally, amongst the male and female issue; others again amongst the male issue equally, to the exclusion of the females; and in

Malabar and Canara we find the females inheriting to the exclusion of the males. Some nations acknowledge succession by right of representation, and the right to inherit in the order of proximity. The diversity upon this subject that prevails amongst different nations is still greater when we come to deal with collateral succession, and the arbitrary character of the rules are still more obvious.

Difficult to reduce rules to general principles.—It is impossible to reduce the canons of inheritance which are recognised as the law of any country to any general or leading principle without assuming some maxim not necessarily or naturally connected with such canons.

For those whose duties require them to understand the rules and maxims of the Hindu law of inheritance, close study and application are necessary, for a knowledge of this subject cannot be attained by a hasty reference to authorities when occasion arises.

Comparison between English and Hindu law favourable to latter.—On a comparison between the English and Hindu codes, the latter in point of simplicity will be found to possess the advantage. It is true it may be difficult at times to distinguish what the latter commands from what it commends, or to reconcile the conflicting doctrines of the different schools, or the discordant reasonings of commentators, or the varied opinions of pundits, so as to gather from them what the law upon any given branch of the subject really is. *Sir Thomas Strange* encourages the English student in his investigations by the assurance, "that in pursuing them he is relieved from much of the toil inherent in the study of the correspondent branch under his own law, as arising with reference to real property, from the division of inheritances into different kinds, and the distinctions of estates as regarding the quantity of interest taken in them with the doctrine of estates in expectancy, the whole of which together has in progress of centuries given rise to a body of learning, in parts so nice and abstruse, and upon the whole so various and intricate, as to have occasioned often despair in the study of it, a branch of learning, in fact, to be acquired and retained only by the most severe study and uninterrupted practice."

Hindus are a patriarchal people.—It must not be forgotten that the Hindus are a patriarchal people, several families living together as one, connected in blood and united in interests, with various dependents, all entitled to provision out of the aggregate fund or common stock, but subject always to separation in the Southern schools, as well as to the exclusion of any one or more from participation in the inheritance for causes hereafter explained.

Co-proprietors.—This unity of interests constitutes amongst such families what is termed co-parcenery, but for which we would substitute co-proprietorship, as conveying the more accurate relation of the parties composing an undivided family. *See* Index, "Co-parcenery," "Joint-tenancy."

Co-parcenery, with its incident of survivorship, differing in this particular from co-parcenery with us, and resembling rather joint-tenancy.* So that on the death of a Hindu parcener the succession to his rights (with the exception of property separately acquired by him) vests in the other remaining members,—his sons, if he have any, representing him as to his undivided rights, while the females of his family continue to depend upon the common fund till a partition take place, which may never happen, or their marriage.

Line of descent.—It will be seen in the course of this chapter, that the Hindu law of inheritance comprehends the deceased's family and his near relations—viz., his issue, male and female; his widow, who takes immediately in default of sons—a term which includes grandsons and great-grandsons. On exhaustion of this line of *descent*, the succession *ascends* to his parents, brothers, nephews, and grand-nephews, this line continuing upwards to the grandfather and great-grandfather, the grandmother and great-grandmother, the latter being given precedence by those who have preferred the mother to the father. The succession then runs downwards to their respective issue, including daughters' sons, but not daughters, the whole being preferred to the half blood; then follow the more remote kindred whom we shall presently enumerate.

In proportion as the claimant becomes remote, the particulars vary with different schools and authors presently pointed out.

In default of natural kin, the series of heirs in all the classes, except that of Brahmins, closes with the preceptor of the deceased, his pupil, his priest hired to perform sacrifices, or his fellow student, each in his order, see *post;* and failing all these, the lawful heirs of the *Shetrya*, *Vysya*, and *Sudra*, who are learned and virtuous Brahmins, resident in the same town or village with the deceased, *Jim. Vahana.*

If an estate should vest by succession in a Brahmin—as he, being such, cannot perform obsequies for one of an inferior caste—the duty may be discharged by substitution of a qualified person, equal in class with the deceased. In all cases where the heir is under disabilities, he must take the same course, paying the person employed for his services. The king, too, where he takes by escheat, must cause obsequies to be performed for the deceased, *Vishnu Purana.*

The Hindus give the agnate succession the preference, the succession of females being deemed exceptions. But see Malabar and Canarese law, *post.*

* It really resembles tenancy in common more than joint-tenancy, there being unity of interest, which may be unequal; unity of time in creating the right, which may be different; but in all cases unity of possession.

Females cannot on account of their sex perform obsequies. They do not, therefore, confer any benefit, and are generally disqualified from inheriting. From this rule there are only four exceptions for special reasons, viz., the widow, the daughter, the mother, the grandmother. According to the Benares and Mithila schools, the females above mentioned inherit only when the family is divided. In an undivided family females are not admitted as heirs, *Elberling*, unless on exhaustion of male undivided members, *Stra. Man.*, except in Malabar and Canara.

There are two modes of devolution of property:—

1. From a sole separate owner.
2. From a female.

Property of a united owner cannot be considered as devolving upon the rest, they being joint proprietors by birth. In the second class the property will, in part, be affected by the rights of collateral sharers.

But even in undivided families, a widow takes the self-acquired property of her husband.

No daughter can claim until after a surviving widow.

Meaning of heritage.—In Hindu law, "Heritage, Daya," signifies that wealth which becomes the property of another solely by reason of relation to the owner, *Mitac.*

Solely here excludes any other cause, such as purchase, or the like; and "relation," or the relative condition of parent and offspring, must be understood of that other person, a son or kinsman, with reference to the owner of the wealth, *Balam Bhatta.*

Wealth which becomes the property of another (as a son, or other person bearing relation), in right of the relation of offspring and parent, or the like, which he bears to his father or other relative who is owner of that wealth, is signified by the term "heritage," *Subodhini.*

Wealth includes in Hindu law personal as well as real property, movable as well as immovable property, which is again divided into property ancestral and self-acquired, and again into joint and separate. The distinction in our law between real and personal property does not exist amongst the Hindus. Both species with them descend to the legal heirs. Their law of inheritance includes what with us forms the law of administration. Their law comprehends every possible claimant on the property of a person deceased, as well as any description of property of which, during his life, he was seised or possessed.

Wealth not re-united.—Wealth not re-united, nor put back again into a common stock, and still admitting of partition, is heritage. By not re-united, I mean to exclude wealth never before joint, and now first united for the purposes of gain, or the like; because the term, partition of heritage, does not apply to the dividing of [wealth] thrown together by merchants, *Mayukha.*

In like manner we must also exclude re-united property, in the sense in which that term will hereafter be defined, even as we find in the *Smriti Sangraha:* "That which is received through a father, and that received through a mother, is described by the term heritage;" and in the *Nighantu*, it is said the learned define heritage to be wealth of a father which admits of partition. The word "father" is merely put to denote relations in general, as a part for the whole, *Mayukha*.

Right of the natural family to inherit property acquired by adoption.—We may remark here that the natural family have no right to succeed to property on the death of an adopted son, which the latter has acquired by reason of his adoption. A member of a Hindoo family cannot as such inherit the property of one taken out of that family by adoption. The severance of a person adopted from his natural family is so complete, that no mutual rights as to succession to property can arise between them, *Sri Nevasa Ayyangar* v. *Kuppanyyangar ; Rayan, Krishnamachariyar* v. *Kuppanayyangar*, 1 *Mad. H. C. R.* 180; affirming *S. A.* No. 1 of 1859; *M. S. D.* 1859, p. 81.

When an adopted son dies without issue.—When an adopted son dies without issue, property which he has inherited from his adopted father goes to the natural heirs of the latter, *M. S. A.* No. 71 of 1858, *M. S. D.* 1859, p. 265.

Whether a mother succeeding to estate of her son takes by way of inheritance.—In the case of a widow, all the property falls strictly under the head of inheritance, so says the *Mitac.* But where widows succeed to their husbands' property in default of sons, the course of decision in the Madras courts has ruled that she only possesses a life-interest, and that after her death the property devolves upon her husband's heirs. If we are to consider the *Mitac* as an authority, we may readily imagine various other cases where a woman may inherit, and the question may be fairly raised, whether property inherited from other than a husband should not be classed in schools following the doctrine of the *Mitac*, under the head of *stridhana?* This has been doubted by the High Court of Madras in *Bachiraja* v. *Venkatappadu*, 2 *Mad. H. C. R.* 402, in an elaborate judgment, wherein the question was considered whether a mother succeeding as heir to her son took the estate by way of inheritance, and whether, having so inherited, the property became her *stridhana*. The Court held that the estate taken by the mother was merely a life-estate, and that she had no power of alienation.

Death opens up the inheritance.—The devolution of property arises either on natural or civil death; save in Bengal, the son is not a co-heir with his father, and inherits in the strictest sense of the word after the parent's death, *Narada*, 1 *ib.* 276. Among the Hindus no new right accrues to the heir on the death of the father, for male issue from the very moment of birth are co-proprietors with the father, as regards ancestral property, on whose death only a larger development of share arises. If a father has four sons, by virtue of the vested right in the issue, any one of them may bring a suit for partition, in which case he would receive one-fifth of the ancestral property as his individual share; whereas, if the partition took place upon the death of the father, he would get one-fourth of that property.

Natural death.—Natural death consists of two classes—viz., 1. known; 2. presumed.

The instances where natural death is known are so familiar as to require no comment here.

Presumption of death.—Death may be presumed when the proprietor has been absent without tidings for a long period, or where he has voluntarily retired from the world by joining a religious community.

The sages consider that long absence is equivalent to death. The law has therefore assigned various periods of absence, varying from twelve years upwards, according to the age of the person at the time of his departure, within which, if he is not heard of, the heir may take possession, keeping certain fasts, then burning an image of his ancestor made of *cusa*, and performing for him his funeral rites, *Jim. Vahana.* In this case, where the heir is residing in a distant country, the inheritance is kept open to the seventh in descent from the person deceased, which is an extension of the rule limiting the right to the fourth in descent, *Jim. Vahana, Vrihaspati.*

The English law limits the period of absence to seven years. The Hindu law varies the period according to the age of the absentee, twenty years for one between thirty and thirty-five; fifteen if between forty and forty-five, and twelve for one between sixty and sixty-five. *Macnaghten* says, "After twelve years' absence death is presumed. In the English law the principle seems to be that a man who has any interest in the property would take care that his existence was made known, while with the Hindoos he has the benefit of being assumed to be alive during the ordinary duration of life."

Civil death.—Civil death takes place when one has voluntarily retired from the world by joining a religious community. Crime, too, unexpiated, *Sir Thomas Strange* says, opens up the inheritance to the heirs, and "Disqualification for inheritance" and "Partition." "Unexpiated," is presumed to mean so long as the sentence or punishment shall not have been completed.*

Loss of caste.—Formerly loss of, or degradation from, caste operated as a deprivation of the right of inheritance. But it has now no effect as a cause of civil death in matters of property. See Act xxi. of 1850, *Abraham* v. *Abraham, Moore's In. Ap.* 227. It is not necessary that the heir should have been actually born when the

* It is doubtful whether in the present day the doctrine would be maintained.

inheritance falls in. It suffices if he has been begotten and afterwards born alive. When born with vitality, it is of no moment how soon after he may die ; the right of inheritance is acquired, and the inheritance devolves on the heirs of the child, *Elberling.*

Three classes of heirs.—There are three classes of heirs—viz., 1. *Sapindas*, a term derived from *Pinda*, the funeral rice-ball or cake, and those who participate in offering it to the deceased are called Sapindas. These also offer oblations of water. 2. *Samonodacas*, a term derived from *Oodaca*, water, and who offer water only, being of a remoter class of relationship with the deceased, and consequently excluded from offering rice-balls unless on failure of the sapindas. 3. *Bundhus*, a term which signifies cognate kindred lying beyond the *Samonodacas*, *Mitac.* These as such make no offerings unless on failure of the *Sapindas* and *Samonodacas*, when they make offering of the *Pinda*, as do the *Samonodacas* on failure of *Sapindas*, *Stra. Man.*

The sapindas are of two grades—viz., the nearer and the remoter, the former of whom offer and partake of the rice-ball entire, the latter, who offer and partake of merely the wipings of the hands. The *Samonodacas* also are divided into two grades, but there is no distinction between them as to the offerings they make, *Menuvurtha Mooktavalee or Menu.*

Limit of Sapindas.—The nearer sapindas are the three in direct descent from the person to be traced from, and the three in ascent above him and their descendants to the second degree, *Smriti Chandrika ;* also the wife, daughters, daughters' sons, mother, and paternal grandmother, *Smriti Mooktha Palum.* The limit is the grandson of the great-grandfather. The rest are the remoter sapindas.

The Sapinda extends to the sixth in descent.—They extend to the sixth male in direct descent from the person to be traced from, and the sixth male in direct ascent, and the direct male descendants of these latter to the sixth degree. The brothers and their male descendants to the fifth degree come in thus as the descendants of the father, or the first in direct ascent. The wife, daughters, and daughters' sons, the mother, and the paternal grandmother are also embraced among the Sapindas, *Saraswatee Valasa ; Varada Rajeyum ; Smriti Mooktha Palum.* The female line extends no further. The remotest embraced in the line of Sapindas is the four times great-grandson of the four times great-grandfather.

Limit of Samonodacas—Extends to the sixth male below and the sixth above the male *Sapindas*, and the direct male descendants of the latter six to the sixth degree, *Mitac. ; Smriti Chandrika ; Smriti Mooktah Palum.*

Mr Strange, in his *Manual*, § 313, says the collaterals in the above list are brought in on the principle that they have some common ancestor with the person to be traced from, to whom they, as well as he, offer oblations, this constituting participation in offering.

Bundhus.—The *Bundhus* are of three kinds—viz., such as are in parallel grade to the individual himself, who are the sons of his own father's sister, the sons of his own mother's sister, the sons of his aunt, and the sons of his mother's maternal uncle must be considered as his own cognate kindred; such as are parallel to his father, who are the sons of his father's paternal aunt, the sons of his father's maternal aunt, and the sons of his father's maternal uncle, must be deemed his father's cognate kindred; and such as are parallel to his mother, who are the sons of his mother's paternal aunt, the sons of her maternal aunt, and the sons of her maternal uncles, *Mitac.*

The following enumeration of heirs shows the order in which each class of relations takes direct from the person to be traced from. It is not an order according to which each succeeds to the other. On the property coming to an individual, the descent would commence afresh in his line, and will fall upon his own immediate heirs.

For example, should the inheritance devolve upon a brother's son, in default of nearer relatives, his heir would not be the paternal grandmother of the person from whom the property came. It would descend primarily to the new inheritor's male issue, and so onwards; and should it devolve on a female relative—for instance, on a daughter—it would go on from her according to the rule of descent in the female line to be hereafter explained.

Madras—

Sons.
Sons' sons.
Sons' grandsons.
Widow.
Daughters.
Daughters' sons.
Mother.
Father.
Brothers.
Brothers' sons.
Paternal grandmother.
Paternal grandfather.
Paternal grandfather's sons (*i.e.*, the uncles).
Paternal grandfather's sons' sons (*i.e.*, the cousins).
Paternal great-grandfather.
His sons.
And sons' sons.

After those, the remoter Sapindas come in, each in their order, and then the Samonodacas in their order, and, lastly, the Bundhus in theirs.

In Bengal, in default of brother's grandsons, the sister's son inherits, but not in the provinces which follow the *Mitac.*

In *Elberling's Treatise on Inheritance* it is laid down that sons of different sisters take according to the number born, as well as unborn, and even unbegotten at the time of their uncle's death.

Elberling is a Bengal authority, but discusses the authorities of the Benares school as well. He says also that, according to the schools of Benares and Mithila, they, sisters' sons, are excluded, as they belong to a different family. See *post.*

For the order of succession in Bengal school, see *post.*

For that of Bombay, see *post.*

For that of the Mithila school, see *post.*

For that of Malabar and Canarese schools, see *post.*

In the case of a sole separate owner, no question of collateral heirs can arise until the lineal descendants are first exhausted.

In the case of an undivided owner being a co-heir, his property will in part be affected by the rights of collateral sharers.

The direct descent does not in general go beyond the putthar, except where one of them is absent without tidings, and then his lineal descendants to the sixth degree may claim the inheritance.

Section II.

Male issue—In default of—Adopted son—Law applicable to both alike—Issue includes sons, grandsons, and great-grandsons—Great-great-grandsons—When death presumed from absence—Performance of obsequial rites—Keystone to the law of inheritance—The grandson—Benefit to the soul of the ancestor is not the only principle—The mere act of solemnising exequial rights gives no title to inheritance—By birth co-proprietor with his father—Heirs presumptive and apparent—Several wives—Sons born after partition—Illegitimate children—Sons of Englishman by Brahmin woman separated from husband—Marriage with bastard's daughter—Bastard's right to maintenance—Sudra bastard's right to inheritance—Rebuttability of presumption of legitimacy when opportunity for sexual intercourse—Right of a son by a female slave—Illegitimate son of a Shetriya by a Sudra—Entitled to maintenance—Minor—Undivided family—Primogeniture—Public and private property of a rajah—Evidence of descent of zemindar's estate—Self-acquired property.

Male issue.—The first in order of Hindu heirs is a man's legitimate male issue. The legitimate son is one procreated on a lawfully wedded wife, *Mitac.*

In default of—adopted son—Law applicable to both alike.—In default of such issue, a legally adopted son becomes such heir. *See* Adoption. As between issue of the body and an adopted son, the

Hindu law of inheritance makes no difference. The adopted son, however, takes the entire estate only in the event of the failure of a legitimate son, and as the adopted is a substitute for such son, he succeeds to his adopted father's estate exactly as if he were a legitimate son, the law of inheritance being equally applicable to both.

Where the sons may have divided from their father, and received their portions, they nevertheless succeed to their father's remaining property as first in descent.

Issue includes sons, grandsons, and great-grandsons.—In Hindu law the term "issue" includes not only all the sons a man leaves behind him, but sons' sons also, or sons of the latter, or great-grandsons, *i.e.*, the sons, the grandsons, and great-grandsons. The whole have by the Hindu law ever constituted but one heir, so that if the son have died in the lifetime of his father, leaving a son, and that son also dies leaving one, and then the great-grandfather dies, the great-grandson succeeds as his grandfather would have done had he survived; and according to *Vyjayante*, a commentary on *Vishnu*, the right of representation in all these cases vests likewise in the widow; but according to other authorities she is only entitled to maintenance, to be supplied her by her father-in-law, and on his death by his heir. But here, as far as the fourth in descent, the right of lineal representation stops, unless there has been an absence in a distant country, when it extends beyond the fourth, as far as the seventh degree, *Vrihaspati*.

Great-great-grandsons.—So that supposing the intermediate descendants to have failed, and a son of the great-grandson to survive at the death of the proprietor, he would not inherit, save as a mere remote sapinda; but the widow of the deceased, the next in the series, would succeed in preference, though in the event of the great-grandson surviving his ancestor, and then dying, the property so inherited by him would devolve upon his son, in consequence of its having vested in the father.

The grandsons and great-grandsons inherit *per stirpes*.

When death presumed from absence.—Where the death of the owner is presumed from absence, he being unheard of, and his descendants also are absent and unheard of, any of them, up to the sixth from him, on appearing, will be entitled to inherit as of the male issue, taking precedence of the widow, 1 *Stra. H. L.*, 125. The inheritance is kept open to the remotest *sapinda* in this branch, on the presumption that an intermediate descendant may have survived to transmit it to him, *Stra. Man.*, § 324. See *ante*, pp. 75, 226.

Performance of obsequial rites—Keystone to the law of inheritance.—The keystone of the whole Hindu law of inheritance is the birth of a son, in which event the father is delivered from Put, and if he have no son he is required to adopt one whose adoption effects the same deliverance. The table of descent is clearly laid down in the various schools of law. No one has a right to succeed or perform the funeral rites, except a person enumerated therein, and in the order established. It is the position that he occupies in the table that gives the right to inheritance, which is rather subject to the duty of performing the funeral ceremonies of the deceased.

The series of heirs is naturally adjusted by the amount or degree of benefit which each is supposed to confer upon the deceased. The son is preferred because he presents the greatest number of beneficial offerings, and he saves his parent from Put, *Jim. Vahana.*

The grandson.—The same degree of efficacy is attributed in default of their respective fathers to the grandson and great-grandson, which reaches the fourth in descent, but not beyond ; for *Menu* says, "But the fifth has no concern with the gift of the funeral cake."

Accordingly some benefits are derived from the great-grandson as well as from the son. The term "son," in the texts of *Menu, Vishnu, Yajnavalchya,* &c., extends to the grandson, for as far as that degree descendants equally confer benefits by presenting oblations of food in the prescribed form in monthly obsequies, *Jim. Vahana ;* and this accounts for representation stopping with the great grandson.

In *Jim. Vahana* it is said, accordingly, Since inheritance is in right of benefits conferred, and the order of inheritance is regulated by the degree of benefit, *Srikrishna,* the equal right of the son, the son's son, and the grandson, is proper for their equal pretensions, are declared in the text. By a son a man conquers worlds, &c., *Jim. Vahana,* and in other similar passages, where it is said, upon this principle, ministering equally to the peace of their departed ancestor, if he leave a son, and the son of a son, and the son's son of a third son, they take equal shares of his estate, because they confer the benefit equally, *Jim. Vahana.*

Benefit to the soul of the ancestor is not the only principle.—This benefit to the soul of the ancestor, although it is the general, is not the sole and universal principle ; payment of the ancestor's debts, as well as nearness of kin, or proximity by birth, also form considerations in the Hindoo law of inheritance.

And although the table of inheritance, on failure of the great-grandson, opens up the succession to the widow, yet the property after her death reverts to the lineal kindred of the husband ; at all events, as far as the seventh person, or the sixth degree of ascent or descent, *Menu, Jim. Vahana.*

The right to inherit is therefore connected with the power to benefit, so that the title of a son lawfully begotten on a wedded wife is preferred before any other heir, which accounts for the anxiety of a Hindu for male issue, or his substitute by adoption.

The mere act of solemnising exequial rites gives no title to inheritance.—But it is not to be concluded, therefore, that the rights of inheritance and performance of obsequies go together, otherwise it might be assumed that the mere act of solemnising the funeral rites would give a title to the succession which would create a scramble for priority amongst conflicting claims. All the rule establishes is, that the person being the nearest of kin, the most competent, is bound to the due performance of exequial rites for the benefit of the deceased to whose property he has succeeded. The performance of funeral rites by an individual, not in propinquity of relationship to the deceased to qualify him for the act, will not confer on him the right to inherit, for such performance of funeral rites is only evidence of a nearer relationship, and may therefore be always rebutted by other evidence. In a case where a widow died, leaving a daughter and a brother surviving her, and the brother performed the widow's funeral ceremonies, it was held that the daughter was entitled to the estate, *Colebrooke* remarking that the brother's pretensions were founded on passages of Hindu law, purporting that the succession to the estate and the right of performing obsequies go together.

Female relatives, to a very limited extent, may offer funeral oblations. They do so by proxy—it not being permitted to them to recite passages from the Vedas.

By birth Hindu co-proprietor with his father.—By birth every Hindu is a co-proprietor with his father in his ancestral property.

By birth he acquires a vested interest in the property, *Mitac. Suboudhini.* But the extent of that interest is a question discussed in the Hindu books, and upon which differences of opinion exist in the various schools.

In Bengal inheritance is defeasible during the life of the father by gift or other alienation, including will, requiring the concurrence of the sons only in the instance of land inherited, though valid without it.

In Benares and Southern India his power of alienation was more limited. The power of alienation may be anticipated by partition, without the consent of the father, if warranted by law, or voluntarily on his part, according to the doctrine of all the schools.

Sir Thomas Strange says, This power, however, may be limited by adverse possession in a stranger for twenty years, citing *Yajnavalchya, Vyasa and Brihaspati.* But *Mr Ellis* denies this to be the law of Southern India. He says *Vignyanswara* (*Mitacshara*), after a long argument, ruled that it is the perishable produce only of land that cannot be recovered after the expiration of twenty years, and of other property after ten years, such land or other property having been enjoyed to the exclusion of the owner by his default or in his view. With regard to land, he holds that if legal acquisition can be disproved, even after the expiration of a hundred years (considered as the measure of the life of man), ownership is not established by possession, and he accordingly declares that "even beyond the period of memory, if there exist a current tradition of the illegality of the acquisition, the enjoyment is not valid." And it is observable that, to render it so in any case, it must have been in view of the owner. In fact, according to the original and correct doctrine of the Hindu law, enjoyment or possession can never be cause of ownership; it is a presumption of it only; but if the want of original title can be shown, the possessing holder may at any time be divested of the property. This applies not only to land but to property of every description. The Hindu canon is, "Acquisition must be shown;" all else is exception. *Menu* says, "He who enjoys without ownership for many hundred of years, the lord of the earth shall inflict on that criminal the punishment ordained for thieves."

Of course these rules are now subject to the law of limitation, Act xiv. of 1859. See last Chapter.

Heirs presumptive and apparent.—The Hindu law recognises the distinction of heirs known in English law as apparent and presumptive. With the Hindus they are styled Heritages not liable to obstruction, and liable to obstruction. The former are called *Apratibandha*, answering with us to the heir-apparent, whose right, if he outlive his ancestor, is indefeasible. The latter is called *Sapratibandha*, those remoter heirs, as brothers, uncles, &c., whose right is liable to obstruction by the intermediate birth of nearer ones, so that their title is not apparent but presumptive only.

Several wives.—Sons equal in number by each inherit by representation according to their mothers.

Sons born after partition.—Where sons are born after the partition, they succeed to the father's share to the exclusion of the divided sons; so if there be no after-born son the divided sons succeed as heirs to their father's share, provided their father's wife be not living.

All sons get equal shares, and not according to the mother's. But in some parts the mothers represent equal shares, and their sons get equal parts of these shares.*

Illegitimate Children.—By the Hindu law illegitimate children do not inherit unless in the Sudra class, see *Chuoturya Run Murdun Syn* v. *Sahub Purhulal Syn*, 7 *Moore's In. Ap.* 18. They are, however, a charge upon the inheritance, *Menu*, and are entitled to maintenance. Even among Sudras, if there are illegitimate sons, daughters, or sons of daughters, they get only half of what they would have got had they been legitimate, the rest being shared among the legitimate children.

In No. 124 of 1861, a question arose whether the grandson of a divided uncle took along with, or in preference to an illegitimate

* Putnibhaga, the term applied to this mode of division, receives no countenance from the High Court of Madras.

son. The decision was that he did neither—the decision giving no further claim on the brother's property. *Sir Thomas Strange* says, In one description of the *Pauner Bhava*, or son of a twice married woman, which occurs still in some instances of the fourth order, illegitimate sons continue to participate with legitimate ones if there be any, and if there be none, nor daughters, nor daughters' sons, they are then not distinguishable in point of inheritance from legitimate ones.

The status and right of the sons of an Englishman by a Brahmin woman living apart from her husband.—When a Brahmin woman residing apart from her husband lived with an Englishman, and had two sons by him, it was held that the sons are Hindus, and that their rights are determined by those of the class of Hindus to which they belong, and that they are to be regarded as *Sudras*, or as a class still lower, and that in the absence of preferable heirs they inherit the property of the mother, and of each other; if not, she is a mere prostitute, and of the cognation or relationship between her and her offspring there exists no doubt whatever, *Myna Bai* v. *Oottaram*, 2 *Mad. H. C. R.* 196.

Marriage with bastard's daughter—Bastard's right to maintenance—Sudra bastard's right to inherit—Rebuttability of presumption of legitimacy where opportunity for sexual intercourse.—The Hindu law, independently of special usage or custom, does not make illegitimacy an absolute disqualification for caste, so as to affect in the relations of life not only the bastard, but also his legitimate children.

The Hindu, unlike the English law, recognises a bastard's relation to his father and family.

By birth, and without any form of legitimation, bastards of the three twice-born classes are now recognised as members of their father's family, and have a right to maintenance.

In the case of Sudras, the law has been, and still is, that bastards succeed their father by right of inheritance.

The presumption of legitimacy where there has been opportunity for sexual intercourse, is not irrebuttable, *Pandaiya Tĕlaver* v. *Puli Tĕlaver*, 1 *Mad. H. C. R.* 478. See "Marriage," p. 23.

Right of a son by a female slave—Illegitimate son of a Shetriya by a Sudra woman.—An illegitimate son of a Shetriya, one of the three regenerate castes, by a Sudra woman cannot, by Hindu law, succeed to the inheritance of his putative father.

Entitled to maintenance.—He is, however, entitled to maintenance out of the estate. It would be otherwise if he were the son of a Sudra, as the illegitimate children of that caste are entitled to succeed to the inheritance of their father, *Chuoturya Run Murdun Syn* v. *Sahud Purhulal Syn*, 7 *Moore's In. Ap.* 18.

Minor.—If the heir be a minor, a guardian should be appointed for him, to whom the care of his property should be committed, until he is of age to take possession himself. See title "Minority." Where sons or their issue are minors, full shares are reserved for them, under the charge of guardians, either specially appointed or assumed as such by the law. In general, minority ceases on completion of the age of sixteen. In any of the three superior classes on his ending his studentship, and returning home from his preceptor, *Menu*, the *Ratnacara*. Zemindars are minors until eighteen, by *Madras Reg.* v. of 1804.

The natural guardians are the father, mother, elder brother, and paternal relatives. Any one of them, however, may be superseded by a decree of a court, and incompetency in any one passes the right of guardianship on to the next. Although we have said a guardian should be appointed, yet it is not necessary that he should be specially appointed as such, for the person entitled to be a guardian will always be assumed in law to be such. See "Minority."

With regard to the appointment of guardians, see *Mad. Reg.* v. of 1804, and Act ix. of 1861 of the Legislative Council of India.

It will have been seen from the foregoing, that property under the Hindu law descends lineally, and vests in the legitimate male issue before the female. See *Malabar and Canara Law.*

Undivided family.—According to the law of inheritance, all legitimate sons living in a state of union with their father at the time of his death succeed equally to his property.

Primogeniture.—The right of primogeniture was never a great favourite with the Hindus; it, however, formerly prevailed to a certain extent. But with other usages it has been abolished. *Talevar Sing* v. *Pahlwan Sing*, 3 *S. D. A. Rep.* 203. Formerly the first born son was entitled, if he possessed extraordinary merit, bodily, mental, or moral, to the most valuable chattel, or the best room in the best house. The eldest son is the managing member where there are sons by different wives, and one party claimed that the estate should be distributed according to the number of wives, without reference to the number of sons born by each, a distribution technically called *putnibhaga*, averring that such had been the kulachar or immemorial usage of the family; but the court determined that the distribution amongst them should be made not with reference to the mothers, but with reference to the number of sons; being of opinion that although in cases of inheritance the kulachar or family usage has the presumptive force of law, yet to establish kulachar it is necessary that the usage should have been ancient and invariable.

Public and private property of a rajah.—*Semble.* There is a distinction between the public and private property of a Hindu sovereign, as upon his death his private property goes to one set of heirs, and the raj and the public property to the succeeding rajah.

The general rule of the Hindu law of inheritance is partibility. The succession of a single heir, as in the case of a raj, is the exception, *Secretary of State in Council of India* v. *Kamachee Boye Sahaba*, 7 *Moore's In. Ap.* 476.

Evidence of descent of Zemindar's estate to eldest son.—In a suit by a younger brother against the eldest brother for partition of a zemindary estate, it was held that family usage and custom for eight generations for the zemindary estate to descend entire to the eldest son, to the exclusion of the others, was evidence that it was not *divisible* property, *Rawut Urjun Sing* v. *Rawut Ghunsiam Sing*, 5 *Moore's In. Ap.* 169. So family usage for fourteen generations, by which the succession of the raj zemindary of Tirhoot had uniformly descended entire to a single male heir, to the exclusion of the other members of the family, has been upheld, *Baboo Singh* v. *Maharaja Singh*, 6 *Moore's In. Ap.* 164.

The *competency* to benefit the deceased in the solemnisation of exequial rites forms the consideration for the succession, whilst the *order* of succession is regulated by the *degree* of benefit conferred, *Jim. Vahana.* Benefits conferred by the nearest of kin are regarded of more importance than those offered by one more distantly allied.

Self-acquired property.—The self-acquired property of a co-parcener immovable and movable, vests wholly in his male issue as far as the great-grandson. Failing male issue, it goes to his united brothers and their line.

In *Varadiperumal Udaiyan* v. *Ardanari Udaiyan*, 1 *Mad. H. C. R.* 412. *Mr Justice Holloway* says, "I have always understood that in this Presidency, at least, the law was clearly that the im movable property of an undivided member of a Hindu family may go to his surviving co-parceners, whether such property was self-acquired or ancestral. During his life he is entitled to the separate enjoyment of his self-acquired immovable property, with the right, if he have no male issue, to alienate the same. On his death, without male issue, if not previously alienated, it devolves on his co-parceners. But his widow, whether childless or not, has no title to anything but maintenance. The author of *Mitacshara* was clearly of *Daresvara's* opinion, *Mitac.* ch. ii. s. i. § 8. "The rule deduced from the texts that the wife shall take the estate, regards the widow of a separated brother." And it may reasonably be inferred that an author who lays down that a widow inherits when her husband was divided, was also of opinion that she would not inherit when the deceased was undivided."

In the *Sivagunga* case, it was ruled that even where the family was undivided, the widow inherited the self-acquired property of her husband in preference to his male kin, 9 *Moore's In. Ap.* 539.

On failure of male issue the succession is thus enumerated in the

Mitacshara, ch. ii. s. i. § 2. The wife and the daughters also, both parents, brothers* likewise, and their sons.† Gentiles, cognates, a pupil, and fellow student. On failure of the first amongst these, the next in order is indeed heir to one leaving no male issue. This rule extends to all classes and persons, *ib.* ch. ii. s. i. § 3. 1 *Morl. Dig.* 319; 1 *Moore's In. Ap.* 132.

This rule or order of succession extends to all tribes, whether the *Murdhavasikta* and others in the direct series of the classes, or *Suta*, and the rest in the inverse order, and as comprehending the several classes, the sacerdotal and the rest, *Mitac.* ch. ii. s. i. § 4.

SECTION III.

INHERITANCE BY FEMALES.

Heirs differ according to form of marriage—Woman's fee—Betrothed females—Widow—A daughter—Self-acquired property—Right of widow with a power to adopt which has not been exercised by her—The widow of a son cannot claim through her husband if he has died during the life of his father—Whether the widow is entitled to inheritance or merely to maintenance—Several wives—Indivisible and self-acquired property—Grounds of the widow's right of succession—Widow's right to succeed to her husband's ancestral property—The widow's right of succession to self-acquired property of her husband, who was a member of an undivided family—Self-acquired immovable property—Nature of a widow's tenure—In nature of estate tail—Widow's right to accumulations of joint estate—Maintenance—Widow's power over her husband's property—Widow's right in undivided estate—Widow must be chaste—Consequences of infidelity—Abandonment of blameless wife—Wife's special property—Where wife dies without issue—The husband surviving—Son-in-law—Where widow leaves issue on re-marriage—Daughters—Daughter's right after death of sonless widow—Their order of succession—In Bengal—Benares—Bombay—Mithila—Applicable in every possible case—Self-acquired property—Daughter's son—Mithila school—Order of succession—Daughter's grandsons—Daughter's daughters—Succession in descending lines stops with daughter's son—Daughter's daughter—Where one of several daughters who succeeded as maiden dies, leaving sons and sisters—Where one of several daughters who had as married women succeeded dies, leaving sons, sisters, and sister's sons—On failure of daughter's issue estate reverts to father's heirs.

Females inherit only in divided families, *Elberling*, or on exhaustion of male undivided members, *Stra. Man.;* even in an

* Balam Bhatta includes sisters.

† Balam Bhatta includes daughters of sons.

undivided family a widow takes the self-acquired property left by her husband, *Shivagunga* case, 9 *Moore's In. Ap.* 539. No daughter can claim until after any surviving widow.

Property vesting in a female descends first to her daughters, the unmarried having preference over the married, and the unendowed over the endowed, then to her daughter's daughter, daughters' sons; sons; and sons' sons, *Stra. Man.*, *Mitac.;* the distinction also prevailing in favour of those who have or may have sons, *Stra. M.*

That which a widow has derived from her husband on the exhaustion of the male line, goes to his kindred in their order.

Heirs differ according to form of marriage.—That which a woman may have received in gift from her own family returns to the donors, if alive, should her marriage have been of a disapproved species, namely, *Racshasa*, *Asoora*, or *Paishacha*. If the donors are dead it goes to her husband and his kindred.

If the marriage were of the disapproved sort, failing the son's son, the property would go to her mother, afterwards to her father, and after him to his heirs. Should the marriage have been of an approved species, namely, *Brahma*, *Daiva*, *Arsha*, *Prajapatya*, or *Gandharva*, the above gifts go to the husband and his kindred, *Mitac.*, *Smriti Chandrika.*

Macnaghten says stridhun, which has once devolved in succession, is ever after governed by the ordinary rules of inheritance. This is true to a certain extent if the stridhana devolves on a male. But if on a female it continues to be regarded as stridhun, according to the doctrine of the *Mitac.* to which *Macn.* refers in the passage from which the quotation is taken.

Woman's fee.—The woman's fee, or the gratuity given to her on her marriage by the bridegroom for purchase of household utensils, cattle, &c. (*Smriti Chand.* Mayukhum), as an exception, goes to her brothers of the whole blood.

Betrothed females.—Any nuptial presents a female may have received from her intended husband in anticipation of marriage, are returnable to him on her death unmarried, the charges on both sides being first deducted therefrom. The whole brothers shall have the ornaments for the head and other gifts presented to the maiden by her maternal grandfather, or her paternal uncle, or other relations, as well as the property which may have been regularly inherited by her. For *Baudhayana* says, the wealth of the deceased damsel let the uterine brethren themselves take. On failure of them, it shall belong to her mother, or if dead to her father, *Mitac.*

Widow.—In default of sons, grandsons, and great-grandsons, the inheritance descends lineally no farther, and the widow succeeds, her place being assigned her in every enumeration of heirs next after sons, and before daughters. According to the Bengal law, whether her husband has separated, or was living as a member of an undivided family, she takes his property, *Jim. Vahana.* But, according to the other schools, the widow succeeds to her husband's property only where he was separated from his brethren, an undivided brother being held to be the next heir. The widow, however, is in such case entitled to maintenance, *Mitac.*

The author of the *Smriti Chandrika* cites *Brihaspati*, and *Prajapati* as his authorities for the doctrines laid down in chap. xi. respecting a widow's right of succession. *Brihaspati* ordains that the widow of a deceased man who left no male issue, takes his share notwithstanding kinsmen, a father, or uterine brother be present. *Prajapati* referring to the widow, observes, "Having taken his moveable and immovable property, the precious and the base metals, the grains, the liquids, and the clothes that are duly offered at his monthly and half-yearly repasts," see *Mayūkha. Brihaspati* again observes, "Whatever property a man possesses of any kind after division, whether mortgaged or otherwise, the wife shall take after the death of her husband, with the exception of fixed property." What the meaning of the exception "fixed property" is, does not clearly appear, but in accordance with the universally received opinion, the widow of a man dying without male issue, who is separate from his parceners, is entitled to succeed to all her husband's property. The author of the *Smriti Chandrika* observes, "The purport of the text is, whatever is the property of a deceased husband, whether consisting of movables or immovables, whether pledged or otherwise, the widow alone takes where the husband was a divided member of the family." But somewhat inconsistently in the following paragraph says, "in respect to the exception of fixed property." This exception is applicable to a *Patni*, who has not even a daughter, for if it were held to be applicable to any widow generally, the passage would be inconsistent with that of *Prajapati* already cited. No authority is quoted to justify the doctrine, that to entitle a widow to succeed to immovable property she should have a daughter.

According to the doctrine of the *Smriti Chandrika* (translator's summary), which is of great and paramount authority in Southern India, a widow being the mother of daughters, takes her husband's property, both movable and immovable where the family is divided.

A daughter.—The translator omits to notice the absence of authority in his summary. The *Mitac.* very clearly lays down the right to succeed in the widow as being irrespective of the necessity of having daughters; *Vradhanlanee, Vrhad, Vishnu, Katyayana,* and *Brihaspati*, are cited in support of the author's views. These authorities place no such restriction on the widow's right of succession as the author of the *Smriti Chandrika* has done. According to the Bengal law, *Jimuta Vahana* says, a widow succeeds whether her husband was divided from his co-proprietors or not.

The *Vyavahara Mayukha* (Bombay School) agrees with the *Mitac.*, and although he had the text of *Brihaspati* before him, which the author of the *Smriti Chandrika* construes to mean that a widow who succeeds to immovable property should have a daughter, he does not draw this distinction. And it has been held at Bombay, that the widow of a Hindu who died without male issue might give away her husband's property in *krishnarpana*, "grant of lands in propitiation of *krishna*," notwithstanding the existence of a sister's son, provided she herself have no son, or other near heir of her own, whose rights would be affected by such gift of their inheritance to another.

The widow of the deceased husband without male issue is sole heir to his movable and immovable property, as she takes before the daughters.

Self-acquired property.—By the law of inheritance, as prevailing in the southern parts of India, separate acquired estate descends to the widow in default of the male issue of the deceased husband, *Katama Natchiar* v. *Rajah of Shivagunga*, 9 *Moore In. Ap.* 539.

When the estate is in the nature of a principality, impartible and capable of enjoyment by only one member of a family at a time, it descends to the widow in default of male issue, *Katama Natchiar* v. *The Rajah of Shivagunga*, 9 *Moore's In. Ap.* 539, *ib.* See *post*, "Partition."

A Hindu widow, whether childless or not, stands next in the order of succession. Daughters can only succeed on failure of their mothers. If there are two wives, and one dies leaving a daughter, the daughter always inherits after the widow, and would get nothing till the death of the surviving widow, who would take all the property.

Where A. had two wives, B. and C.; and B. predeceased A., leaving three daughters; and C. survived A., and was childless. Held that C. succeeded to A.'s property in preference to the three daughters, *Perammal* v. *Venkatammal*, 1 *Mad. H. C. R.* 223.

The law is the same in Bengal. If a wife shall die in the lifetime of her husband, A., she, the deceased wife, having left a daughter B. If A., the father of B., shall then die, leaving a childless widow, C. and his daughter B. surviving him, C. shall first take the estate, and upon her death it shall go to B.

A Bengalee bequeathed all his property, movable and immovable, to his family idol, and directed that his property should never be divided by his (four) sons, &c., in succession, but that they should enjoy the surplus proceeds only, and in the event of disagreement between the sons and family, directed that after the expenses attending the estate, &c., and maintenance of the family, and whatever nett produce and surplus there might be, should be divided annually among the members of the family. At the date of the will the family were joint in estate, food, and ownership. The accumulations of the income were divided as directed. One of the sons of the testator died, leaving three sons, one of whom also died without issue, leaving a widow. Held, that the direction contained in the will that the property should go in the male line, did not exclude the widow of the grandson of the testator, and that the widow was entitled to a third share of a fourth part of the property, and accumulation without prejudice to her rights as a Hindu widow when the property should be divided, *Sonatum Bysack* v. *Sreemutty Juggutsoonaree Dossee*, 8 *Moore's In. Ap.* 66.

As to the capacity to inherit in Bombay, see *Laroo* v. *Sheo*, 1 *Borr.* 71; *Ichharam Shumbhoodas* v. *Prumanund Baeechund*, 2 *ib.* 471.

Right of widow with a power to adopt which has not been exercised by her.—A childless Hindu in Bengal authorised his widow to adopt a son at his decease; the widow did not exercise that power, and many years after her husband's death brought a suit as widow, claiming his succession in the family estates. Held, that the mere fact of there being authority given her by her husband to adopt a son, did not before her adoption had actually taken place supersede and destroy her personal right as widow to sue, *Ramundoss Mookerjea* v. *Mt. Tarinee*, 7 *Moore's In. Ap.* 169.

The widow of a son cannot claim through her husband if he has died during the lifetime of his father.—A son married and died in the lifetime of his father, the father previously to his death disposed of his property for the support of his daughter, a sister, and the son's widow. The widow of the son claimed it as hers. *Mr Colebrooke* was of opinion that, according to the *Mitacshara*, the daughter would have inherited in preference to the son's widow, though the author of the *Vaijayante*, and a few other writers, hold differently.

A widow whose husband died in the lifetime of his father has no right to claim a share of her father-in-law's estate, nor does there exist any supposed case in which she could inherit or participate in it. To make such relation an equal participator with the wife is very erroneous.

Whether the widow is entitled to inheritance, or merely to maintenance.—According to the Benares and Southern India school, when the family is undivided, the widow is only entitled to maintenance, *Mitac.*

Sir Thos. Strange says, When the husband died before consummation, it has been held that his widow is entitled to maintenance only. But *Mr Strange*, in his *Manual*, says, that it gives her a right of inheritance. *Sir Thomas Strange* cites the case of *Vencataratnam* v. *Vencamamal*, *S. C. Mad.* 1824, for his proposition. But the case can hardly be considered law. *Mr Strange's* opinion is certainly more conformable to equity, for it is but fair if she is to suffer all the disabilities of widowhood she should also enjoy the advantages. Consummation, according to Hindu law, is a non-essential of marriage, and therefore, whether consummation has taken place or not, her rights should not be affected in the one case any more than in the other.

Several wives.—It has been held that where there is a plurality of wives, and no sons by any, the one first married being the one who is to be considered as having been married, from a sense of duty succeeds, to the exclusion of the others, each of whom takes after her in succession in her order of marriage.

Mr Justice Arnould, in the case of the goods of *Dadoo Mania, Ind. Jur.* 25th Oct. 1862, p. 59, said, In Bengal the two wives take the whole estates for life, and on the death of one the whole survives to the other, upon whose death it goes to the collateral heirs of the husband. In Madras it has been held that the eldest widow succeeds, the other widows being entitled during her life to maintenance only, the second widow succeeding on the death of the first. But see *Strange's Man.*, where the author lays it down that in Southern India the wives are viewed as on an equality, and inherit equally, and considers the following passage from the *Mitacshara*, ch. ii. s. i. § 5 (omitted in *Colebrooke's Translation*), which the editor owes to *Vakil Srinivasacharay.* "The singular number," "wife," signifies the kind; hence if there are two widows, one the mother of daughters, and the other childless, the former alone takes the immovable estate, and the movable property is equally divided amongst them.*

When there are several widows, those with issue, daughters, take the immovable estate in equal proportions, to the exclusion of those without issue. The personal property all share alike, 1 *Saraswatee, Velasa.*

We are not aware of any decision on the subject, and doubt much whether *Mr J. Strange's* view would be upheld if the subject were mooted.

Indivisible and self-acquired property.—Of course the senior widow takes property which is in its nature indivisible, as a zemindari, &c. It was formerly held that the widow took property only when her husband was a divided holder; but, in the *Shivagunga case*, 9 *Moore's In. Ap.* 539, it was ruled that, even when the family was undivided, the widow inherited the self-acquired property of her husband, in preference to his male kin. In this case the property of the zemindar had been confiscated for disloyalty by the then zemindar. It was then conferred upon a younger brother, and was consequently held to be self-acquired, and another undivided elder brother could not take in preference to the widow of the second zemindar. See "Partition."

Where there are two united brothers who die in succession without male issue, each leaving a widow, the widow of the last survivor alone inherits; because the property, on the death of the

* "Several wives belonging to the same or different castes, (they) divide the property according to the shares prescribed to them and take it."

brother who deceased first, went by survivorship to the other, and from him passed to his widow.

Where one of two united brothers dies, leaving a daughter, she does not succeed—the property passes to the surviving brother and his line.

Grounds of the widow's right of succession.—The ground upon which the widow's right of succession is based is the assistance rendered by her to her husband in the performance of his religious duties. But if the doctrine of *Sir Thomas Strange, supra*—viz., that it is "a right vested in her by marriage, to be perfected on the death of her husband without leaving male issue," be correct, the performance of religious duties is not a very satisfactory reason for the rule.

Sir Colley Scotland, in delivering judgment in the case of *Viras Vami Gramini* v. *Ayyasvami Gramini,* 1 *Mad. H. C. R.* 475, says—"It seems to us that the real ground upon which the widow's right of succession is placed in the *Daya Bhaga* is the authority of *Brihaspati,* who says, that "a wife is declared by the wise to be half the body of her husband, equally sharing the fruit of pure and impure acts. Of him whose wife is not deceased, half the body survives;" adding, by way of question, "How then should another take his property while half his person is alive?" So that the right, in truth, rests upon the oneness of husband and wife, and not upon the existence of a separate estate and interest of the husband in the property during his life. Such a separate estate, as a matter of inference, might be deduced as well from the descent of the father's undivided share to sons, which is common to both schools of law, as from its descent to his widow, which is peculiar to the Bengal school."

Widow's right to succeed to her husband's ancestral property.—A widow's right to succeed to her husband's ancestral property is only as his immediate heir.

A widow can only inherit family property where there has been a partition among the co-parceners, of whom her husband was one; or where the whole property has vested in her husband by the death of all the other co-parceners.

The widow of an undivided Hindu, who leaves a co-parcener surviving him, has, like the widow of a divided Hindu, who leaves male issue, merely a right to maintenance.

Where, therefore, a widow sued for a Palaiyappattu, as heir to the surviving brother of her husband, it was held that the suit must be dismissed, *Peddamuttu Viramani* v. *Appu Rau,* 2 *Mad. H. C. R.,* 117.

Widow's right of succession to self-acquired property of her husband who was a member of an united family.—In a united Hindu family, where there is ancestral family property, and one of the members of the family acquires separate estate, on the death of that member such separate acquired estate does not fall into the common stock, but descends in the same manner as if the deceased had divided from his co-sharers, *i.e.*, to the male issue, if any, of the acquirer, or in default to his daughters, who, while separated, take their father's share in the ancestral property, subject to all the rights of co-parceners, yet inherit the self-acquired estate free from such rights. Where property belonging in common to an united Hindu family has been divided, the share of a deceased member of the family goes in the general course of descent of separate acquired property;* but if there is a co-parcenership between the different members of the united family, survivorship follows. Upon the principle of survivorship the right of co-parceners in the undivided estate overrides the widow's right of succession; but with respect to self-acquired property of a member of a united family, the other members of the family have neither community of interest, nor unity of possession; therefore, the foundation of the right to take by survivorship fails, *Katama Natchiar* v. *Rajah of Shivagunga*, 9 *Moore's In. Ap.* 539.

The grounds of the decision in this case are given in *Grady's Hindu Law*, p. 260, *et seq.* See the explanation of the case given at p. 268.

Self-acquired immovable property.—An undivided Hindu is entitled during his life to the separate enjoyment of his self-acquired immovable property; but such property will, in the event of his death without male issue, and previous disposition thereof, devolve on his surviving co-parceners, and his widow is entitled only to maintenance, *Varadiperumal Udaiyan* v. *Ardanari Udaiyan*, 1 *Mad. H. C. R.* 412.

The learned editor has appended the following as a note to this case: "But see *Menu*, cited 2 *Stra. H. L.* 250, from a copy of a paper in the handwriting of *Sir W. Jones*: If the husband has been a co-heir, and died before partition, his brothers, and the next order inherit his undivided share, but his wife takes all his divided property, and the opinion of a Mofussil pundit cited. The judgment of the Lords of the Judicial Committee of the Privy Council in *Katama Natchiar*, v. *Rajah of Shivagunga* (30th May 1863), principally rests on the passage last cited, which the reporter has been unable to find in *Menu*, or elsewhere.

This would seem to be a misconception of the learned editor. The Lords of the Privy Council appear to rest their judgment more upon analogy than upon the texts referred to.

Nature of the widow's tenure.—The nature of the tenure by which a widow holds property which has devolved upon her by the death of her husband has given rise to much discussion, and the arguments relied on have been supported by analogies drawn from the English law of real property.

* This is not strictly correct—in most cases it would be ancestral property.

The wife has not an absolute proprietary right, neither can she in strictness be called a tenant for life, for the law provides her successors, and restricts her use of the property to very narrow limits. She cannot dispose of the very smallest part, except for necessary purposes, and certain other objects particularly specified.

It follows then, that she can be considered in no other light than as a holder in trust for certain uses; so much so, that should she make waste, they who have the reversionary interest have clearly a right to restrain her from so doing. What constitutes waste must be determined by the circumstances of each individual case. The law has not defined the limits of her discretion with sufficient accuracy, and it was probably never in the contemplation of the legislator that the widow should live apart from, and out of the personal control of her husband's relatives, or possess the ability to expend more than they thought right and proper. In assigning a motive for the ordinance, that a widow should succeed to her husband, and at the same time that she should be deprived of the advantages enjoyed by a tenant for life even, it seems most consistent with probability, that it originated in a desire to secure against all contingencies, a provision for the helpless widow, and thereby prevent her from having recourse to practices by which the fame and honour of the family might be tarnished. By giving her nominal property she acquires consideration and respectability, and by making her the depositary of the wealth, she is guarded against the neglect or cruelty of her husband's relatives. At the same time, by limiting her power, a barrier is raised against the effects of female improvidence and worldly inexperience. This opinion receives corroboration from the distinction that prevails in the Benares school, which may he said to be the fountain and source of all Hindu law.

By the Hindu law of inheritance a childless widow takes as heir, but it is only a special or qualified estate, *The Collector of Masulipatam* v. *Cavally Vencata Narrainapah*, 8 *Moore's In. Ap.* 550.

In nature of an estate tail.—The interest of a Hindu widow succeeding to the principality of her husband is similar to that of a tenant entail by the English law as representing the inheritance, *Katama Natchiar* v. *The Rajah of Shivagunga*, 9 *Moore's In. Ap.* 539.

The widow in Western India has only a particular estate for life in the immovable separate property of her deceased husband, *Jumiyatram* and *Uttamram* v. *Bai Jamna* 2 *Beng. H. C. R.* 10.

Widow's right to accumulations of joint estate—Maintenance.—A Hindu testator, after devising his real and personal estate absolutely, amongst his five sons, said, in clause 11, " Should any amongst my said five sons die, not leaving any sons from his loins, nor any son's son, in that event neither his widow, nor his daughter, nor his daughter's son, nor any of them, will get any share out of the share that he has obtained of the immovables or movables of my said estate. In that event of the said property, such of my sons and son's sons as shall then be alive, they will receive that wealth according to their respective shares. If any one act repugnant to this, it is inadmissible. However, if any sonless son shall leave a widow, in that event she will only receive 10,000 Company's rupees for her food and raiment." The family remained joint, Surrupachuntar, one of the sons, died, but leaving a widow his heir-at-law:—held, that upon the death of her husband without male issue his interest in the capital of the estate determined, and that his widow became entitled to hold, and enjoy as a Hindu widow, a fifth part of the accumulations from the testator's estate from the time of his death to the death of his son, Surrupachuntar, and that she was also entitled absolutely in her own right to the interest and accumulations which, since her husband's death, had arisen from such fifth part of the accumulations.

She was declared entitled to the 10,000 rupees given by the will, with residence in the family dwelling-house, and participation in the means of worship, the amount of her maintenance as a Hindu widow being left open by the Judicial Committee, as that point could be raised on further directions after taking the accounts, *Sreemuttee Soorjeemoney Dossee* v. *Denobando Mullick*, 9 *Moore's In. Ap.* 125.

Widow's power over her husband's property.—It must be observed that a widow has not the same power over property inherited by her from her husband as she has over her stridhana, or woman's property; and that the descent of one differs from the other. Her stridhana goes to her heirs. Her husband's property reverts, after her death, to his heirs. See "Stridhana."

A deed of arrangement and release in the English form between members of a Hindu family, in respect of certain joint-estate, claimed by a childless Hindu widow, of one of the co-heirs, in her character of heiress, and legal personal representative of her deceased husband, declared that she was entitled to the sum therein expressed, as the share of her deceased husband, "for her sole absolute use and benefit." Held, that these words were not to receive the same interpretation as a court of equity in England would put upon them, as creating a separate estate in the widow, but that the deed must be construed with reference to the situation of the parties, and the rights of the widow by the Hindu law, and that, as the deed recited that she claimed and received the money as her husband's share in the joint-estate, as the heiress and personal representative of her deceased husband, such words must be construed to mean, that it was held by her in severalty from the joint-estate, and as a Hindu widow she had only a life-estate in the *corpus*, the same at her death devolved as assets of her deceased husband, upon his personal representative in succession, *Sreemutty Rabutty Dossee* v. *Sibchunder Mullick*, 6 *Moore's In. Ap.* 1.

Widow's right in undivided estate.—Upon the principle of survivorship, the right of the co-parceners in an undivided estate overrides the widow's right of succession, *Katama Natchiar* v. *Rajah of Shivagunga*, 6 *Moore's In. Ap.* 540.

Widow must be chaste.—Chastity seems to be the only condition imposed upon the widow's right of inheritance. *Sir Thos. Strange* says, Chastity is a necessary title to inheritance, adultery subjecting her to degradation from caste, for the loss of which she forfeits her right to inheritance. See *Grady's Hindu Law of Inheritance*, p. 269, in which this subject is fully treated.

Consequences of infidelity.—If adultery be committed with a man of low caste, it is said that the wife's life is in her husband's power. Some writers protect her person in cases of infidelity with men of the higher caste. But all agree as to forfeiture of inheritance in the former case. She is subjected to extreme mortification, bare necessary subsistence, and her husband may marry again, though her own marriage may remain undissolved.

Adultery with another man's wife among the Hindu is punishable, if committed with a priest, by ignominious tonsure, and in other cases with loss of life, and the case may be proved from circumstances. But in the Queen's courts it would be actionable, as it does not come under either of the two subjects which these courts are called upon to administer according to native law. See *Civil Procedure Code*, s. 1.

The criminal code punishes by imprisonment and fine the man, while the woman is allowed to escape unscathed, *Indian Penal Code*, Act xlv. of 1860, s. 497.

The husband is not entitled to damages from the adulterer, the Hindu law not providing for discretionary damages on any account.

Abandonment of a blameless wife.—If a husband abandons a blameless wife he is punishable, but his wife is entitled to a third of his property as a separate maintenance, *Yajanvalchya*. And there seems to be no reason why she should be deprived of any of her rights of inheritance on failure of male issue.

Wife's special property.—Besides the contingency of succeeding as heir to her husband, a Hindu wife has special rights of two kinds —viz., 1. *Stridhana*, or women's property consisting of money, land, jewels, or other ornaments; and, 2. Whatever is not stridhana. This is possessed by the wife, subject to the direct and unlimited control of her husband. Thus, what she acquires by her industry, or obtains from strangers, or inherits on failure of nearer heirs. *Sir Thomas Strange* cites with reference to these two sources of the wife's property, the following passage from *Jagannatha*:—"No argument is found to show why a woman should not have independent power over that which she has gained by arts, or which has been given her by a stranger on a religious consideration, or through friendship, but should have independent power over that which was received as a bribe."* The same learned author adds, It is necessary also, in every case of ornaments belonging to her, to distinguish between such as were given to her by her husband, or some of her relations, on, before, or connected with her marriage, and those worn by her occasionally, and not having been so given, the latter not being her property, but her husband's, descendable to his heirs, she surviving; but it is otherwise if they were habitually worn by her, in which case they are not partible. See *Stridhana.*

Where wife dies without issue, the husband surviving.—If the wife die in the lifetime of her husband without issue, her property will go to him, or his sapindas (nearest kinsmen), allied by funeral oblations, provided the marriage was in an approved form; if otherwise, to her father. There seems some doubt whether this rule applies to that part of her property only which is acquired at the time of her marriage.

The son-in-law never takes, as he is not in the line of heirs.

In *Rajchundra Das* v. *Dhunmani*, 3 *S. D. A. Rep.* 362, it was determined that, according to the Hindoo law as current in Bengal, on the death of the widow who had claimed her husband's property, her daughter will inherit, to the exclusion of her husband's brother, if the daughter has, or is likely to have, male issue; and on her death, without issue, her father's brother will inherit, to the exclusion of her husband.

Where she leaves issue.—Where the wife leaves issue, her property will go to her immediate descendants, whether daughters or grand-daughters. The latter take *per stirpes—i.e.*, according to the root; the unmarried or unendowed of the one or other taking first. Where there are daughters and grand-daughters, it vests in the daughters exclusively, subject to such a provision for grand-daughters as usage may warrant. Daughters take equally, subject to the above, of married and unmarried; and failing the latter, the husband and his relatives.

On re-marriage.—Except among some of the lower castes, no widow could marry again; but Act xv. 1856, § 1, now permits it —provided no such widow marrying again shall inherit the property of her first husband, unless he allows it.

Daughters.—Assuming that the deceased has left neither sons nor a widow, but daughters, they come next in succession. The daughter takes as a principle in her own right, in default of the widow, who has precedence.

In *Jim. Vahana* it is said, the daughter's right of succession is declared. *Menu* and *Narada* say, The son of a man is even as himself, and the daughter is equal to the son: how then can any

* **Meaning the gifts presented as an inducement to marriage.**

other inherit his property, notwithstanding the survival of her who is, as it were, himself ? *Menu.* *Narada* places her right of inheritance on the ground of her continuing the line of succession : "On failure of male issue, the daughter inherits ; for she is equally a cause of perpetuating the race, since both the son and the daughter are the means of perpetuating the father's line," *Narada.*

The line of descendants here intends such descendants as present funeral oblations ; for one who is not an offerer of oblations confers no benefits, *Jim. Vahana.* Her son only presents such oblation.

Daughter's right after death of sonless widow.—A Hindu, an inhabitant of Bombay, entitled to separate movable and immovable property, died without male issue, leaving a widow, four daughters, a brother, and the male issue of other deceased brothers. The widow is entitled to the movable property absolutely, and to the immovable property for life. Subject to the widow's interest the immovable property descends to the daughters absolutely, in preference to the brother and the issue of the deceased brothers, *Pranjeevandass Toolseydass* v. *Dewcooverbaee,* 1 *Bomb. H. C. B.* 131. This case was decided by the High Court of Bombay. The judgment of *Chief-Justice Sausse* is set out in a note to 9 *Moore's In. Ap.* 528, and will be seen in *Grady's Hindu Law of Inheritance,* p. 273. See *Rangasvami Ayyangar* v. *Vanjulatammal,* 1 *Mad. H. C. R.* 28 ; and *Perammal* v. *Venkatammel, ib.* 223 ; see also *Koomua Chunder Roy* v. *Seetakunth Roy,* 1 *W. R. Cal.* 750.

This decision seems to be correct, with the exception of that point which refers to the distinction drawn between movable and immovable property, no reason appearing for such distinction.

In the *Mitacshara,* on the right of a daughter and daughter's son, it is laid down on failure of her (that is, the widow), the daughters inherit, is as follows. Thus *Katyayana* says, Let the widow succeed to her husband's wealth, provided she be chaste, and in default of her, let the daughter inherit, if unmarried. This expression is shown in the following sections in the *Mitacshara* not to be restrictive but preferential only, as between married and unmarried daughters. See the judgment of *Chief-Justice Sausse* in *Venayak Anandroo* v. *Lakshimi,* 9 *Moore's In. Ap.* 532, *ante.*

Sir Thomas Strange says, The right of daughters to succeed in default of sons and widows is not to be confounded with that of the appointed daughter under the old law. That appointment was one of the many substitutions for a son, and by a fiction, now obsolete, regarded as one.

The appointed daughter derived her title from the will and act of her father. The daughter succeeding derives hers from the law, having regard to the general principle of conferring at his obsequies benefits on the deceased, *Menu.*

Their order of succession.—Daughters take in common. If there is but one unmarried daughter, she takes the whole inheritance first, to the exclusion of her sisters during her life. After the decease of the single daughter the married next enjoy it.

Among daughters, the unmarried take first. After them, the married daughters having male issue, or with probability of having it, and the widowed daughters with male issue. All of which three latter classes inherit jointly, *Smriti Chandrika.*

After these, the barren married and the sonless widowed daughters succeed. These also take jointly, *Mitac.*

Those with male issue, or the probability of it, are preferred, because the performance of the funeral rites can be continued from generation to generation better by their sons than others. In each class the unendowed take before the endowed, *Mitac.*

What constitutes endowment is not settled. But *Mr Strange* considers that it should be sufficient for maintenance, *Stra. Man.* § 330. Daughters in each class succeed jointly, and share alike. But this relates to succession from the father. If succession be derived from the mothers, where the father may have had a plurality of wives, the daughters take by succession, according to their mothers, *Stra. Man.*

In Bengal.—According to the Bengal school, the unmarried daughter is first entitled to the succession. If there be no maiden daughter, then the daughter who has, and the daughter who is likely to have, male issue, are together entitled to the succession,* and on failure of either of them the other takes the heritage. Under no circumstances can the barren daughters or widows destitute of male issue, or the mothers of daughters only, inherit the property, *Jim. Vahana.*

In Benares.—This rule does not obtain in the Benares school, that school holding that a maiden is, in the first instance, entitled to succeed; failing her, the married daughters succeed; the indigent, excluding the wealthy daughters; but in default of the former, the latter are competent to inherit. But no preference is given to the daughter who has, or is likely to have, male issue, over a daughter who is barren, or a childless widow.

In Bombay.—It has been held by the High Court that, as between two married daughters, the circumstance of having a son is no qualification on this side of India, giving the married daughter having a son a prior claim to inheritance of her parents' property over the married daughter not having a son, such priority of claim

* A distinction is made by *Srikrishna,* in his commentary on *Jim. Vahana,* in respect of unmarried daughters. He is of opinion that the daughter who is not betrothed is first entitled to the inheritance. In her default, the daughter who is betrothed. But this doctrine is not indorsed by any other authority, and the author of *Dayarahasya* expressly impugns it as untenable. —*Macn. Prin. H. L.* 21, n.

depending on the several daughters being respectively endowed, (*sadhan, i.e.*, with wealth,) or unendowed, (*nirdhan, i.e.*, without wealth,) the unendowed daughter having the preference.

In Mithila.—The Mithila law gives the preference to the unmarried over the married daughter.

Failing her, the married daughters are entitled to take. There is no distinction made amongst the married daughters; and one who has, or is likely to have, male issue is not preferred to one who is widowed and barren; nor do indigence or wealth give a preferable title. This school divides the property equally between poor and rich, mothers and childless. See *Chintamani*, 293.

Applicable in every possible case.—In Bengal, the above rule of succession is applicable in every possible case.

But in other schools, only where the family is divided; for, according to the doctrine of those schools, even the widow, to whom the daughter is postponed, can never inherit where the family is united, nor can the mother, daughter, daughter's son, or grandmother. The father's heirs, in such case, exclude them. But though the schools differ on other points, they concur in opinion as to the manner in which such property devolves on the daughter's death in default of male issue.

According to the Southern authorities, it classes as her stridhana, and descends accordingly to her heirs; but he cites no authority. In a note to the same page, he comments on the passage of *Sir Thomas Strange*, already quoted, wherein he treats property devolving on a daughter by inheritance as the daughter's stridhana, and descendible as such. *Macn.*, however, at p. 38, cites the *Mitac.*, which treats property acquired by means of inheritance as stridhana. See *ante*, "Stridhana."

According to the law of Bengal, also, it reverts to her father's heirs. *Sir Thomas Strange* asserts that property devolving upon a daughter by inheritance is classed by the Southern authorities as stridhana, and descends accordingly to her heirs.

It should seem, therefore, that the husband takes no interest in the *corpus* of such property. Nor has the daughter any power over it beyond her life-interest. *Sir Thomas Strange* says, The daughter's own power over it is greater than that of the widow of the deceased, whose condition is essentially one of considerable restraint.

Macnaghten mentions a curious case which arose in Bombay, involving the daughter's right of inheritance. Of two widows, one had two sons, and the other a daughter. On the death of the latter widow, it became a question who was to succeed to her property, whether her daughter, or the rival widow's sons? Various authorities were consulted, and they inclined to the opinion that the daughter was not entitled to succeed as heir, inasmuch as property, which had devolved on a widow, reverts at her death to her husband's heir, among whom the daughter would have ranked in default only of her own brothers.*

Woman's separate property goes to her daughters unmarried and unprovided for, *Goutama*, *Mitac.*

Self-acquired property.—It may safely be stated as a true proposition that property, which is not ancestral, is self-acquired, in whatever way the property may have been obtained, whether by gift or purchase, or labour, mental or physical, or otherwise. When a zemindary was escheated on the death of the last zemindar, the Government granted it anew to a distant relation of his. This was treated as self-acquired property in *Katama Natchiar* v. *The Rajah of Shivagunga*, 9 *Moore's In. Ap.* 595. That case has decided that *all* self-acquired property devolves in the same way as the family property of a divided member. Failing male issue, therefore, a widow takes the self-acquired property of her husband. No doubt, on the failure of male issue and a widow, the daughter would take, 9 *Moore's In. Ap.* 616.

Upon the effect of this ruling, the Lords Commissioners of the Privy Council, in the case of *Raja Suraneni Vankata Gopala Narasim ha Row Bahadoor* v. *Raja Suraneni Lakshmi Vankama Row*, 13th July 1869, "deemed it right to make a remark upon one passage in the otherwise very learned and able judgment of the Court below. The passage is this, 'If it (that is, the zemindary) was not partible, and the brothers were, as the plaintiff contends, undivided at the brother's death, the widow would, according to the decision of the Privy Council in the Shivagunga case, be entitled to the whole estate, so that, whether the plaintiff's own view, or that which we here take is correct, the plaintiff is not entitled to suceeed in this action.'" Now, that seems to proceed upon a singular misapprehension of the effect of the Shivagunga case. "It is immaterial, as I said before (said Sir L. Peel, in delivering judgment), to the decision of this case, because it is admitted that the zemindary was not impartible." But the Shivagunga case was this—the family was shown to be undivided, but the impartible zemindary was shown conclusively to have been the separate acquisition of the person whose succession was the subject of dispute. The ruling of this Court was that in that case the zemindary should follow the course of succession as to separate property, although the family was undivided; but if that zemindary had been shown to have been an ancestral zemindary, as this case, the judgment of the Court would no doubt have been the other way.

Daughters' sons.—According to the law of Bengal and Benares, the daughters' sons inherit in default of the qualified daughters.

Vishnu says, If a man leave neither son, nor son's son, nor [wife nor female] issue, the daughter's son shall take his wealth, for in

* This case is very obscure. It does not appear whose was the property or how the widow succeeded, there being sons.

regard to the obsequies of ancestors, daughters' sons are considered as sons' sons. This is not found in *Vishnu's Institutes*, but cited under his name in the *Smriti Chandrika*, note to *Mitac.*

Menu likewise declares, "By that male child whom a daughter shall produce from a husband of an equal class, the maternal grandfather becomes the grandsire of a son's sons. Let that son give the funeral oblation, and possess his inheritance."

As to the law of Mithila, see *Chintamani*, 294, and see 1 *W. R.* 75 *Cal.* sp. no.

A Hindoo died possessed of self-acquired property in land, leaving no sons, or sons' sons, but one widow, Rambai, and two daughters, Jamna, his daughter by Rambai, and Suraj, his daughter by an elder wife, who predeceased him. Rambai succeeded to all her husband's property as his sole surviving widow, and held it for her life. Suraj died in Rambai's lifetime, leaving two sons. Held, that the daughters, as co-heiresses, took an estate in remainder, vested in interest on their father's death, and that such vested right on the death of one of them during the widow's lifetime passed by inheritance to her sons, who, upon the widow's death, became entitled to enter into possession of their mother's moiety as her representatives, *Jamiyatram* and *Uttamram* v. *Bai Jamna*, 2 *Bomb. H. C. R.* 10.*

Mithila school.—But the right of daughters' sons is not recognised by the Mithila school. The *Vivada Chandra*, the *Vivada Ratnakara*, and *Vivada Chintamani*, authorities current there, do not enumerate daughters' sons amongst the series of heirs.

Order of Succession.—If there be sons of more than one daughter, they take *per capita*, and not as the sons' sons do, *per stirpes*. *Sir Thomas Strange* states, that where such sons are numerous, when they do take, they take *per stirpes*, and not *per capita*. But this authority supports a contrary view. *Jagannatha* there lays down the following rule :—"Again, if daughters' sons be numerous, a distinction must be made. In that case, if there be two sons of one daughter, and three of another, five equal shares must be allotted ; they should not first divide the estate in two parts, and afterwards allot one share to each son."

This principle was maintained also in the case of *Ramdhaun Sein* v. *Kishenkant Sein*, 3 *Sudr. D. A. R.* 100, 1821, where it was determined that grandsons by different mothers claiming their maternal grandfather's property take *per capita* and not *per stirpes*, *Macn.*

Daughters' grandsons.—Daughters' grandsons are not in the line of heirs, *Stra. Man.*

Daughters' daughters.—*Macnaghten*, *Cons. H. L.* 6, says, In the line of the daughters' male issue the descent stops with their

* See observations on this case in *Grady's Hindu Law of Inheritance*, p. 278.

sons. It does not extend to the female issue, *M. D.* 27 of 62, *Stra. Man.*

On failure of daughters' sons, among Soodras, illegitimate sons succeed, that is, to full shares. Half shares they are always entitled to, if there are legitimate sons' daughters, or sons of daughters, the illegitimate sons of Sudras get half shares.

The question was raised, but not decided, whether the interest of a daughter in the estate of her deceased father is of the same nature as that of a widow, 6 *Moore's In. Ap.* 433.

Succession in descending line stops with daughter's son.—The succession in the descending line from the daughters does not proceed beyond her son, the funeral cake stopping with him. It is the daughter's son who is the giver of funeral oblation, not *his* son, nor the daughter's daughter, for the funeral oblation ceases with him, *Jim Vahana*, which, *Sir Thomas Strange* says, is an answer to the claims of the son's son, grounded on the property having belonged to his father.

Daughter's Daughter.—According to the commentary of *Balam Bhatta,* the daughter's daughter inherits in default of daughter's sons. He grounds this opinion—for which, however, there is no authority in *Vignaneswara's* text—upon the analogy which this author has admitted in another case between the succession to a woman's separate property, and the inheritance of the paternal estate, note to *Mitac.*. It has been held, that where two of four daughters died during the lifetime of their mother, and one of them left a daughter, who sued her aunt for a fourth of the property in right of her mother, there was no legal foundation for the claim, 2 *S. D. A. R.* 290 *Bengal,* 1810. Moreover, when there are daughters' sons, their right of succession is postponed, for it is a right deduction that the succession of the daughters' son is next after the daughter, *Jim. Vahana,* so that he comes in after the other daughters of the deceased.

Where one of several daughters who succeeded as maiden dies, leaving sons and sisters.—If one of several daughters who had as maidens succeeded to their father's property die, leaving sons and sisters, and sisters' sons, then, according to the law of Bengal, the sons alone take the share to which their mother was entitled, to the exclusion of the sisters and the sisters' sons.

In conformity with this doctrine it was held, that property inherited by a daughter goes at her death to her son or grandson, to the exclusion of her sister and her sister's son, 2 *S. D. A.* 26.

Where one of several daughters who had as married women succeeded dies, leaving sons, sisters, and sisters' sons.—If one of several daughters, who had as married women succeeded their father, die, leaving sons, sisters, or sisters' sons, according to the same law the sisters exclude the sons; and if there be no sister, the property will be equally shared by her sons and her sisters' sons. This distinction seems to prevail in Bengal only.

On failure of daughter's issue estate reverts to father's heirs.—This is a moot point, whether on failure of issue the inheritance so descending on the daughter goes, like her stridhana, to her husband surviving her, or to those who would have succeeded, had it never vested in such daughter?

Jim. Vahana says, If a maiden daughter, in whom the succession has vested, and who has been afterwards married, die, without bearing issue, the estate which was hers becomes the property of those persons, a married daughter, or others who would regularly succeed if there were no [unmarried] daughter in whom the inheritance vested, and in like manner succeed on her demise after it has so vested in her (see 1 *Morl. Dig.* 319). It does not become the property of her husband, or other heirs, for that [text which is declaratory of the right of husband and the rest] is relative to a woman's peculiar property (stridhana). Since it has been shown, that on the decease of the widow, in whom the succession had vested, the legal heirs of the former owner, who would regularly inherit his property, if there were no widow, in whom the succession vested—namely, the daughters—and the rest, succeed to the wealth—therefore the same rule concerning the succession of the former possessor's next heirs is inferred, *à fortiori*, in the case of the daughter and grandson, whose pretensions are inferior to the wife's (see *Daya Krama Sangraha*), so that if the daughter die without issue her father's next heirs succeed. See *Stridhana*.

Section IV.

PARENTS.

Property ascends—Mother—Father—Mother restricted in alienation—Where father had other wives—Brothers divided—Sisters not included—Order of succession amongst brothers—Title rests on funeral benefits—Re-united brothers—Brothers' sons or nephews—Sonless widow of undivided brother cannot separate and take his share, and daughter of former wife cannot take father's share—Brothers' grandsons—Nephews' sons, or grand-nephews—Brothers' daughters—Daughter-in-law—United family—Widow—Daughter's son—Sister—Bombay—Sisters' sons—Nieces or sisters' daughters—Succession after sister's son in Bengal—Remote kindred—Sakulyas—Spiritual preceptor—Benares—Sapindas—Mithila—Bombay—Spiritual preceptor—Pupil—Southern India—Religious order—Dancing-girl—Prostitution—Its gains recognised—Samonidacas—Lands endowed for religious purposes—What law governs parties who migrate from one district to another where a different school of law prevails— Caranese law—Aliya Santana—Division of family property—Malabar—Castes following the Maroomakatayam rule—United females—Succession as Karnaven—No right to partition—The principle of partition—Alienation—Property assigned by Naya females—Judgment against Karnaven—Charges on property—Self-acquired property—Widowhood—Management by females—Maintenance—Account from Karnaven—Succession to management—Anandraven's right to maintenance.

Property ascends.—In default of issue in the descending line, the inheritance ascends, the property passing to the parents. But a difference of opinion has prevailed in the various schools as to which parent should take the precedence. Some give the preference to the father, some to the mother, and some to both jointly. The father inherits according to the Bengal school.

Mother—Father.—But the mother succeeds to the exclusion of the father, according to the other schools. *Jim. Vahana* (and other authorities in Bengal) says that in the term *pitru*, "both parents" (contained in the text of *Yajnavalchya*), "the priority of the father is indicated, for the father is first suggested by the radical term *pitri*, and afterwards the mother is inferred from the dual number, by assuming that one term of two which composed the phrase is retained." But both the Benares and Mithila schools prefer the mother to the father. The *Mitacshara* founds its preference of the mother on the use of the term *matapitru* (mother and father), rather than that of *pitara* (parents), and arguing thence, according to Hindu logic, that the omission of the one, and the retention of the other, show the intention to be to give the mother the preference. In the *Mitacshara*, reliance is placed on the propinquity of the mother to the son; it is there said, "Therefore, since the mother is the nearest of the two parents, it is most fit that she should take the estate."

But on failure of her the father is successor to the property, according to the same school.

The commentator *Balam Bhutta* is of opinion that the father should inherit first, and afterwards the mother, upon the analogy of more distant kindred, where the paternal line has invariably the preference before the maternal kindred, and upon the authority of several express passages of law.

Nanda Pandita, author of commentaries on the *Mitacshara* and on the institutes of *Vishnu*, had before maintained the same opinion. But the elder commentator of the *Mitacshara*, *Visvesvara*, has in this instance followed the text of his author in his own treatise, entitled *Mădăna Parĭjăta* (honey flower), and has supported *Vignaneswara's* argument both there and in his commentary, named *Suboudhini*.

Srikara maintains that the father and mother inherit together, and the great majority of writers of eminence (as *Apararka* and *Kalamakara*, and the authors of the *Smriti Chandrika*, *Madanaratna*, *Vyavahara Mayukha*, &c.) give the father the preference. *Jimuta Vahana* and *Raghunandana* have adopted this doctrine. But *Vachespati Misra*, on the contrary, concurs with the *Mitacshara* in placing the mother before the father, being guided by an erroneous reading of the text of *Vishnu*, as is remarked in the *Veramitrodaya*. The author of the latter work proposes to reconcile these contradictions by a personal distinction. If the mother be individually more venerable* than the father, she inherits; if she be less, so the father takes the inheritance. But this is very fanciful.

Others again exclude the father altogether, and on failure of the mother pass the inheritance to the paternal grandmother, as the surer means of preserving the property in the same tribe, upon the ground that the father succeeding, the estate becomes a paternal one, and as such may devolve, as well on sons belonging to a mixed class, as on issue by a wife of his own, whereas if taken by the grandmother it descends as a maternal one to persons of the same class only, viz., to her daughters and their representatives, *Dharesvara*, *Mitac.* But the force of this argument ceased ever since marriages with women of inferior classes became illegal.

Assuming the father to take first, in default of him the mother takes. Her interest, however, is not absolute, and is of a nature similar to that of a widow. But this rule seems to be more than doubtful.

In a case of property which had devolved upon a mother by the decease of her son, the law officers of the *S. D. A.* held that the rules concerning property devolving on a widow equally affect property devolving on a mother. On her death the property devolves on the heirs of her *sons*, and not on *her* heirs. But *vide*, with reference to the Madras school.

Although *Jagannatha* admits the point to be uncertain, yet it is evident that the bias of his judgment was in favour of the father, upon the ground of his comparative efficacy in performing obsequies to the deceased, arguing by analogy to the ground of preference to the son of a daughter, who succeeds as well to both parents as to the brother, *Jim. Vahana*.

Of a son dying childless and leaving no widow. *Menu*, according to the gloss of *Coollooca Bhutta*, says that the father and mother shall take the estate. This, according to Hindu reasoning, establishes in the father the right of prior enjoyment. Other versions of the same text, omitting the father, have been construed to suppose the father dead, *Mitac.*, *Jim. Vahana*, *Menu*.

Amidst all these conflicting authorities, *Sir Thomas Strange* adds,

* As to the pre-eminence of the mother, see the *Vivada Changarnava*, *Menu*, *Vyasa*, the *Puranas*.

Reason ought to decide between the contending views, with *Jagannatha*, in favour of the father, upon the principle that "if two texts differ, reason, or that which it best supports, must in practice prevail, when the reason of the law can be shown."

That the father takes first is the doctrine of the Bengal school, founded on *Vishnu* and *Menu*, resting the subsequent title of the mother on her claims of having borne the deceased, and nursed him in his infancy.

Mother restricted in alienation.—In whatever order the natural mother inherits, she is, like the widow, taking as such, restricted from alienating the estate, unless for necessary subsistence, or for pious purposes beneficial to the deceased, and for this only to a very limited extent.

Where the father had other wives.—Should the father of the person to be traced from have had other wives besides the mother of the individual, they do not inherit. The property passes exclusively to the individual's mother.

It is said in *Stra.*, that step-mothers are excluded, but the Hindu law authorities he has referred to do not support him. It has, however, been held that a step-mother cannot take by inheritance from her step-son. *Lalla Jotee Lall* v. *Musat Dooranee Kooer*, 1 *W. R.* 173 Cal. sp. no.

Brothers divided.—If the *father* be dead, brothers share the estate,* according to *Menu*. Of him who leaves no son, the *father* shall take the inheritance, *Menu*. *Macn.* says, In default of father and mother, brothers inherit.

Sisters not included.—*Nanda Pandita* and *Balam Bhutta* consider this as intending brothers and sisters, in the same manner in which "parents" have been explained mother and father, and, conformably with a rule of grammar, they give the inheritance to the brother first, and in his default to the sister. This opinion is controverted by *Kamalakara*, and by the author of *Vyavahara Mayukha*, *Mitac.* Sisters are not enumerated in the order of heirs.

Order of succession amongst brothers.—Those that are of the whole blood take the inheritance in the first instance, under the text of *Menu*: "To the nearest sapinda the inheritance next belongs." Since those of the half blood are remote, through the difference of the mothers, *Mitac.*, and take only on failure, or in default of the whole brothers. If there be no uterine (or whole brothers), those by a different mother inherit the estate, *Jim. Vahana.*

Macn. says, The order of succession is, first, the united brothers of the whole blood; second, the divided brothers of the whole blood; third, the united brothers of the half-blood; fourth, the divided brothers of the half-blood. A divided brother of the whole blood takes in preference to a divided one of the half-blood.

This order of succession supposes that the deceased had only

* See "Sister," *infra*.

uterine or half-brothers, and that they were all united, or all separated; but if a man die, having a uterine brother separated, and a half-brother associated or re-united, these two will inherit the property in equal shares.

Assuming the mother to have succeeded the father, on her death the property devolves on the brother, for *Vishnu*, who declares that "if the father be dead, it appertains to the mother," proceeds to say, "on failure of her it goes to the brothers,"* and here the pronoun refers to the mother. It appears, also, from the passage of *Yajnavalchya*, "both parents, brothers likewise," that the brother's succession takes place in the case of the death of both parents, *Jim. Vahana.* On the death of the mother the residue of the estate devolves on the brother as next heir, in the order of succession; and not like a woman's peculiar property on her son and daughter, for it is the case of an estate devolving on a woman, *Jim. Vahana, Chudamani.*

Stridhana, or women's peculiar property, being the mother's, descends on her death to her daughters.

Sir Thomas Strange says, But if the property was not *stridhana,* but was inherited by her from her son, it passes in Bengal to *his* heirs, and not to hers, *Jim. Vahana,* who on failure of a son of the owner, or on failure of widow, or of a daughter, or of parents, are his brother or brothers. †

Title rests on funeral benefits.—The title of the brother, as in other instances, rests on the benefits he confers by the offer of oblations in which the deceased owner of the property participates, and in presenting others which the deceased was bound to offer, and in this respect occupying his place, *Jim. Vahana.*

The uterine brother takes first, for he presents oblations to six ancestors, which the deceased was bound to offer, and three oblations in which he participates, while the half-brother presents none to ancestors.

But as he presents three, in which the deceased participates, he is therefore superior to the nephew, who accordingly, though son of a uterine brother, is postponed in the succession to his uncle of the half-blood, *Jim. Vahana*—a preference, nevertheless, that has been censured.

It has been suggested that the succession differs where the property has been inherited, and where it has been acquired by the deceased; but this has not been established.

Re-united brothers.—When brothers separate and afterwards re-unite, and then again separate, should any share have lapsed by

* That is, the brothers of him through whom she succeeded—that is, her son. This text must refer to a divided family; for if united, the inheritance must pass direct to the brothers, and not to the mother.

† This, of course, assumes a separation, for if a son had united brothers, the property could not have devolved upon the mother.

death, &c., during the state of re-union, such share goes in equal parts to the re-united brothers of the whole blood and the sisters of the whole blood. Failing brothers of the whole blood, it goes to re-united brothers of the half-blood, and sisters of the same mother, to all in equal shares, *Mitac.*

Although in the succession to the estate of a grandfather the right of representation exists—that is to say, the son of a deceased son inherits with his uncle—yet where the property comes to the brother after the death of his brother's widow, the son of another brother, who died during the life of the widow, has no right to claim a share of the inheritance, because during the life of his widow the father of the son had not even an inchoate right to the property. It had never appertained to him.

In the case of *Rudrachundra Chowdhi* v. *Samhhu Chandra Chowdhri*, 3 *S. D. A. R.* 106, a question arose as to the relative rights of a brother and a brother's son to succeed on the death of a widow to property which had devolved on her at the death of her husband, they being the next heirs. In the succession to the estate of a grandfather the right of representation undoubtedly exists; that is to say, the son of a deceased son inherits together with his uncle. Not so in the case of property left by a brother, the brother's son being enumerated in the order of heirs to a childless person's estate after the brother, and entitled to succeed only in default of the latter. In the case in question the deceased left two brothers and a widow; the widow succeeding, one of the brothers died during her life, leaving a son; on her death this son claimed to inherit together with his uncle. The opinion of the pundits in favour of the justice of his claim was based upon the fallacious supposition, that on the death of the first brother the right of inheritance of his other two surviving brothers immediately accrued, and that the dormant right of the brother who died subsequently was transmitted to his son; whereas, in point of law, during the life of the widow neither brother had even an inchoate right to the property, and as it had not vested in them, the one who died could not have transmitted to his son a right which never appertained to himself. This doctrine was supported in *Musst. Jymani Dibia* v. *Ramjoy Chowdhri*, 3 *S. D. A.* 289.

Brothers' sons or nephews.—In default of brothers, their line having been exhausted, their sons inherit, *Vishnu*, *Jim. Vahana*, *Mitac.*, *Daya Krama Sangraha.* In the same order, as to division and union, the whole being preferred to the half-blood, *Jim. Vahana*, *Daya Krama Sangraha.* As the nephew of the half-blood confers less benefits compared with the brother's son of the whole blood, since the mother and grandmother of the deceased owner do not participate in the oblations presented by the nephew of the half-blood to the father and grandfather of such deceased owner, (*Jim. Vahana*, *Mitac.*, *Daya Krama Sangraha*), so the united succeed before the divided.

In case of competition between brothers and nephews, the nephews have no title to the succession, for their right of inheritance is declared to be on failure of brothers [both parents, brothers likewise, and their sons], *Mitac.* However, when a brother has died leaving no male issue (nor other near heir), and the estate has consequently devolved on his brothers indifferently, if any one of them die before a partition of his brother's estate takes place, his sons do in that case acquire a title through their father, and it is fit therefore that a share should be allotted to them in their father's right at a subsequent distribution of the property between them and the surviving brothers.

The sonless widow of an undivided brother cannot separate and take his share, nor can the daughter of a former wife take her father's share.—Where three undivided brothers lived and ate together with the mother, but traded separately, but two of the brothers died, one leaving a widow and a daughter by a former wife, the other a widow and two sons, it was held that the brothers and descendants of the two deceased could not be considered as a divided family, and the widow and her sons will be permitted to possess their father's share; but the widow of the other brother cannot be permitted to separate and take her husband's share; nor has the daughter by a former wife any right to separate and take her father's share because he died without previous separation and leaving no son; the other members of the family are, however, bound to maintain the widow and daughter, *Mt. Raj Koonwur* v. *Mt. Dhun Koonwur*, 1 *Borr.* 207.

But with regard to succession of brothers' sons there is this peculiarity, that if a brother's son, whose father died previously to the devolution of the property, claim *jure representationis*, they take *per stirpes* with their uncle, being in that case grandsons inheriting with a son; but when the succession devolves on the brother's sons alone as nephews, they take *per capita* as daughters' sons do. In the *Suboudhini* it is stated that the succession cannot under any circumstances take place *per capita*. But this opinion is rejected.

He maintains, also, that daughters of brothers inherit. In this opinion he is joined by *Narada Pandita*, but the doctrine is also rejected.

Sir Thomas Strange says, That, unlike sons of daughters they take *per capita*, not claiming *jure representationis*, as if their fathers had had a vested interest in their brothers' property before their decease; whereas the right only vested in them by the demise of the owner, their fathers being at the time dead.

Elberling, p. 78, says, In default of brothers, brothers' sons succeed in the same order as brothers; *Vishnu, Daya Krama Sangraha, Daya Bhaga, Mitac.* They take according to numbers,*

* The reason is, that they do not inherit in right of their father, but in their own right; and as their right is equal, their share must also be equal, *Mitac.*, ch. ii. s. iv. § 7, note.

and not by representation as grandsons. Brothers' sons are totally excluded by the existence of brothers, but when a brother has once succeeded, his share devolves of course, on his death, on his sons, and not on his surviving brothers, even though he happens to die before a partition of the estate takes place, *Mitac.*

Amongst brothers' sons, associated and unassociated, all of the whole blood, the succession devolves exclusively on the associated brothers' sons, *Daya Krama Sangraha.* In like manner, in the case of associated and unassociated brothers' sons, all of the half-blood, the succession devolves on the associated brothers of the half-blood, *Daya Krama Sangraha.*

But if the son of the whole brother were unassociated, and the son of the half-brother associated, then they both inherit together.

Where, however, two nephews were either associated or unassociated with the deceased, one of the whole, the other of the half-blood, then in both instances the succession devolves on the nephew of the whole blood.

The sons of brothers who have demised before the property falls in, do not succeed while there are surviving brothers to take the inheritance.

Brothers' grandsons.—Brothers' grandsons are not in the direct line of heirs; but *Mr Justice Strange* says they come in ulteriorly as more remote *supindas.*

Nephews' sons or grand-nephews.—Nephews' sons or grand-nephews next take in the same order, and in the same manner as nephews. But with them the succession in the male line from the father direct stops.

In default of brothers' sons, their grandsons inherit in the same order,* according to the law as current in Bengal. But the law of Benares, Mithila, and other provinces, does not enumerate the brother's grandson in the order of heirs, but assigns to the paternal grandmother the place next to the brother's son, *Mitac.*

The brother's great-grandson, though a lineal descendant of the owner's father, is excluded by the paternal uncle, for he is not a giver of oblations, since he is distant in the fifth degree. Thus *Menu* says, "To three, must oblations of water be made; to three, must oblations of food be presented; the fourth in descent is the giver of these offerings, but the fifth has no concern with them," *Menu,* by this passage the fifth in descent is debarred, *Jim. Vahana, Daya Krama Sangraha.*

Brothers' daughters.—Brothers' daughters do not inherit.

Daughter-in-law does not succeed to her mother-in-law, being excluded equally with sisters and sisters' sons.

* No re-union, after separation, can take place with a grandson's brother. Re-union can take place only with the following relations:—The father, the brother, and paternal uncle, *Brihaspati,* cited in *Jim. Vahana,* ch. ix. s. i. 30.

Succession in united family.—Where brothers are united, the succession differs in some respects from that which prevails where they are divided. The estimated share of each brother vests successively in his sons, sons' sons, and sons' grandsons, as in the case of individual property. Failing these, however, the next in the line of succession are the surviving brothers, amongst whom the lapsed share vests equally. The great-great-grandson of the deceased brother would not take it, unless kept open for him by the survival of his father, or grandfather. From the brothers the lapsed share would vest in their male issue, as far as the great-grandson. After that it would pass to the widow of the last survivor of any of these.

Widow.—The widow of these previously demised would not participate. When there may be male issue of the undivided brothers, it passes from one cousin to another to the remotest degree while united, and on all these failing, then to the widow of the last survivor. It finally goes to divided relatives in their order.

A., one of four brothers in joint-possession of ancestral property, separates himself in food, worship, and estate, leaving his three brothers jointly possessed of their undivided three-fourth shares. A. dies unassociated, leaving a son and heir, B. The three brothers continue, and die associated, two without heirs, and the third leaving a son and heir, C. B. has no claim to any part of the undivided three-fourth shares as against C., who takes the whole absolutely, *Jaudubchunder Ghose* v. *Bonodbeharry Ghose*, *Hyde's Beng. H. C. R.*, 1866, p. 214.

Distant undivided relatives take before the widow.

Where there are two brothers who have not divided, and they die in succession without male issue, each leaving a widow, the widow of the last survivor alone inherits; this is, because on the decease of the brother who first died, the entire property vested in the surviving brother, and so passed on to his widow. Where one of two undivided brothers dies, leaving a daughter, she does not succeed; the property passes on to the surviving brother and his line.

Daughter's son.—The succession in the male line from the father direct, having stopped with the nephews and grand-nephews, failing heirs of the father, down to the great-grandson, the succession devolves on his daughter's son, in preference to the uncle of the deceased, in like manner as it descends to the owner's daughter's son on failure of the male issue, in preference to the brother, *Jim. Vahana, Daya Krama Sangraha.*

The succession of the grandfather's and great-grandfather's lineal descendants, including the daughter's son, must be understood in a similar manner, according to the proximity of the funeral offering. Since the reason stated in the text, "For even the son of a daughter delivers him in the next world, like the son of a son."

Menu, ix. § 139, is equally applicable, and his father's or grandfather's daughter's son transports his *manes* over the abyss by offering oblations of which he may partake, *Jim. Vahana.*

Accordingly, *Menu* has not separately propounded their right of inheritance, for they are comprehended under the two passages, "To three must libations of water be made," &c., and "to the nearest kinsman (sapinda) the inheritance next belongs," *Menu. Yajnavalchya* likewise uses the terms gentiles or kinsmen (*gotraja*) for the purpose of indicating the right of inheritance of the father's and grandfather's daughter's son, as springing from the same line in the relative order of the funeral oblation, and for the further purpose of excluding females related as sapindas, since these also spring from the same line, *Jim. Vahana.*

Sister.—The general principle is that females are incompetent to inherit. The sister, therefore, being no offerer of oblations, is excluded from the heritage. But the right of succession of the widow, and certain others—viz., the daughter, the mother, and the paternal grandmother, is reserved by express texts without any contradiction to this maxim, *Jim. Vahana*, and notes.

Bombay.—According to the law of inheritance prevailing in Bombay, sisters succeed to the estate of their deceased brother, if the estate had been separately acquired by their father in preference to their father's brothers' sons, *Vinayak Anundrow* v. *Luxumeebaee*, 9 *Moore's In. Ap.* 538; 1 *Bomb. H. C. R.* 117.

Sister's son.—In default of brother's grandsons, the sister's son inherits in Bengal, *Jim. Vahana*, but not in the provinces which follow the *Mitacshara; Rajchunder* v. *Goculchund*, 1 *Beng. R.* 46, *ante*, 1805; 1 *Morl. Dig.* 327; *Doe d. Kullammah* v. *Kuppu Pillai*, 1 *Mad. H. C. R.* 90, affirming *R. A.*, No. 33 of 1858; *M. S. D.*, 1858, pp. 209, 211, *S. A.*, No. 84 of 1860; *M. S. D.*, p. 245, 1860. In *Elberling's Treatise on Inheritance*, § 178, &c., it is laid down that sons of different sisters take according to the numbers born, as well as unborn, and even unbegotten, at the time of their uncle's death, *Bijia Deby* v. *Unnapoorna Deby*, 1 *S. D. A.* 162; *M. Solookhuna* v. *Ramdolal Pande*, *ib.* 324. *Elberling* is a Bengal writer, but discusses the authorities of the Benares school as well. At the close of § 178, he says, that according to the schools of *Benares* and *Mithila*, the sister's sons are excluded, as they belong to a different family.

In the Southern India schools the paternal grandmother is ranked next to the brother's son, and the sister's son also is excluded from the enumerated heirs, *Rajachunder Narrain* v. *Goculchunder Goh.* 1 *S. D. A. R.* 43. The suit was there brought by a sister's son, against the paternal uncle's son, for the recovery of land in Bengal, the estate of a deceased Hindu. The Court held that, according to *Bengal* law, the plaintiff was heir; according to the *Mithila* law, the defendant.

M

The writers in the Bengal school differ as to the rights of succession between the whole and half blood, some maintaining that an uterine's sister's son excludes the son of a sister of the half blood : but according to the most approved authorities there should be no distinction.

Nieces, or sisters' daughter.—The observations we have made with reference to a sister apply to the claims of nieces, or sisters' daughters, who are nowhere enumerated in the order of heirs, although *Nanda Pandita* and *Balaam Bhutta* maintain that daughters also of sisters have a right of inheritance, an opinion which has been refuted. On a question as to whom does the land of a Hindu woman descend, she having left her surviving two nieces and a grandson of a third, the pundit answered, As between the grandson of a deceased niece, and the surviving sisters, the grandson succeeds. The two surviving their sister can have no claim, having no issue. It is held in the *Smriti Sindheeva*, in the chap. of *Jim. Vahana* treating on woman's property, that a female, having no issue, shall never succeed to land; the same is repeated in the *Smriti Chandrika*, *Saraswati Vilasa*, and *Verderajyah.* Upon which *Mr Sutherland* remarks, that he regards the opinion as very inaccurate. See the erroneous doctrine that women inherit only through having male issue, controverted in the *Mitacshara*, ch. ii. s. i. Here the right of the grandson to succeed can only be through his grandmother; therefore he can have no right to a larger share than that to which she would have been entitled. In fact, however, I think he has no right to any share. The doctrine of representation does not apply to the case of succession to the estate of an aunt, or great-grandaunt, and the right of his grandmother had never vested. It is worthy of consideration whether either of the three sisters could have any right at all to succeed to the estate of their deceased aunt. In the series of heirs the niece is nowhere enumerated; and my pundit agrees with me that the estate would escheat rather than descend to nieces, and *à fortiori* to the grandson of a niece.

Succession after sisters' sons.—In the Bengal school the succession, after the sister's son, according to *Daya Krama Sangraha*, and *Macn.*, passes to the—

Brother's daughter's son.*
Paternal grandfather.
,, grandmother.
,, uncle.
,, son.
,, grandson.
,, grandfather's daughter's son.

* *Jagannatha* says, that "the son of a son's, and of a grandson's daughter, and the son of a brother's, and of a nephew's daughter, and so forth, claim succession in the order of proximity before the maternal grandfather." But this opinion is not supported by any authority.

Paternal uncle's daughter's son.
,, great-grandfather.
,, ,, grandmother.
,, ,, grandfather's brother.
,, ,, grandfather's son.
,, ,, grandfather's grandson.
,, ,, great-grandfather's daughters' son.
,, ,, ,, grandfather's brother's daughter's son.

On failure of the foregoing, the inheritance passes in the maternal line to the—

Maternal grandfather.*
,, uncle.
,, son.
,, grandson.
,, daughter's son.
,, great-grandfather.
,, great-grandfather's son.
,, great-grandfather's grandson.
,, great-grandson and daughter's son.
,, great-great-grandfather.
,, great-great-grandfather's son.
,, great-great-grandfather's grandson.
,, great-great-grandfather's great-grandson and daughter's son.

Remote kindred—Sakulyas.—In default of all these, the property goes to the remote kindred in the descending and ascending line, as far as the fourteenth in degree, then to the—

Spiritual preceptor.

The pupil.

The fellow-student;† those bearing the same name; those descended from the same patriarch.

Brahmins learned in the vedas or holy books; and, lastly, the king, by escheat, with the exception of Brahmin's property, which must be distributed among other Brahmins; but see 8 *Moore's In. Ap.* 500, where it has been held that a Brahmin's estate is also liable to escheat.

Even amongst the Bengal writers this order of succession does not generally prevail, *Srikrishna Tarkalankara,* in his commentary on the *Daya Bhaga,* after the sisters' sons places the paternal uncle of the whole blood, the paternal uncle of the half blood, the son of the paternal uncle of the whole blood, the son of the paternal uncle of the half blood, their grandsons successively—

The paternal grandfather's daughter's son.
,, grandfather.
,, grandmother.

* See note on previous page.

† A fellow-hermit is heir to an anchorite, his pupil to an ascetic, and his preceptor to a professed student of theology.—2 *Stra. H. L.* 248.

The paternal grandfather's whole brother.
" " half-brother.
their sons and
grandsons successively.
" great-grandfather's daughter's son.

The *Sapindas ;* the maternal uncle and the rest, who present oblations which the deceased was bound to offer.

The mother's sister's son.

The maternal uncle's sons and grandsons.

The grandson of the son's son, and other descendants for three generations in succession.

The offspring of the paternal grandfather's grandfather, and other ancestors for three generations.

Samanodacas, these connected by obsequial offerings of water.

In the *Vividanavasetu*, a digest compiled by the order of *Mr Hastings*,* *Vivadasararnava* and *Vividabhungarnava*, a digest compiled at the request of *Sir W. Jones* by *Jagannatha*, and usually cited as the Digest, the series of heirs are thus enumerated :—After the sister's sons—

The grandfather.
The grandmother.
The uncle.
The uncle's son.
" grandson.
" great-grandson.
Grandfather's daughter's son.
Great-grandfather.
Great-grandmother.
" " son.
" " grandson.
" " great-grandson and daughter's son.
Maternal grandfather.
" uncle.
" " his son.
" " grandson.
The deceased's grandson's grandson (in the male issue).
His great-grandson and his
Great-great-grandson.
Then the ascending line succeed.
The paternal great-grandfather's father.
" " son, grandson, and great-grandson.

Jagannatha assigns a place next to the maternal uncle's grandson, to the maternal great-grandfather, and the maternal great-great-grandfather and their descendants. He also is of opinion that of the male descendants of the paternal grandfather and great-grand-

* This is considered of doubtful authority.

father, those related by the whole blood should exclude those of the half blood.

All these authorities concur in the order of enumeration, as far as the sister's son. *Mr Colebrooke* says, Where there is any difference of opinion, reliance may with safety be placed on the *Daya Krama Sangraha* of *Srikrishna.*

The works to which we have referred are of the greatest authority in Bengal. Differences of opinion prevail amongst writers of less note, but it is unnecessary to refer to them more particularly, 1 *Macn. P. H. L.* 31.

Spiritual Preceptor.—In default of all relatives, property vesting in a male will pass to the acharyar, or spiritual preceptor, the pupil, fellow-student in theology; learned Brahmins; and, lastly, always excepting the property of Brahmins, the estate escheats to the Crown, *Mitac.* and *infra.* See *ante.* Property vesting in a female, except in the instance of Brahmins' escheats, in default of relatives, *Stra. Man.* § 358.

Property vesting in a Brahmin, whether male or female, on failure of relatives, should go to any learned or venerable priest, and then to any pure Brahmin, *Menu, Narada, Mitac.* The Privy Council, however, have determined that it escheats to the Crown as any other property, *Collector of Masulipatam* v. *Cavaly Vencata Narainapah,* 8 *Moore's In. Ap.* 500.

The Crown would now therefore undoubtedly claim the property in supersession of the teacher, &c., and their rights; for, such a rule seems to be merely directory, and comes under a principle which our Courts cannot carry out or adjudicate upon, as being too indefinite in its nature, and incapable of being carried out universally. Even a much clearer rule, that the Crown could not take the property of Brahmins, has been overruled by the Judicial Committee of the Privy Council on the ground—

1. That even Hindu law does not say that the King cannot take the property, but merely says it would be a great sin if he kept it, his duty being to bestow it upon the virtuous Brahmins.

2. Escheats are not governed by Hindu law, for rights attaching to property are dependent on the religion and law of the person holding it. Property without an owner cannot be governed by the law of the last holders, and there being no other holder, the law of the person taking it governs the whole question.

Benares.—According to the law as prevailing in Benares, in default of the son and son's son and grandson, the widow (supposing the husband's estate to have been distinct and separate) succeeds to the property under the limited tenure above specified. But if her husband's estate were joint, and held in co-parcenery, she is only entitled to maintenance.

In default of the widow, the maiden daughter inherits. In her default, the married indigent daughter. In her default, the married wealthy daughter. Then the daughter's son. But the *Vivadachandra*, *Vivadaratanakara*, and the *Vivadachintamani*, authorities which are current in *Mithila*, do not enumerate the daughter's sons amongst the series of heirs. The mother ranks next in the order of succession. *Balaam Bhutta* gives the inheritance to the father first; so *Nanda Pandita;* so *Apararka*, *Kamalakara*, author of *Vivadatandava;* the authors of the *Smriti Chandrika*, *Madanaratna*, *Vyavahara Mayukha*, *Vivada Chandrika*, *Ratnakara;* and the authorities current in Benares prefer the father.

In default of the father, brothers of the whole blood succeed, and in default, those of the half blood. In their default, sons inherit successively.

The paternal grandmother.
,, grandfather.
Paternal uncle of the whole—of the half blood,—their sons in succession.
Paternal great-grandmother.
,, great-grandfather.
,, son and grandson successively.
,, great-grandfather's mother.
,, ,, father.
,, ,, brother.
,, ,, brother's son.

Sapindas.—In the same order to the seventh degree, which includes only one degree higher in the order of ascent than the heirs above enumerated.

Samanodacas.—In default of sapindas, samanodacas succeed. These include the above enumerated heirs in the same order, as far as the fourteenth in degree.*

In default of the samanodacas, the Bundhus or cognates succeed. These kindred are of three descriptions; personal, paternal, and maternal. The personal kindred are the sons of his own father's sister; the sons of his own mother's sisters, and the sons of his own maternal uncle. The paternal kindred are, sons of his father's paternal aunt, the sons of his father's maternal aunt, and the sons of his father's maternal uncle. The maternal kindred are, the sons of his mother's paternal aunt, the sons of his mother's maternal aunt, and the sons of his mother's maternal uncle.†

In default of them, the acharya or spiritual preceptor, the pupil,

* The term *Gotraja*, or Gentiles, has been defined to signify sapindas and samanodacas by *Balaam Bhutta*, and in the *Suboudhini*, &c.

† See *Mitac.* In this series no provision appears to be made for the maternal relations in the ascending line; but *Vachespatimisra*, in the *Vivida Chintamani*, assigns to the maternal uncle and the rest a place in the order of succession next to the samanodacas; and *Mitramisra*, in *Viramitrodaya*, expresses his opinion that, as the maternal uncles' son inherits, he himself should be held to have the same right by analogy.

fellow-student in theology, learned Brahmins, and lastly the estate escheats to the crown.

Mithila.—The order of inheritance in *Mithila* corresponds with the above. In *Gungadutt Jha* v. *Sreenarain*, and *Musst. Leelawutee*, 2 *S. D. A. R.* 11, it was held that, according to the *Mithila* law, claimants of succession, as far as the seventh (*sapindas*), and even the fourteenth in descent (*samanodacas*) in the male line from a common ancestor, are preferable to the cousin by the mother's side of the deceased proprietor, *i.e.*, his mother's sister's son. Had the case been decided according to the Bengal law, the mother's sister's son would have succeeded, he taking between the *sapindas* and *samanodacas;* for it was there held that the son of a maternal uncle (who is also a *bundhu*) takes the inheritance before the lineal descendants from a common ancestor, beyond the third in ascent, *Rschoorun Mohapater* v. *Anund Lal Khan*, 2 *S. D. A.* 35.

Bombay.—There is a considerable difference between the above order of inheritance and that current in the West of India. In the *Vyavahara Mayukha*, the heirs after the mother are thus enumerated :—

The brother of the whole blood.

Son.

Paternal grandmother.

Sister.*

The paternal grandfather, and the brother of the half blood, who inherit together.

Sapindas.

Samanodacas, and

Bundhus inherit successively according to the degree of proximity. Maternal, or mothers' cognate kindred, are the sons of his mothers' paternal aunt, of his mothers' maternal aunt, and of his mothers' maternal uncle, *Mitac.*

Spiritual preceptor.—The acharyar, or spiritual preceptor, succeeds them.

Pupil. — Then follow the pupil, the fellow-student in theology, learned Brahmins; and lastly, the ruling power, which, in this instance, would be the Empress of India.

Southern India.—The order of succession, according to the law of Southern India, does not appear to differ from that current in *Benares.*

Religious order.—Holy mendicants, devotees, hermits, ascetics, student in theology resigning all worldly ties, have their title as heirs to those to whom they are by nature related, and their property is transmissible amongst themselves, *Jim. Vahana, Mitac., Daya Krama Sangraha.* In Bengal the rights and possessions of the religious order of *Sanyasis* or *Gosaiys* pass to their *chelas* or adopted

* See 1 *Borr. Bombay Reports*, 71 ; 2 *ib.* 471. A sisters' grandson, 3 *Morris*, 156.

pupils, *Beng. R.* 1806, pp. 73, 92; *ib.* 1807, p. 144; *ib.* 1810, p. 246; *Bomb. R.* 397; 1 *Stra. H. L.* 150.

Dancing-girl.—The property of a dancing-girl must pass to her female issue first, then to her male, as in the case of other females. On failure of her issue it will go to the pagoda to which she is attached. *Mr Strange* relies upon the pundits' opinion, but they cite no authorities.

With prostitutes, the tie of kindred being broken, none of their relatives who remain undegraded in caste, whether offspring or other, inherit from them; for this position the proceedings of the Sudr Court of Madras, dated 11th Nov. 1844, and 7 *S. D. A.* 273, are referred to, as authorities. *Mr Strange* adds, Their issue after their degradation succeed, but for this no authority is cited. But the latter position appears to be supported by the judgment of the *H. C.* in *Mayna Bai* v. *Uttaram*, 2 *Mad. H. C. R.* 196; 8 *Moore's In. Ap.*, wherein it is ruled that there is no authority against the existence of heritable blood between the woman and her "illegitimate offspring."

Prostitution, its gains recognised.—The trade of prostitution is recognised and legalised by Hindu law, *Chalakonda Alasani* v. *Chalakonda Ratnachalam*, 2 *Mad. H. C. R.* 56.

The learned editor appends the following note to this case:—"In *Anundrow Gunpet* v. *Bapoo Gungadhur*, the High Court of Bombay seemed to think that as the legislature discountenanced prostitution by enacting ss. 372, 373 of the *Penal Code*, it was time to withdraw the sanction of the profession of a prostitute, which had been given by the decision in *Tara Munee Dosea* v. *Motee Buneanee*, and in *Morris' Bomb. R.* 1851, p. 137."

"Quære, If this is law, *samhandha* or relationship can only be destroyed by *Ghatasphotana*. Moreover, if it be said that by Hindu law a woman loses caste by becoming a prostitute, and therefore cannot inherit, Act xxi. of 1860 applies. If then she *can* inherit, why should not her undegraded relatives inherit from her?"

Lands endowed for religious purposes.—These lands, although the management of them passes by inheritance, subject to usage, are not heritable as private property, see *Elder Widow of Rajah Chattersim* v. *Younger Widow*, *Beng. R.* 1807, p. 103; *Marain Dass* v. *Bindhasan Dass*, *ib.* 1814, p. 481.

What law governs parties who migrate from one district to another where a different school of law prevails.—Upon a question whether the *Mithila* or *Nuddea* law was to regulate the succession, the test to be applied is the form and character of the religious rites and ceremonies, and the usages of the family.

When, therefore, a family of Bengali Sudra Sutgops had migrated at a remote period from the south-west of Bengal, where the Nuddea law prevailed, to the district of Poornea, where the Mithila law was in force, and had adopted and performed their religious rites and ceremonies according to the law of Mithila, the lords of the Judicial Committee of the Privy Council held, affirming the decree of the Sudr Court, that the Mithila law in such case governed the right of succession, *Rany Pudmavati* v. *Baboo Doolar Sing*, 4 *Moore's In. Ap.* 259. Upon a claim to the inheritance of a zemindary in Midnapore, which had been in possession for a long period anterior to the institution of the suit of a family of *Gutgop* Brahmins, who had migrated from Bengal to Midnapore, but had retained their laws and performed their religious ceremonies according to the *Daya Bhaga*, and other authorities in force in Bengal, the lords of the Judicial Committee held, affirming the judgment of the Sudr Court, that the *Daya Bhaga Sastras* must govern the descent, and not the *Mitacshara*, which prevailed in Midnapore, *Rany Srimutty Dibeah* v. *Rany Koond Luta*, 4 *Moore's In. Ap.* 292. Where a family emigrates from Mithila to Bengal, the presumption is that they have preserved the religious rites and customs prescribed by the Mitac. law, unless the contrary be proved, *Koomud Chander Roy* v. *Seata Kanth Roy*, 1 *W. R.* 75, sp. no.

A deed purporting to be a deed of gift of a zemindary was executed to a stranger by the widow of the zemindar last seised, who died without issue. The deed was made with the confirmation of the *Bundhus*, the mother's brother's sons, the heirs, held to be valid by *Daya Bhaga Sastras*, as against a party claiming the succession according to the *Mitacshara*, as being descended in the seventh remove in the male line from the common ancestor.

Canarese law—Aliya Santana—Division of family property. —This term is derived from *karn aliya*, son-in-law, and *sri satana*, offspring; see *Chamier's*, "The Land Assessment, and the Landed Tenures of *Canara*," *Mangalore*, 1853, pp. 16, 86, where it is stated that the rule was introduced into *Canara* about the beginning of the third century. *Mr Justice Strange* says, In *Canara* a similar system (speaking of Malabar law) of inheritance obtains, which is termed Aliya Santan. In Malabar, the Brahmins do not follow this rule. In its details the law of Aliya Santan corresponds with that of *Maroomakatayam*, saving that the principle that the inheritance vests in the females in preference to the males is in practice better carried out in Canara, where the management of property vests ordinarily in females, while in Malabar the males commonly administer thereto.

In Canara, females only are recognised as the proprietors of family property, and division cannot be enforced by one of the members of a family governed by the law of Aliya Santan. This system differs only from that of Malabar in more consistently carrying out the doctrine that all rights to property are derived from females, per *Mr Holloway, J.*, *Munda Chetti* v. *Timmaju Hensu*, 1 *Mad. H. C. R.* 380.

Malabar.—In the province of Malabar, among the great body of its inhabitants, a different rule of descent prevails from what exists in other districts of the Presidency, Canara excepted. In these two provinces the descent runs in the female line. A man's sons are not in the line of his heirs, his property goes to his

Sisters.
Sister's sons.
Sister's daughters.
Sister's daughter's sons and daughters.
Mother.
Mother's sisters, their children.
Maternal grandmother.
Her sisters, and their children.

Failing these and their stock, in the same way of descent, it goes, as in the other parts of the Presidency, to the man's disciple and fellow-student, and then escheats, *Stra. Man. H. L.* § 382.

This rule of descent is termed *Maroomakatayam*, or Nepotism, in the female line. *Mr Justice Strange* says, The origin thereof is conceived to be thus:—It is alleged that Parasooramen, the first king of Malabar, introduced Brahmins into the district, and gave them possessions therein; and to prevent these properties from being split up, decreed that they should vest in the elder brothers, whom alone he permitted to contract marriage. The sons of these were to be accounted as sons for the whole family. The junior members, being without wives, were permitted to consort with females of lower castes; the offspring of these unions not being legitimate, could not take rank as Brahmins, or inherit from their fathers. Their inheritance was hence made to follow from their mothers. The lower castes fell into the same system of promiscuous intercourse amongst themselves. With them the females, before attaining maturity, go through a form of marriage, the bridegroom not necessarily taking the position of husband. After maturity they may consort with whom they please, and with as many as they please, provided that the connection be with members of their own, or some higher caste. The offspring succeed to the estate in the mother's family; it being obvious that parentage cannot be traced out in the line of the male.

Castes following the Maroomakatayam rule are all, except Brahmins and Aka Podwals, a class of pagoda servants, the artisans, —viz., carpenters, brass, black, and gold smiths; the Cheromars or slave tribe; the Malayers and the Paniars, with whom the rule of descent is to sons. The Fecars or toddy-drawers, and the Mookwas, or fishermen of North Malabar follow the rule, while those to the South observe Makatayam or descent to sons. In North Malabar, most of the Moplas, although Mohammedans, follow also the rule of female descent in this respect, having conformed to Hindu usage in the times of the ascendancy of the Hindus.

United families.—The adherents to the female line of descent form united family communities called *Tarawads*. The remotest member is acknowledged as one of the family if living under subordination to its head, and taking part in its religious observances. The senior male, of whatever branch, is the head of the family, and is termed *Karanaven*, the other members being termed *Anandraven*.

Succession as karanaven.—The position of karanaven belongs to the senior relative of the deceased karanaven, and not to the nearest in blood to the deceased. Thus, a mother's sister's daughter's son, being the senior, is preferred to a mother's sister's son. He would be preferred also to a sister's son, who is nearest in descent. Each member of the tarawad has a right to succeed by seniority to the management of the family property, *Kunigaratu* v. *Arrengaden*, 2 *Mad. H. C. R.* 12.

The right of the eldest member of a Nambudiri family to manage the illom is absolute, and where a junior member has in fact managed it, then this is presumed to have been with the permission of the former, who may, at any time, take up the actual control, *Nambiatan Nambudiri* v. *Nambiatan Nambudiri*, 2 *Mad. H. C. R.* 110.

No right to partition.—The head of the family has entire control over the concerns and property of the family, to which he has to administer for the good of the whole. The unity of the family may not be broken up by any member claiming his share, and forcing on a division, or incurring debt, and charging it on the property, *ib.* 387. The family may, however, by common consent, come to a division amongst themselves, and the courts would uphold it, and would doubtless grant relief where a wrong was inflicted upon an individual member.

But a division cannot be enforced by a co-sharer, nor by a creditor.

The principle of partition.—The division would be according to the taveries, or branches of the family ; that is, the property would be divided primarily according to the number of the sisters of the common ancestor, these giving rise to the branches, and afterwards among their progeny.

Alienation.—The karanaven can alienate all movable property, ancestral or self-acquired, at his discretion. But as to immovable property, whether self-acquired or ancestral, he must have the written assent of the chief anandraven.

The absence of concurrence of an anandraven, living in discord with the karanaven, would not, however, vitiate the act of the karanaven in alienating immovable property, the rule requiring the assent of the anandraven to such alienation implying that the family is a united one.

A karanaven may raise money on mortgage for the use of the family without the assent of the anandraven. It is only in making absolute alienation that their concurrence is necessary. The signature of the latter is not required to give validity to bonds executed by the karanaven.

According to Malabar law a sale of family property is valid when made with the assent, express or implied, of all the members of the tarawad, and when the deed of sale is signed by the karanaven and the senior anandraven, *if, sui juris, Kondi Menon* v. *Srangin-reagatta Ahammada*, 1 *Mad. H. C. R.* 248. Such signature is *primâ facie* evidence of the assent of the family, and the burden of proof of dissent lies on those who allege it.

The assent of the anandraven is necessary to a sale of tarawad by a karanaven. The chief anandraven's signature to the instrument of sale is sufficient but not indispensable evidence of such assent, *Kaipreta Ramen* v. *Makkaiyil Mutoren*, 1 *Mad. H. C. R.* 359.

Property assigned for Nayar females—Judgment against karanaven.—Property assigned by males of a Nayar family, for the support of their females, is still family property, and liable as such to be taken in execution to satisfy a judgment against the karanaven, *Parrakel Kondi Menon* v. *Vadakentil Kunni Penna*, 2 *Mad. H. C. R.* 41.

Charges on property.—Debts to be chargeable on the family property must have been contracted for the use of the family by the karanaven, or other member managing under his sanction. The debts of individual members cannot be charged on the property, nor one contracted by the head of the family for his own use. The debtor's estimated share in the family property is not liable for individual debts. The presumption is that a debt contracted by karanaven was for the use of the family. The presumption would be the other way, where the debt was contracted by the anandraven.

A karanaven may be superseded for incompetency, loss of caste, old age, deafness, blindness, dumbness, madness, disgraceful conduct, and dissipation of the family means. When put aside, either by the family, or legal process, he is to be replaced by the next senior competent male member.

Self-acquired property.—Self-acquired movable property—*i.e.*, what has been obtained by individual exertion, and without aid from the family funds—belongs exclusively to the acquirer, and may be disposed of by him at his pleasure. Females may hold it, as well as males. On demise, it descends, in the case of males, to their sister's sons, or nearest anandraven ; and in the case of females, to their issue, male and female.

By the law of Malabar, all acquisitions of any member of a family, which he has not disposed of in his lifetime, form part of the family property.

The acquirer may, during his lifetime, hold, alienate at once, and encumber his self-acquisitions. A karanaven in possession of the family funds is presumed to have made all acquisitions with them, and for the benefit of the corporate body. But such presumption is not irrebuttable, and his alienation, or charge of such acquisitions made during his lifetime may be valid, *Kallati Kunju Menon* v. *Palat Erracha Menon*, 2 *Mad. H. C. R.* 162.

Widowhood.—There is nothing analogous to the case of widowhood, as elsewhere existing. Females, whether in alliance with males or not, reside in their own families.

Management by females.—In theory, the property is held to vest in the females only, the males having right of management and claim to support. Practically, the males are co-sharers with the females. In default of males, females succeed to the management of the family property. In some families, the management devolves on them in preference to the males. In such cases, the senior female takes.

Maintenance.—All members of the family, even the remotest, are entitled to maintenance. It seems an anandraven's right to maintenance is merely a right to be maintained in the family house, *Kunigaratu* v. *Arrungaden*, 2 *Mad. H. C. R.* 12.

Account from karanaven—Succession to management—Anandraven's right to maintenance.—An individual member of a tarawad, governed by the Maroomakkatayam rule, has no right to an account from the karanaven, *Kunigaratu* v. *Arrungaden*, *supra*.

CHAPTER X.

PARTITION.

SECTIONS.

SECTION I.

Definition of partition of heritage—Inheritance includes succession to the goods of any relative—Partition may take place where no property—Three modes of disposing of property—Presumption in joint family that all the property is joint—But need not be joint in all respects—Each can only claim his own share—May be total or partial—Need not attach upon the whole of the property—But presumption that a division of the whole was intended—The law of succession follows the nature of the property—Agreement to divide may be enforced by the widow—Effects subsequently discovered—Re-distribution by consent—Where inequality caused by fraud—By concealment—Re-union—Condition of co-heirship destroyed by partition—Status of native Christians—The law regulating the succession—The estate of a native Christian of pure Hindu blood—Madras regulations—Effect of conversion to Christianity—Hindu law—Rights of members of undivided Hindu family—Severance of partnership—Hindu writers treat partition under inheritance—Sons co-proprietors with father—Right to maintenance out of ancestral property—Payment of debts previous to division—Payment or apportionment with consent of creditors—Postponement with consent of creditors—Mode of providing for payment—Debts contracted after division—Initiation of younger brothers, sisters—Marriage of daughters.

Definition of partition of heritage.—The natural condition of a Hindu family is that of union. *Narada* declares, Where a division of the paternal estate is instituted by sons, that becomes a topic of litigation called by the wise partition of heritage, *Mayukha, Jimuta Vahana, Mitac.* The word "sons" includes (by synecdoche) grandsons and the rest, and in the same way by "paternal" (is intended the estate of) the grandfather and the rest, and this definition of partition of heritage has been declared, *Mayukha, Mitac.* Partition is the adjustment of diverse rights regarding the whole, by distributing them on particular portions of the aggregate, *Mitac.*

Inheritance includes succession to the goods of any relative.—The expressions "paternal," and "by sons," both indicate any relation, for the term "partition of heritage" is used for a division of the goods of any relation by any relatives, *Narada, Menu, Jim. Vahana, Mitac.* Partition consists in manifesting [or particularizing by the casting of lots or otherwise] a property which had arisen in lands or chattels, but which extended only to a portion of them, and which was previously unascertained, being unfit for exclusive appropriation, because no evidence of any ground of discrimination existed, *Jim. Vahana*, or partition is a special ascertainment of property, or making of it known [by reference of a particular share to a particular person].

Partition, in its most general sense, comprehending, as well the division of the paternal property during the life of the father, as that which usually takes place, at some period or other, among co-heirs, is adjusting, by distribution, the possession of different parties to a pre-existing right.

The definition holds good in the case even of a single article; the right to which may be shared, as provided by *Vrihaspati; Jim. Vahana.*

Partition may take place even where there is no property.—Even where there is total failure of common property, a partition may also then be made, by the mere declaration, "I am separate from thee." A partition may even be a mere mental distinction. This exposition clearly distinguishes the various qualities of the term, *Mayukha.*

Three modes of disposing of property.—In Hindu law there are three modes of disposing of property—

1. By partition.
2. By alienation or gift.
3. By will.

In Malabar, no *one* member can call for a division, nor an account of the property from the managing member, nor can he claim to live on any particular portion of the property. In fact, in these respects, all obey absolutely the managing member, who, however, may be set aside for mismanagement.

In Madras any male member within the four degrees of affinity —*i.e.*, the father, son, grandson, or great-grandson—can compel a division.

In Bengal the father's consent is necessary.

Presumption in joint family that all the property is joint.—The presumption of Hindu law with respect to a joint undivided family is, that the whole property of the family is joint estate, and the *onus* lies upon a party claiming any portion of such property as his separate estate, to establish that fact, *Gopeekrist Gosain* v. *Gungapersaud Gosain*, 6 *Moore's In. Ap.* 53; *Dhurm Dass Pundey* v. *Mt. Shama Soondri Dibiah*, 3 *ib.* 229, 240; *Luximon Row Sadasew* v. *Mullar Row Bajee*, 2 *Knapp P. C.* 60, *Gour Chunder Rai* v. *Hurrish Chunder Rai*, 4 *Beng. S. D. R.* 164; 1 *Stra. H. L.* 225.

But need not be joint in all respects.—Yet the law does not require that a joint Hindu family should be joint in all respects, 9 *Moore's In. Ap.* 539.

Each can only claim his own share.—No general division can be compelled by any one member. Each can claim only his own share, but loses all claim to property subsequently obtained.

May be total or partial.—A division may be either total or partial, *Rewun Persad* v. *Mt. Radha Beeby*, 4 *Moore's In. Ap.* p. 168.

It may be partial, both as to number of shares and amount of property.

It need not attach upon the whole of the property.—It is not, therefore, necessary, where the partition is general, that it should attach upon the whole of the property; a part only may be distributed, keeping what remains for future division or to descend in the course of inheritance. The circumstance of a few articles remaining undivided would be no impeachment of a partition otherwise valid.

Presumption that a division of the whole was intended.—Where the division is partial, the presumption will always be that a division of the whole was intended, and so the divided member may sue for his share of the remainder; the whole being regarded as constructively divided already. He, in fact, holds a dual position, being divided as to part, and undivided as to part; but the presumption as to the latter being against him, he must adduce strong proof to show that this part was really undivided.

The law of succession follows the nature of the property.—It has been held in the *Shivagunga Case*, 9 *Moore's In. Ap.* 539, on the authority of 1 *Macn. H. L.* 53, that when a residue is left undivided upon partition, what is divided goes as separate property; what is undivided follows the family property; that which remains as it was, devolves on the old line; that which has changed and becomes separate devolves in the new line—in other words, the law of succession follows the nature of the property, and the interest in it, *Temmi Reddy* v. *Achama*, 2 *Mad. H. C. R.* 325.

Agreement to divide may be enforced by widow.—An agreement between two heirs to separate, whether partially carried into execution, or not carried into execution at all, may be enforced by action by the widow of a deceased parcener, *Raja Suraneny Lakshmy Venkama Row*, appellant, v. *Venkata Gopalla Narasimha Row Bahadoor*, respondent, 3 *Mad. H. C. R.* 40.

This case was brought by appeal to the Privy Council on 13th July 1869, and the Lords Commissioners, in delivering judgment, said that they found it impossible to distinguish the arrangement which has been come to in this case from the arrangement which has been entered into in the case of *Appovier* v. *Rama Subba Aiyan*, 11 *Moore's In Ap.* 75, in which this committee held that, although the agreement for a partition had not been carried out by actual partition by metes and boundaries of the property, it was nevertheless binding upon the contracting parties, and operated as a division of the family. Their Lordships observe, that the judgment delivered by Lord Westbury was in fact an affirmance of the judgments of two of the Courts below, and was fully supported by the authorities then before the Court. It is, however, satisfactory to find, in the present case, that the High Court of Madras, not adverting to the case in Moore, which probably had not then come to their knowledge, has, in its learned judgment, arrived at the same conclusion, and that upon independent and upon the earlier authorities. The passage which they quote from the *Mitacshara* fully supports the proposition involved in the judgment. The passage runs thus :—"If partition be denied or disputed, the fact may be known and certainly obtained by the testimony of kinsmen, relatives of the father or of the mother, such as maternal uncles and the rest, being competent witnesses as before described." That is one mode of proving division. It then goes on in the disjunctive, "or by evidence of a writing or record of the partition," which we have here, and then it says, "It may also be ascertained by separate or unmixed house and field ;" that is, if other evidence of partition be wanting it may be supplied by proof that the houses and fields had been actually divided, and were held separately.

Effects subsequently discovered.—And although a division, when once made, is final, and cannot ordinarily be re-opened, yet, if effects which were not embraced in the division made be subsequently discovered, they may then be divided—as to which the family is not yet therefore divided. But this, although so treated in the books, cannot be regarded as an exception to the rule of finality of the division.

Parties may consent to re-distribution where original unequal.—But by consent of the co-heirs, if, for any cause not understood at the time, the division may prove to have been unequal or defective, the shares may be re-distributed. As this is effected by the consent of the parties, it can hardly be considered an exception to the rule of the finality of the division.

Where inequality caused by fraud.—If indeed the inequality had been brought about by fraud, then the Courts would grant redress. But the fraud must be clearly proved.

Concealment of common stock.—And if any of the co-heirs conceal any of the common property, with a view of defrauding his coheirs of their shares therein, upon a division, he forfeits his share, *Mitac.*

Reunion.—There may be a re-union and a subsequent partition. But this can only be effected by fathers and sons, brothers and paternal uncles, and nephews; more distant relations, as grandchildren, cousins, &c., may club their resources together, but cannot return to the position of an undivided Hindu family, *post*, p. 426.

In case of a re-union, after-born sons, and the re-united members, share the property exclusively. See *post*, "Re-union."

Condition of co-heirship destroyed by partition.—The condition of co-heirship may be destroyed by partition of the joint property, each co-heir taking his appointed share. The effect of such division is to vest the divided share absolutely in each separate member, and in his line after him.

Status of native Christians *—The law regulating the succession—The estate of a native Christian of pure Hindu blood—Madras regulations, II. of 1802, s. xvii.; and III. of 1802, s. xvi. cl. i.—Effect of conversion to Christianity as to succession—Hindu law—Rights of members of undivided Hindu family—Severance of partnership—The *Lex Loci* Act, No. xxi. of 1850. —The status of native Christians, and the law of succession and inheritance, as administered in the Mofussil, in respect to their rights and properties, were considered by the Privy Council in the case of *Abraham* v. *Abraham*, 9 *Moore's In. Ap.* 195.

The *Madras Regulation* II. of 1802, s. xvii., provides that in cases coming within the jurisdiction of the Zillah Courts, for which no specific rule may exist, the judges are to act according to justice, equity, and good conscience; and the *Madras Regulation* II. of 1802, s. xvii. cl. i., prescribes that in suits before the native Court, regarding succession, inheritance, caste, &c., the Hindu law, with respect to Hindus, and the Mohammedan law, with respect to Mohammedans, are to be considered the general rules by which the judges are to form their decisions. Held that the latter regulations applied to Hindus and Mohammedans not by birth only, but by religion.

Held also, that in case of succession to the estate of a deceased Hindu of pure native blood, who had married a European wife,

* Native Christians, and East Indians, are appellations given to two different classes.

and who professes with his family the Christian religion, and whose ancestors for generations had embraced Christianity, that such a case was within the provisions of *Madras Regulations* II. of 1802, s. xvii., and was to be decided by reference to the usages of the class to which the deceased attached himself and the family to which he belonged.

Upon the conversion of a Hindu to Christianity, the Hindu law ceases to have any continuing obligatory force upon the convert.

The convert may renounce the old law by which he was bound, as he renounced his old religion, or, if he think fit, he may abide by the old law, notwithstanding he has renounced the old religion. For though the profession of Christianity releases the convert from the trammels of the Hindu law, yet it does not of necessity involve any change of the rights or relations of the convert in matters in which Christianity has no concern, such as his rights and interests in, and his power over the property. The convert, though not bound as to such matters, either by the Hindu law or by any other positive law, may, by his course of conduct after his conversion, have shown by what law he intended his rights to be governed. He may do so either by attaching himself to a class which in this respect has adopted and acted upon some particular law, or by having himself observed some particular law, family usage, or custom.

The *Lex Loci* Act xxi. of 1850, does not apply where the parties have ceased to be Hindus in religion.

A member of an undivided Hindu family having become a convert to Christianity, held that such circumstance amounts by the Hindu law to a severance of the union.

Hindu writers treat partition under inheritance.—The Hindu law writers treat partition under the head of inheritance, to which it bears an affinity, inasmuch as it is founded on a claim of succession having its origin in birth; although, in the lifetime of the father, inchoate and contingent, either upon his consent, or upon the will of the sons. In these cases, the right of the sons becomes absolute as if the father were dead.

Sons co-proprietors with father—Right to maintenance out of ancestral property.—This contingent right makes the sons in some sense co-proprietors, or in a certain sense co-parceners with the father in the family property, giving them during the life of the father certain claims for support, &c., upon it that he cannot altogether defeat. But these claims, deriving their right from birth, attach more upon ancestral than upon self-acquired property of the father. Upon partition the law regulates the distribution of the former, whilst the latter is left more to his discretion, *Jim. Vahana, Mitac., Vishnu, Nagalinga Mudali* v. *Subbiramaniya Mudali,* 1 *Mad. H. C. R.* 77.

Payment of debts previous to division.—Previous to division provision should be made for all charges upon the family property, such as maintenance, family debts, &c., for where partition takes place during the lifetime of the father, it must be regarded as a descent of the property. And as debts by the Hindu law attach upon the property of the debtor, it follows that such property would be liable to the debts of the ancestor into whosesoever hand it would come. The co-sharers amongst whom it would be divided would therefore be liable to the creditors to the extent of their respective shares at least. *Ratyayana* says, "The debts of the father, one incurred by a parcener himself on account of the debts of the father, and one specially his own—debts so incurred, must be examined on a partition with the kinsmen." *On account of the debts of the father*, incurred for the sake of discharging the father's debts; *specially his own* (contracted by other than himself), for the maintenance of his family. The same author says, "A debt contracted by a brother, a paternal uncle, or a mother, for the support (of the family), must be fully discharged by the co-heirs when partition is made," *Mayukha.*

Payment or apportionment with consent of creditors.—From the text of *Narada* it results that co-heirs making a partition may apportion the debts of their father or other predecessor with the consent of the creditors, or must immediately discharge the debts, for such is the purpose of ordaining a partition of the residue after payment of the debts, *Jim. Vahana, Mayukha.*

Postponement with consent of creditors.—A partition should be made by sons of the wealth of their deceased father which remains after discharging his debts; or, with the consent of the creditors, the partition may take place first, and the debts be afterwards discharged, *Daya Krama Sangraha.*

Narada declares, What remains of the paternal inheritance, over and above the father's obligations, and after payment of his debts, may be divided by the brethren, so that their father continue not a debtor. Here, from the expression, "so that the father remain not a debtor," it appears that the debts may be cleared off subsequently to the partition, otherwise it would be unmeaning, *Daya Krama Sangraha.* A son living with a father is liable for a debt contracted by him for the common concern, where the latter is afflicted with an incurable disease, the same as though he were dead.

Mode of providing for payment.—The mode of providing for these liabilities usually adopted is by setting aside a portion solely for the purpose of meeting those charges, and dividing the rest, or by apportioning those charges among the members who have taken their shares. But in this case, as on dissolution of partnership, the consent of the creditors to a separation of liabilities is required to bind them.

Debts contracted after division.—The debts and charges incurred after division bind the members individually who incur them.

So, also, if a father incur debts after a division, his after-born sons will be jointly liable for them, just as in an undivided family.

Initiation of younger brothers and sisters.—On a partition after death of the father, the elder brothers shall, out of the wealth of the father, perform investiture and other ceremonies for those younger brothers and unmarried sisters who have not had those ceremonies performed, *Brihaspati*, *Mayukha*, "Charges on Inheritance."

Uninitiated brothers should be initiated by those for whom the ceremonies have been already completed, *Yajnavalchya*, *Mayukha*, *Mitac.*

Marriage of daughters.—But sisters should be disposed of in marriage, giving them as an allotment the fourth part of a brother's own share—meaning that a fourth part of such share as would be allotted to a son of such class as the sister [happens to be] being given to each sister [according to her rank they are to be initiated], *Yajnavalchya*, *Mayukha*, *Mitacshara.*

SECTION II.

WHO ARE OBJECTS OF PARTITION.

Inherent right of each heir to obtain partition—In Madras male issue may enforce division from the father—One son may claim it—The right of after-born sons—Partition postponed until delivery of pregnant women—Father must reserve two shares of self-acquired property when wife not past child-bearing—Son born after partition made by father—Several sons so born—Where born after father's death—Re-union with father lets in the sons to share with after-born son—Sons born after adoption, where there are no after-born nor united sons—Minors—May claim through guardian if evidence of malversation—Where infant bound by acts of guardian—Guardian may refer the question, whether division should be according to Patni Bhaga or Putra Bhaga—Charge on zemindary by manager or guardian—Re-union of minor—Evidence of—Whether minor can enter into division and execute a deed—Illegitimate children—Of Englishman by Hindu woman—Rights governed by Hindu law—Joint family—Yet partnership differs from joint Hindu family, defined by that law—On death of each, his lineal heirs entitled to enter partnership—Illegitimate sons do not inherit even movables—Entitled to maintenance—Sons of a man by a woman of higher class—Illegitimate sons of Sudras—Failing son, daughter, and daughter's son—Failing son among Sudras, daughter's son takes equal shares—Daughters cannot claim, though when property descends they may divide equally—Partition among brothers alters the line of descent—Among daughters, has not the same effect—No woman can compel division—Where married according to approved species—Woman's fee or gratuity—Wife entitled to a share—Widow's rights in Bengal—In Benares—Mother shares equally with sons.

Inherent right of each heir to obtain partition.—It is an inherent right in each co-heir, by the Hindu law, to obtain a partition, *Jim. Vahana.*

Sons are the immediate objects of partition by the father, including male offspring as far as great-grandsons. They on partition, as well as inheritance, share *jure representationis*, *Daya Krama Sangraha.*

In Madras male issue may enforce division from the father.—In Madras any male member within the four degrees of affinity, viz., the father, son, grandson, or great-grandson, may compel a division of ancestral property, *Nagalinga Mudali* v. *Subbiramaniya Mudali*, 1 *Mad. H. C. R.* 77.

One son may claim it.—So one son may claim it, the rest preferring to remain in union. All may jointly sue for their respective shares, though in enforcing division from the father, each may claim for himself alone.

The right of after-born sons.—In the distribution of property, the law chiefly regards the interest of the sons, and takes especial care that none of them are excluded from participation, whether they be already in existence, or come subsequently into existence by after-birth, the law making special provision for such a case, although different opinions prevail as to whether the share of such sons is to be supplied by the father out of his share, or by the brothers out of theirs. *Mr Justice Strange* lays it down, that in *any* case they are always a charge on the father only; but *Sir Thomas Strange* adopts a more reasonable rule. If the pregnancy be apparent at the time, it has been said that the division should be postponed, or the share set apart to abide the event. But should the pregnancy be unknown, and therefore not anticipated, and a son, who was in the womb *at the time*, be born after, he should obtain his share from the brothers by contributions, just, in fact, as if he had been born. Should, however, a son be *subsequently begotten*, he must be provided for out of the remainder of the father's property, succeeding to the whole exclusively, or dividing it with such of the brothers as may have become re-united to the common parent, any acquisition by a re-united parent, through is own industry, or individual wealth, belonging exclusively to the son born after partition, and not to him in common with another re-united; and on failure of after-born issue, the sons who had already received their shares take by inheritance what their parents leave.

Partition postponed until delivery of pregnant women.—

Partition amongst brothers must be postponed until after the delivery of such of the women as are childless but pregnant, *Vashishtha, Mayukha.* See *Mitac., Jim. Vahana.*

A father must reserve two shares of self-acquired property for himself when his wife is not past child-bearing.—In a case cited by *Macnaghten,* the question is asked, Can a person divide his self-acquired landed property between his two sons by his senior wife, reserving something for his own maintenance, while his junior wife is pregnant, or while there is a probability of such wife bearing children? And the reply given is, That he is incompetent, without reserving two shares of his wealth, to divide his self-acquisitions, whether real or personal, between his two sons by his elder wife, while his junior wife is pregnant, or while there is a possibility of such wife's bearing children; for "who acts otherwise than the law permits has no power in the distribution of the estate." "They who are born, and they who are yet unbegotten, and they who are actually in the womb, all require the means of support, and the dissipation of their hereditary maintenance is censured." "If the sons were separated from the father (while his wife was pregnant), but not known to be so, the son who is afterwards (born of that pregnancy) shall receive his share from his brother."

Macn. says, It should not be supposed that, according to Bengal law, there is a fixed period for a father's distribution of his own acquired property of whatever description. Having exclusive control over his own acquisitions, he may distribute them in greater, less, or equal shares to his sons, and may reserve to himself whatever he chooses, whether half or two shares, or three. His choice alone determines the time of making partition of his own acquired wealth, and the distribution does not operate to debar a male child born subsequently thereto, for his right still subsists over the paternal estate, as appears from the following passage of the *Daya Bhaga:* —" If a father, having separated his sons, and having reserved for himself a share according to law, die without being re-united with his sons, then a son who is born after the partition shall alone take the father's wealth; and that only shall be his allotment. But if the father die after re-uniting himself with some of his sons, that son shall receive his share from the re-united co-heirs. If the sons were separated (from the father) while his wife was pregnant, but not known to be so, the son who is afterwards born (of that pregnancy) shall receive his share from his brothers. Not one only, but even many sons begotten after a partition, shall take exclusively the paternal wealth. All the wealth which is acquired by the father himself, who has made a partition with his sons, goes to the son begotten by him after the partition." Under the term "all," wealth, however considerable, which is acquired by the father, goes to the son begotten by him after partition." "But the followers of the Benares school maintain that the father is subject to the control of his sons, in regard to the immovable estate, whether acquired by himself, or inherited from his father or other predecessor. And in conformity to such opinion it may be held that a father is incompetent to distribute his self-acquired landed estate, until his wife is past child-bearing, though that is not distinctly stated in the *Mitacshara* in the chapter treating of the right of one born after partition."

Son born after partition made by father.—If a son is born after partition made by a father, he will be sole heir to the property retained by the father. If none have been retained, the other sons are bound to contribute to a share out of their portions.

Several sons so born.—So if several sons be born after partition made by the father, their portions are also to come from their father's share, *Stra. M. H. L.* § 258, citing *Mitac.* ch. i. s. vi. § 2, which does support him, and he and they succeed to the exclusion of the divided sons; but if any of these have re-united with the father, they will share with him.

After father's death.—*Yajnavalchya* states a distinction at a partition after the father's death, with respect to a son born immediately afterwards by a mother, a stepmother, or brother's wife, where pregnancy was uncertain. "When the sons have been separated, one who is [afterwards] born of a woman equal in class shares the distributions." The partition is to be thus effected: Something is to be contributed by all the brothers or others [who had previously shared], each something out of his own share, until the [posthumous son's] share is equal to their own, *Mayukha*; see *Mitac.*, *Jim. Vahana.* Sons with whom the father has made a partition, should give a share to the son born after the distribution, *Vishnu*; see *Jim. Vahana*, after allowing for subsequent expenses and income, *Yajnavalchya*, *Mayukha*, *Mitac.*, *Jim. Vahana.*

"One born [to a man] separated [from his sons] will alone take the father's wealth," *Brihaspati*, see *Mitac.*, *Jim. Vahana.* "All the wealth which is acquired by the father himself, who has made a partition with his sons, goes to the sons begotten by him after the partition; those born before it are declared to have no right," *Mayukha*; see *Jim. Vahana*, *supra.* "As in the wealth so in the debts likewise, and in gifts, pledges, and purchases." "They have no claims on each other except for acts of mourning and libations of water." If there be nothing but debts, then that [son] is not even bound to pay those debts, without receiving a share from those formerly separated; for as is afterwards shown, "he who takes the estate must be made to pay the debts for it," *Mayukha.*

Re-union with the father lets in the sons to share with after-born son.—A son born after a division shall alone take the paternal wealth, or he shall participate with such of the brethren as are re-united with the father, *Menu*, *Mitac.*, *Jim. Vahana.*

Sons born after adoption.—Where a son has been adopted, and there are other sons born after the adoption, the adopted son is entitled to but one-fourth of what forms the share of each of the after-born sons, *Elberling.*

Where no after-born nor united sons.—Where there are no after-born sons, nor sons still remaining in union, the divided sons inherit the father's share.

Minors.—If necessary a division may be made during the minority of any son, and his share should be securely set apart, with the approbation of the guardian, or of the representative of the sovereign. But if this should be neglected, he must, within a reasonable time after attaining his majority, object, and demand his fair share. If not, he will be barred of his remedy after the lapse of the statutory period, or after acts on his part of positive ratification, or tacit acquiescence. But mere silence does not prove ratification, or acquiescence, as the Sudr Court, Dec. 1852, p. 107, seems to have thought. There must be something done under these circumstances, showing—

1. A full knowledge of his rights.
2. An abandonment of them.

May claim through guardian if evidence of malversation.—A minor of himself cannot claim a division, but may do so through his guardian, and this only in case there is a reasonable ground to fear that his interests are in danger. There must be evidence of such malversation as will endanger the minor's interests if his share be not separately secured, *Svámiyár Pillai* v. *Chokkalingham Pillai*, 1 *Mad. H. C. R.* 105. It may be a question to what particular share a minor may be entitled, but this being raised alone affords no warrant for claiming a partition in his name. When he comes of age he will himself claim what may be his due. In the meantime there can be no valid objection to the property remaining in its normal state of joint inheritance, *ib.* See *Alimelammal* v. *Arunachellam Pillai*, 3 *Mad. H. C. R.* 69.

His guardian, or, if he have none, any relation not interested, may institute a suit for the purpose. His share being separated, must be secured for him until he attains his age; otherwise, as against him, a partition would be void. *Mr Colebrooke* says, "The sovereign, or his representative, as guardian of the minor, is competent to authorise a partition. . . . Nothing has been found in the law to prohibit the demand of a partition for the benefit of a minor," 3 *Dig.* p. 544, text, ccccliii. 2; 2 *Stra. H. L.* 362. In another case he says, "It does not appear that the original partition would have been void if the due allotment for the minor had been securely set apart with the approbation of his guardian, or of the representative of the sovereign. In the case as set forth, the share stated to have been set apart for the minor in the hands of the defendants, was never delivered to him by them, nor had the partition been ratified for him by his guardian," 2 *Stra. H. L.* 361

A division of property took place in 1837 between A., the mother and guardian of the plaintiff, a minor, and B., the husband of two childless widows, the defendants in a suit to recover possession of the property, on the ground that the division did not bind the plaintiff. The Court held that there being no proof of fraud, or that undue advantage had been taken of the plaintiff's minority, and in the absence of proof of gross inequality in the distribution of the property, the division was valid and binding on the plaintiff, *Nallappa Reddi* v. *Balammal*, 2 *Mad. H. C. R.* 182.

Where infant bound by acts of guardian.—All acts of the guardian of a Hindu infant, which are such as the infant might, if of age, reasonably and prudently do for himself, must be upheld when done for him by his guardian. Such a guardian may bind his ward by referring to a panchayat of their caste a question of customary partition, *Temmakal* v. *Subbammal*, 2 *Mad. H. C. R.* 47.

Guardian may refer question whether division should be according to Patni Bhaga or Putri Bhaga.—Where a Sudra died leaving two widows, one with an only son, an infant, and the other with two sons, held that the guardian of the infant might refer the question, Whether the deceased's estate should be divided according to the *Patni Bhaga* (division according to wives), or *Putra Bhaga* (division according to sons) ?

Charge on zemindary by manager or guardian of minor.—A bond executed by a Hindoo and guardian of an adopted son during his minority, the object of which was first to pay off a debt due by her deceased husband charged upon the zemindary, and next to discharge certain debts contracted by her in the management of the zemindary, the validity of which was recognised by her adopted son after he became of age, upheld without determining the question raised of the power of a Hindoo widow, as guardian of a minor, to create a charge on the zemindary during the minority of her adopted son, *Chetty Colum Coamra Vencatachella Reddyar* v. *Rajah Rungasawmy Streethmunth Jyengar Bahadoor*, 8 *Moore's In. Ap.* 319.

Re-union of minor, evidence of.—Where a division has taken place between the members of a Hindu family, one of whom is a minor, and the minor continues to live with the father after the division, and their shares become mixed together, it does not follow that there was a re-union. A re-union from that circumstance is not conclusively established. It is only evidence from which a re-union may be inferred. Passages abound in writings of Hindu lawyers in which this distinction seems not to have been borne in mind, and the passage quoted from the *Mitacshara* is of that character, *Kuta Bullyviraya* v. *Kuta Chudappavuthamulu*, 2 *Mad. H. C. R.* 235.

Whether minor can enter into division and execute a deed.—This case appears to be principally decided upon a deed of release alleged to have been executed by the minor after attaining his majority; but it is doubtful whether the point of Hindu law raised during the trial has been correctly determined. The father and a grown-up son divided the family property, the adult son receiving his share, and the father retaining his own share as well as the share of his minor son. The question arises, Could the minor son have entered into a division, and execute a deed of division? The father, in ascertaining the share to which the adult parcener was entitled, would, of course, be obliged to take into account the amount of property to which the parceners remaining united would be entitled, and the fact of one parcener insisting on division, and separating his interests, does not necessarily constitute the parceners who remain united, separated in consequence of the mere circumstance of their shares having been estimated in order to determine the share of the outgoing parceners. Even if a division between the parceners who do not separate can, under these circumstances, be considered to have taken place, the *Mitacshara* shows that a re-union ensued between the father and minor son. At § 2, s. ix. ch. ii., we find the author says, Effects which had been divided, and which are again mixed together, are termed re-united. He to whom such appertain is a re-united parcener; and at § 3 he observes, *Brihaspati* declares, He who being once separated dwells again, through affection, with his father, brother, or paternal uncle, is termed re-united. With such of the brothers as may have become re-united to the common parents, any acquisition by a re-united parent, through his own industry or individual wealth, belongs exclusively to the son born after partition, and not to him in common with another re-united; and on failure of after-born issue, the sons who had already received their shares take by inheritance what their parents leave, *Mitac.* ch. i. s. vi. § 16; 1 *Stra. H. L.* 183. See further on the subject, "Minority."

Illegitimate children.—In those cases where illegitimate children would inherit on the death of their father, they will share on partition during his life; if not, they are entitled to maintenance, see p. 97.

Illegitimate children of Englishman by Hindu woman—Rights governed by Hindu law—Joint family—Yet partnership differs from joint Hindu family, defined by Hindu law—On death of each, his lineal heirs entitled to enter partnership.—H., an Englishman, had five children by two Madras Hindu women, one a married one of the Brahmin caste, living apart from her husband. The children were brought up as Hindus, and lived together as a joint family. H. devised an estate to the children in equal shares. Held, that the children were Hindus, and their rights were to be governed by that law, *Myna Boyee* v. *Cotaram Myaram*, 8 *Moore's In. Ap.* 400. That, being children of a Christian father, by different Hindu mothers, although constituting themselves co-parceners in the enjoyment of the property, after the manner of a joint Hindu family, yet that the partnership so constituted differed from the co-partnership of a joint Hindu family, as defined by the Hindu law, and that at the death of each son, his lineal heir, representing their parent, would be entitled to enter into that partnership.*

A suit having been instituted by one of the children against his brothers for partition of the estate, a razinamah was executed, by which the shares and the amount to be paid to each were ascertained, with provision against alienation by sale, mortgage, lease, or security of any separate share. Held, that each co-sharer might nevertheless alienate by will.†

Illegitimate sons do not inherit even movable wealth.—But the son by a Sudra woman, not legally married, does not obtain a share even of the movable property. "The son of a Brahmin, a Kshetriya, or a Vaisya, by a woman of the servile class, shall inherit no part of the estate [unless he be virtuous, nor jointly with other sons unless his mother was lawfully married]. Whatever his father may give him, let that be his own," *Menu, Mayukha;* see *Mitac., Jim. Vahana.*

Heirs entitled to maintenance.—*Brihaspati* declares this distinction after the father's death: "The virtuous and obedient son, born by a Sudra woman to a man who has no other offspring, should obtain a maintenance, and let kinsmen take the residue of the estate, *Mayukha,* see *Jim. Vahana.* A son by a Sudra woman born unto a man who leaves no [legitimate] offspring shall, if he be strictly obedient like a pupil, receive a provision for his maintenance." *Gautama, a provision for his maintenance,* or as a means of livelihood, *Mayukha.*

Sons of a man by a woman of a higher class.—The same author says, "Sons termed pratiloma ‡ [shall have an allotment] similar to that of the son produced by a woman of the servile class." *Sons termed pratiloma,* meaning those produced by a woman higher than the begetter with respect to class, *Mayukha.*

Illegitimate sons of Sudras.—"Even a son begotten by a Sudra on a female slave may take a share by the father's choice. But if the father be dead, the brethren should make him partaker of the moiety of the share," *Yajnavalchya, Mayukha, Mitac., Jim. Vahana. Choice,* the pleasure of the father. From specifying *by a Sudra,* it is clear that a son, by a twice-born man on a female slave,

* Query, Whether such a right of inheritance enures to collaterals?

† Where the opinion given by the native law officers is apparently irreconcilable with the opinions of approved text-writers on the Hindu law, those who give the opinion should be asked to explain that which appears *primâ facie* irreconcilable, so that they may show on what ground an apparent exemption from the general law is inferred; whether a general custom, modifying texts or local usage, family customs, or other exceptional matters? *ib.*

‡ *Pratiloma* means against the hair.

does not obtain a share even by the father's choice. Neither after the death of the father will he get the half, nor in the absence of sons, or other [heirs], will he get the whole. This is the argument of the *Madana Ratna* and others, *Mayukha*, *Mitac.* But simple maintenance, *Mitac.*

Failing son, daughters, etc., illegitimate sons take full shares. —Failing son, daughter, and daughter's son, the illegitimate sons come in for full shares in a Sudra's property, but their obtaining shares during their father's lifetime depends upon his pleasure, *Mitac.*

Failing son, daughter's son takes equal share.—Among Sudras, failing a putra, the son of a daughter becomes co-heir, *Mitac.*

Daughters cannot claim.—Daughters can neither claim nor share in division.

Though when property descends they may divide equally.— Daughters can divide property descending to them in equal shares as sons, of course, by consent.

Partition among brothers alters the line of descent.—Partition among brothers creates a new line of succession tracing from the deceased brother.

Among daughters has not the same effect.—*F. Macn.*, 55, says, On failure of male issue of a brother who has divided off, the right of the female relatives, namely, of the widow or daughters, accrues. Partition among daughters has no such effect, since on the lapse of one co-sharer, if married, her share vests in her own line; if unmarried, in her brother's, *Mitac.*

Women cannot compel division.—No women can compel a division. A *wife* can only claim maintenance from her husband, but no *share* in the property; and a widow inherits in the case of a divided family, so that no division is necessary. In an undivided family she gets only maintenance, unless she inherits the self-acquired property of her late husband.

Where married according to approved species.—That which a woman may have received in gift from her own family returns to the donors, if alive, and her marriage be of a disapproved species. If the donors are dead, it goes to her husband and his kindred. If the marriage be of an approved species, it goes to her husband and his kindred, which does not support him, and *Smriti Chandrika*, which does. Gifts made by a man in anticipation of marriage, should the woman die before the marriage takes place, are returned to the intended bridegroom. See "Stridhana."

Woman's fee or gratuity.—*Mr J. Strange* says, The woman's fee, or the gratuity given her on her marriage by the bridegroom, for the purchase of household utensils, cattle, &c., as an exception goes to her brothers. For this he cites the *Mayukha*, without reference to the particular part. Chapter iv. s. x. of that work treats of woman's property, and does not support this rule. *Mr J.*

Strange likewise refers to the *Smriti Chandrika*, which does not support him. But the *Mitacshara* supports the rule, but says, "to the brothers of the whole blood," a distinction which *Mr J. Strange* does not notice.

Wife entitled to a share.—In the case of equal participation between a father and his sons, a share belongs also to the wife, if no separate property had been given to her. *Yajnavalchya* says, "If he make the allotments equal, his wives, to whom no separate property had been given by the husband or father-in-law, must be rendered partakers of like portions;" and he adds, "or if any had been given, let him assign the half." *The half*, meaning as much as, with what had been before given her as separate property (stridhana), will make it equal to a son's share. But if her property be [already] more than such share, no share [belongs to her], *Mayukha, Mitac., Daya Krama Sangraha, Jimuta Vahana.* Where she does not participate, she must depend upon the reservation to be made by her husband for himself and the remaining members of the family, which, with reference to property acquired by him, may be to any extent that he may deem expedient. Where peculiar property has been bestowed on some of the wives, the other wives destitute of male issue must be rendered by the father partakers of wealth to the same amount, *Daya Krama Sangraha.* But if such property have not been given, then she must be rendered equal sharer with the sons, *i.e.*, where the sons are made equal sharers, *Daya Krama Sangraha.*

In the case, however, of peculiar property having been given [to all the wives], then they will only receive half a share by the rule of analogy observed in the case of a superseded wife who has received peculiar property, and who is entitled to receive only half the gratuity [otherwise] given to a wife on her supersession, *Yajnavalchya, Jim. Vahana, Chudamani.*

Widow's rights in Bengal.—*Sir W. H. Macn.* says, At any time after the death, natural or civil, of their parents, the brethren are competent to come to a partition among themselves of the property, movable and immovable, ancestral and acquired; and according to the law as received in the province of Bengal, the widow is not only entitled to share an undivided estate with the brethren of her husband, but she may require from them a partition of it, although her allotment will devolve upon the heirs of her husband at her decease. See *Bhyroochund Rai* v. *Russookmunee*, 1 *S. D. A. R.* 28; *Neelkaunt Rai* v. *Munee Chowdrain*, *ib.* 58; *Rani Bhawani Dibia* v. *Ranee Soorujmuni*, *ib.* 135.

In Benares.—But in the Benares school the reverse of this doctrine prevails. See *Duljeet Singh* v. *Sheomunook Singh*, *ib.* 59.

Mother shares equally with sons.—"Let the mother also take an equal share," *Yajnavalchya.* Mothers receive allotments according to the shares of sons, *Vishnu, Jim. Vahana.*

In another *Smriti* it is said, "A mother, if she be dowerless, shall in a partition by sons take an equal share." The meaning is, that if she have dower she shall take only as much as, with that dower, will make her an equal sharer with her sons. But no share belongs to her if her property be more than such share, *Mayukha*.

In a case before the High Court of Bombay, after citing the above passages, *Arnould, J.*, said, This doctrine has been followed by the late Supreme Court in the case of the goods of Chepajuddoo, decided on the 22d of June 1861, a note of which was furnished by the Chief-Justice, where the Court, after consideration, and obtaining answers from the Shastres of the Sudr Adawlut, and at Poona, held that, "If there be more than one widow, each is entitled to an equal share of the property." It appears from these answers, that although the author of the *Mayukha* cites no text in support of his opinion, such texts are to be met with in the *Viramitrodaya*, an authority of the *Benares* school, and *Macn.* "Prins. of Hindu Law," a work of authority in Bengal. It is also said, p. 19, that if there be more than one widow, their rights are equal. The case in *Morton's Reports*, p. 314, shows that this rule was acted upon by the Supreme Court as early as the year 1791; and in 1 *Morley's Digest* (§ 15), we find an instance of its being acted on in the North-Western Provinces in 1850. On these authorities we hold that the widows in this case are *prima facie* entitled to equal shares of the property, and it remains to be considered whether either of them is disentitled by misconduct to her share; and if not, then whether we ought to grant administration to them jointly, or to one only; and if the latter, to which of them. After asking, Is the elder widow, then, deprived of her right by the misconduct proved? the learned judge proceeds to discuss the questions of infidelity and incontinence, and to point out discrepancies in the authorities on the subject, adding, In Bengal two widows take the whole estate for life, and on the death of one the whole survives to the other, upon whose death it goes to the collateral heirs of the husband, 1 *Morl. Dig.* 313. In Madras it has been held that the eldest widow succeeds, the other widows being entitled during her life to maintenance only, the second widow succeeding on the death of the first, 1 *Mad. Sel. Dec.* 456, 457, *S. R. A.* of No. 11, 835; 2 *ib.* 44. But see *Strange's Man. of H. L.* 2d ed. § 326, where the author lays down that in Southern India the wives are viewed on an equality, and inherit equally; and he considers the following passage from the *Mitacshara*, ch. ii. s. i. § 5 (omitted in *Colebrooke's* translation), which the editor owes to *Vakeel Srinivasacharya*, "The singular number 'wife' signifies the kind, hence if there are several wives belonging to the same or different castes, (they) divide the property according to the shares prescribed to them, and take it." In the goods of *Dadoo Mania*, 1st September 1862, *Ind. Jur.* Oct. 25, 1862, page 59.

Sir Thomas Strange, pp. 136, 137, has laid down decidedly, When a man has left more widows than one, and no son by any, she who is first married, being the one who is considered as married from a sense of duty, succeeds in the first instance, the others inheriting in their turn as they survive. He quotes as an authority 3 *Dig.* 461, 489, 486. *Mr Strange's Man. H. L.* 326, does not assign any reason for supporting the conclusion that a clause between clauses 5 and 6 in *Colebrooke's* translation of ch. ii. s. i. of the *Mitacshara* has been omitted; and until the authenticity of his assertion be proved, we must conclude that *Colebrooke* is correct. In clause 5 *Mr Colebrooke* translates a passage from *Suboudini*, which appears to us to support the view of *Sir Thomas Strange.* Clause 6, which should follow the supposed omitted clause, is not in harmony with the existence of such a clause. Neither does any other passage in the whole chapter of the *Mitacshara* support the conclusion that such clause ever existed.

Macn., *P. H. L.* p. 19, which appears to be the same passage as that referred to in the above-quoted judgment of *Sir J. Arnold*, when drawing the distinction between the law current in the Bengal and other schools, observes, that if there be more than one widow, their rights are equal; for this position he attests *El. H. L. Ap.* 59, which has reference to a totally different subject, namely, a claim to maintenance preferred by a wife against her husband. It is singular that *Macnaghten* should have referred to *Sir Thomas Strange's* work as his authority, seeing that it expresses a totally different opinion at pp. 136, 137.

SECTION III.

MODE OF PARTITION.

Where no common property, partition may take place—By arbitration, by adjustment, by lot, by suit—Without writing—Among co-heirs.

Where no common property, partition may take place.—Even where there is a total failure of common property, a partition may also then be made by the mere declaration, "I am separate from thee." A partition may be a mere mental distinction. This exposition clearly distinguishes the various qualities of this term, *Mayukha.*

By arbitration, by adjustment, by lot, by suit.—Partition may be made openly in the presence of arbitrators, or privately by adjustment, or by casting lots, *Sancha* and *Lichita*, *Jim. Vahana.* If no amicable arrangement can be arrived at, the object may be effected by a suit to enforce division.

Without writing.—A division may be effected without an instrument in writing, *Rewun Persad* v. *Mt. Radda Beeby*, 4 *Moore's In. Ap.* 168. According to Bengal law, a writing is merely used *in memoriam rei*, and a written instrument is not essential to the validity of any disposition of property, 2 *Macn. Prin. H. L.* 147, n., 168, n. Though not necessary, it is proper to execute a deed of partition or release, which is the best evidence of partition. But partition without such an instrument cannot be set aside by any of the co-heirs on that ground, as doubts regarding the fact can be solved by parol evidence, *ib.* 168, n. See *Mantena Rayaparaj* v. *Chekuri Venkataraj*, 1 *Mad. H. C. R.* 100; *Doe d. Rajah Sri Krist* v. *E. In. Co.* 6 *Moore's In. Ap.* 267.

Verbal evidence of partition is as conclusive as though it had been written, *Doe d. Gocoolchunder Mitter* v. *Tarrachurn Mitter*, 1 *Morl. Dig.* 485, § 55.

A memorandum of separation between two brothers, one of whom had neither agreed to nor signed it, is not binding on him, and on the death of his brother he is entitled to succeed to the whole property, to the exclusion of the deceased brother's widow; she is entitled, however, to maintenance, *Gopal Rao Pandoorung* v. *Ruma Baee*, 2 *Borr.* 625; 1 *Morl. Dig.* 485, § 51.

Among co-heirs.—As on partition by the father, *ante*, p. 339, so here by the co-heirs partition may take place by arbitration, adjustment, or lot, or by suit in court. Although it is not made indispensable, yet the law prescribes a written instrument, and it is always better to have it. *Brihaspati* says that a record of partition which brothers [or other co-heirs] execute after making a just division by mutual consent, is called the written memorial of the distribution, *Mayukha*.

Sir Thomas Strange, in terms eulogistic of the instruments and agreements of the Hindus, says, They are models in their way. Penned in general by the village accountants (*conocopolies*),* while they express everything that is material, they do so with a compactness and precision not easily surpassed. A regular instrument of partition being entitled according to its purport, the things distributed by it are specified by name, and may be inventoried on the back, the amount being noted also in figures to preclude any fraudulent insertion subsequent. But they are considered to be best enumerated in the body, and this so as to show what each has received, that the fairness of the division may appear. With the date the names of the parceners are inserted, designated by those of their fathers', the same names among Hindus being usually common to many, for which reason the paternal names of the drawer of the instrument, and of the witnesses to it, are added. Where it is holograph [or wholly written by the hand of the writer], there is the less necessity for witnesses, but they are in all cases recommended, *Vrihaspati*, *Yajnavalchya*. The greatest credit attaches to

* Putwaree, Canoongo.

such an instrument, executed in the presence of, and attested by the rajah and his officers, by which is to be understood simply a public authenticated attestation. What the law expects in general is, that it should be attested by kinsmen; the want of whom, however, and the consequent substitution of more distant relations, or even of neighbours, is always open to be explained. Such, in fact, is the order in which witnesses for this purpose are classed; *kinsmen* being described as persons allied by community of funeral oblations, or as sprung from the same race; *relations*, as maternal uncles; and other collateral and distant relations of the family.

SECTION IV.

PERIOD OF PARTITION.

Conflicting opinions in different schools—According to the Bombay school there are three periods at which partition of ancestral estate takes place after death of parents—During joint lives, if the mother be past child-bearing—(3.) Or with the father's consent at any time—Circumstances justifying partition without father's consent—Where father incapable, partition with consent of eldest son—This opinion refuted—In Bengal two periods of partition—In Madras are four periods—(1.) By the father's desire—(2.) On his retiring from worldly affairs—(3.) Demise of the father—(4.) When the father is addicted to vice, is old, disturbed in intellect, diseased—Enumeration by Colebrooke—In Bengal the right to partition is at the father's instance, except in case of civil death and degradation—Menu does not support the doctrine of compulsory division—He refers only to the recovery of lost ancestral property—The mention of sisters has reference to disposal in marriage—The doctrine of the cessation of the mother to bear children is not generally adopted—In Bengal the volition of the father and the mother's incapacity must co-exist—Provisions for after-born sons—The rule with regard to mother being past child-bearing refers to any wife—The vice and disease must be such as to produce degradation from caste—Age, impairment of mind, and bodily disease are not causes of partition, but of appointment of son as manager—His acts bind the family property, but consent necessary to alienation.

Conflicting opinions in different schools.—There have been very conflicting opinions expressed upon this branch of our inquiry by different writers in the several schools, who assign various periods for the attaching of the son's claim to partition. One of these was the death of the father. As we have treated of the descent of property on the natural demise of the father, under the head of Inheritance, it more properly coming under that division, it is of course excluded to a certain extent from our consideration here. We say to a certain extent; for, as almost all writers on Hindu law include it, either expressly or impliedly, under the head of partition, we must necessarily, in referring to their opinions, follow their example. *Viramitrodaya. Mitac.* says, But in the case of his (the father's) demise, the successor's own choice is of course the reason (of partition).

According to the Bombay school, there are three periods at which partition of ancestral estate takes place after death of parents.—1. "After the [death of the] father and mother, the brothers being assembled, must divide equally the *paternal* [and *maternal*] estate; but they have no power over it while their parents live [unless the father choose to distribute it"], *Menu.* By inserting the word "*and,*" the consummation of [both their] deaths is not required. Even thus, in the *Madana Ratna* and *Smriti Sangraha,* "a partition of the father's wealth may take place even while the mother lives, for this reason, that without her husband the mother does not, from her independence, also derive ownership. A partition of the mother's wealth may also take place in like manner while the father is alive; for if there be issue, the lord of the wife is not lord of the wife's wealth, *Mayukha.*

During joint lives, if the mother be past child-bearing.—2. This is opposed to the text of *Brahaspati:* "On the demise of both parents, participation among brothers is allowed, and even while they are both living it is right, if the mother be past child-bearing." So *Narada:* "Let sons regularly divide the wealth when the father is dead, or when the mother is past child-bearing, and the sisters are married, or when the father's sensual passions are extinguished," *Mayukha.*

In partition, however, of the mother's property by sons, the assumption of course is, that there are no daughters, as these would take first, *Mitac., Yajnavalchya, Jim. Vahana.*

Or with the father's consent at any time.—3. *Goutama:* "After the demise of the father, let sons share his estate, or while he lives, if the mother be past child-bearing, if he desire partition. From this expression, *if he desire,* partition is declared legal also before the mother is past child-bearing by the father's wish alone,* *Mayukha.*

Circumstances justifying partition without father's consent.—*Narada:* "A father who is afflicted with disease, or influenced by wrath, or whose mind is engrossed by a beloved object, or who acts otherwise than the law permits, has no power in the distribution of

* The following note is appended :—" 5. *Colebrooke, Mitac.* 260, But I have here followed the translation given in *Jim Vahana,* p. 24, as more conformable to the doctrine of the *Mayukha,* which allows only three periods of partition. The *Mitac.,* on the other hand, asserts four, and in support of this doctrine divides this very text of *Goutama* into three portions."

the estate." *Harita:* "If the father be free from desire, old, perverted in mind, or long afflicted with disease, partition of his wealth [may be made]." *Free from desire*, according to the *Madna Ratna*, means without desire of partition. *Perverted in mind*, following practices contrary to law. "The sense is, that partition may be made even against the will of [such a] father," *Mayukha.*

Where father incapable, partition with consent of eldest son.—*Harita** says, that when the father is incapable, partition takes place by the concurrence of the eldest son. But if he be decayed, remotely absent, or afflicted with disease, let the eldest son manage the affairs as he pleases. So *Sankha* and *Likhita:* "If the father be incapable, let the eldest son manage the affairs of the family, or, with his consent, the next brother conversant with business," *Mayukha.*

This opinion refuted.—*Jim. Vahana* says, The alleged power of sons to make partition when the father is incapable of business [by reason of extreme age, &c.], has been asserted through ignorance of express passages of law [to the contrary]. Thus *Harita* says, "While the father lives sons have no independent power with regard to receipt, expenditure, and bailment of wealth. But if he be decayed, remotely absent, or afflicted with disease, let the eldest son manage the affairs as he pleases. So *Sankha* and *Likhita* explicitly declare, "If the father be incapable, let the eldest son manage the affairs of the family, or, with his consent, a younger brother conversant with business. Partition of the wealth does not take place if the father be not desirous of it; when he is old, or his mental faculties are impaired, or his body is afflicted with a lasting disease, let the oldest like a father protect the goods of the rest, for [the support of] the family is founded on wealth. They are not independent while they have their father living, nor while the mother survives."

In Bengal two periods of partition.—*Jim. Vahana* says, There are two periods of partition, one when the father's property ceases, the other by his choice while the right of property endures, *Jim. Vahana;* and the author of that work denies the right of the sons to enforce partition in the life of the father against his consent, on the ground that the sons have not ownership while the father is alive, and free from defect. But three periods must not be admitted. The author here opposes the doctrine maintained in the *Mitacshara*, as is remarked by the commentators, *Achyuta*, *Srikrishna*, and *Mahesvara.*

In Madras are four periods.—The *Mitacshara* mentions four periods—†

1. **By the father's desire.**—One period of partition is when the

* *Sankha, Stokes, H. L.* book 196, n.; *Mitac.* ch. i. s. ii. n.

† This section refers to the law governing the division of property generally, *Nagalinga Mudali* v. *Subbiramaniya Mudali*, 1 *Mad. H. C. R.* 77.

father desires separation—"When the father makes a partition," *Goutama, Mitac.*

2. On his retiring from worldly affairs.—Another period is while the father lives, but is indifferent to wealth and disinclined to pleasure, and the mother is incapable of bearing more sons, at which time a partition is admissible, at the option of sons, against the father's wish, as is shown by *Narada*, who premises partition subsequent to the demise of both parents. "Let sons regularly divide the wealth when the father is dead;" and adds, "or when the mother is past child-bearing, and the sisters are married, or when the father's sensual passions are extinguished." Here the words, "Let sons regularly divide the wealth," are understood, *Mitac.*

3. Demise of the father.—*Goutama* likewise having said, "After the demise of the father, let sons share his estates," states a second period, "or when the mother is past child-bearing," and a third, "while the father lives, if he desires separation."

4. When the father is addicted to vice, is old, disturbed in intellect, diseased.—So while the mother is capable of bearing more issue, a partition is admissible by the choice of the sons, though the father be unwilling, if he be addicted to vice or afflicted with a lasting disease. *Sankha** declares, "Partition of inheritance takes place without the father's wish, if he be old, disturbed in intellect, or diseased."

Enumeration by Colebrooke.—*Colebrooke's Annotations.* There are four periods of partition—One while the father lives, if he desire partition; another is when the mother ceases to be capable of bearing issue, and the father is not desirous of sexual intercourse, and is indifferent to wealth, if his sons then require partition, though he do not wish it. Again, another period is while the mother is yet capable of bearing issue, and the father, though not consenting to partition, is old, or addicted to vicious courses, or afflicted with an incurable disease, if the sons then desire partition. The last period is after the decease of the father, *Visvesvara*, in the *Madana Parijata.*

There are four periods of partition in the case of wealth acquired by the father, *Visvesvara* in the *Suboudhini.*

Four periods of partition amongst sons have been stated by the author (*Vignyaneswara*), which are compendiously exhibited in a twofold division by the contemplative saint *Yajnavalchya.* Here three cases may occur under that of distribution during the life of the father, viz., with or without his desire for separation; the case of his not desiring it being also twofold—1st, When the mother has ceased to be capable of bearing children, and the father is disinclined to pleasure, &c.; 2d, When the mother is not incapable of

* Cited as Harita in the *Mayukha*, p. 343.

bearing issue, but the father is disqualified by vicious habits, or the like, *Suboudhini.*

The doctrine of the Eastern writers, *Jim. Vahana*, &c., who maintain that two periods only are admissible (viz.), the volition of the father and his demise, and not any third period; and that the text relative to the mother's incapacity for bearing more issue regards the estate of the paternal grandfather, or other ancestor, is refuted, *Balam Bhutta, Mitac.*

We hold that while the father survives, and is worthy of retaining uncontrolled power, his will alone is the cause of partition. If he be unworthy of such power in consequence of degradation, or of retirement from the world, or the like, the son's will is likewise a cause of partition. But in the case of his demise, the successor's own choice is, of course, the reason. By this mode the periods are three. Else there must be great confusion, in the uncertainty of subject and accident, if many reasons, as extinction of worldly propensities, and so forth, must be established collectively and alternatively. Thus the mention of certain reasons in some texts, and the omission of them in others, are suitable; for the extinction of temporal affections, and the other assigned reasons, indicate the single circumstance of the father's want of uncontrolled power, since it is easy to establish that single foundation of the text, *Viramitrodaya, Mitacshara.*

Partition then attaches *with* the father's consent, or *without* it, under the circumstances mentioned.

In Bengal the right to partition is at the father's instance, except in case of civil death and degradation.—*Sir Thomas Strange* says, "No Hindu can, according to the law, as it prevails in the Bengal provinces, under any circumstances, call upon his father to divide his property with him. The father may abdicate in favour of one, or of all, according to the limits imposed upon him by law, if he thinks proper; but with the exception of two cases, partition amongst the Hindus in the lifetime of the father, whether of ancestral or of acquired property, would seem to be at the father's will, not at the option of the sons, *Menu*, ch. ix. § 104; *Sancha* and *Likhita, Narada, Vyasa, Goutama, Baudhayana, Jim. Vahana, Mitac.* (See *Nagalinga Mudali* v. *Subbiramaniya*, 1 *Mad. H. C. R.* 77.) The excepted cases being that of his civil death *by entering into a religious order*, and that of *degradation*, working a forfeiture of civil rights," *Menu*, and even in these cases it is the law alone that operates, casting upon the sons, by right of birth, the succession by anticipation.*

Menu does not support the doctrine of compulsory division.—*Sir Thomas Strange* says, "A text of *Menu* is referred to as showing that of ancestral property belonging to the father, the sons may

* But the British Legislature have enacted that this circumstance shall not interfere with an individual's right in property, Act xxi. of 1840.

at their pleasure exact a division of him, however reluctant; and it is true [as has been already intimated], that their claim upon property descended is stronger than upon what has been otherwise acquired. But the inference drawn in the *Mitacshara* is at variance with the current of authorities, including *Menu* himself, whose obvious meaning in the text referred to is simply that ancestral property *recovered* without the use of the patrimony classes upon partition with property *acquired*, not to mention that the text in question is differently rendered in the translation we have of the "Institutes" by *Sir W. Jones*, in which it has nothing to do with partition by the father, but regards partition among brothers after his death. Moreover *Jagannatha*, in his digest, virtually negatives the inference deduced from it and other correspondent texts which he examined, concluding that "if it be against the father's inclination, partition, even of wealth inherited from the grandfather, shall not be made." The passage in the *Mitacshara*, ch. i. s. v. § 11, alluded to is: — "*Menu* likewise shows that the father, however reluctant, must divide with his sons at their pleasure the effects acquired by their paternal grandfather, declaring as he does, If the father recover paternal wealth not recovered by his co-heirs, he shall not, unless willing, share it with his sons, for in fact it is acquired by him." The passage in *Menu* is as follows :—" And if a son, by his own efforts, recover *a debt or property unjustly detained* which could not be recovered before *by his father*, he shall not, unless by free-will, put it into parcenery with his brethren, since in fact it was acquired by himself;" that if a father recover property which had been acquired by an ancestor, and taken away by a stranger, but not redeemed by the grandfather, he need not himself share it, against his inclination, with his sons, any more than he need give up his own acquisitions, *Mitac.*

He refers only to the recovery of lost ancestral property.—But the inference is not warranted by the text cited, nor indeed by other authorities. *Menu* does not in this text discuss the division of ancestral property, but simply declares that lost paternal wealth, when recovered by the co-heir, shall be treated as self-acquired property. Moreover, the text in question is differently rendered by *Sir W. Jones, Menu*, where it appears to refer to partition among brothers after the father's death, and *Jagannatha* opposes the inference drawn from it, adding, that if it be against the father's inclination, partition, even of wealth inherited from the grandfather, shall not be made. *Jagannatha* says, that of patrimony inherited, a partition may be obtained by application to the king in a certain case—viz., if sons be oppressed by a stepmother—but for this he cites no authority. *Macn.* confirms this; but *Sir Thomas Strange* virtually negatives the position.

The father cannot make a partition of his ancestral immovable property unless the mother is past child-bearing. With regard to his self-acquired estate, consisting of movable and immovable property, and ancestral property lost, but recovered by the father, his own consent is alone requisite to partition.

The Benares and other schools differ from the Bengal as to the division of ancestral estate. According to the former, the sons may enforce it, if the mother be past child-bearing, although the father retain his desire for sexual intercourse, or, as it is termed, worldly affections, and he is opposed to partition.

The mention of sisters has reference to disposal in marriage.—The mention by *Narada*, " Of the sisters being married," does not intend a distinct period, but inculcates the necessity of disposing of them in marriage, *Jimuta Vahana.*

The doctrine of the cessation of the mother to bear children is not generally adopted.—The doctrine with reference to the period when the mother ceases to bear issue, does not appear to be generally adopted, unless it has tended to induce the husband to withdraw from the world, that circumstance alone justifying the claims of the sons, which does not support him.

But though the cessation of child-bearing may not entitle them to a partition without the consent of the father—

In Bengal the volition of the father and the mother's incapacity must co-exist.—Yet in Bengal it has been held that it cannot take place even *with* his consent, if the mother continues capable of child-bearing, it being necessary that the volition of the father and the mother's incapacity should co-exist, because after-born children have by birth a special interest in ancestral property, *Narada, Jimuta Vahana, Srikrishna, Daya Krama Sangraha, Balam Bhutta, Mitac.*

Provisions for after-born sons.—There is, however, a provision made for this contingency, *Menu, Mitac., Daya Krama Sangraha,* although there are different opinions as to whether the shares of after-born sons should be supplied by the father, or by the brothers who have received theirs.

Where the pregnancy is apparent at the time of partition, it should either be postponed or a share set apart to abide the event. But if it were not known, should a son who was at the time in the womb be born afterwards, he should obtain his share from his brothers by contribution, while a subsequently begotten one should have recourse only to the remaining property of the father, succeeding to the whole exclusively, or dividing it with such of the brothers as may have become re-united to the common parent. Any acquisition by a re-united father, through means of his individual wealth or personal exertions, belonging exclusively to the son born after partition, and to him in common with another re-united, and where there is no after-born issue, the sons who had received their shares take by inheritance what their parents leave, *Mitac.*

The rule with regard to mother being past child-bearing refers

to any wife.—This denotes generally any wife of the father, *Srikrishna.* Since the condition is stated by way of illustration, it intends generally the impossibility of further male issue. If, therefore, it be possible that the father should have issue by another wife, partition should not be made, *Achyuta.* Even then, when the father's wife is incapable of bearing issue, partition is by the father's choice, *Srikrishna,* note to *Jim. Vahana;* so the postponement of partition is admissible lest sons born after his retirement, if his passions be not extinguished, and his wife accompany him to the wilderness under the option allowed by the law ("if she chose to attend him"), *Menu,* should be thus deprived of a maintenance. But if he retire to the wilderness at the latter period described by the legislator, *Menu,* there is nothing to prevent partition at that time, since the cessation of the mother's courses must have previously taken place, *Srikrishna, Jim. Vahana.*

The vice and disease must be such as produce degradation from caste.—*Sir Thomas Strange* says, Adverting to the various opinions that have been entertained on the question, the practical difference among them, says an eminent commentator, *Colebrooke,* regards chiefly the cases of vice and profligacy with lasting disease, and consequent disqualifications and incapacity, subjoining, however, that without consent of the head of the family it is not in such cases allowed by the prevalent authorities of Bengal, unless the vice or disease be such as to induce degradation from caste.

Age, impairment of mind, and bodily disease, are not causes of partition, but of appointment of son as manager.—*Harita* says, "If he (the father) be decayed, remotely absent, or affected with disease, let the eldest son manage the affairs as he pleases." So *Sankha* and *Likhita* explicitly declare, "If the father be incapable, let the eldest (son) manage the affairs of the family, or, with his consent, a younger brother conversant with business. Partition of wealth does not take place if the father be not desirous of it. When he is old, or his mental faculties are impaired, or his body is afflicted with a lasting disease, let the eldest, like a father, protect the goods of the rest, for the support of the family is founded on wealth. They are not independent while they have their father living, nor while the mother survives," *Jim. Vahana.* Primogeniture does not give any title to the management, but capacity for business, though, where the qualifications are equal, the eldest would have the preference, *Menu.*

His acts bind the family property, but consent necessary to alienation.—The acts of the managing member, when for the uses of the family, are binding upon it, but in alienating the property, the consent of the co-partners, expressed or implied, is necessary.

SECTION V.

PARTITION AGAINST FATHER'S CONSENT OF ANCESTRAL PROPERTY.

Of ancestral property—In Bombay, sons entitled to division of ancestral property—Ancestral property lost but recovered, as self-acquired, not within the rule—Madras school—Sons or grandsons may compel a division of ancestral property—Partition without the father's consent is illegal—But with his consent binds him, though absent at the time—But without his consent does not bind the son who made it—Partition of self-acquired property without the consent of the father—What is self-acquisition—Explanation of acquisition by learning—Bengal school—Not if joint-stock used in acquisition—Bombay school—Lost property acquired—Applies to movable property in Madras: in Bengal and Bombay, to both—Bengal school—Ancestral property recovered—Special rule with regard to land recovered—Madras school—In Madras sons have some interest in self-acquired immovable property—Undecided whether son can compel division of self-acquired immovable property—Self-acquired movable property—The owner may divide it as he likes—Retraction—Enumeration of subjects of acquisition—The acquisition must be made without charge to the patrimony—If such acquisition obtained from common stock—Exception with regard to acquisitions by learning—Exception with regard to wealth acquired without detrimemt to the paternal estate—Gifts from father, &c.—Where acquisitions by valour are distributable—Gifts of affectionate kindred—Soudayacam—Wealth acquired by labour, employment in agriculture—Other exemptions from partition—Brothers living in union are entitled to the lands purchased by their acquisitions in proportion to the funds contributed by them respectively—Property acquired by brothers should be distributed among them according to the labour and funds employed by each—Acquisitions made by means of the patrimony—Lands purchased by one co-heir with borrowed money—Property exclusively acquired by one co-heir is not to be shared by his brethren—Interest of father in wealth acquired by united sons—Where one brother associates with another in developing his property—House built on joint land—Augmentation of the common fund—Acquisitions by unassisted labour—By joint funds or personal labour—Self-acquisitions without the aid of joint funds—Exception in case of land, the recovery of which entitles acquirer to a fourth over and above his own—Yautuca—A united half-brother shall not participate in the self-acquisitions of his co-proprietors—Improvement of undivided property—Agreement between members respecting expenditure of self-acquired funds—Benamee purchased by a member of a joint family does not render the property self-acquired—Fraudulent concealment of common property.

Of ancestral property—In Bombay, sons entitled to division of ancestral property.—Partition of ancestral property may take place without the father's consent in Bombay. *Brihaspati* declares partition in some cases without his wish: "The father and sons are equal sharers in houses and lands derived regularly from ancestors; but sons are not worthy [in their own right] of a share in wealth acquired by the father himself when the father is unwilling." From which it results, "that sons are worthy of a share in property acquired by the grandfather, or other [ancestor], even though the father do not wish it," *Mayukha.* This doctrine has been followed in a case in the High Court at Madras, *Nagalinga Mudali* v. *Subbiramaniya*, 1 *Mad. H. C. R.* 77.

Ancestral property lost but recovered, as self-acquired, not within the rule.—But this rule does not apply to ancestral property where such property has been lost, and could not be recovered by the ancestor, but has been recovered by the efforts of his son, and at his sole expense. Such property classes as self-acquired property, and follows the rule applicable to property gained by science, valour, or the like, *Menu*, *Vishnu*, *Brihaspati*, *Mayukha.*

Madras school—Sons or grandsons may compel a division of ancestral property.—We have seen that in the Bengal school the opinion is, that under no circumstances can a son exact from his father a division of ancestral property except in cases of civil death, (entering a religious order), or of degradation of caste, working a forfeiture of civil rights, these two exceptions being applicable to Hindu law in general. But with regard to the law of the Madras Presidency and elsewhere in the Peninsula, *Sir Thomas Strange* holds, that partition of ancestral property independent of the father's will is authorised, but only under circumstances which would justify it—viz., when the father has become superannuated, the mother past child-bearing, and the sisters also married; while *Mr Justice Strange* holds, that sons may, irrespective of all circumstances, compel a division, citing the *Mitacshara.* The point has recently been decided by the High Court of Madras, in conformity with *Mr Strange's* opinion, holding that sons or grandsons may compel a division against the will of the father or grandfather of ancestral property, leaving the question open as to a division of acquired property, *Nagalinga Mudali* v. *Subbiramaniya Mudali*, 1 *Mad. H. C. R.* 77. See the comments upon this case in *Grady's Hindu Law of Inheritance*, p. 351.

Partition without the father's consent is illegal.—A. had three sons; the youngest absconded, and the father followed to make inquiries after him; the other two remained at home. In the absence of the father the eldest son adjusted the proportion of his father's share of the joint property by arbitration. Held that any partition of joint property made by arbitration without the father's permission cannot be considered as lawful.

But with his consent binds him, though absent at the time.—But if the father left directions with the eldest son to adjust the dispute regarding his share of the immovable property, held in union with his co-heirs, which was accordingly done by arbitration, but the father, on his return, was not satisfied with the adjustment, the partition of the estate is good and binding, even though the father, after his return, wish to recede from it.

But without his consent does not bind the son who made it.—A person had an only son, who, in his father's absence, chose an arbitrator, and caused a partition of his father's ancestral immovable property, which was held in union with his other co-heirs, and the father having returned home, dissented from the partition, and then died. The son who caused the partition wishes to recede from it. Held that the partition of the father's joint immovable and other property, made by the award of an arbitration during the father's absence, without his express permission, and to which the father after his return did not consent, is illegal, and the son who caused it to be made may recede from it.

Partition of self-acquired property without the consent of the father.—Upon a consideration of all the authorities, it will be seen that the sons have no claim by reason of birth or otherwise to what is self-acquired, and called the father's wealth, as distinguished from that which has come to him by descent, and denominated ancestral estate. It is true that on his decease the sons will become entitled to self-acquired property if it has not been otherwise disposed of, *Brihaspati, Jim. Vahana,* but they cannot enforce a partition of it against the father's will, as they can of ancestral property. In the *Mayukha, Brihaspati* is cited in support of this view. He draws the distinction between the two classes of property, and while he admits the right of the sons in the one case, he denies it in the other. He says, "Fathers and sons are equal sharers in houses and lands derived regularly from ancestors, but sons are not worthy [in their own right] of a share in wealth *acquired by the father himself* when the father is unwilling," *Jim. Vahana, supra.*

What is self-acquisition.—What a brother has acquired by his labour without using the patrimony, he need not give up to co-heirs; nor what has been gained by science, *Menu, Mayukha, Jim. Vahana.* What a man gains by his own ability without relying on the patrimony, he shall not give up to the co-heirs, nor what he acquired by learning, *Vyasa, Mayukha, Jim. Vahana.*

Explanation of acquisition by learning.—Wealth gained through science which was acquired from a stranger while receiving a foreign maintenance, is termed acquisition through learning, *Katyayana, Mayukha.*

Bengal school.—So in Bengal, *Jim. Vahana, Menu,* and *Vishnu,* are cited as declaring that "What a brother has acquired by his labour without using the patrimony, he need not give up without his assent, for it was gained by his own exertion," * *Jumeeyut Lal* (pauper) v. *Huqeequt Rai*, 2 *Macn. Prin. H. L.* 155; and the reason for the exception is thus explained, Since the patrimony is not used, there is no exertion on the side of the others through the means of the common property, and since it was obtained by the man's own labour, there is no corporeal effort on the part of the rest, it is therefore the separate property of the acquirer alone; for the phrase, "It was gained by his own exertion" is stated as a reason; and *Vyasa* ordains what a man gains by his own ability, without relying on the patrimony, he shall not give up to the co-heirs, nor that which is acquired by his learning, *Jim. Vahana.*

Since it is expressed in general terms, "What he gains solely by his own ability," all property so acquired being his own, is not common, but as the gains of science, though obtained by the man's own ability, are shared by parceners equally or more proficient in knowledge, the phrase "Nor that which is acquired by learning" is subjoined for the sake of excluding illiterate, or less learned parceners, *Jim. Vahana.* So a present from a friend, or a gift at nuptials, does not appertain to the co-heirs, *Yajnavalchya, Jim. Vahana.* So wealth acquired by learning, and anything given by a friend, received on account of marriage, or presented as a mark of respect, *Menu.* So what is gained by science or earned by valour, or received from affectionate kindred, *Vyasa.* So what is gained by valour, the wealth of a wife, what is acquired by science, and any favour conferred by a father, *Narada.*

Not if joint stock used in acquisition.—But if the common goods be employed in the acquisition of wealth by valour, it follows the rule of ancestral property, and is distributable against the volition of the father, *Vyasa.* So he who maintains the family of a brother studying science shall take, be he never so ignorant, a share of the wealth acquired by science, *Narada.* What has been gained by a learned man without using the paternal estate, he need not give up to an unlearned co-heir, but he must share it with a learned co-heir, *Goutama, Katyayana, Srikrishna, Jim. Vahana.*

Bombay school—Lost property acquired.—The *Mayukha* points out that, although in the strict sense of the term the estate may have been ancestral, yet, if it were a debt, or property unjustly detained and lost to the ancestor, but regained by the personal exertions of his son, and at his sole cost, it passes into that class of property which is denominated self-acquired, and ranks with wealth acquired by science, valour, or the like, and partakes of its incidents, one of which is, that it does not come into co-parcenery with sons, and is therefore not liable to partition, unless by the free will of the father, *Menu, Vishnu, Mayukha.*

Applies to movable property in Madras: in Bengal and Bom-

* See *Mitac.* ch. i. s. iv. § 10, where a different reading is given to the second half of the text.

bay, to both.—This applies to movable property in Madras, and is the doctrine of the Bengal and Maharashtra schools, with respect to both movable and immovable property.

In the grandfather's property also partition in some cases depends on the father's pleasure, see *Menu* and *Vishnu*. "And if a father by his own efforts recover [a debt or property unjustly detained], which could not be recovered before [by his father,] he shall not, unless by his free will, put it into parcenery with his sons, since in fact it was acquired by himself," *Brihaspati*. "Over the grandfather's property which has been seized [by strangers], and is recovered by the father through his own ability, and over [anything] gained by him through science, valour, or the like, the father's full dominion is ordained. He may give it away at his pleasure; or he may defray his consumption with such wealth, but on failure of him the sons are entitled to equal shares," *Mayukha*.

Bengal school—Ancestral property recovered.—And the same rule prevails in Bengal as in Bombay with reference to hereditary property taken away, and which has been recovered, *Yajnavalchya*, *Jim. Vahana*, *Menu*. *Brihaspati* says, "Over the grandfather's property which has been seized [by strangers], and is recovered by the father through his own ability, and over [anything] gained by him through science, valour, or the like, the father's full dominion is ordained. He may give it away at his pleasure, or he may defray his consumption with such wealth; but on failure of him, the sons are pronounced entitled to equal shares," *Jim. Vahana*.

Special rule with regard to land recovered.—Thus the rule must be understood in the instance of any such hereditary property, other than land, exactly as in the case of property not hereditary, but acquired by the man himself, *Jim. Vahana*. *Sankha* propounds a special rule regarding land: "Land inherited in regular succession, but which had been formerly lost, and which a single [heir] shall recover solely by his own labour; the rest may divide according to their due allotments, having first given him a fourth part, *ib.* § 38. So that ancestral lands, when recovered by any member without the aid of family funds, may be regarded as self-acquired; but not being so considered, the acquirer may claim one-fourth of it, and then divide the rest among the whole family, he getting a second share by this division. Here, again, he may treat it as self-acquired, and it is of his own mere choice that such lands go to the family.

Madras school.—In the *Mitacshara*, the passage before cited from *Yajnavalchya* is relied on. Upon which the following exposition is given :—"That which had been acquired by the co-parcener himself without any detriment to the goods of his father or mother, or which has been received by him from a friend (see *Rewun Persad* v. *Mt. Radha Beeby*, 4 *Moore's In. Ap.* 162, *per Wigram arguendo*), or obtained by marriage, shall not appertain to co-heirs of brethren.

Any property which has descended in succession from ancestors, and had been seized by others, and remained unrecovered by the father and the rest through inability, or for any other cause, he among the sons who recovers it, with the acquiescence of the rest, shall not give up to the brethren or other co-heirs ; the person recovering it shall take such property."

In Madras sons have some interest in self-acquired immovable property.—The sons certainly possess some interest in self-acquired immovable property in Madras, inasmuch as there a father cannot alienate his self-acquired immovable property without the concurrence of his sons; and failing sons, their sons' grandsons, *Mitac.*

Undecided whether son can compel division of self-acquired immovable property.—But it does not appear to be yet decided whether a son can compel a father to divide against his will separate acquired immovable property. The decision of the High Court at Madras has reference only to ancestral property, and the *Mitacshara* is silent with respect to compulsory division of self-acquired immovable property.

Self-acquired movable property—The owner may divide it as he likes.—Self-acquired movable property cannot be divided by a court of law, unless the owner choose to share it. *Sir Thomas Strange* lays it down that he must divide it in equal shares, he taking a double portion ; but the more correct and reasonable rule is that of *Mr Justice Strange*, that he may divide it in any manner he pleases, keeping what he likes for himself.

Retraction.—Both authorities agree in saying that such shares of acquired property may be recalled by the father in case of subsequent indigence, *Harita*, cited in the *Vivada Chintamani.* But this perhaps is merely *directory*, for no retraction of voluntary gifts is allowed in England ; this recall of the shares, therefore, must be regarded as of doubtful authority.

Enumeration of subjects of acquisition.—"What is gained by the solution [of a difficulty] after a prize has been offered must be considered as acquired by science. What has been obtained from a pupil, or by officiating as a priest, or for [answering] a question, or for determining a doubtful point, or through display of knowledge, or by success in disputation, or for superior skill in reading, are gains of science, and not subject to distribution," *Mayukha*, *Jim. Vahana.*

The law is the same in regard also to artisans, and to increase of price. A prize which has been offered for the display of superior learning, and a gift received from a votary for whom a sacrifice was formerly performed, or a present from a pupil formerly instructed, are the acquisitions of science. What is otherwise acquired is [the] property [of co-heirs]. What is won by surpassing another in learning, after a stake has been deposited, is the acquisition of science, and impartible. So what is obtained by the boast of learning, what is received from a pupil, or for the performance of a sacrifice, *Brihaspati*, *Bhrugu*, *Mayukha.*

"Solution," "Display," "Superior reading," "In regard also to artisans," "Increase of price," "Performance of a sacrifice," are explained in *Mayukha.*

The acquisition must be made without charge to the patrimony.—Here the phrase "Anything acquired by himself without detriment to the father's estate" must be everywhere understood, and it is thus connected with each member of the sentence; what is obtained from a friend without detriment to the paternal estate; what is received in marriage without waste of the patrimony; what is redeemed of the hereditary estate without expenditure of ancestral property; what is gained by science without use of the father's goods; consequently, what is obtained from a friend as the return of an obligation conferred at the charge of the patrimony; what is received at a marriage concluded in the form termed *Asoora*,* or the like; what is recovered of the hereditary estate by the expenditure of the father's goods; what is earned by science acquired at the expense of the ancestral wealth; all that must be shared with the whole of the brethren, and with the father, *Mitac.*, *Narada*, and *Katyayana;* see *Laximon Row Sudasew* v. *Mullar Row Bajee*, 2 *Knapp's P. C.* 60, 63; *Menu.*

If such acquisitions obtained from common stock.—If, however, in any of those cases the acquisition was not obtained without loss or detriment to the paternal estate, then the rule of indivisibility does not apply, *Katyayana.* Yet *Brihaspati* has ordained that wealth shall be partible, if it be gained by learned brothers, who were instructed in the family by their father, or paternal grandfather [or uncles], and it is the same if wealth were acquired by valour [with assistance from the family estate], *Brihaspati*, *Mayukha.*

If the rule be carried out to its legitimate results, it is so general in its operation, there is no possible case in which it will not apply, for all men are indebted to their paternal estate for their acquisitions in one sense.

But even in cases coming within the exception, although the acquisitions may be divisible, the acquirer is entitled to a double share. "He amongst them who has made an acquisition may take a double portion of it," *Vasishta*, *Mayukha*, see *Jim. Vahana.*

Exception with regard to acquisitions by learning.—A further exception has been engrafted on the rule in regard to the acquisition of wealth through learning. He who maintains the family of a brother studying science, shall take, even though not told (that is, not promised), a share of the wealth gained by science, *Narada*, *Mayukha.* See *Madana Ratna*, *Mitac.*, *Jim. Vahana.*

* For at such a marriage wealth is received by the father or kinsman of the bride, *Mitac.* p. 269, ch. i. sec. iv. n. 6.

Exception with regard to wealth acquired without detriment to the paternal estate.—" His own acquired wealth, a learned man may, if he please, give up to unlearned co-heirs," says *Goutama. Katyayana* says, No part of the wealth which is gained by science need be given by a learned man to his unlearned co-heirs ; but such property must be yielded by him to those who are equal, or superior in learning." A learned man need not give a share of his own acquired wealth without his assent to an unlearned co-heir ; provided it were not gained by him using the paternal estate. But, according to *Madana*, this prohibition applies only where there exists other property for those brothers who are present ; but on failure of other property [a share of it] even must be given to them, *Mayukha, Jim. Vahana.*

Gifts from the father, &c.—That is impartible which has been given by the father or other [person]. " That which may have been given by the paternal grandfather, or father, or mother, is not to be taken back, any more than wealth acquired by valour or the wealth of a wife," *Brihaspati : Narada.* Excepting what is gained by valour, the wealth of a wife, and what is acquired by science, which are three sorts of property exempt from partition, and any favour conferred by a father ; *Katyayana,* So that which is taken under a standard it not distributable, also what is seized [by a soldier] in war, after routing the forces of the enemy, and after risking his life for his lord, is spoil taken under a standard. When a soldier performs a gallant action, despising danger, and favour is shown him by his lord, whatever property is then received by him shall be considered as gained by valour, *Mayukha,* 3 *Jim. Vahana.*

Where acquisitions by valour are distributable.—There is an exception to this rule where gains by valour, or the like, are obtained by one of the brothers, by means of any common property, such as a vehicle, or weapon, or the like. To him two shares should be given, and the rest should share alike, *Vyasa, Mayukha ;* see *Jim. Vahana.*

Gifts of affectionate kindred—Soudayacam.—That which is received by a married woman or by a maiden in the house of her husband, or of her father, from her husband, or from her parents, *Vyasa ;* what is received with a damsel equal in class at the time of accepting her [in marriage], is wealth received with a maiden, which, like wealth acquired by learning, is impartible, if it be acquired without detriment to the father's estate, *Mayukha.*

Wealth acquired by labour, employment in agriculture.—*Menu* says, And if all of them, being unlearned, acquire property [before partition] by their own labour, there shall be an equal division of that property [without regard to the first born], for it was not the wealth of their father—this rule is clearly settled, *Mayukha.*

Other exemptions from partition.—*Menu* says, Clothes, vehicles, ornaments, prepared food, water, women, sacrifices, and pious acts, as well as the common way, are not liable to distribution. Clothes, conveyances, and ornaments, belong respectively to the possessor, if they are of equal value. If the value of one article be more or less than the value of another, then let them be divided, *Mayukha;* see *Mitac.* 272, *Jim. Vahana.* This subject is fully discussed in the *Mayukha.*

Brothers living in union are entitled to the lands purchased by their acquisitions in proportion to the funds contributed by them respectively.—Two brothers living jointly had acquired wealth by their separate exertions, with which they purchased lands. The proportions in which they contributed did not appear, but the proportion contributed by the respondent was much greater than that contributed by the appellant. It was held that the property acquired by the brothers while living jointly, without using the paternal estate, became his exclusive property, and that purchased by the respondent became his own estate. If the property was purchased with a greater share of the respondent's funds, the less sum being contributed by the appellant while they were living together, each is entitled to share the estate in proportion to the funds respectively contributed by them to the purchase of the property. Whatever property may be ascertained to have been purchased by each of the parties, each is entitled to, and such portion should be considered the exclusive property of each; but where the proportionate contribution of each may not be determined, there is no rule in the law by which the respective shares to which each is entitled can be ascertained, *Yajnavalchya, Jim. Vahana, Dayarushasya, Koshul Chuckrawutee* v. *Radhanath Chuckrawutee,* 2 *Macn. Prins. H. L.* 154.

Property acquired by brothers should be distributed among them according to the labour and funds employed by each.—A father died, leaving four sons, and some self-acquired landed property. Afterwards the sons living united purchased by their respective acquisitions some lands, and annexed them to the original estate. The property is distributable, if there is any means of discriminating how much either of funds or labour was contributed by each of the brothers, according to their respective contributions,—the ancestral property going to them equally,* *Vyasa, Ramchunder Das* v. *Gungadhur Mahtee,* 2 *Macn. Prins. H. L.* 160.

By the law of Mithila, whatever is acquired by sons living jointly with their father is divisible amongst them all, *Dhun Sing* v. *Dewlut Sing,* 1 *Morl. Dig.* 478.

* This supposes that the funds used for the acquisition had not been derived from the ancestral estate. In that case, the rule is, that a double share only goes to the acquiring brother. The brethren participate in that wealth which one of them gains by valour or the like, using any common property, either a weapon or a vehicle: to him two shares should be given; but the rest should share alike, *Vyasa, Jim. Vahana,* p. 111, ch. vi. s. i. § 14.

Acquisitions made by means of the patrimony.—With regard to acquisitions made through means of the patrimony, the *Mitacshara* lays down two rules, which do not appear very clear or easy to be applied in practice. At § 29, s. iv. ch. i. it is stated, that whatever is acquired at the charge of the patrimony is subject to partition; but according to the text of *Vasishta*, the acquirer shall in such case have a double share. What is here meant by the words, "At the charge of the patrimony," does not distinctly appear; for we find at § 31 a rule laid down in apparent contradiction of the above text, "Among unseparated brethren, if the common stock be improved or augmented by any one of them through agriculture, commerce, or similar means, an equal distribution nevertheless takes place, and a double share is not allotted to the acquirer." *Mr Strange, M. H. L.* § 276, following § 29 of the *Mitacshara*, conceives that it has reference to "a distinct acquisition." But what is meant by a distinct acquisition, apart from augmentation of the common stock, is difficult to conceive. *Mr Colebrooke*, 2 *Stra. H. L.* 283, calls it a "separate acquisition;" and in all probability *Mr Strange* has followed *Mr Colebrooke*, who, however, does not explain the distinction between the texts of the *Mitacshara*, if any distinction in reality can be drawn between them, so as to reconcile the apparent contradiction in the rules. *Mr Ellis* would appear to have arrived at a better construction, in which he would seem to have been followed by *Sir Thomas Strange*, 1 *H. L.* 220, 221. *Mr Ellis* says, With respect to the division among the brothers, the better mode is—1st, To divide the property descended from the ancestors into equal shares; 2d, To divide what has been acquired by the possessors into unequal shares, giving a larger share to the acquirer, leaving the proportion to the common consent of the co-parceners, or, in case of dispute, to the discretion of the judge. The law, though it mentions a specific proportion, intending it as an example, not as a precept, 2 *Stra. H. L.* 383, 384.

Jimuta Vahana, throughout ch. vi. of the *Daya Bhaga*, s. i. § 23, would appear to argue in favour of the proposition of *Mr Ellis.* He says, that where the exertion of one is merely through the joint property, and the other contributes to the acquisition by his person and wealth, it is a rule suggested by reason, that the one shall have a single share, and the other two. Hence, likewise, it follows, that if the joint stock be used, shares should be assigned to each person in proportion to the amount of his allotment, be it little or much, which has been used. The *Mayukha* follows the text of the *Mitacshara* already cited.

Lands purchased by one co-heir with borrowed money.—Lands purchased by one member of an united family with borrowed money cannot be claimed by another who has not joined in the transaction. But if it happened with his consent, then he is entitled to participate, and must pay the debt proportionably.

Property exclusively acquired by one co-heir is not to be shared by his brethren.—The father of the appellants and the grandfather of the respondent were a joint family. A purchase of a zemindary by the latter, with the produce of his separate industry, and without any aid from friends, ancestral or paternal, no one else can participate in it, citing *Menu, Vishnu, Jim. Vahana.*

Interest of father in wealth acquired by united sons.—In wealth acquired by sons while living in union with the father, he has a co-ordinate interest; but if it were obtained irrespective of the father or his property, it is the sons.

Where one brother associates with another in developing his property.—If one brother has acquired property individually, and in developing it associates another brother with him, they are each entitled to a share, or moiety, of such property. See *Abraham* v. *Abraham*, 9 *Moore's In. Ap.* 529.

House built on joint land.—If one build a house on ancestral land with separate funds of his own, such house would not be property in which shares might be claimed by co-parceners; they would only have a claim on him for other similar land equal to their respective shares. Such is the custom or unwritten law, *Khodeeram Serma* v. *Tirlochun*, 2 *Macn. Prins. H. L.* 152, and authorities quoted.

Augmentation of the common fund.—The augmentation or improvement of the common stock by one of the co-heirs does not entitle him to an extra share, if the increase be gradually added to the property, and is not, in the strict sense, self-acquired, *Mitacshara; e.g.*, the managing member may trade with the funds so as greatly to increase them; he gets, however, only his regular share.

Acquisitions by unassisted labour.—But, according to the Bengal school, an acquisition made by one co-heir by means of his own unassisted and exclusive labour entitles the acquirer to a double share.

By joint funds or personal labour.—Where an estate is acquired by one of four brothers co-parceners, either with the aid of the joint funds, or with the personal aid of the brothers, two-fifths should be given to the acquirer, and one-fifth to each of the other three, 1 *S. D. A. R.* 6. But according to the law as current in Benares, the fact of one brother having contributed personal labour, while no exertion was made by the other, is no ground of distinction. If the patrimonial stock were used, all the brethren share alike, 1 *Macn. Prins. H. L.* 52.

Self-acquisitions without aid of joint funds.—If the joint stock have not been used, he by whose sole labour the acquisition has been made is alone entitled to it. It may, indeed, be difficult at times to determine what constitutes a joint stock, in consequence of the difficulty of laying down any general rule that can with propriety be applied to every case. Each must, therefore, be decided upon its own merits.

Exception in case of land, the recovery of which entitles acquirer to a fourth over and above his own.—Where landed property, lost to the family, may be recovered by a co-heir without aid from the family resources, and made available to them, the recoverer is entitled to a fourth of such property, over and above his own, as a special remuneration, and the rest is divisible among himself and the other co-heirs, *Sankha, Mitac. Sir Thomas Strange* says, Whether by this is to be understood a fourth of the whole property recovered, or only a fourth of an equal share added to a share, seems uncertain. It has been held, that if lands are acquired by the labour of one co-parcener, and partly by the funds of another, each is entitled to half a share, but if they were acquired by the joint labour and capital of one, and by the labour only of the other, two-thirds should belong to the former, and one-third to the latter; but there is hardly any principle of Hindu law to support this.

The acquirer takes a double share on partition where ancestral property has been used in making the acquisition, 2 *Macn. Prins. H. L.* 158.

Yautuca.—Land purchased for a boy by means of his yautuca is not liable to partition. Yautuca signifies anything received at the time of marriage. The term is generally used to signify donations given at the time of each of the sancaras or ceremonies, 2 *Macn. Prins. H. L.* 159.

A united half brother shall not participate in the self-acquisitions of his co-proprietor.—Two half-brothers lived together in unity, one of them, without separation, went to a foreign country, where he obtained a situation, and purchased lands. According to the doctrine contained in *Jim. Vahana* and other law books, the brother of the half blood has no title to participate in the property, from the circumstance of his continuing with the acquirer as a member of a joint and undivided family when the acquisition was made, 2 *Macn. Prins. H. L.* 161.

Improvement of undivided property.—Money expended in the improvement or repair of undivided property enjoyed by a Hindu family in common, is spent on behalf of all the members alike, and all partake of the benefit arising from the outlay, should a division take place.

Agreement between members respecting expenditure of self-acquired funds.—There is no rule of Hindu law precluding one member of an undivided Hindu family, though living together, from entering into an agreement with his co-proprietors for the repayment of self-acquired funds which had been expended on the improvement or repairs of the family property, particularly where portions of it have been occupied by each of the members living separately, *Muttusvami Gaundan* v. *Subbiramaniya Gaundan,* 1 *Mad. H. C. R.* 309.

Benamee purchase by a member of a joint family does not

render the property self-acquired.—The presumption of Hindu law in a joint undivided family, is that the whole property of the family is joint estate, and the *onus* lies upon a party claiming any portion of such property as his separate estate to establish that fact, *Dhurm Dass Pandey* v. *Mt. Shama Soondri Dibiah*, 3 *Moore's In. Ap.* 229; *Gopeekrist Gosain* v. *Gungapersaud Gosain*, 6 *Moore's In. Ap.* 53.

Where a purchase of real estate is made by a Hindu in the name of one of his sons, the presumption of the Hindu law is in favour of its being a *benamee* (*i.e.*, a purchase by the father in another's name for his own benefit) purchase, and the burden of proof lies on the party in whose name it was purchased, to prove that he was solely entitled to the beneficial interest in such purchased estate. Purchase of a *talook* in Bengal by a Hindu in his eldest son's name, the conveyance, though in the English form of lease and release, was held to be a *benamee* purchase, and the son in whose name it was purchased was declared to be a trustee for the father, and the talook, part of the father's estate at the time of his death, *Gopeekrist Gosain* v. *Gungapersaud Gosain*, 6 *Moore's In. Ap.* 53. With reference to the practice of benamee transactions, see *Grady's Hindu Law of Inheritance*, p. 365.

Fraudulent concealment of common property.—Effects which have been held by one co-heir from another, and which are discovered after the separation, let them again divide in equal shares. This is a settled rule, *Yajnavalchya*, *Mayukha;* see *Mitac*, *Jim. Vahana.* *Menu** says, "When any common property whatever is brought to light after partition has been effected, that is not a [fair] partition, it must be even made over again," *Mayukha.*

When *before* a division a member conceals or removes a part of the family property with intent to defraud, he shall lose all share in the property when it is divided.

But should this fraud be committed after division, he will not be divested of his share, so that such acts bar the remedy, but not his right to the property which would fall to his share.†

Fraud alone, and not impiety, profligacy, &c., would bar inheritance in modern courts of law.

* The text is not found in the Institutes.

† On the death of the father, dissensions arising among his heirs, the collector took upon himself to attach the property. One of the sons entered the house and took away part of the property, and for this was convicted of burglary, for which fraudulent crime he was afterwards deprived by the *Sudr Court*, on appeal, of any share in the property. The law, or justice, of this decision is not apparent to ordinary minds.

Section VI.

DISTRIBUTION OF SHARES—I. BETWEEN FATHER AND SONS—II. BETWEEN CO-HEIRS.

1. *Equal distribution of ancestral property rule of all schools—In Madras sons may demand partition and take* per stirpes—*In Benares unequal distribution of ancestral property, and of immovable self-acquired property prohibited—According to* Mac. Cons. *if once made, valid—This opinion discussed and refuted—Opinions of old authorities—Father entitled to two shares of ancestral property—Father and only son—The doctrine of the* Mitac. *as to the equal participation of father and son, and the right of the latter to acquire partition rejected—As to self-acquired property—Property acquired by use of patrimony—Lost property acquired by sole exertions—Sons may dispute unequal division—Each son may demand his share at different periods—Or may renounce—May resume share in case of indigence.*
2. *Between co-heirs—Ancient rule—Equal division—Partition after the father's death—Disproportionate enjoyment—The co-heirs are not called upon to deduct their legitimate expenditure—Division is made of the balance, after deducting expenses—But extravagant excess may be deducted from him who indulges in it—Drones not allowed to share in accumulations—Sons take* per capita—*Other than sons take* per stirpes—*One son requiring partition, no exception to rule as to equality of shares—Amongst sons of different brothers is according to their fathers—One of four grandsons, co-heirs having died, his son is entitled to claim partition from his uncles—Brother's sons also share with their uncles—The son of the great-grandson will not take, being in another line of heirs, unless the direct line is exhausted—This refers to a re-united family only —This limitation is intended in the case of residence in another district—Distribution according to the mothers—But not where the sons vary in number—Property descends in co-parcenery—Exception—Condition of undivided family previous to partition—Manager's acts important—Consent of co-sharers necessary to valid alienation of joint property beyond the alienor's shares—In Bengal, assignment of co-proprietor's own share even before partition—In Madras, co-sharer may alien his share which is liable to be sold in execution on a judgment obtained for a tort.*

Equal distribution of ancestral property rule of all schools.—1st, Between father and sons; 2d, Between co-heirs. The rule (which is alike binding according to the doctrine of every school) is, that as to ancestral property, whether real or personal, land or movables, the division must be strictly equal, *Daya Krama San-*

graha, Mitacshara. "In wealth acquired by the grandfather, whether it consist of movables or immovables, the equal participation of father and son is ordained," *Brihaspati, Jimuta Vahana.* The meaning is, that the participation shall be equal and uniform, and the father is not entitled to make a distribution of greater or less shares at his choice, as he may do in the instance of his own acquired goods. It does not imply that the shares must be alike, *Jimuta Vahana.* Probably this means that it is not imperative, that each individual should receive the same class of property.

In Madras sons may demand partition and take per stirpes.— In Madras it has been held, as we have seen, that a son, or even a grandson, of his own pleasure may compel a division of ancestral immovable property. Each of the latter stands, as to his share, in the exact position of the person he represents (his father), *i.e.*, he gets the share that would have fallen to him if he had claimed a division.

In Benares unequal distribution of ancestral and immovable self-acquired property prohibited.—In the Benares school an unequal distribution by the father of *ancestral* property, of whatever description, as well as of *immovable* property *acquired by himself*, is prohibited ; and of his own personal acquisitions he cannot, according to the same law, reserve more than two shares for himself, and any unequal distribution of real property is illegal, for the maxim *factum valet* does not apply in the Benares school.

According to *Sir Thomas Strange*, relying on the old Bengal authorities (and *Mr Strange*, who relies upon his father), the father has a right to two shares for himself out of the ancestral property. But the other rule, as laid down by *Mr Strange*, prevails in Southern India, and it is laid down in the *Mitac :* "A father has no right to a double share."

Ancestral property is equally divided between a father and his sons in Eastern India.

In the Bengal school the father may make unequal distribution of self-acquired property as well as movable ancestral property, and of property of whatever description recovered by himself, retaining for himself as much as he pleases ; and should he make an unequal distribution, or without any just cause exclude any of his sons, the act would be sinful, but not invalid. But with regard to ancestral immovable property and estate, to the acquisition of which his sons may have contributed, they are entitled to equal shares, but the father may retain a double share of it, as well as of acquisitions made by his sons.

According to Macn. Cons., if once made, valid.—*Macnaghten in Considerations on H. L.* ch. "Gifts—unequal distribution," in discussing the subject with reference to the Bengal law, which he admits is surrounded with difficulty, arising from conflicting opinions, is evidently biased in favour of the opinion that a gift of even the entire ancestral movable property, if once made, is valid though sinful.

This opinion discussed and refuted.—*Macn.* (*Prins. H. L.* 45) differs from this view, first, Because the doctrine for which I contend has been established by the latest decision, 2 *S. D. A.* 214 ; and, secondly, Because the only authority for the reverse of this doctrine consists in the following passages from *Jim. Vahana*:—"The texts of *Vyasa* exhibiting a prohibition are intended to show a moral offence ; they are not meant to invalidate the sale or other transfer. Therefore, since it is denied that a gift or sale should be made, the precept is infringed by making one, but the gift or transfer is not null, for a fact cannot be altered by one hundred texts ;" and the learned author adds, "If these passages are to be taken in a general sense, if they are to be held to have the effect of legalising, or at least of rendering valid, all acts committed in direct opposition to the law, they must have the effect of superseding all law, and it would be better at once to pronounce those texts alone to be the guide for our judicial decisions. The example adduced by the commentator to illustrate these texts clearly shows the spirit in which this unmeaning though mischievous dogma was delivered ; he declares that a fact cannot be altered by a hundred texts, in the same manner as the murder of a Brahmin, though in the highest degree criminal and unlawful, having been perpetrated, there is no remedy ; or, in other words, that the defunct Brahmin cannot be brought to life again. . . . . But what renders this conclusion less disputable is, that the texts of *Vyasa* in question occur in the chapter of the *Daya Bhaga* which treats of self-acquisitions, and has no reference to ancestral property. If any additional proof were wanting of the father's incompetency to dispose of ancestral real property by an unequal partition, or to do any other act with respect to it which might be prejudicial to the interests of his son, I would merely refer to the provision contained, ch. iii. s. vii. § 10, of the translation of the extract from the *Mitacshara* relative to judicial proceedings. The rule is in the following terms :—'The ownership of the father and son is the same in land which was acquired by his father,' &c. From this text it appears that in the case of land acquired by the grandfather the ownership of father and son is equal, and therefore if the father make away with the immovable property so acquired by the grandfather, and if the son has recourse to a court of justice, a judicial proceeding will be entertained between the father and son. The passage occurs in a dissertation as to who are fit parties in judicial proceedings, and although the indecorum of a contest wherein the father and son are litigant parties has been expressly recognised, yet, at the same time, the rights of the son are declared to be of so inviolable a nature that an action by him for the maintenance of them will be against his father, and that it is better there should be a breach of moral decorum than a violation of legal right.

The question as to the extent to which an unequal distribution made by a father in Bengal should be upheld has been amply discussed in a case decided in the Court of *S. D. A.* (2 *S. D. A. R.* 214) in 1816. It was there determined that an unequal distribution of ancestral immovable property is illegal and invalid, and that the unequal distribution of property acquired by the father, and of movable ancestral property, is legal and valid, unless when made under the influence of a motive which is held in law to deprive a person of the power to make a distribution. It was declared, in a note to that case, that the validity of an unequal distribution of ancestral immovable property, such as is expressly forbidden by the received authorities on Hindu law, cannot be maintained on any construction of that law by *Jimuta Vahana* or others. *Jagannatha*, in his *Digest*, maintains a contrary opinion. He says, that if a father infringing the law absolutely give away the whole or part of the immovable ancestral property, such gift is valid, provided he be not under the influence of anger or other disqualifying motive; and admitting this doctrine to be correct, it must be inferred *à fortiori* that he is authorised to make an unequal distribution of such property, but the reverse of this doctrine has been established by the mass of authorities, which will be found collected in the case above quoted, 1 *Macn. P. H. L.* 45.

Opinions of old authorities—Father entitled to two shares of ancestral property.—When a father makes a partition of the ancestral property, he may take two shares for himself, and allot to each of his sons a single share; for the text of *Brihaspati*, which declares "the father may himself take two shares at a partition made in his lifetime," relates to ancestral wealth, *Daya Krama Sangraha.* It must not be supposed that this text refers to the father's own wealth, since it would contradict the texts of *Vishnu* and the rest, which declare that what a father may in such case take depends entirely upon his own will, and as he may take a greater or less share, at his pleasure, the restriction of two shares only would be useless.* A father has not the power to make an unequal distribution of ancestral property, consisting either of land, or a corrody, or slaves, even though any of the causes before mentioned, namely, the superior qualifications of one particular son, &c., should exist; and the text of *Yajnavalchya*, which declares "the ownership of the father and son is the same in land which was acquired by his father, or in a corrody, or in chattels" (slaves), is intended to restrain the exercise of the father's will; for although contrary to the received opinion [of equal ownership between father and son], it is impossible that as long as the father, the owner of the ancestral property, continues to survive, his sons should have ownership therein.

* See *Macn.* opinion, *ante*, p. 370, where this subject is discussed, and the correct rule laid down.

But the father possesses a power in regard to ancestral property other than land (and the descriptions above mentioned), such as pearls, gems, similar to that which he has in the disposal of his own acquired wealth. *Yajnavalchya* declares, "The father is master of the gems, pearls, and corals, and of all [other movable property], but neither the father nor the grandfather is so of the whole immovable estate."

Here, by the specification, in the first instance, of gems, pearls, and corals, and afterwards by the use of the word *all*, gold and other effects, exclusive of the three descriptions of property, consisting of land, &c., are intended. The word *whole*, again, which occurs in the second portion of the above text, is made use of for the purpose of showing that a prohibition does not exist against a gift of immovable property not incompatible with the due support of the family. Thus it is stated in *Daya Bhaga.*

In like manner, a father may at his pleasure allot to his son the deduction of a twentieth from his own acquired wealth, or to the ancestral property. *Yajnavalchya* says, "If a father make a partition, let him separate his sons at pleasure, and either dismiss the eldest with the best share, or, if he choose, all may be equal sharers." Here the first half of this text relates to a father's own acquired wealth, and the last refers to ancestral property. This is the opinion stated in the *Daya Bhaga, Daya Krama Sangraha.*

Father and only son.—*Narada* allows a double share to a father, but this has been explained to relate to an only son, *Mayukha, Jim. Vahana. Brihaspati* declares, however, that the father is entitled to only an equal share with an only son in ancestral property, *Mayukha, Jim. Vahana,* so *Yajnavalchya;* for the ownership of the father and son is the same in land which was acquired by the grandfather or in a corrody * or in chattels (which belonged to him). *Mayukha,* § 13 ; *Mitac.* ch. i. s. v. § 3 ; *Jimuta Vahana,* ch. ii. § 9. So *Katyayana,* when the father and the sons even take all that which has been made upon the commonwealth, in equal shares, it is called a legal partition, *Mayukha,* ch. iv. s. iv. § 13. A text in *Yajnavalchya,* and another in *Narada,* to a contrary effect have

* A corrody signifies what is fixed by a promise in this form : "I will give that in every month of Kartiki" (October or November.) The author explains corrody *nibandha* as signifying anything which has been promised deliverance annually or monthly, or at any other fixed period. Srikrestna Raghunandana in the Daya tata cites from Kalpwataru this definition : "A fixed amount granted by the king or other authority, receivable from a mine or similar fund. *Nibandha* is enforced in Wilson's Gloss to be in law fixed on immovable property, also a corrody or fixed allowance granted by the Raja or person in authority to be received from the proceeds of a manufactory or estate. Corrody is also known to the English law. *Corodium,* signifies a sum of money or allowance of meat, bread, drink, money, clothing, lodgings, and such like necessaries for sustenance due to the king, from an abbey or other house of religion whereof he was founder towards the sustentation of such an one of his servants as he thought fit to bestow it upon.

been explained as relating to former ages, § 14, "or the meaning of the text (*Yajnavalchya supra*) may be as set forth by *Dhareswara*." A father occupied in giving allotments at his pleasure has equal ownership with his sons in the paternal grandfather's estate. He is not privileged to make an unequal distribution of it at his choice, as he is in regard to his own acquired wealth. So *Vishnu* says, When a father separates his sons from himself, his will regulates the division of his own acquired wealth. But in the estate inherited from the grandfather the ownership of father and son is equal, *Jimuta Vahana*. This is very clear, "When the father separates his sons from himself he may, by his own choice, give them greater or less allotments if the wealth were acquired by himself; but not so if it were property inherited from the grandfather. The father has not, in such case, an unlimited discretion."

The doctrine of the Mitacshara as to the equal participation of father and son, and the right of the latter to acquire partition, rejected.—Hence (since the text becomes pertinent, by taking it in the sense above stated, or because there is ownership restricted by law in respect of shares, and not an unlimited discretion) both opinions (of the *Mitacshara* and others, *Srikrishna* and *Achyuta*), that the mention of like ownership provides for an equal division between father and son in the case of property ancestral, and that it establishes the son's right to require partition, ought to be rejected, *Jim. Vahana*. It is consequently true (since the texts above cited do not imply co-ordinate ownership) that the father has his double share of wealth inherited from the grandfather or other ancestor, and that a distribution takes place at the will of the father only, and not by the choice of his sons, see *Srikrishna Chudamani*, and *Achyuta*.

As to self-acquired property.—As to self-acquired property, whether his sons co-operate or not in its acquisition, although the disposition of it is more in the discretion of the father, he must not make distinctions in its distribution upon improper or arbitrary grounds, or from caprice, as for instance on behalf of the issue of a favourite wife, nor when the father's mind is labouring under disqualifying influences, such as anger, sickness, &c., *Menu*, *Jim. Vahana*, *Narada*, *Daya Krama Sangraha*, *Bhowannychurn Bunhoojea* v. *Heirs of Ram Kaunt B.*, 2 *S. D. A.* 202, 3 *Dig.* 544, 1 *Stra. H. L.* 194, 2 *ib.* 317 and *Katyayana*.

This restriction on his volition in the distribution of it, is incompatible with the doctrine that he can do with it as he pleases, *ante*. Bengal authorities only are quoted in support of it. As to the Mithila law—

Property acquired by use of patrimony.—It will be borne in mind that although property may have been self-acquired, yet if it were obtained by the father at the expense of ancestral wealth, or if the patrimony were used in its recovery, it enters into the category of that class of property, and regarded as such.

Lost property acquired by sole exertions.—While, on the other hand, property which was ancestral, but which had been lost by the ancestor, and was recovered by the son at his sole expense, without the use of ancestral property, is regarded as self-acquired.

Sons may dispute unequal division.—Should any other principle be adopted in the distribution without the concurrence of the sons, it may be disputed by them, for the sons have the power of resisting an unequal distribution as well as of claiming division.

Each son may demand his share at different periods.—We have seen that a division, at the instance of some of the sons, may take place; in that case the other sons may, at any time, require a distribution of their shares.

Or may renounce.—But should a son not be desirous of participation, he may waive his right to a share by acceptance of a trifle in satisfaction. *Yajnavalchya* says, "The separation of one who is able to support himself, and is not desirous of participation, may be completed by giving him some trifle which will have the effect of binding his heirs who might, without renunciation, still claim partition," *Menu, Mitac., Jim. Vahana, Mayukha.*

May resume share in case of indigence.—It is said the father may resume, in case of indigence, what he has so shared with his sons. The correctness of this last rule is doubtful. There is no case in English law where a gift, the possession of which passes at the time to the donee, has been resumed.

2. Between co-heirs.—We have now to treat of the division of property after the death of the father amongst the co-heirs; but before passing on, we shall pause for a moment to take a bird's-eye view of the state of a Hindu family previous to partition. In Hindu law, the presumption is in favour of union, as the primary state of every Hindu family is that of association, *Dhurm Dass Pundey* v. *Musst. Shama Soondri Debiah*, 3 *Moore's In. Ap.* 229, 1 *Stra. H. L.* 225. On the death of the father undivided, the ancestral property devolves upon the co-heirs undivided, and so long as they remain in that, the normal state of a Hindu family, they enjoy community of interest, although the management of the family concerns may devolve upon one member thereof. The eldest son generally having the first claim, but his pretensions are subject to the concurrence of the rest, and to his character and habits of business. On that male member of the family (except in *Malabar* and *Canara*, where the female is preferred, and even there a male member is manager) in whom these qualifications unite, the management falls, *Jim. Vahana.*

Ancient rule.—It is unnecessary here to do more than refer to the ancient rule with regard to the assignment of shares into twentieths, fortieths, and eightieths amongst the eldest, middle-most, and youngest, and the right of the eldest son to the least chattel, &c.

Equal division.—The rule that now prevails is, that among the sons the partition must be equal. The mode by equal division is the only one adopted in the present age, because younger brothers are now-a-days seldom met with who entertain this great veneration (referring to an additional share) for the eldest son, and elder brothers deserving of it are (equally) rare, *Daya Krama Sangraha, Mayukha, Jim. Vahana.*

We have elsewhere observed, under the head of "Charges on the Inheritance," that the debts and other charges must be provided for before partition. These, of course, can only be ascertained on settlement of the accounts of the family, and division of the liabilities among the co-heirs, or by special allotment of the property to meet the demand, as when provision of maintenance is in question. But this is mere matter of private arrangement, and cannot oust the creditors of their right to follow the property, notwithstanding its partition. If the enjoyment have been disproportionate, the co-heirs are liable to account for it. We have also seen, under the head of "Disqualifications for Inheritance," p. 98, that there are certain moral, physical, and mental defects, which, as they exclude from the performance of obsequies, likewise exclude from inheritance. Making allowance for these, the division of both ancestral and acquired property must in general be equal, without deductions for the eldest son. *Harita* ordains equal distribution without deduction. *Usanas* says, "The distribution among brothers born of women of the same tribe is ordained to be made equally." *Paithinasi* says, "When the paternal inheritance is to be divided, the shares shall be equal." *Yajnavalchya* also declares, "Let the sons divide equally the effects and the debts after the death of both parents." Where deductions take place, it can only be by consent of the brethren, *Jim. Vahana, Mitac., Daya Krama Sangraha.*

Partition after the father's death.—An equal partition after the death of the father is declared in another, *Smriti* (*Yajnavalchya, Mitac., Jim. Vahana*). Let sons divide equally both the effects and the debts after (the demise of) both parents, *Harita.* When the father is dead, the partition of the inheritance should be made equally, *Mayukha.*

Disproportionate enjoyment.—The enjoyment of common property in disproportionate or unequal shares—some of the co-heirs having more, some less, of the shares when divided—must nevertheless be equal, the law taking no account of greater or less expenditure, unless the difference be such as to exclude all idea of proportion, the object entirely selfish, or the circumstances of a kind to include fraud.

The co-heirs are not called upon to deduct their legitimate

expenditure.—Whatever excess has been expended by one brother, in consequence of his having a large family, should not be taken into account at the time of partition, but a partition should be made of the wealth which is actually forthcoming, *Daya Krama Sangraha. Narada* declares, "Among unseparated kinsmen, let not one restore what has been expended." A partition should take place of the visible wealth collected for income and expenditure.

The division is made of the balance after deducting expenses.—Having compared the amount of the wealth which had accumulated at the time when no partition had taken place with the amount expended, a division should be made of the balance actually remaining; so what has been laid out, with prudence and without excess, on initiation of a son, or the nuptials of a daughter, are not to be accounted for, for these are charges upon the joint wealth.

But extravagant excess may be deducted from him who indulges in it.—But if there have been extravagant excess at these ceremonies, to the detriment of the common fund, the co-heir indulging in such extravagance will receive his share diminished in proportion to such excess; though, if the debt incurred exceed his share, it is said that the law does not direct that the excess shall become a debt.

Drones not allowed to share in accumulations.—In Bengal, a lazy knave, or drone, may be deprived of participating in the property acquired by augmentation or improvement. But this rule does not extend to Southern India. *Jagannatha* says, "Should any one of undivided brothers, through laziness or knavery, make no exertion for gain, not striving to improve the existing stock, and acquire further wealth, by agriculture or the like, he may be debarred from his share of that which has been added by the rest of the brethren, subject to a trifle being given him for his maintenance, and without prejudice to his claim for a share of the original stock." But in Southern India this is denied—there being no exception there to the right of sharing, all participating equally, without reference to their contribution to the common stock, except in the one case only—viz., with the consent of the co-heir, *Mitac., Menu.*

Sons take per capita.—These shares are given to the sons irrespective of their mothers; that is, whether they be by the same mother or not, they take *per capita*. Their shares are not governed by the number of the mothers from whom they have sprung, not even among Sudras. The same rule of equality of shares for sons prevails for all classes, *Judgment of Sudr Court in R. A.* 20 *of* 1846, *Stra. Man. H. L.* 251.

Other than sons take per stirpes.—Where, however, other than sons claim a division, they inherit *per stirpes*—standing in the position of those through whom they derive their claim, and receiving amongst them all only what he would have got had he divided.

Thus: A. has two sons, B. and C.; B. has one son, D.; C. has two sons, E. and F.

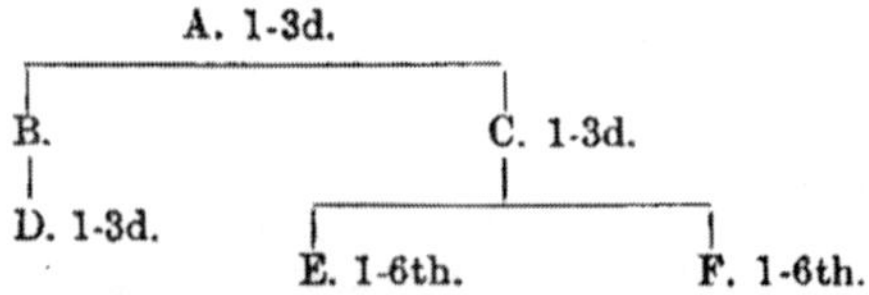

Here A.'s property is divided into three shares. A. gets one share, one-third; one share, another third, claimable by B., goes to D.; and the other third share, claimable by C., goes to E. and F., one-sixth to each.

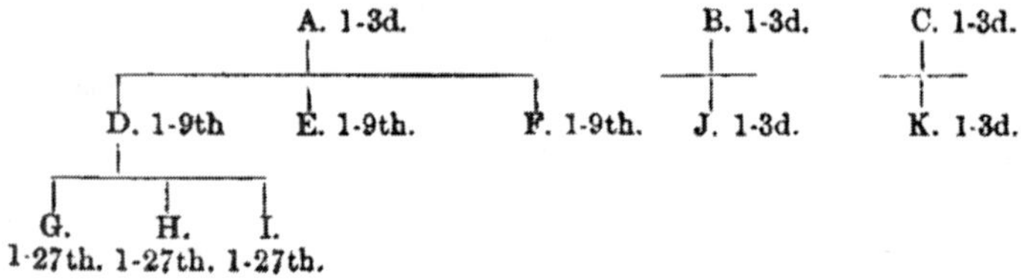

The property was originally divided amongst three brothers, A., B., C.; each takes a one-third share. A. leaves three sons, D., E., F., amongst whom he divides his one-third portion, which gives to each a one-ninth share. D. leaves three sons, G. H. I., who are likewise entitled to an equal division of D.'s one-ninth share, so that each would receive a twenty-seventh part. J. and K., B. and C.'s adopted sons, each take their adopted father's one-third share.

Again, A., B., and C. are brothers. A. dies, leaving a son, D., who claims and receives his father's one-third share of the property; B. and C. remain united. B. dies without issue, his share vests in C. The divided nephew, D., has no claim thereon. Had D. not divided off previously to the death of B., the whole of the family property would have been enjoyed in common by himself and C.; but in consequence of his having divided on the death of B., C. takes the whole property on the death of B., as sole surviving member of a joint family.

The law says, "That on the death of a divided co-heir, after the enumeration of various classes of heirs, or failure of those of higher degree, brothers of the whole blood take the inheritance in the first instance; if there be none, then brothers by different mothers, and on failure of brothers of either class, brothers' sons share the heritage in the order of their respective fathers; but brothers' sons or nephews have no title to the succession during the existence of their uncles," *Mitac.* We have not seen this doctrine applied to claims to succession of the nature of the case we had supposed. For instance, if D. had not been a divided nephew, and had been living in union with B. and C. at the period of B.'s death, the question might be raised, whether he was entitled to share the whole of the property equally with C., or whether he ought not to be restricted to the share of his father, A. and C. taking the share of B., or two thirds of the whole paternal inheritance? We do not recollect of any case wherein the question has been raised, but certainly consider this one likely to arise. *Jim. Vahana* agrees with the Benares school in respect to the succession of a brother to the share of his deceased separated brother.

One son requiring partition, no exception to rule as to equality of shares.—It can hardly be considered an exception to the rule of equality of shares that any son may, in exclusion of the rest, be its sole object, the rest of the family and the property remaining in union with the father as before; for such son, on separation, can only receive his due share.

Amongst sons of different brothers is according to their fathers.—*Yajnavalchya* declares the mode of division of ancestral estate among the sons of different brothers: "Among grandsons by different fathers, the allotment of shares is according to the fathers." It means, that if there be one son of one, two sons of a second, and three sons of a third [or the like], their shares will be solely according to the number of the fathers, and not the number of the sharers themselves, *Mayukha, Mitac., Jim. Vahana.*

One of four grandsons, co-heirs, having died, his son is entitled to claim partition from his uncles.—The eldest of four brothers, who had received movable and immovable property by gift from their maternal grandfather, died, leaving a son, the complainant, and then their mother died. Afterwards two of the surviving brothers died, one leaving a daughter, who was mother of male issue, and the other a widow, as their heirs. A part of the property was undivided, another portion was divided, and in the exclusive possession of the several individuals specified. The complainant, the son of the eldest brother, sued for partition of the estate, and the defendant, one of the uncles, admitting the inchoate right of the plaintiff, stated that while he is alive the brother's son cannot have an equal share with him. The question was, Is the property a fit subject of partition while one of the four brothers exists, or will the surviving brother be entitled to a superior portion? It was answered, All the grandsons were equally entitled to the gift of their maternal grandfather, and should one of them die during the life of the mother, leaving a son, his son has the exclusive right to the property to which his father was entitled, whether divided or undivided. The following is the doctrine of the *Mitac.*, *Jim. Vahana*, and other books of law, *Brihaspati*:—"All the brethren shall be equal sharers of that which is acquired by them in concert."

With regard to separately-acquired property, the brothers may enter into contracts with each other.

Brothers' sons also share with their uncles.—*Katyayana* says, "Should a younger son die before partition, his share shall be allotted (by the elder brother) to his son, provided he had received no fortune from his grandfather." "That son's son shall receive his father's share from his uncle, or from his [uncle's] son, and the same [proportionate] share shall be allotted to all the brothers according to law. Or [if that grandson be also dead] his son takes the share; beyond him succession stops." The *younger son* (*anuja*) denotes also that the eldest [is bound to portion off his brother's son] stops at the great-grandson, *Mayukha*.

The son of the great-grandson will not take, being in another line of heirs, unless the direct line is exhausted.—We must thus understand it: "The son of the great-grandson, or the rest, will not on the death of the father [grandfather, and great-grandfather, without interval, after the death of the great-great-grandfather,] obtain his wealth, being of another [line], so long as his son or other [heirs] are alive. In default of a son, grandson [and great-grandson], in the general [family] only, he also will take [the succession]," *Mayukha*.

This refers to a re-united family only.—This does not refer to an undivided family, but to a re-united one. For it is said by *Devala*, "Partition of heritage among undivided parceners, and a second partition among divided relatives living together [after re-union], shall extend to the fourth in descent. This is a settled rule;" and "Be it debt, or a written contract, or a house, or arable land, descended from his grandfather, he shall take his due share of it when he comes, even though he had been very long in a foreign country. If a man leave the common family and reside in another province, his share must undoubtedly be given to his male descendants when they appear." It means between the great-great-grandfather and his sons, separated when in a state of union, and afterwards re-united, *Mayukha, Jim. Vahana*. In both, the text is assigned to *Brihaspati*.

This limitation is intended in the case of residence in another district.—This refers to those fixed in the same district, because where they reside in different districts it will descend even to the fifth, as is declared by *Brihaspati* in treating of residence in other lands: "Be he the third person, or fifth, or even the seventh [*i.e.*, in the second, or fourth, or even in the sixth degree], he shall receive the share that gradually descends to him on full proof of his birth and family name," *Mayukha*.

Distribution according to the mothers.—*Brihaspati*: "If there be many [sons] sprung from one father, alike in number and in class, but born of rival mothers, partition must be made by them according to law, by the allotment of shares to the mothers." So *Vyasa* says, "If there be many sons of one man, by different mothers, but equal in number, and like by class, a distribution among the mothers is approved," *Mayukha, Jim. Vahana.*

But not where the sons vary in number.—"Among brothers who are equal in class, but vary in regard to the number [of sons produced by each mother], the shares of the heritage are allotted to the males [not to their mothers]," *Brihaspati, Mayukha.*

Property descends in co-parcenery.—Wherever there are several sons, they take, as one heir, the property descending to them as co-parceners, and they enjoy it in community under one manager, as we have seen.

Exception.—There is, however, one exception to this general rule in favour of the Crown. *Menu*, ch. ix. § 323, speaks of a dying king duly committing his kingdom to his son. But this rule is based upon usage rather than law, *Jagannatha.* So the same exception extends to principalities and the great zemindaries. See *ante*, "Inheritance." *Beemlah Dibeh* v. *Goculneth, Beng. R.* 1805, p. 32; *Rumgunga Deo* v. *Doorgamunee Jobrai, Beng. R.* 1809; *Urjun Manie Thakoor* v. *Rumgunga Deo, Beng. R.* 1814, p. 469.

Condition of undivided family previous to partition.—We have seen that the management devolves upon some male member of the family, where they continue to live in association, *Jim. Vahana.*

Manager's acts important.—The manager regulates the dealings and transactions of the family, and his acts are of importance not only to the association, but also to the creditors. As to the power of manager or guardian to alienate ancestral property, see 6 *Moore's In. Ap.* 393, *ante*, p. 79. *Sir Thomas Strange* says, In his capacity as manager, all his acts and disbursements, to be of validity, must be for the general good, if not for the immediate and indispensable maintenance of the whole, for objects chargeable upon the common stock, including works of piety, which it concerns all should not go unperformed; with this difference, that where his acts have been for the support of the family, the charge is in its nature binding upon the joint property, though the remedy may be eventually against him only by whom it was incurred so acting; whereas, if in the course of trade, or for charitable purposes, in order to its being so, it must have had the consent of the rest express or implied, *Mitac.*

It is important for creditors, therefore, to ascertain whether the family with whom they are dealing be separated or united. It being necessary in the latter case to see that the transaction is one that will bind the co-heirs, otherwise the common stock will not be liable, *Prannath Das* v. *Calishunker Ghoosal, Beng. R. ante*, 1805, p. 51; *Sheva Dass* v. *Bishonath Dobee, ib.* 46. *Mr Colebrooke*, upon this point, says, That a mortgage, sale, or gift, by one of several joint owners, without the consent of the rest, is invalid for others' shares. In Bengal law it is clear that it is good for his own share, and for that only, *Colebrooke* and *Ellis, Daya Krama Sangraha.* But he would be liable to penal consequences, and the Court would probably enforce a separation in such case. In other provinces it is as clear that the act is invalid as it concerns others' shares; *Mr Colebrooke* remarking, that the only doubt which the subtlety of Hindu reasoning might raise would be, whether it be maintainable even for his own share, the property being undivided.

Consent of the co-sharers necessary to valid alienation of joint property beyond the alienor's share.—I take the law to be, that the consent of the sharers, express or implied, is indispensable to a valid alienation of joint property beyond the share of the actual alienor, and that an unauthorised alienation by one of the sharers is invalid beyond the alienor's share as against the alienee. But consent is implied, and may be presumed in many cases, *Mitac.*

In Bengal assignment of co-proprietor's own share even before partition.—But in Bengal there may be an assignment of the co-proprietor's own share even before partition, since a common property is already vested in him, *Jim. Vahana, Srikrishna Daya Krama Sangraha.*

In Madras co-sharer may alien his share which is liable to be sold in execution on a judgment obtained for a tort.—According to Hindu law, current in Madras, a member of an undivided family may alien his share of the family property, to which, if a partition took place, he would be individually entitled, and such share is liable to be sold in execution on a judgment obtained for a tort, *Virasvami Gramini* v. *Ayyasvami Gramini*, 1 *Mad. H. C. R.* 471.

The judgment in this case will be found set out in *Grady's Hindu Law of Inheritance.*

Section VII.

AS TO THE RIGHT TO DEMAND PARTITION AMONG CO-HEIRS.

1. *The right to demand partition*—2. *The property to be divided*—3. *How division takes place*—4. *Evidence*—*Wife cannot claim in her own right where there are sons, neither can a daughter*—*One member may divide*—*During life of the mother*—*In Bengal*—*In every province except Bengal*—*Where there are several widows with sons*—*Effects of the two modes of division*—*Amongst Sudras*—*Stepmothers and grandmothers*—*Widow of husband separated from his co-heirs*—*Daughter*—*Where brothers and sisters are of the same tribe*—*Division presumed to be general*—*Whether an only son is entitled to demand partition from his uncles*—*The son of one of five whole brothers, though his father was insane, is entitled, on par-*

tition, to one fifth of property acquired by joint funds—Absentees entitled to share as far as the seventh in descent—But those at home as far as fourth—Minor—Period of absence—What constitutes a foreign country—After-born sons—Pregnant widow of a co-heir—Land goes to the son borne by the wife of equal class alone—The right to a share may be renounced.

We have still to consider—

1. The right to demand partition—2. The property to be divided—3. How division takes place—4. Evidence.—To resume our inquiries as to partition among co-heirs, and—

1. As to right to demand partition.—The right to demand a partition exists only in those who are considered as heirs. This, of course, excludes those who have only a right to maintenance, and, consequently, the female members of the joint family, who have certainly an interest in the property, but only to the extent of their maintenance. *Sir Thomas Strange* says, that the interest which a wife has in partition by or in the life of the husband is merely incidental.

Wife cannot claim in her own right where there are sons—Neither can a daughter.—The wife cannot claim it in her own right, *Apastamba.* A daughter takes nothing as of right during her father's lifetime. She is equally barred from calling for it after his death. Where there are male issue, therefore, the widow or widows are entitled to maintenance only, for they cannot present the funeral cake, *Devala.*

One member may divide.—Partition may take place with reference to one or more members of the family, leaving the rest still undivided, or all may join in it and afterwards may become re-united. See "Re-union."

During life of the mother.—It has been thought by some that it could not take place during the mother's life in consequence of a forced construction having been placed on the precept of *Menu,* "After the death of the father and mother, the brothers may divide the paternal and maternal estate." But it is manifest that *Menu* in this passage was treating of two classes of property, one of the father, and the other of the mother; and with that terseness of expression which is peculiar to almost all ancient writers in most languages, he united the two branches of his subject in one sentence, so that what he really meant to express was, that after the death of the father the brothers may divide the paternal estate, and that after the death of the mother they may divide the maternal estate; and accordingly the author of the *Smriti Chandrika* has explained the meaning to be that the death of the one and of the other has reference distributively to their several property, so that there may be a division of the father's property during the mother's life, and *vice versâ,* there being no reason to await the demise of both in order to divide what has belonged to either, neither having ownership in the other's property where there are children. Inasmuch, then, as the wife has no ownership in the property of the husband during his lifetime, nor the husband in that of his wife during her lifetime, on the death of either, without children, the survivor may succeed by virtue of inheritance.

In Bengal.—In Bengal the lawfulness of division during the mother's life is denied, *Jim. Vahana*. But this opinion is construed by his commentator, *Srikrishna*, as importing that the partition is valid, but not morally right; and by *Ragh. Dayatatva*, that if it be made, a share is ordained for the mother; and by *Kasirama* on *Dayatatva*, that it is not laudable, not that it is null.

In every province except Bengal.—And *Mr Colebrooke*, after a careful examination of every material passage applicable to the point, was of opinion that a division during the mother's life was allowable throughout every province, with the exception of Bengal.

Sir W. H. Macn. says, Partition may be made also while the mother survives. This rule, though at variance with the doctrine of *Jim. Vahana*, has nevertheless been maintained by more modern authorities, and is universally observed in practice, 3 *Dig.* 78.

According to the *Jim. Vahana, Raghunandana, Srikrishna*, and other Bengal authorities, when partition is made by a father, a share equal to that of a son must be given to the childless wife, not to her who has male issue. But the doctrine laid down by *Harinatha* is, that if the father reserve two or more shares, no share need be assigned to the wives, because their maintenance may be supplied out of the portion reserved. The *Vivadarnavasetu* holds that the wife is entitled to an equal share where the father gives equal shares to his son, but that where he gives unequal shares, and reserves a larger one for himself, he is bound to allot to each of his wives from the property reserved to himself as much as may amount to the average share of a son, *Misra, Daya Krama Sangraha*.

The doctrine laid down by *Jagannatha* is, that if the wife have received from any quarter wealth which would ultimately have devolved on her husband, such wealth should be included in the calculation of her allotment. But if she received the wealth from her own father or other relative, or from the maternal uncle or other collateral kinsman of her husband, it should not be included, her husband not having any interest therein.

The law of Benares, Mithila, and elsewhere, differs from the Bengal school on this subject, and is not in itself uniform or consistent. *Vignyneswara* ordains, "When the father by his own choice makes all his sons partakers of equal portions, his wives, to whom peculiar property had not been given by their husband or father-in-law, must be made participants of shares equal to those of sons." But if separate property had been given, the same authority subsequently directs the allotment of half a share, "or if any had been given, let him assign the half."

According to *Madhavacharya*, if the father by his own free will make his sons equal participants, he ought to make his wives, to whom no separate property has been given, partakers of a share equal to that of a son; but if such property has been presented to her, then a moiety should be given. *Kamalakara*, the author of the *Vividatandava*, declares generally, that whether the father be living or dead, his wives are respectively entitled to a son's portion. But *Sulapani*, in the *Dipakalika*, maintains, that if the father makes an equal partition among his sons by his own choice, he must give equal shares to such of his wives only as have no male issue; and *Helayudha* lays it down, that wives who have no issue male are here intended.

Misra ordains, "That when he reserves a greater part of his fortune, and gives some trifle to his sons, or takes a double share for himself, the husband must give so much wealth to his wives out of his own share alone. Accordingly, the separate delivery of shares to wives is only ordained when he makes an equal partition," *Daya Krama Sangraha*. *Macn.* sums up the argument thus: "In case of an equal partition made by a father among his sons, his wives who are destitute of male issue take equal portions; where he reserves a large portion for himself, his wives are not entitled to any specific share, but must be maintained by him; and where unequal shares are given to sons, the average of the shares of the sons should be taken for the purpose of ascertaining the allotments of the wives. The same rules apply also to paternal grandmothers in case of partition of the ancestral property."

Where there are several widows with sons.—There are two modes of division adopted where there are several widows with sons, varying in number by each, some more, some less, called *Patni Bhaga*, or division by wives, or *Putra Bhaga*, or division by sons. If the number of sons by each wife be equal, the allotment may be to the mothers, according to the former mode of division, leaving it to them to subdivide among the sons. This appears very fair. But the principle upon which this mode is adopted being that the division to the wives must always be an equal one (*Coleb.*), where the number of sons by each varies, its effect is very different. Thus, if one wife has one son, another three, and a third six, and each wife takes a third of the property, it is clear that the shares of the sons will be very different in each case. So unnatural a mode of division is allowed only among Sudras, and even among them only where there is a custom for it, and which must be strictly proved, *Sumrun Singh* v. *Khedun Singh*, *Beng. R.* 1814, p. 443. *Mr Ellis* says, "I know not that any authority admits *Patni Bhaga* to be the true rule. It is only allowed by some, and entirely rejected by others."

Effects of the two modes of division.—The division by *Putra*

Bhaga must always be unequal with respect to the children of each *venter*; for if there be two wives, and one son by either first or second of the two, he takes half the estate; and if there be a dozen by the other, they take no more among them. In the present case, dividing by *Putra Bhaga*, the three sons would take each one-third of the estate, and the mother and sisters would be jointly provided for. If by *Patni Bhaga*, the son of the first marriage takes one half, and provides for his own mother only; those of the second take one half also, and provide jointly for their mother and sisters. If the order had happened to be reversed, and the single son been of the second marriage, he, though the younger brother of the four, would still have got half of the whole estate. These are the effects of the two modes of division which I have taken this opportunity of explaining—an explanation which, I think, clearly shows that no judge should allow of the division of *Patni Bhaga* if he can avoid it. *Mr Ellis*, in another case, says, In many parts of the southern countries the custom of dividing the property in equal shares to the *venter*, and afterwards equally between the sons of the several *venters*, is so strongly established that it must be allowed to supersede the general law.

Amongst Sudras.—Where a Sudra died leaving two wives, one with an only son, an infant, and the other with two sons, held that the guardian of the infant might refer the question whether the deceased's estate should be divided according to *Patni Bhaga* or *Putra Bhaga*. *Temmakal* v. *Subbammal*, 2 *Mad. H. C. R.* 47. It was decided in another case that among Hindus in the Madras Presidency, the division must be by sons, and not by wives. *Ex relatione, Mr Justice Strange.*

Stepmothers and grandmothers.—*Vyasa* declares [the right] to share even of a stepmother and paternal grandmother. "Even childless wives of the father are declared equal sharers, and so are all the paternal grandmothers or wives of the paternal grandfather, they are declared equal to mothers." From this word *all* the step-grandmothers also are to be included, *Mayukha, Vishnu, Jim. Vahana.* See *Lalla Jotee Lall* v. *Musst. Dooranee, Kooer*, 1 *W. R.* 173, Cal. Sp. No.

Widow of husband separated from his co-heirs.—From the texts of *Yajnavalchya, Menu, Narada, Katyayana*, and others, cited in the *Mitacshara, Viramitrodaya, Vyavaharamadhaya, Vyavahara, Mayukha*, and other authorities, it would appear that if the four individuals being descended from the same grandfather have not been separated from each other, the widow (respondent) of one of them is only entitled to her food, raiment, and a house for her residence. But if her husband have been separated from his co-parceners, then she is entitled to inherit his property, 2 *Macn. Prins. H. L.* 169.

But the allotment of shares to the wife does not imply separation, the conjugal intercourse remaining after partition among sons, *Apastamba*. Her share, when assigned to her, is more in the nature of alimony than *stridhana*, or *the peculiar property of a woman*, and is resumable by her husband if necessary.

Daughter. — Daughters can neither claim nor share division. Unmarried daughters take nothing during their father's life, *Mitac.*, *Narada*. The law gives nothing to a married daughter where male issue is left.

Where brothers and sisters are of the same tribe.—On division among brethren to the unmarried daughters, such portions are allotted as may suffice for the due celebration of their nuptials. This portion has been fixed at the fourth of the share of a brother, *i.e.*, if there be one son and one daughter, the whole paternal estate should be made into two parts, and one of these two parts made into four, the daughter takes one of these fourths; so, if there be two sons and one daughter, the estate should be made into three parts, and one of these three made into four, the daughter takes one of these; so, if there be one son and two daughters, the estate is divided into three parts, and two of these parts made into four, the daughters each take one of these fourths, *Mitac.* It must be similarly understood in any case of an equal or unequal number of brothers and sisters. Where brothers and sisters are of different tribes, see *Mitacshara*. And *Macn.* adds, But according to the best authorities, these proportions are not universally assignable, for when the estate is either too small to admit of this being given without inconvenience, or too large to render the gift of such portion unnecessary to the due celebration of the nuptials, the sisters are entitled to so much only as may suffice to defray the expenses of the marriage ceremony. This provision for the sisters is not an absolute right, although it is a charge upon the inheritance. It is intended more to uphold the general respectability of the family, *Macn. Cons. H. L.* 103; *Sir W. H. Macn. P. H. L.* 51.

Division presumed to be general.—In any case of division, *all the members* are *primâ facie* presumed to have divided the whole property, and any one who denies having got any share will have to give very strong evidence of the partial division, either in respect of shares or amount, with reference to any particular portion of the property. See *Dec.* 118 of 1859; 1 *Sel. Dec.* p. 52; *Dec.* 87 of 1861.

Whether an only son is entitled to demand partition from his uncles.—*Menu* says, "Brothers being assembled, shall divide the inheritance." This text has been used for the purpose of showing partition cannot take place at the instance of a single co-heir; but *Jimuta Vahana* says that partition takes place by the will of any one (of the co-heirs).

A member of an undivided family died, leaving three brothers undivided, and a son of eight years of age under charge of one of his uncles. The son on coming of age called upon his guardian uncle to account for his father's share of the property, which the uncle refused to do, alleging that the nephew was only entitled to share in common with his uncles and cousins. *Mr Colebrooke* held that the right of the nephew to receive his father's share from his uncle is explicitly declared in a passage of *Katyayana* (cited 3 *Dig.* p. 7, text lxxix.), and the power of any one of the co-heirs to exact partition of the joint property may be gathered from the *Mitac.*, and is distinctly affirmed by *Jim. Vahana.*

Nephews whose fathers are dead are entitled as far as the fourth in descent to participate equally with the brethren, and these take *per stirpes.*

The son of one of five (whole) brothers, though his father was insane, is entitled, on partition, to one fifth of property acquired by joint funds.—It appeared that the estate was jointly purchased by the four defendants and the plaintiff's father, who were whole brothers, and living jointly; but that at the time of the purchase the father was insane, and the plaintiff a minor, who had since attained his majority. If one of the five brothers was mad, and all of them were undivided, and the four purchased the estate with the joint funds of all five, although the deed of sale be drawn out in the name of the four sane brothers, still if the plaintiff be free from similar defect of madness, he is entitled on partition to one fifth of the property; but if the property were purchased without aid of the joint funds, he has no right to share, *Vivadaratnacara, Vivadachintamani, Mitacshara,* &c., 2 *Macn. Prins. H. L.* 165. On the death of a father or *other owner of property,* neither an impotent man, nor a person afflicted with elephantiasis, nor a madman, nor an idiot, nor one born blind, nor one degraded for sin, nor the issue of a degraded man, nor a hypocrite or impostor, shall take any share of his heritage. For such men, except those degraded, let food and clothes be provided, and let the sons of such as have sons take the shares of their parents, if themselves have no similar disability. *Devala* cited in the *Vivadaratnacara,* "On partition of co-heirs, all the wealth left by their father, or by his father, and what they themselves have acquired by their joint efforts, shall be divided among them." *Katyayana,* "What they themselves have acquired, excepting that for which there is a cause of severalty." The term *self-acquired* here means acquired with the use of the father's funds, *Vivadachintamani,* 1 *Macn. P. H. L.* 165.

Absentees entitled to share as far as the seventh in descent.—Where consent cannot be obtained in consequence of some of the members of the family residing in a foreign district, or province, or collectorate, the partition may, nevertheless, proceed, the law requiring the preservation of his share until his return, as far as the seventh in descent, *Brihaspati, Jim. Vahana.* But query, how far the statute of limitations would prevent this rule from applying?

But those at home as far as fourth.—But descendants only as far as the fourth degree of one who had remained all along in this country are entitled to share his wealth; for it has been formerly declared that the fifth in descent and the rest confer no benefits on the deceased owner, since they are not competent to present funeral oblations to him at solemn obsequies, *Daya Krama Sangraha.* His right is therefore barred after the fourth in descent. See *Devala, Brihaspati.*

Minor.—It may be enforced on behalf of minors. See "Minority."

Period of absence.—The period allowed in such cases varies according to the age of the party at the time of his leaving home for a foreign country. *Sir Thomas Strange* says, The period is generally twenty years, although, in one place, it is said that the law presumes him dead after twelve years, if no tidings have been heard of him, and requires his son to perform obsequies for him.

What constitutes a foreign country.—Difference of language, intervention of a mountain, or great river, and distance, where intelligence is not received within ten nights, have been held to be essential in the consideration of what constitutes a foreign country. But probably none of those circumstances would, in the present day, be much relied on; the departure from one province, or district, or collectorate, for another, affording a surer criterion. Thus, where a Canarese went to reside in Telingana, or a Tamulian in Benares, or a Bengalee in Bombay.

After-born sons—Pregnant widow of a co-heir.—Should any of the widows of the co-heirs happen to be pregnant at the time of their death, or be supposed to be so, the partition should be postponed, or a share set aside to abide the contingency of her having an after-born son. On failure of that contingency, such share falls in, and becomes distributable in like manner as the other property, subject to the maintenance of the widow. But should the event happen without anticipation, then the share of such son, not having been reserved, must be allotted by contribution among the parceners who have divided.

On division being made after the death of a brother, who may have demised without male issue, a share must be taken out of the divided shares for his posthumous son, should his widow bear one to him, *Mitac.*

Grandsons claiming by representation are only entitled to their father's share, the aggregate sons of each being entitled *per stirpem*, and not to an equality individually with their uncles and cousins. Although grandsons have a right in the grandfather's estate equally with the sons, still the distribution of the grandfather's property must be adjusted through their fathers, and not with reference to themselves. The meaning is, if unseparated brothers die, leaving male issue, and the number of sons be unequal, one having two sons, another three, and another four, the two receive a single share in right of their father; the other three take one share appertaining to their father, and the remaining four similarly obtain one share due to their father. So, if some of the sons be living, and some have died, leaving male issue, the same method should be observed; the surviving sons take their own allotments, and the sons of their deceased brothers receive the shares of their own fathers respectively, *Mitac.*, *Yajnavalchya*, *Katyayana.*

Land goes to the son borne by the wife of equal class alone.—Land obtained by acceptance of donation must not be given to the sons of a Shetriya, or other wife of inferior tribe; even though his father give it him, the son of a Brahmin may resume it when his father is dead, *Brihaspati*, *Mitac.*, *Jim. Vahana*, *Devala*, *Mayukha.* The son begotten on a Sudra woman by any man of a twice-born class is not entitled to a share of land, but one begotten on her being of equal class, shall take all the property [whether land or chattels]; thus is the law settled, *Mitac.*, *Jim. Vahana*, *Mayukha.*

Of land acquired by purchase, and the other modes also; yet he does obtain a share of the [movable] wealth, *Mayukha.*

The right to a share may be renounced.—The same rule holds on a partition amongst co-heirs as between father and son; where one does not want a share he may waive his right by acceptance of a trifle, which shall ever after operate as an estoppel in respect of his claim, *Menu.* But he cannot renounce his share, unless he is able to maintain himself, *Mitac.*

Yajnavalchya treats of a case "where a man wishes to give up his right to participate in a share. The separation of one who is able to support himself, and is not desirous of participation, may be completed by giving him some trifle." According to the *Mitacshara*, it means, that "anything whatever may be given for the sake of preventing the desire being entertained by his sons of receiving a share of the heritage," *Mayukha*, *Menu*, *Mitac.*, *Yajnavalchya.*

SECTION VIII.

UPON WHAT PROPERTY PARTITION ATTACHES.

Upon what property partition attaches—What property is incapable of division—Jaghire—A jaghire or other grant acquired at the expense of the patrimony does not belong exclusively to the acquirer—Though science should have been the means of acquisition—The acquirer takes a double share—Bengal Pallyam—Enam villages—A Shrotriyam—A corrody—A shrotriyam is inalienable—Offices attached to Pagoda—Lands endowed for religious purposes—Women—Where one member has more jewels, &c., than another—Books, tools, &c.—

Regalities and zemindaries—Lands granted to maintain rank, &c.—Nuptial gifts—Annuity—Dues attached to the office of Kurnam—Self-acquisitions—The acquisitions of a man made by his own means alone is not divisible amongst his brothers—Half-brother—Joint funds—Acquisitions by one of four brothers, with the aid of his father's funds and labour, will, on partition, be made into ten parts, of which five will go to the father, two to the acquirer, and one to each of his brothers; if acquired without any aid, into two parts, the father taking one, and the acquirer one, the brothers having no right to any share—Acquisitions made by a man jointly with his brother's four sons, by means of joint funds, will be divided into two portions, of which one will be taken by the acquirer, and the other be shared equally by the four sons of his brother—Younger brother joined with elder in management of self-acquired property—Incidental expenditure—Divisibility of gains of science—In respect of what acquisitions the rule applies—Gift by a friend—Nuptial gifts—Gifts must be made to the donee—Exception to the rule—Property recovered—Where landed property lost to the family, and recovered by a co-heir without aid from the family resources, he is entitled to a fourth—Gains by valour—Special property—Alienation may be effected for support of the family, not otherwise—Managing co-heir has power to bind parceners for a debt contracted for the concern.

Upon what property partition attaches.—We have already seen that there are two descriptions of property which are the subjects of partition, the one ancestral, the other self-acquired. Upon partition in the lifetime of the father, there is a difference with reference to the distribution of these two classes of property, the father having no discretion with regard to the former, while with regard to the latter the distribution to some degree depends upon his will and discretion. This distinction, however, does not prevail among co-heirs, whose right attaches on both kinds, and who are entitled to an equal division of everything, unless, indeed, things used for religious purposes, which remain in common.

What property is incapable of division.—There are certain species of property which form an exception to the general rule of Hindu law, viz., that property held in association is divisible amongst the co-heirs. These cases are governed more by usage than general law, and will depend upon the terms of the grant.

Jaghire.—The owner of an extensive jaghire died, leaving two sons, the elder of whom succeeded to it, the younger accepting some villages as his portion. The jaghire was in possession by descent of the great-grandson (by adoption) of the owner, and the great-grandson by the younger branch now set up a claim to a share of it, and upon a question submitted to the pundit as to the claimant's right, he answered, As to the divisibility of a jaghire, it is stated in ancient books, that the crown was entailed upon the eldest son, the rest provided with means for their livelihood, being left to conquer for themselves new countries, . . . therefore a kingdom is not divisible. Mr Ellis remarks upon this case, That this is a very good opinion, . . . a jaghire is a fief (it may be hereditary or not), held under such conditions, and for the performance of such services, as the grantor pleases to prescribe. The jagirdar possesses no powers except such as are necessary for the collection of the revenues in the country assigned to him, or such as may be specially conferred by the terms of his grant. Such tenure, therefore, can bear no resemblance to what the law calls *Rajiyam*, the enjoyment of sovereign power, paramount or subordinate. The latter cannot be divided, for division would destroy it, and it is a maxim that nothing shall be divided which would be destroyed by the Act. But the effects and private estate of a sovereign prince may and ought to be divided like the property of others amongst his children. *Mr Thackaray* says, The succession of zemindaries has never been regulated by the common Hindu law of inheritance, but by the usage of the country or the pleasure of Government. Had they been divisible, we should not have found so many of ancient date still existing as we do; *Beemlah Dibeh* v. *Goculneth, Beng. R.*, 1805, p. 32; *Koonwur Bodh Singh* v. *Sconath Singh, ib.* 1813, p. 415; *Ramgunga Deo* v. *Doorgamunee Jobrai, Beng. R.* 1809; *Uerjun Manie Thakoor* v. *Ramgunga Deo, ib.* 469, 1814.

Mr Thackaray is not accurate in arguing that the succession of ancient zemindaries depends on the pleasure of Government. It depends more on the custom of the family.

A jaghire or other grant acquired at the expense of the patrimony does not belong exclusively to the acquirer.—One of three whole brothers, living jointly in possession of their paternal estate, acquired a jaghire or pension in land, and obtained a few villages as a grant from his father-in-law. If the jaghire had been gained at the expense of the patrimony, it must be divided among all the brothers; but if it has been acquired solely by the labour of one brother, without the aid of the paternal estate, in this case it will not be shared by all the brothers, as it becomes the exclusive property of him who acquired it. So the villages may have been acquired by the father-in-law with his own money, and given by him to his daughter's husband, and in this case they cannot be shared by all the brothers. As *Menu* says, " What a brother has acquired by his labour, without using the patrimony, he need not give up, without his assent, for it is gained by his own exertion."

Though science should have been the means of acquisition.—The estate will be acquired at the expense of the patrimony, if it was obtained out of something taken from the patrimonial estate, or if the acquirer, having been supported at the expense of the ancestral property, had studied science, by means of which he held a situation, and obtained a jaghire; for according to Hindu law, any property acquired by an unseparated brother by means of science, which science he was enabled to obtain by assistance from his father's funds, will be participated by his brothers.

The acquirer takes a double share.—Whether the jaghire be acquired by the direct use of the patrimony, or through science gained by its means, the acquirer is entitled to two shares, and the other brothers to a single share each. He among them who has made an acquisition may take a double portion of it, *Brihaspati*, *Aghoree Shewchurnram* v. *Aghoree Kurtaram*, 2 *Macn. Prins. H. L.* 167.

Bengal.—According to the Bengal law, an acquirer using joint stock has two shares, but the Benares school propounds an exception to this maxim, and they support an equal division in cases of addition to or improvement of the original property, without any separate acquisition. The *Mitacshara* says, "Among unseparated brethren, if the common stock be improved, or augmented by any one of them, through agriculture, commerce, or similar means, an equal distribution nevertheless takes place, and a double share is not allotted to the acquirer.

A polliyam is explained in *Wilson's Glossary* to be a tract of country subject to a petty chieftain. In speaking of *polliyars* he describes them as having been originally petty chieftains, occupying usually tracts of hill or forest, subject to pay tribute and service to the paramount state, but seldom paying either, and more or less independent, but as having at present, since the subjugation of the country by the East India Co., subsided into peaceable landholders. A *polliyam* is in the nature of a raj.* It may belong to an undivided family, but it is not the subject of partition. It can be held by only one member of the family at a time, who is styled a *polliyar*, the other members of the family being entitled to a maintenance or allowance out of the estate, *Naragunty Lutchmee Davamah* v. *Vangama Naidoo*, 9 *Moore's In. Ap.* 66.

It is somewhat similar in its nature to a Gwatwal tenure, which was upheld by the Judicial Committee of the Privy Council in *Rajah Selamund Singh Bahadoor* v. *Bengal Government*, 6 *Moore's In. Ap.* 101.

The succession to the Naragunty *polliyam* in Madras, being ancestral estate, held to vest in the nearest undivided male cousin of the *polliyar* last seised who died without issue male, in preference to the widow.

* A *polliyam* is in the nature of a zemindary, the succession to which is regulated by the deed of permanent settlement, which recognises the order of inheritance according to law and custom. It is only when the custom of the family has been proved to exist limiting the succession in a particular manner, or when an estate is proved to have been an ancient zemindary, that it descends contrary to the ordinary rules of Hindu law, 3 *Morley Dig.* pp. 187 189, "Inheritance by Custom."

The following question was propounded by the Court to the pundits of the Sudr Adawlut :—This *polliyam*, the ancestral property of a family said to be undivided, has descended to an adopted son, K., and on his death, without male issue, is taken possession of by his widow, L. The *polliyam* is now claimed by H. and J., the cousins of I., the adoptive father of K., as their inheritance. Is such claim valid, or is L., the widow of the adopted son K., who died without male issue, entitled to succeed to the *polliyam?* The pundits answered as follows :—The Hindu law books, *Vignyaneswara*, &c., declare that all the members of an undivided family have a joint right in their ancestral property, although only one of them, being capable, continues in possession thereof. I., who had no issue, was not justified in adopting K., a stranger, as a son, to the exclusion of his undivided cousins H. and J. ; but as he adopted him, he, K., became a member of the said undivided family ; and the said H. and J. being his undivided cousins, still retain their joint right to the ancestral family property. It is only when a family is divided that a widow succeeds to the estate of her husband, who died leaving no son ; but when the family is undivided the right of succession is not in the widow, but in the undivided cousins. This being the rule of the Hindu law, H. and J., the undivided cousins of I. and K., are alone entitled to inherit the ancestral *polliyam* referred to in the question. L., the widow of K., has no right to succeed to it.

The pundits consulted by the Court, said the Judicial Committee in delivering judgment, as to the rule of Hindu law, on the assumption that the plaintiffs had established their allegations by evidence, were of opinion that they were entitled to succeed. This view was adopted by the Court below, and no objection to the decision upon this point has been urged at our bar.

Enam villages.—Enam villages, granted by the Government to the grantee and his heirs-male, for services rendered to the state, are governed by the principles of Hindu law respecting the partition of the father's estate among his heirs. There is nothing peculiar in the case, the division is according to Hindu law,* *Bodhrao Hunamont* v. *Nursing Rao*, 6 *Moore's In. Ap.* 426. Enam grants are not, by the Hindu law in force in the Southern Mahratta country, distinguishable from other ancestral real estate, and are divisible among the heirs of the grantee.

A Shrotriyam.—Originally a shrotriyam was an assignment to a shrotriya or Brahmin well read in the *Vedas*, 2 *Dig.* 290 ;† it is conferred by Government, in consideration of the individual merits of the grantee. The succession to the property would be regulated either by law, or by the terms of the grant. Supposing the grant to be exclusive, it would not be partible among collaterals, *Purtaub*

* Of course the grant may regulate the descent.

† Cruti (κλυτός), in contradistinction to *Smriti* law, note by *Stokes*, *Sundaramurti Mudali* v. *Vallinayakki Ammal*, 1 *M. H. C. R.* 465.

Bahaudur Sing v. *Telukdhasse Sing*, *Beng. R.* 1805, p. 101. And consequently, upon the death of the shrotriyumdar, leaving sons, it would descend (not to the eldest merely, but) to all the sons in common; the uncles would not share in the inheritance, 1 *Stra. H. L.* 210. In one case, the grantee being dead, leaving sons and daughters, a dispute arose between the eldest son and the uncles as to whom it belonged, whether to the lineal representatives of the deceased exclusively, or to them only in common with their uncles? The pundit replied to this point, The first and the other sons are to enjoy the property in question equally, defraying out of what they have the necessary expenses of the family, and getting the daughters married. Property acquired by the deceased and his brothers, through their joint industry, or the use of their patrimony, which was in common, the latter are interested in together with the sons of the deceased; for his separate acquisitions vest exclusively in his descendants. In remarks upon this case, *Mr Colebrooke* refers to *Mitacshara*, ch. i. s. iv. § 10, 31, where a reference is made to the text of *Menu*, "What a brother has acquired by his labour, without using the patrimony, he need not give up to his co-heirs."

Mr Ellis says, A *shrotriyam* granted for public services is an honourable reward to the individual, and an inducement to others to act as he has done. But the honour and inducement are both lost by its becoming the same as ancestral property, and being subject to endless division. Of divisible property the daughters would be entitled to a share on division taking place before their marriage, but it does not appear that they can demand a division. *Mr Thackaray* says, The brother of the deceased shrotriyumdar can have no claim upon any grounds. It was not ancestral property, but given by the Government as a reward for services to the individual. The Government never would have granted it if they had thought an idle brother could have claimed a share.

And *Mr Sutherland* says, I am inclined to concur in the general accuracy of the pundit's opinion, nor can I find anything inconsistent with the grant, that the estate should be enjoyed by the heirs of the grantee according to their legal interests. Any practical inconvenience which, in the course of time, might be experienced would be ascribed, not to the law, but to the want of explicitness in the grant. In the present case, the estate having been acquired by the exclusive exertions of the grantee, his brothers have clearly no right to participate in it.

As to the interest of the unmarried daughters, doubt certainly presents itself. I cannot but regard as more correct, more consistent with the genius of the Hindu law, the opinions of those writers who admit the right of unmarried daughters to receive from their deceased father's estate merely what may be sufficient to provide for their marriage. Texts, however, of *Menu* and *Yajnavalchya* are adduced which mention the fourth part of a brother's share as the unmarried sister's allotment; and *Vignyaneswara* in the *Mitacshara* denies that the mention of a quarter of a share can be construed as used indefinitely, and as merely intending that a sufficiency to provide for the daughter's marriage should be given. This author accordingly contends, that after the decease of the father, the unmarried daughter participates in the inheritance, receiving one fourth of what would be her share were she male, *ib.* The doubt thrown out by *Mr Ellis* above, viz., "that the honour and inducement by its becoming the same as ancestral property, and being subject to endless division," is not very satisfactorily met by the remark of *Mr Sutherland*, viz., that "any practical inconvenience which in the course of time might be experienced, would be ascribed, not to the law, but to the want of explicitness in the grant." *Sir Thomas Strange*, 1 *H. L.* 210, adopts the opinion of *Mr Sutherland*, 2 *ib.* 367: "As to this leading to endless divisibility, the objection being inherent, cannot be helped, unless obviated by the terms of the grant importing a particular limitation, since otherwise the law must prevail."

There is no doubt that ordinarily self-acquired property goes to the sons as co-heirs of the acquirer, but the distinction has not been drawn between such property which follows the ordinary course of descent and that which is granted as an honourable reward to an individual, and as an inducement to others to act as he has done; and although it may be argued with some show of reason that "heirs" in Hindu law does not refer to an only son alone, but includes all the sons as co-heirs, and that therefore a shrotriyam descends to all the heirs in co-parcenery, and is divisible, yet the intention of the Government in making this particular description of grant must have been that it should operate as an exception to the rule, and should go to the eldest son, see *Regulation* iv. of 1831, *Mad.*. The consideration for the grant, and the objects of the grant, are purely exceptional. There must be some reason for limiting the grant to the grantee and his heirs. There is no such limitation with reference to any other self-acquired property. In a note to 2 *Stra. H. L.* 366, it is said, It would seem from this (the observation of *Mr Ellis* above quoted), to have been *Mr Ellis's* opinion that the grant, on the death of the grantee, should inure not to his heirs generally, but to a select one, according to the notion expressed by him in the following remarks in speaking of the conocopily of a village:—"I doubt whether the maravurtanah, &c.—perquisites of office granted for the performance of specific duties—can be 'accounted the same as household property.' On the contrary, it appears to me that they cannot so be accounted. For what is the real nature of them? Are they not given for the subsistence of the office, enabling him to apply his whole time and attention to the accounts of the village, and would not the division of them among a number, for whose maintenance they cannot adequately provide, destroy their object? Again, does not the law that regards the grant of *a corrody* apply to these and similar perquisites? and has not the grantor, or he who pays, a right to see that they are appropriated according to the original intention under which they were granted? I have no doubt but it applies, and that similar official perquisites, though certainly heritable, are not divisible, nor ought they to descend by primogeniture. The most capable of the direct, or, in their default, of the collateral descendants of the first grantee, should be selected for the performance of the duties of the office, who should enjoy the whole perquisites."

A shrotriyam is inalienable.—A *shrotriyam* has been held to be inalienable, except for the holder's life-interest, *Sundaramurti Mudali* v. *Vallinayakki Ammal*, 1 *Mad. H. C. R.* 465.

A corrody.—A *corrody* seems to be an incorporeal hereditament. It is the grant of an annuity assigned upon some particular fund. It signifies what is fixed by a promise in this form, " I will give that in every month of Kartiki," *Jim. Vahana.* Deliverable annually, monthly, or at any other fixed periods, *ib.* note by *Srikrishna*. Where one of an undivided family, being the conocopily of a village, received the *Mara Vurtanah, Bazar Vurtanah*, and other dues, a question was submitted to a pundit as to whether he was accountable for them to his co-parceners, notwithstanding he alone discharges the whole duty. His reply was, that brothers undivided must, without reservation, equally share all the cattle and household goods left by their father, and the *Mara Vurtanah* being considered the same as household property, it follows that the perquisites in question are divisible.

Upon this *Mr Colebrooke* remarks, " If the office be hereditary in the family, the dues or profits appertaining to it must be subject to be shared. But in such case it classes with immovables; and corrodies and the dues belonging to it cannot be reckoned household property."

Sir Thomas Strange, 1 *H. L.* 209, says, But a corrody being the grant of an annuity assigned upon some particular fund, if made to one of an undivided family and his heirs, with nothing in it to control the operation of the law, would, upon the death of the grantee leaving sons, descend in common, and be divisible among them on partition, *Katyayana, Mayukha.*

Offices attached to padogas.—So with regard to the various offices attached to pagodas and other religious houses of the natives; *teertam* or holy water, either of some sacred spring or a mixture of liquids in which the sacred images have been washed; and *prasadum* or holy food, prepared in the pagoda for the consumption of holy men; and the rights of Brahmins attendant upon funerals and the like, which, however some of them may be disposable by regulating the periods of their enjoyment, as they are in general hereditary, so are they common and divisible, 3 *Dig.* 375. *Mr Colebrooke* says, The hereditary privileges of the family, with the income arising from them, are divisible among heirs like other patrimony, under the general rules of inheritance. At most of the religious establishments of the Hindus, and at their great temples, the various offices attached to them are considered as hereditary, together with the perquisites belonging to them.

Lands endowed for religious purposes.—Lands endowed and set apart for religious purposes are not inheritable, and therefore not divisible, though the management of them may be so, *Elder Widow of Rajah Chutter Sein* v. *Younger Widow of Rajah Chutter Sein, Beng. R.* 1807, p. 103.

Women.—Women are not partible, *Jim. Vahana, Mayukha, Mitac.*; this term is supposed to apply to the wives of co-heirs.

Clothes, vehicles, ornaments, prepared food, water, women, and furniture, for repose or for meals, are declared not liable to partition, *Jim. Vahana, Mitac.* Clothes which have been ordinarily worn must not be divided, *Mitac.*, *Daya Krama Sangraha.* On the principle of appropriation things become impartible; what is used by each person belongs exclusively to him, *Mitac.* But clothes of value, as court dresses and the like, worn only on particular occasions in which all are interested, remain for common use, and are not liable to partition; but if they are sold the proceeds are.

Where one member has more jewels, &c., than another.—It appears that if one member of the family have more jewels or apparel than another, the excess should be divided, *Mitac.* What clothes had been usually worn by the father must be given after his death at partition to the person who partakes of food at his obsequies. "The clothes and ornaments, the bed and similar furniture, appertaining to the father, as well as his vehicle and the like, should be given, after perfuming them with sacred drugs and wreaths of flowers, to the person who partakes of the funeral repast, *Brihaspati, Mitac.*

Books, tools, &c.—*Sir Thomas Strange* says, books, tools, and implements of art belong generally to those who can best employ them, the rest taking to other parts of the property, unless where the whole consists of nothing else, in which case there must be a general distribution or a sale, and equal division of the proceeds.

Regalities and zemindaries.—Regalities and ancient zemindaries which have vested in the eldest son are impartible, on the principle that royalty is indivisible. But the personal property of the king or zemindar are an exception to the rule, and are partible. *Judgment of Sudr. Court in R. A.* 11 *of* 1816 *and* 64 *of* 1848; *Dec.* 12 *of* 1850; 1 *S. D.* p. 141. Lands purchased with the profits of these regalities, &c., are partible property. But though the former are not partible, the younger sons are entitled to a maintenance, which ought to be apportioned with reference to the dignity of the family and the extent of the possessions of the reigning son; and it would seem that they are also entitled to a residence, either in the family mansion or elsewhere.

Lands granted to maintain rank, &c.—Land specially granted to maintain the rank and dignity of a family, *Judgment of Sudr. Court in R. A.* 5 *of* 1850; *Sudr. Dec.* 94 *of* 1851, *and* 74 *of* 1858; *Stra. M. H. L.* § 280, iii., or settled by Government on the eldest son. But land purchased with the surplus profit of these estates ranks as personal property, and may be divided. But this will, of course, depend upon the terms of the grant.

Nuptial gifts.—Nuptial gifts received by a man with his wife are exclusively his, even although the joint property bears the expenses of the marriage; as the expenditure is incidental only, it does not render them partible. So what is received at a marriage in the form termed Asoora, at which presents are made by the bridegroom to the father or kinsman of the bride.

Annuity.—An annuity descending to the sons of an annuitant is divisible.

Dues attached to the office of kurnam.—Dues attached to the office of kurnam are, in an associated family, in practice brought into the common stock, but after separation, inasmuch as the dues are inseparable from the office, they belong exclusively to the person performing the duties. The kurnam and conocopoly, in the sense *Sir Thomas Strange* uses the latter term, perform the same duties.

Self-acquisitions.—This is the subject with reference to which questions upon the divisibility of property most frequently arise. We have more than once remarked that property amongst Hindus is either ancestral or self-acquired, or it may be both. The subject of ancestral property has been already fully discussed, and that of self-acquired property partially, the more complete elucidation of which now becomes necessary.

The common stock of an undivided family may be augmented, and improved during their joint occupation by the different members of the family, and the question whether these accretions are the sole property of him through whose instrumentality they accrued, or whether they become the joint property of the common family, and therefore liable to division as ancestral property (partaking of the nature of both), depends in a great measure upon whether they arose from the employment of the common stock, or by the sole original and independent exertions of the individual; and if the former, the benefit arising from such augmentation or improvement accrues to all alike, without regard to the degree in which each contributed to its augmentation. And such accretion may be said to be of the nature of ancestral property; at all events, it follows the law of that class of property as to the incident of divisibility. If, on the other hand, its acquisition is not attributable to the use of the joint stock, but is solely due to the original and independent exertions of the individual acquirer, then, upon partition, his co-heirs will have no right to a share, although during its accretion he continued undivided from them, and he enjoyed in common with them all the advantages of union, *Mayukha, Jim. Vahana, Mitacshara, Daya Krama Sangraha.*

The acquisition of a man made by his own means alone is not divisible amongst his brothers.—Whenever property, movable or immovable, may have been gained by a co-parcener without detriment to the paternal estate, such acquisition becomes his sole property, and his brothers have no claim to it. Should there have been joint labour or funds used, the acquisition must be equally divided among the brothers, as declared by *Menu* and *Yajnavalchya.*

Half-brother.—A brother, whether of the half or whole blood, cannot share the acquisitions exclusively made by his brother without the use of the patrimony; but if it were made with the use of the joint funds, according to the law as current in Bengal, the acquirer should have twice as much as the rest of the co-parceners, but to any augmentation in the nature of an increment this rule does not apply, and all the brethren share equally. "Among unseparated brethren, if the common stock be improved or augmented by any one of them through agriculture, commerce, or similar means, an equal distribution nevertheless takes place, and a double share is not allotted to the acquirer," *Mitac.*

Whether the joint stock contributed to the acquisition is sometimes a nice question; and *Mr Ellis* says, "The judge must determine, on an equitable consideration of the circumstances of the case, whether the acquisitions of any of the individual parceners have been made without such use of the family property as in law would render them divisible."

Where brothers are living in union, the law will imply that acquisitions are made by the use of the family property. But when the contrary is shown, they are not divisible. *Mr Ellis* was of opinion, in one case where the defendant acquired learning without the aid of the family property, that if he had been educated by his father the case would have been different, for it must have been at the expense of the family had it been so, and in that case *the acquisition would by consequence have been family property. Sir Thomas Strange* adds a *quære* as to the position in italics, and if *Mr Ellis* be correct, there is scarcely any self-acquisition that would not in one sense have been obtained through the instrumentality of the family property; for a man's education is always conducive more or less to the acquisition of wealth. Probably what *Mr Ellis* meant to say was, that after the death of the father, if the common stock is employed in educating any of the co-heirs, and he, by means of that education, accumulates wealth, the ancestral property has sustained detriment by the expenditure on the education, there being no moral or legal obligation on the co-parceners to apply the common fund for any such object. His observation must be read with reference to the facts of the case upon which he writes, and there the defendant educated himself, and it was sought to show that the common stock was used for that purpose. At all events, it would be a strange doctrine, in the absence of more direct authority on the subject, to hold that because a parent, in the exercise of, at most, a moral obligation, disburses some of the ancestral property in educating his son, that all the acquisitions of that son arising primarily or secondarily from such education were derived from the employment of the common stock, and therefore divisible. It must, however, be admitted that *Mr Ellis's* remarks are specially directed to a case where the son was educated by the father. Such an expenditure seems more properly to come within the category of an incidental one.

Joint funds—Acquisitions by one of four brothers with the aid of his father's funds and labour, will, on partition, be made into ten parts, of which five will go to the father, two to the acquirer, and one to each of his brothers; if acquired without any aid, into two parts, the father taking one, and the acquirer one, the brothers having no right to any share.—In both cases, the acquirer's sons are entitled to the portion to which their father was entitled, *Daya Bhaga, Daya Tatwa*, and other authorities. The text of *Katyayana* cited in the above authorities, "A father takes either a double share or a moiety of his son's acquisitions of wealth." Here the father has a moiety of the goods acquired by his son at the charge of his estate; the son who made the acquisition has two shares, and the rest take one a piece. But if the father's estate had not been used, he has two shares, the acquirer as many, and the rest are excluded from participation, *Daya Bhaga*.

Acquisitions made by a man jointly with his brother's four sons, by means of joint funds, will be divided into two portions, of which one will be taken by the acquirer, and the other be shared equally by the four sons of his brother.—Supposing one of the two undivided brothers to have died, leaving four sons, his brother, and a son, him surviving, and the family to have subsequently separated in respect of food only; and after the elder brother's death, their property being undivided, and lands having been acquired by means of their joint funds and labour in the name of the surviving brother's son, and that son to have managed the estate; in this case the property will be made into two shares, of which one will go to the four sons of the deceased brother, in right of their father, and the remaining one to the surviving brother. The portion which will go to the four sons of the deceased brother will be equally shared by them, *Daya Bhaga, Daya Tatwa*, and other authorities. But it must be understood in this case, that the sons of the deceased brother did not individually contribute anything to the acquisition. The right they derived was from their father, and in virtue of his contribution.

Younger brother joined with elder in management of self-acquired property.—If a younger brother is associated with an elder in the management of property acquired solely by the latter, he is entitled to his share, *Abraham* v. *Abraham*, 9 *Moore's In. Ap.* 195.

Incidental expenditure.—Where the expenditure is incidental to the acquisition, and has not been made for the express purpose of gain, the expenditure does not give the gain a partible character. Thus the expenditure of wealth for nourishment, maintenance, or otherwise, must necessarily be made by a person remaining at home, and though it contribute to the end, yet, as it was not designed for the acquisition of wealth, it cannot be considered as the cause of the acquisition, since that is similar to the sucking of the mother's milk, *Visvarupa, Jim. Vahana.* Hence [because its being actually intended for that purpose is a requisite to its being the cause of the acquisition, *Mahesvare*], though much wealth belonging to the father have been expended in festivity at the son's initiation, or at his wedding, what is obtained by him in alms during his austerities as a student, or received on account of his marriage, is not common, for that expenditure of wealth was not made with a view to gain. So that, to give the acquisitions a joint character, there must have been a joint labour, or the common fund must have directly contributed to the gains, *Jim. Vahana.*

Divisibility of gains of science.—The ordinary gains of science are divisible when such science has been imparted at the family expense, and acquired while receiving family maintenance; otherwise, where the science has been imparted at the expense of persons not members of the learner's family, *Chalakonda Alasani* v. *Chalakonda Ratnachalam*, 2 *Mad. H. C. R.* 56. See the observations on this case in *Grady's Hindu Law of Inheritance*, p. 405.

In respect of what acquisitions the rule applies.—Wealth acquired by learning,* anything given by a friend, received at or on account of marriage, or presented as a mark of respect to a guest, gains by science or by valour, or wealth received from affectionate kindred, belongs to him who acquired it. Hereditary property which had been taken away but recovered, acquisitions by labour, as agriculture, service, merchandise, what a man gains by his own ability without relying on the patrimony, the wealth of a wife, *Mayukha, Jim. Vahana, Mitacshara, Daya Krama Sangraha.* Each of these have received extended significations. Acquisition by learning is explained to be wealth gained through science, which was acquired from a stranger while receiving a foreign maintenance, *Katyayana.*

The Sanscrit word for science (*vidya*) is derived from the word *vid*, to know, and signifies any knowledge or skill, *Jim. Vahana.* In

* See the enumeration of acquisitions by learning, *Mayukha*, ch. iv. s. vii. 5.

fact, in all cases whatsoever wherein superior skill is required, the wealth gained is technically denominated the acquisition of science, *Jagannatha.*

It includes what was gained by solution [of a difficulty] after a prize has been offered, what is obtained from a pupil, or by officiating as a priest, or for answering a question, or for determining a doubtful point, or through display of knowledge, or by success in disputation, or for superior skill in reading. It extends to the arts; what is won from another, as a stake at play, or a fee for a correct opinion between two litigants on a point of law; so in a contest between two persons respecting their knowledge of sacred ordinances, or in any other contest respecting their attainments; what is won by beating another at play; what is gained by painters, goldsmiths, and other artists. Having taken gold or the like belonging to the joint stock, and having made bracelets or similar things, the value which is thus superadded by the skill of the artist to the price of the gold, &c., is an acquisition made through science, *Srikrishna, Jim. Vahana, Mayukha, Katyayana, Daya Krama Sangraha.*

Gift by a friend—The importance of gifts or presents from a friend is enhanced, "since it is in such modes that acquisitions are usually made without expenditure," particularly among Brahmins, *Jim. Vahana, Menu. Sir Thomas Strange* says, With regard to a gift, in order to its vesting separately, it must have been pure in its motive and personal in its object, for if it were in return for something previously given, it would be liable to be considered as common property, common property having been used in obtaining it. Not that wherever there have been mutual gifts, the gifts to the co-parcener are necessarily partible. It depends upon whether the one have been in consideration of the other, a present made with a view to a return. A gift under such circumstances loses the nature of one, *do ut des;* it is too like a contract, the result of which is common.

Nuptial gifts.—*Menu* says, Anything received on account of marriage is not partible. *Katyayana* says, What is received by a damsel equal in class at the time of accepting her [in marriage], let a man consider as wealth received with the maiden; it is deemed pure, and promotes increase [of prosperity]. But let him know that to be received on account of marriage, which is accepted by him with his bride, *Mayukha,* § 13,* and is not partible; what is received at a marriage concluded in the form termed *asoora,* or the like; or at such a marriage wealth is received from the bridegroom by the father or kinsman of the bride, *Mitac., Menu.*

Gifts must be made to the donee.—The gift must be made to the donee, for if anything be given to one expressly in considera-

* In the 3d *Dig.* 363, this text is attributed to *Menu,* but it is not found there.

tion of his being the son of a person named, all the sons of that person are entitled to partake on the ground of common relationship, *Srikrishna* and *Achyuta*, *Jim. Vahana.**

Exception to rule.—An exception in a case or two may be made to the precept that acquisitions without the use of the common stock, or by joint exertion, are not divisible. Thus treasure found by an unseparated brother is one instance, and the receipt of anything given by a stranger through commiseration is another. These, although not obtained by means of the joint fund, nevertheless are divisible, *Jim. Vahana.*

A practice, however, prevails amongst virtuous people of dividing wealth gained by receipt of presents without expenditure of joint property, either from a feeling of mutual affection, or manly sentiment, or upon the erroneous notion of *Srikara* and others, that property acquired before separation is impartible, and they have done it voluntarily. But this is not founded on uniform practice, *Jim. Vahana.*

Property recovered.—Even property inherited from the paternal grandfather which has been long lost, and is not recovered by the rest through inability or through aversion from the efforts requisite for its recovery, belongs exclusively to the father, if recovered by him at his own expense, and by his own labour, and is not common property, *Jim. Vahana*, *Mitac.*, *Mayukha*, 3 *Dig.* 365, requires the acquiescence of the other sons; and *Sir Thomas Strange* adds, Unless there appear to be an abandonment of them, by which silent neglect on their part may be evidence, the onus of proof of acquiescence should be upon the party claiming. C. and B., represented respectively by the appellant and respondent, were descended from R., who in his lifetime was proprietor of two of the villages in dispute. About the time of his death, one V., having joined the French during an engagement, took possession of these two villages. C. and B. thus lost their patrimony, and they separated, and from that time until the death of B., a period of eighty years, the intercourse between their respective descendants ceased. After C.'s death and separation, B. procured assistance from the E. I. Company, subdued V., and recovered possession of the two villages which had been formerly taken from the family. A share in them is now claimed by the descendants of C., and the question was, Whether the villages were the particular acquirement of B., or were included in the patrimony?

The pundit replied, If during the time that C. and B. were in possession of their patrimonial estate it was seized by their enemy V., and subsequently recovered by B., without aid from the patrimony, he and C. having antecedently separated, the general conclusion would be that it is B.'s as his particular acquirement. But to

* This rule has been supported in a case in the Madras High Court, but believed not to be reported.

be certain, it is necessary to know whether their separation took place with the intervention of relations and witnesses with deeds of division; and further, whether the recovery subsequently by B. was with the privity and acquiescence of the sons and grandsons of C. The acquiescence alluded to, means a writing purpórting, "You will subdue back our patrimonial property, which was seized and possessed by a stranger, and enjoy it yourself; I shall expect no part of it." It is further necessary to know with reference to a passage of *Vyasya, Jim. Vahana*, ch. vi. s. i. § 14, whether in the re-conquest of the property in question, money, carriages, arms, or other things belonging to the patrimony were used, and in what, if any, degree, or whether the recovery were made exclusively of it. If upon examination it appears that B. acted on the occasion without the warrant, or cession from the original co-parceners or their representatives, notwithstanding his merit and continued enjoyment for a length of time, the property is still liable to division, more especially if obtained by means common to him and them, one fourth being previously deducted as his remuneration for the recovery. With respect to the village obtained during the collectorate of *Mr Place*, the right to it, whether it is to be considered as sole or joint, depends upon its having been acquired or not by the employment of the patrimonial property.

And *Mr Colebrooke* remarks upon this case, The acquiescence spoken of by the pundit is required by the restriction stated in the *Mitacshara*, commenting on a passage of *Yajnavalchya*. See *Mitac.* When no division has taken place, *i.e.*, if the brethren were not separated in their interests and concerns, the patrimony which is recovered is recovered to the use of all the heirs, allowing however one fourth as remuneration to him who recovered it. See *Sancha*, cited *Mitac.*

And *Mr Ellis* says, This is an excellent and very correct opinion of the pundit; but it may be convenient to explain the general law upon which it turns. If at the time an estate is divided any part of the assets belonging to it, in whatever shape they may exist, be not forthcoming so as to enable an actual division of them to be made, either the parceners must come to some mutual agreement regarding them prospectively to the recovery, or the right to such property wi l continue to rest in them jointly, their heirs and representatives, in the same manner as if no division had ever taken place. Hence the pundit properly says, "It is necessary to know whether the separation took place with the intervention of relations," &c. It is necessary to know, in fact, the exact terms and agreements under which C. and B. separated, for in this case it is not sufficient to prove the mere fact of separation, it must be seen whether any specification were made at the time respecting the villages removed by the act of V. from the possibility of actual division. If it were said at the time, "Whoever recovers the family property let him keep it," the question is at rest. If it was not so said, then B. must have been taken to have been acting for the joint interest in the recovery he effected; the property so recovered, notwithstanding the division, remained joint property, being a portion of the assets that was never divided. In this view he cannot be allowed to appropriate it to his own use, the villages retain their original character of joint family property, and are divisible among the surviving representatives of R., the common ancestor. As to the right of the representatives of C. to cede their claim to B., if they chose to do so, and to that of B. (by the same rule that applies to the actual acquirer of property) to an addition to his shares under certain circumstances with his sole right to the third village obtained after separation from his brother, these require but one remark. It is, That if it can be shown that he recovered the family property first, and used it to acquire the third village, this also becomes divisible, reserving to B. his claim to a superior share.

Where landed property lost to the family may be recovered by a co-heir without aid from the family resources, he is entitled to a fourth.—The recoverer is entitled to a fourth only, instead of a double share. *Sankha* says, " Land inherited in regular succession, which had been formerly lost, and which a single (heir) shall recover solely by his own labour, the rest may divide according to their due allotments, having first given him a fourth part," *Jim. Vahana.* The acquirer has a fourth part in addition to his own regular share—the meaning of the text is, " Having given a fourth part of the land in addition to the person who recovered it, all the co-heirs, together with him, shall take equal shares." It is not understood from the term " the rest," that a fourth part only shall be given to him, for it would be an unequal rule, since the person recovering the land would receive less than his co-heir, if there be one or two sharers unconcerned in the recovery, *Mitac., Daya Krama Sangraha.* This, like augmentation or improvement, might have been treated as self-acquired property.

Sir Thomas Strange says, The claim is to a fourth only instead of a double share; the merit of recovering what has only been withheld not being considered equal to that of making a new acquisition. But whether by this is to be understood a fourth of the whole property recovered, or only a fourth of an equal share added to a share, seems uncertain, *Jim. Vahana, Mitac.* Where the co-heirs consent, of course a more unequal distribution may take place.

Sir Thomas Strange, supra, adds, The effect of the use of the joint stock in rendering separate acquisitions in general common, is attended sometimes with injustice, where, in cases of small patrimony, large fortunes are made by the unaided exertions of enterprising parceners, of which the benefit may eventually be shared by drones, who have in no degree conduced to their accumulation. Nor to obviate this is there any resource where timely separation has been omitted ; a right to the benefit of each other's labours being incident, where co-partnership has continued, and the joint property been instrumental. But where the latter has not been the case, the claim to participate fails, though made by an unseparated member, *Soobuns Lal* v. *Hurbuns Lal*, *Beng. R.* 1805, p. 7. This rule also holds in Madras.

Gains by valour.— *Vyasa* says, "Wealth gained by science, earned by valour, or received from affectionate kindred, belongs, at the time of partition, to him who acquired it, *Jim. Vahana.* So *Narada* excepts from division what is gained by valour, the wealth of a wife, and what is acquired by science. These sources of wealth are joint, if attended with a sufficient cause of joint right. *Srikrishna*, *Mayukha*, *Katyayana* explains gains by valour to be, When a soldier performs a gallant action, despising danger, and favour is shown him by his lord, pleased with that action ; whatever property is then received by him shall be considered as gained by valour. That, and what is taken under a standard, are declared not to be subject to distribution ; what is seized by a soldier in war, after risking his life for his lord, and routing the forces of the enemy, is named spoil taken under a standard, *Jim. Vahana, Daya Krama Sangraha.* But if the family estate were instrumental in its gain, it would be partible, *Mayukha.*

Wherever there has been employment of the joint or common funds, or the joint exertion of the co-heirs in the acquisition of wealth, it is partible, but the acquirer takes a superior share. In all other instances, that of property recovered excepted, a share extra the number that is to divide is given to the special acquirer, beyond his equal share ; and if more than one have been concerned with him, they participate in the excess, *Vasishta.* "He among them who has made an acquisition may take a double portion of it," *Jim. Vahana, Mitac.*

Special property.—There is another class of property which partakes of a kind of middle nature, not being absolutely divisible, because of its incapability to be cut up into sectional parts, yet in which the co-heirs have nevertheless a certain interest. A direct partition in such instances being inconvenient, a virtual one takes place. Such are water in wells and tanks, which must be taken by each according to his exigency, couches adapted to the use of each, and eating and drinking vessels used by each, the path for cows, the carriage road, clothes, and anything worn on the body, books which must go to the learned, the taker giving to the unlearned an equivalent ; so whatever is adapted to the exercise of the arts the artist takes ; so of a dwelling-house and other property of a like nature, pasture land for cattle, *Daya Krama Sangraha, Mayukha.*

These are all more or less modified by local custom, or by usage applicable to the particular class or community ; and *Sir Thomas Strange* says, Equality, subject to convenience, being the object, the means of attaining it appear to be left very much to the suggestions of reason and good sense, having regard to the circumstances of the families, and the nature of the property to be divided.

Alienation may be effected for the support of the family, not otherwise.—The rule being that the family property or patrimony is not to be arbitrarily aliened : a loan, gift, even for a good (as a religious) purpose, sale, or hypothecation, if made by a parcener on his sole account, does not bind the family property unless effected for the support, or interest, or spiritual benefit of the whole. His own share, however, would be bound.

The plaintiff stated that the defendant gave him a bond in the name of his elder brother for a sum due on account of clothes purchased, to which the defendant alleges in answer, that as he did so by direction of his brother, who is living, the latter should have been made the defendant. To which the plaintiff replied, that they are an undivided family, and that the elder brother, not being on the spot, and the defendant having given the bond, though in the name of the elder brother who received the goods, the action is properly brought. The question was, Is it under these circumstances maintainable against the defendant? To which the pundit replied, that the elder brother being alive, though absent, the younger is not liable. Upon which *Mr Colebrooke* remarks, This opinion appears to proceed on the ground of the elder brother being sole manager, and alone personally responsible for debts contracted on the common account. This, however, would not exempt the joint stock and youngest brother's share of it from being answerable for the debt. The absence of the elder, independently of the debt having been contracted by the younger brother in the name of the elder, rendered the younger in this case even personally amenable ; see 1 *Dig.* text clxxx. and following gloss. It would be otherwise if the debt be taken to be contracted on the separate account of the elder brother, in which the younger would not be answerable in consequence of the absence of the elder until the lapse of twenty years, *ib.* clxxv. While *Mr Ellis* says, with respect to the answer of the pundit, Here the letter of the general law is applied without discrimination to a particular case. Where was the estate? Did it remain in the management of the younger brother? Whoever is in the management of the joint estate is answerable for all claims upon it, be he elder or younger.

It will be observed that *Mr Colebrooke* assumes more than the question warranted. *Mr Ellis's* remarks are more strictly according to the law. It must, however, be observed that the act of the younger brother would not bind the family property unless it were intended for the benefit of the family.

Managing co-heir has power to bind parceners for a debt contracted for the concern.—Being the managing member of a family partnership, the elder brother has a power to bind his partners for a debt contracted for the concern, and his brothers will be bound by his act unless they can show that the debt, though purporting otherwise, was contracted for his separate interest, and that the lender was apprised that it was so, *Colebrooke. Mr Ellis* says, Whoever has the management, elder or younger, binds by his acts the other parceners.

The defendant executed a bond to the plaintiff's father for a debt due to him by the father of the defendant. At the time of executing it he (the defendant), his younger uncle, C. R., and his elder uncle's son, T. R., were living together undivided. Three years afterwards they divided their property and lived separately, and the question was, Whether the defendant was liable to pay the whole amount of the bond or his proportion only? To which it was replied, That it appearing that the bond was given by the defendant for a debt due from his father to the father of the plaintiff, was for so much borrowed for the common benefit while living in co-partnership, the amount of the debt should be paid in the proportions in which the several parties divided the estate, and consequently the defendant is answerable for his proportion only, *Vignyaneswara.* Upon which *Mr Colebrooke* remarks, The action is properly brought against the defendant; and the plaintiff should have had judgment against him, leaving him to recover from his uncle and cousin their rateable proportions, the debt having been originally contracted for the common concern, and the payment of it not otherwise provided for on the partition. But if the son had not entered into a new obligation the opinion delivered in this case would be correct, as in such circumstances the son is answerable only for his father's share of the debt contracted by him when acting for his co-heirs.

Under the principles of Hindu law a contract entered into by one parcener authorised to bind his co-parceners is virtually a joint obligation binding on the joint family, and therefore the suit appears to have been improperly instituted, as all the surviving co-parceners were not proceeded against.

The defendant and the husband of the plaintiff were undivided brothers. Their mother died. The defendant, in the absence of his brother, made a gift of land on her death, the defendant being at the time in possession of the family property. The question raised was, Was the gift good as against the absent brother, unauthorised by him? The answer was, Where one brother has the consent of the others for a present, a sale, or a mortgage, all will be bound by it. In the present case the gift in question is as against the absent brother, the same as if it had not been made, notwithstanding the doctrine that a mother is to her son as a divinity; the effect of which is, that a gift of a man out of his own share, with a view to her salvation on occasion of a sacrifice offered to her, will be a gift on good consideration. But the defendant was incapable of making such an one out of lands, the property of both, without joint concurrence. This seems to be a very good opinion, upon which *Mr Colebrooke* remarks, see *Mitac.*, the gift being made for the spiritual benefit of the mother's shade, and, as far as appears, being not excessive for that purpose, according to the religious notions of the parties, seems to come under the description of indispensable duty, for which one brother is competent to make a valid gift without consent of the other; it could not therefore be recalled. The action, however, does not appear to have been brought for this purpose, the donee being no party to the suit, but for that of charging the whole gift against the donor's share of property, in which view also the maxim cited from the *Mitacshara* is averse from the plaintiff's claim, which goes to disallow this disposal of property as for the common concern. And *Mr Ellis* observed, If the husband of the plaintiff had during his lifetime sued the defendant, he might have recovered, as the bringing of the action would have implied that the alienation was made without his consent. Or if the plaintiff had proved not merely that his consent was not given, but that he refused it at the time of the alienation, or disapproved the act as soon as he was informed it had taken place, then she would have been entitled to recover. But the Hindu law will infer * that all charitable acts performed by one parcener, especially one so sacred as that which operates towards the "salvation" of the common mother, are performed on account of, and with the consent of the rest, the contrary not being shown; and, in the present case, the contrary is not shown; as it does not appear that the then living parcener objected to the gift being by his brother, or that he disapproved of it at any subsequent period; had the alienation been made for any common purpose, not charitable, the inference of the law would have been directly the reverse of what I have stated; it would have been that the absent parcener did not consent, unless the contrary were shown; in this case it is that, unless the contrary were shown, he did consent. The pundit has not sufficiently considered these legal distinctions.

Sir Thomas Strange adds, It may be remarked, in addition to the above observations, that had the plaintiff's husband been a minor at the time of the grant in question, it would have been clearly good without his consent, which he would not during minority have been competent to give, *Mitac.* It does not appear that he was a minor; but it is stated that he was absent at the time, which would be equally material, as connected with the occasion of the grant, being the death of the mother, whose ceremonies could not conveniently wait.† Minors ‡ and absentees

* It is doubtful how far the presumption referred to holds good. *Mr Ellis* cites no authority to show the existence of such presumption.

† Gifts not being an essential part of the funeral ceremonies, it is doubtful what *Mr Sutherland* means by referring to them.

‡ It is not clear how far minors are bound by charitable gifts of adult parceners.

stand in many respects in point of Hindu law on the same footing, *Latchemenada* v. *Visvanada*.

Section IX.

EVIDENCE OF PARTITION.

Presumption in favour of association—Rebuttal—Question of division one of fact—Living apart as to food and habitation is not considered a separation such as to disqualify from inheritance—Separate transactions—Gifts—Sureties—Commensality—Separate possession of property—Indication of relinquishment or division of joint property—Division of income does not constitute a division of family—Food separately prepared—Purchase of joint stock property by one co-heir — When brothers lived separate, trading without aid from joint funds—Son—Widows—Division of produce without the land—Presumption where long residence and food taken apart—Evidence of kinsmen—Occasional employment and receipt of supplies for private expenses are not evidence of union—Circumstantial evidence—Joint management of the property—The sonless widow of undivided brother cannot separate and take his share, nor can the daughter of a former wife take her father's share—Separate caste invitations and presents—Presumption that trade carried on by member of undivided family is joint—Possession of property divided—Jagannatha's summing up.

Presumption in favour of association.—The primary or normal condition of a Hindu family is that of union. The law, on account of the multiplication of religious ceremonies, favours partition, but the presumption in law is that of association or union. Appearances are not conclusive. They may lead to the inference of union, when in fact separation is really the state of the family. A family may remain united in interest, although its members are separated as to residence, meals, and ceremonies. So they may continue to reside, eat, and perform their solemn rites and accustomed ceremonies together, and in all respects appear to be united, whilst in truth they are legally divided by a severance of their worldly concerns, *Khodeeram Serma* v. *Tirlochun, Beng. R. ante,* 1805, p. 37. The question of union or partition is, therefore, often difficult of solution, in consequence of the law permitting the transaction to take place in secret, instead of compelling publicity by requiring the intervention of a deed and witnesses. This opens the door to litigation, injustice, and fraud. The creditor, too often mistaking the appearance for the reality, gives his property, relying on the unity of the family, and finds that he has got in exchange an individual for a joint responsibility. Again, if one member of the family wishes for a partition, he may be met on the part of the others by the assertion of division having already taken place. The solution of the difficulty is greatly increased by the conflicting character of the evidence called in support of each side of the case.

Rebuttal.—Of course the presumption alluded to is capable of rebuttal by evidence, showing separate acts amounting to proof of partition having taken place.

Question of division one of fact.—Formerly the question of division was considered one of law, and that a written instrument, or evidence of the performance of rites, cooking food separately, &c., was conclusive evidence for or against the fact of division. It is now, however, settled that it is purely a question of fact, to be judged of from the evidence, no circumstance being so strong as not to be capable of rebuttal; and a considerable difference exists under the Civil Procedure Code as to whether a matter is to be considered a question of law or of fact. For in the latter case no special appeal lies in any suit in which the two lower courts agree as to the facts, even if the higher revokes the decision of the lower. A special appeal lies only to settle a question of law, or custom having the force of law.

Living apart as to food and habitation is not considered a separation such as to disqualify from inheritance. — If of the four brothers of the whole blood, whose paternal movable property was divided, but whose immovable estate was undivided, three lived together, of whom one died, and the associated brothers performed his exequial rites with the joint funds, the other brother who lived apart is entitled to one third of the deceased brother's share of the paternal undivided immovable property, even though he may not have joined in the performance of his exequial rites. This opinion is conformable to the doctrine laid down in *Menu* and other sages, " When all the debts and wealth have been distributed according to law, any property that may afterwards be discovered shall be subject to a similar distribution," *Menu*. Next, " Let brothers of the whole blood divide the heritage of him who leaves no male issue," *Devala*. Again, *Menu* says, " Should the eldest or youngest of several brothers be deprived of his allotment at the distribution, or should any one of them die, his share shall not be lost, but his uterine brothers and sisters, and such brothers as were re-united after a separation, shall assemble and divide his share equally." Association merely in point of food or messing together gives no privilege to those so associated over a brother who messes apart, but whose property continues undivided.

Separate transactions.—In the next place, proof is by the circumstance of separate transaction of affairs, as is stated by *Narada*. Gift and acceptance, cattle, grain, houses, land, and attendants, must be considered as distinct among separated brothers, as also diet, religious duties, the rules of gift, income and expenditure,

Jim. Vahana, Mayukha. Where all invitations and presents are sent by the caste to the two brothers, it is evidence of unity and interest, *Mt. Goolab* v. *Mt. Phool,* 1 *Borr.* 154; 1 *Morl. Dig.* 484, § 46. Separated, not unseparated, brethren may reciprocally bear testimony,* *Mayukha,* ch. iv. s. vii. § 34, become sureties for each other, bestow gifts and accept presents. Those by whom such matters are publicly transacted with their co-heirs may be known to be separate even without written evidence, *Jim. Vahana.*

Gifts.—*Gifts* and *acceptance* having reference to borrowing transactions, *Mayukha. Acceptance of cattle* and the rest, among separated persons, accomplished by each apart, is even the means of generating (sole) ownership; but among unseparated brethren, acceptance by one alone is the origin of the (joint) ownership of the others also. The *rules of gift,* written deeds, or the like. *Income,* entry (or accumulation) of principal and interest, or the like. They who have their income, expenditure, and wealth distinct, and have mutual transactions of money-lending and traffic, are undoubtedly separate, *Brihaspati, ib.* With regard to income and expenditure, with the infinite dealings in which men's interests are concerned, carried on without consulting the others, and this publicly and without reserve, the same inference arises, *Jim. Vahana, Mayukha.*

Sureties.—Husband, wife, father, and son, cannot become sureties for each other before partition, nor reciprocally lend or give evidence for each other, *Yajnavalchya, Mayukha, Jim. Vahana.* With regard to their bearing testimony for each other, the restriction refers only to matters affecting the joint interest, and so raising a direct objection to their competency. But this rule does not now apply as far as evidence is concerned.

The practice of agriculture or other business pursued apart from the rest, and the observance of the five great sacraments, and other religious duty, performed separately from them, are pronounced by *Narada* to be tokens of partition. The religious duties of unseparated brethren is single, *i.e.,* performed by an act in which all join; serving in them, and performing them separately in their respective houses *after* partition. When partition indeed has been made, religious duties become separate for each of them, *Mitac., Mayukka.* But this is by no means conclusive; various circumstances might occur which would necessitate the separate performance of religious ceremonies. By this (reasoning) in every unseparated family, of whomsoever it may consist, father, grandfather, son, son's son, paternal uncle, brother, brother's son, or other (member), the religious duty is even single, *Mayukha, Menu.* As in the unity of place, time, agent, and the like, one agent is by reasoning obtained for several causes as supporting several parts of one act;

* This would now be no evidence of separation, because the courts in India follow the English law of evidence, under which such witnesses are admissible.

so even we may understand from the text that there may be distinct acts of agents otherwise unseparated. Hence, all those religious acts required for performance of sacred as well as of more common rites, even of unseparated brethren, are separate for each, in manner of the distinctions in the nature of a consecrated and a common fire, and the like, though mutually connected. Even so the *shraddha* also of the paternal uncle, brother, son, or other (dying without a son), at the *Amavasya* and other seasons, is even separate by reason of the separation of the deified (person from the parvana rite). But the *shraddha*, &c., of brothers (dying) without maintenance of a sacred fire is to be executed by one instrument or agent only, because all the deified persons are conjoined. In case of separation of place by residence abroad, the *shraddhas* are even separate. The (extra) acts with the fire, requisite for the rites of those who maintained a sacred fire, also, are even separate, but the worship of the household deities are to be done by one agent only. Even so *Sakala* says, Residing with one, dressing of food, worship of a single household deity, and, moreover, one single sacrifice at meals to the manes, show unity. In a family of divided brethren these acts are performed in each house separately, *Mayukha.*

Sir Thomas Strange divides the religious duties into those that are indispensable and voluntary. Amongst the latter he classes sacrifices, consecrations, stated oblations at noon or evening, performance or non-performance of which respects the individual merely, and which may be discharged jointly or severally, so that no inference, one way or the other, can be drawn from their performance.

Where the parties were Sudras. The plaintiff's husband and defendant, being brothers, three years before the death of the former, divided their property, with the exception of a cat, a pillow, a carpet, and a writing-case, and continued to live separate, performing, however, jointly, *pungall,* and the annual ceremony for their father. The plaintiff's husband leaving no son, the defendant performed his funeral obsequies, but under plaintiff's protest. *Quære,* Which is entitled to succeed to the property of the deceased ?

The pundit held that the joint performance of ceremonies proved that no division had taken place, and that the estate of the deceased survived to the defendant. Upon which *Mr Colebrooke* remarks, that this would be a valid conclusion in a doubtful case. *Narada* says, "When partition has been made, religious duties become separate," *Mitac.* The separate performance of religious duties is accordingly evidence of partition, and conversely the joint performance of them affords a presumption of family partnership in a doubtful case, *Mitac.* But it appears from the statement made to the law officer that in this case there was evidence of an actual partition, and the cause turned on a question of fact, which the pundit assumes, from the circumstance above mentioned, against the evidence to which the court seems to have given credit. Joint performance of obsequies is not conclusive evidence of family partnership against other and satisfactory proof of separation. As to a few articles remaining undivided, it would be no impeachment of a partition otherwise valid ; and *Mr Ellis* adds, If the act of division did indeed take place, the joint performance of the ceremonies after (which might proceed from brotherly affection) could make no alteration. Had the division been doubtful, then certainly the joint performance of the ceremonies would be a conclusion against it, a conclusion merely, however, or, as it has been appositely called in another case, a "token," *adyuharana* (I suppose, in the original), not a proof.

Commensality.—A separation from commensality does not, as a necessary consequence, effect a division, or at least of the whole undivided property, *Rewun Persad* v. *Mt. Radda Beeby*, 4 *Moore's In. Ap.* 168. The mere circumstance of messing conjointly is not conclusive proof of co-parcenery, *Khoderam Serma* v. *Tirlochum*, 1 *S. D. A. R.* 35, 1801.

In 1 *Macn. H. L.* 54, it is said the only criterion of division consists in members of the family entering into distinct contracts, and other similar acts, which tend to show that they have no dependence on, or connection with each other.

Separate possession of property.—It is presumed, if they have separate possession of property, *Than Sing* v. *Mt. Jeetoo*, 2 *R. S. D. A.* 320.

Indication of relinquishment or division of joint property.—R., the defendant's brother, borrowed money from the plaintiff. After R.'s death, N., another brother, let some villages to the plaintiff, on an agreement to allow the rents to be applied towards paying R.'s debt, and to execute a writing for the balance. On N.'s death, a balance being due, it was required to know whether the defendant was liable, he and his brothers never having divided, though they lived separate. The pundit replied, That though the defendant and his brothers had never actually divided, yet if he lived alone, unconnected with them, acquiring property independently of the paternal estate, or of aid from them, distinct not only in his dealings, but in his offerings also to their common ancestors, or if the debt contracted was not for the support of the family, he being connected with it, in any of these cases he is not answerable to the plaintiff for the balance, unless he should be in possession of assets belonging to R. See *Yajnavalchya* and *Narada*.

Mr Ellis says, The circumstance here stated, and many others, indicate either division or relinquishment of joint property, but do not constitute absolute proof of it. Notwithstanding the proof of such circumstances, the judge ought to satisfy himself that the separation was such as equitably to release the defendant from responsibility for the acts of his co-parceners. Admitting every circumstance indicating division, still if it appeared that one of the parceners allowed the semblance of an undivided family to exist, either by occasionally asserting or not denying it when asserted, and that a stranger, actuated by impressions so received, lent money or formed contracts with the others, a parcener so acting would be answerable for such debts, and must abide by such contract. This applies, however, in strictness to brothers only. The natural connection between cousins, &c., is not so great, and less therefore is required to establish their separation. Perhaps sometimes it may be incumbent on the claimant to prove their union, which among brothers the law infers.

Separate acquisition is no evidence either way; it is equally consistent with division and unity.

Division of income does not constitute a division of family.—A Bengalee testator, after bequeathing all his movable and immovable property to the family idol, directed that his property should never be divided by his sons, &c., but that they should enjoy the surplus proceeds only, and that the surplus, after deducting the whole of the expenditure, should be added to the *corpus*, and that in the event of disagreement between the sons and family, he directed that after certain expenses, the net produce and surplus should be divided annually in certain proportions among the family. At the date of the will the family were joint in estate, food, and worship. Held that the division of the income arising out of the testator's estate among the members of the family, after the testator's death, did not constitute a division of the family, *Sonatum Bysack* v. *Sreemutty Juggutsoondree Dossee*, 8 *Moore's In. Ap.* 66.

Food separately prepared.—The instance most relied on is the taking food separately prepared, while the parties are residing in the same house. This, too, is but a circumstance, and capable of being explained.

Purchase of joint stock property by one co-heir.—As a purchase of joint stock property may be made by one co-heir from the others, provided all join in it, that would *per se* be no evidence of division.

When brothers lived separate, trading without aid from joint funds—Son—Widows.—Three brothers deceased carried on their concerns in their lifetime separately in different villages for thirty or forty years. No releases appeared among them, nor was there written proof that they had divided. 1. Are they to be considered as having divided, or is it competent for their respective representatives to call for a division? 2. Supposing them to have left one son with widows, to whom does their property belong? Answer of the pundits:—If there be suitable evidence, or visible marks applicable to a divided estate, it is not necessary that there should be a deed of division in writing. If sons, grandsons, or kinsmen have lived long separate, carrying on traffic and other worldly concerns without aid from the common stock, performing also religious ceremonies separately, there will be no ground for a division of such existing separate estates.

Of the property in question, any that remained undivided vests in the surviving son to the exclusion of the widows. *Mr Colebrooke* remarks, The answer to the first question is correct, *Mitac.*

On the second question a difference of opinion exists, whether an undivided residue shall be subject to rules of succession relative to separated or unseparated brethren. Authorities are cited on both sides, but the opinion here given seems the best.

Division of produce without the land.—Distribution of the produce without division of the land does not necessarily constitute a divided family.

Presumption where long residence and food taken apart.—Twenty-five begas of land in one village, and seven in another, formed the ancestral estate of the three appellants, and of the respondent's husband, all of whom descended from the same grandfather. The appellants were possessed of the former, and discharged the rent, the respondent's husband and herself did so for the other seven begas. The appellants resided in the former village, the respondent's husband and herself resided in the latter. It was not clearly ascertained that the lands were formerly divided between the appellants and the respondent's husband, agreeably to their respective shares. From its being specified that the rent due from the twenty-five begas was discharged by the appellants, and that due from the seven begas by the respondent's husband and herself, it may be inferred that the respondent's husband lived separated from his co-heirs, and discharged the rent due on account of the land in his possession by reason of partition having taken place. It is a rule of law that if brothers live apart from each other, and partition is alleged to have taken place so long ago as 1197 *Fuslee,** that no writing on the subject, or other record can be found, and if it be proved that they, for a long time, have lived apart, and have been separate in respect to residence and food, the partition will be presumed.

Evidence of kinsmen.—If a question arise among co-heirs in regard to the fact of partition, it must be ascertained by the evidence of kinsmen, by the record of the distribution, or by separate transaction of affairs, separate possession of house or field, *Mayukha, Jim. Vahana, Mitac.* In the first place, kinsmen, or persons allied by community of funeral oblations; on failure of them, relatives, as signified by the term *bundhu;* in default of these, strangers, *Jim. Vahana. Sankha* says, The family may give evidence if the matter be not known to the relations springing from the same race. Relations sprung from the same race are kinsmen, "family," or relatives (as maternal uncles, and the rest), and may give evidence. But not a stranger, while a person of the family can bear testi-

* In India, a section of a year, a season.

mony; but if these also be uninformed, any other person may give evidence, *Jim. Vahana, Mitac.*

Occasional employment and receipt of supplies for private expenses are not evidence of union.—A member of a Hindu family (among whom there had been no formal articles of separation), who with his father had messed separately from the rest, and had no share in their profits or loss in trade, though he had occasionally been employed by them, and had received supplies for his private expenses, is presumed separate, and is not entitled to a share of the acquisitions of the others of the family, *Rajkishor Rai* v. *Widow of Santoodas*, 1 *S. D. A. R.* 13 (1796).

Circumstantial evidence.—Partition may be inferred from circumstantial evidence, *Doe d. Ramasamy Moodeliar* v. *Vallatah*, 1 *Morl. Dig.* 484, § 42.

Joint management of the property.—The management of the property by the family is evidence that it belongs to them jointly, in opposition to the claim of any one of them singly.

The sonless widow of an undivided brother cannot separate and take his share, nor can the daughter of a former wife take her father's share.—Where three undivided brothers lived and ate together with the mother, but traded separately; two of the brothers died, one leaving a widow and a daughter by a former wife, the other a widow and two sons. It was held that the brother and descendants of the two deceased could not be considered as a divided family, and the widow and two sons will be permitted to possess their father's share, but the widow of the other brother cannot be permitted to separate, and take her husband's share. Nor has the daughter, by a former wife, any right to separate and take her father's share, because he died without previous separation, and leaving no son; the other members of the family are, however, bound to maintain the widow and daughter, *Mt. Rajkoonwar* v. *Mt. Dhunkoonwur*, 1 *Borr.* 207.

Separate caste invitations and presents.—A Hindu Brahmin woman claimed her father's estate from one of his brothers and a son of a second, on the ground of their being separate, as well as under a will of her mother in her favour. The will was held to be void, as, if the three brothers had been *bonâ fide* separate in all their interests, the share of the last brother would have descended to his daughter without the will, and if no separation had taken place the will could not defeat the superior rights of her deceased father's brother and nephew. On investigation, it was found that although the three brothers were so far disunited as to receive caste invitations and presents separately, yet there was no proof as to their carrying on distinct concerns, or having divided among them the family estate, *Bhugawan Goolabchund* v. *Kriparam Anundram*, 2 *Borr.* 24.

Presumption that trade carried on by member of undivided

family is joint.—Where there is no formal separation of interests between brothers, and the parties have lived together as an undivided family till five years after the death of one of the brothers, the presumption clearly is that a trade carried on by the brothers is a joint one, and in the absence of all proof that there was a separation of interests between the members of the family, or that any part of the property was self-acquired by one of the brothers independently of funds, or other aid afforded by the others, the sons of the deceased brother are entitled to share in the whole property of the family, *Bairy Cundappah Chitty* v. *Bairy Cristnamah Chitty*, 1 *Mad. Dec.* 372.

Possession of property divided.—The record of partition which brothers and other co-heirs execute, after making a just distribution by mutual consent, is called the written memorial of distribution, *Brihaspati.* "When a village, a field, and a garden are recorded in the same grant, if any part be occupied they are all legally possessed. Thus, on a partition among brothers, whether village or other land is inserted in a written record of partition, should some part thereof be occupied, and the remainder be not possessed, still the whole land is considered in law as actually possessed, not as property neglected," *Brihaspati*, cited in *Vyavaharamatrica.* In immovable property obtained by an equitable partition, or by purchase, or inherited from the father, or received from the king, a title is gained by long possession, and not lost by silent neglect. Even in property simply obtained, with or without a fair title, which a man has accepted and quietly possessed, unmolested by another, he acquired a title, and in like manner he forfeits one by silent neglect.

By possession, the title over property obtained by an equitable partition, by purchase, or by similar instances, is established, and the silent neglect of the possession constitutes the forfeiture of such property.

"When co-heirs have made a distribution, the acts of giving and receiving cattle, grain, houses, land, household establishments, dressing victuals, religious duties, income, and expenses, are to be considered as separate and (conversely) as proofs of partition," *Narada.*

It will have been seen, therefore, that there is great difficulty in determining whether the family be a divided or an united one. The question is one of importance; it sometimes arises among the members of the family themselves, one member claiming partition, whilst the rest allege that it has already taken place; sometimes amongst creditors, whose interest it is to treat the family as undivided, as they thereby extend the fund, to which they look for payment of their debts, the credit having been given under that impression, though erroneous.

With respect to any one or more of the instances specified, they are but evidence; though the concurrence of all to constitute proof is not required, for those texts are founded on reason, and the reason is equally applicable in every instance, *Jim. Vahana.*

Sir Thomas Strange says, The one the most to be relied on is the taking food separately prepared ; yet as it may be matter of convenience among co-heirs having large families to have separate cookery, dressing their victuals apart, this also is but a circumstance which may be explained, or its effect in point of evidence may be removed by showing not separate but joint preparation of grain for oblations to deities, and the entertainment of guests, as well as for other purposes, which, among united co-heirs, are essentially common. But, in general, a distinct preparation of food, after an agreement to separate, proves partition, and the previous agreement may, in some cases, be inferred from that sole evidence ; but more satisfactorily in proportion as a greater number of the indicated circumstances concur.

The joint performance of obsequies is not conclusive evidence of family partnership in the face of positive evidence to the contrary.

Jagannatha's summing up.—*Jagannatha* sums up this subject thus, In a doubt respecting a prior distribution among those who severally transact commercial affairs, and the like, but without having separated their preparation of food by a previous agreement, what (he asks) is the rule of decision if the dispute concern that property to which the transactions relate ? Deduce the principle of decision (he answers) from reciprocal gift and receipt, for in that case donation, which is an act done for a spiritual end, has been made in contemplation of abundant fruit from liberality to a kinsman. Again, the people know whether these co-heirs have separated their preparation of food by previous agreement or not. Again, do the peasants deliver to them severally the provisions and other dues from their village ? Hence also a principle of decision may be deduced. In like manner the question may be determined by their annual obsequies for a deceased ancestor, and by their worship of *Lakshmi*, or other deities, and the like.

SECTION X.

RE-UNION.

Partition—Definition—A re-union between separate co-heirs may take place—Mitacshara limits re-union to father, brother, or paternal uncle—But it includes all those who make partition—Mode of effecting re-union—Separation after re-union—The superior allotment in right of primogeniture forbidden—Acquirer gets a double share of wealth gained by science, even with aid of common stock—The order of succession of one dying after re-union is an exception to that of obstructed heritage—Exception to the rule that a re-

united brother shall keep the share of his re-united co-heir—The right of whole brothers not re-united and half brothers re-united—Fixed property the uterine brother takes, concealed wealth and animals he shares with those re-united—The son succeeds in all cases—The son of one re-united succeeds before other re-united persons—In other cases, the parents, and first the mother—Then the brother, paternal uncle, &c., equally—The brothers not re-united share with re-united uncles—The wife, if alone re-united—If others re-united, she does not succeed, but must be maintained—Among un-re-united persons succeeding to one re-united with other members of the family, the mother is first, then the father, the eldest wife.

Partition.—After partition has taken place the family may become re-united, and afterwards a second separation may take place.

Definition.—The divesting of exclusive rights in specific portions of property, and re-vesting a common one over the whole, is implied in re-union.

A re-union between separated co-heirs may take place.—*Brihaspati* says, "He who being once separated dwells again, through affection, with his father, brother, or paternal uncle, is termed re-united," *Mayukha, Jim. Vahana, Mitac.* Effects which had been divided, and which are again mixed together, are termed re-united. He to whom such appertain is a re-united parcener, *Mitac.*

Mitacshara limits re-union to father, brother, or paternal uncle.—This re-union cannot take place with any person indifferently, but only with a father, a brother, or a paternal uncle and his nephews, *Jim. Vahana.* But the proper sense is, that this [re-union] arises, even from the joint location of the makers of the [first] partition. For the words, "father," and the rest, are merely as a part to denote the whole of the persons who make the partition, *Mayukha.*

In the Mithila school re-union takes place with the nephew and the rest, *Daya Krama Sangraha.*

But it includes all those who make partition.—Re-union may take place with a wife, a paternal grandfather, a brother's grandson, a paternal uncle's son, and the rest also. "He who being once separated [from the co-heirs] dwells again [in common, is termed re-united]" from joint location [of such a one], the sense of separated brothers [one's own] sons, and the like, does not result, *Mayukha.*

An adult brother, a member of an undivided Hindu family, separated from the family. No regular partition of the estate was made. The lands remained undivided, and each member took his share of the rents. After a short separation, the brother returned to the family, and it was by a deed of *ungshoputtur* or settlement, agreed that the acquisitions made by the elder brother during the separation should go into the joint funds. During the separation, the elder brother purchased a Putnee Talook. Held that the re-union of the brother to the family remitted him to his former *status* as a member of a joint Hindu family, and that he was entitled to share in the purchase, as it must be presumed to have been made out of the funds of the joint estate, *Prankishen Paul Chowdry* v. *Moltrooramohun Paul Chowdry*, 10 *Moore's In. Ap.* 403.

Mode of effecting re-union.—[When two settle thus:] "The present or future wealth of us two is common property, until we make a partition a second time." When there exists such a sign, either by understanding or expressed wish, it is an union, *Mayukha*.

Separation after re-union.—After re-union there may be an entirely new partition.

In that case the shares must be equal. There is not in this instance any right of primogeniture, *Menu, Vishnu, Mayukha*.

The superior allotment in right of primogeniture forbidden.—[The shares must be equal.] This supposes re-union of brothers belonging to the same tribe. But in the case of association of brothers appertaining, the one to the sacerdotal, the other to the military tribe, the rule of distribution must be understood to conform with the original allotment of shares; for the text is intended only to forbid an elder brother's superior portion, as before allotted to him. Accordingly [since unequal partition regulated by difference of tribes is not denied] *Brihaspati*, saying, "Among brethren who, being once separated, again live together through mutual affection, there is no right of primogeniture when partition be again made," prohibits only the assignment of a superior share to the eldest, but does not ordain equality of allotments, *Jim. Vahana, Mayukha, Menu.* Some say that the unequal distribution being set aside by the phrase, the share must in that case be equal, the prohibition of the eldest son's right is repeated, for the sake of making it clearly understood that, although there is to be no inequality in making up the share of the eldest son, yet in the distribution the shares may be even unequal when made up of greater and lesser shares at the time of re-uniting the property, *Mayukha*.

But since the term "eldest son's right" [*jyeshtyam*], and the like, is merely a declaration of the general meaning, therefore, if [the contributions to] the wealth were greater and less, still the share of each must be equal, and the same is the popular practice. Hence, as the foundation of the practice is derived from this text, any supposition of a declaration contrary thereto is at variance with reason, *Mayukha*.

Acquirer gets a double share of wealth gained by science, even with aid of common stock.—"If any one of the re-united brethren acquire wealth by science, valour, or the like [with the use of the joint stock], two shares of it must be given to him, and the rest shall have each a share," *Brihaspati*. See *Jim. Vahana*.

The meaning of the text is, that a double share being established for the acquirer by the phrase, "to the acquirer two shares," then in a partition among [unseparated] brethren not re-united, he gets two shares only in what he has acquired, without detriment to the father's wealth. But in a fresh partition among re-united brethren, he gets two shares of what was acquired by him, even if at the detriment of the re-united property, *Madana*, *Mayukha*.

The order of succession of one dying after re-union is an exception to that of obstructed heritage.—*Yajnavalchya* enumerates the order of those entitled to succeed to the wealth of one re-united: "As of a re-united co-heir the re-united co-heir, so of the uterine brother the uterine brother, which is an exception to the regular succession failing male issue of the wife, the daughters, and the rest, *Mayukha*.

A re-united [brother] shall keep the share of his re-united co-heir, who is deceased, or shall deliver it to a son subsequently born, *Yajnavalchya*, *Mitac*.

The share or allotment of such re-united parcener deceased must be delivered by the surviving re-united parcener to a son subsequently born, in the case where the widow's pregnancy was unknown at the time of the distribution. Or on failure of male issue, he and not the widow, nor any other heirs, shall take the inheritance, *Mitac*.

Exception to the rule that a re-united brother shall keep the share of his re-united co-heir.—"But a uterine [or whole] brother shall thus retain or deliver the allotment of his uterine relation," *Yajnavalchya*. The construction is this, The allotment of a re-united brother of the whole blood who is deceased, shall be delivered by the surviving re-united brother of the whole blood to a son born subsequently; but on failure of such issue he shall retain it. Thus, if there be brothers of the whole blood and the half blood, an uterine [or whole] brother being a re-united parcener, not a half brother who is so, takes the estate of the re-united uterine brother, *Yajnavalchya*, *Mitac.*, *Mayukha*.

The right of whole brothers not re-united, and half-brothers re-united.—"One of a different womb being again associated, may take the succession, not one of a different womb if not re-united. But [a whole brother if] re-united obtains the property, and not [exclusively] the son of a different mother." Here, from the terms, "one of a different womb," "son of a different mother," the half brother alone is not designated, but the paternal uncle and others likewise, *Yajnavalchya*, *Mayukha*, *Mitac*.

The following are the meanings of the terms of this text :—"One of a different womb;" that is, one of a separate womb, [such] the wife, the father, the father's father, the half brother, the paternal uncle and others, if they be re-united, may take the wealth. If not re-united, those of a different womb do not [succeed]. Hence, by reason of the rule respecting fitness and dissimilitude,* the re-union of one of a different womb is declared as the reason for his taking the wealth. A whole brother, termed re-united [by union of the womb], even if not re-united [by re-union of the wealth], will take the property. By this reasoning, the community of womb alone even is declared a sufficient reason. So one re-united, as possessing union of wealth; but if only born of a different mother, he will not take anything whatsoever, *Mayukha.*

So that the one from his re-union, the other from his community of womb, both jointly share and take it [between them]. *Menu* specially determines this very principle in the right of succession among re-united persons, "Should the eldest or youngest of several brothers be deprived of his allotment at the distribution, or if any of them die, his share shall not be lost;" but the uterine brothers and sisters, and such as were re-united after a separation, shall assemble together and divide his share equally," *Mayukha, Mitac.*

Be deprived of means by entering another order, by degradation from sin, or the like.

Uterine must be joined with brothers in construction.

And such as were re-united, i.e., the wife, the father, the paternal grandfather, the half brother, the paternal uncle, and the rest, *Mayukha.*

Fixed property the uterine brother takes, concealed wealth and animals he shares with those re-united.—On this point *Prajapat* states a distinction: "Whatever concealed wealth is brought to light becomes the property of the united parceners; but lands and houses, those not re-united shall entirely take according to their shares," *Mayukha.*

Concealed wealth—what is capable of being hidden by depositing in the ground or otherwise, as gold, silver, or the like; such those re-united, that is, of a different womb, shall take; but landed property the uterine brother [takes]. Kine, horses, and other [animals] the uterine and he of a different womb [shall share]. According to *Madana*, he of a different womb alone, if re-united, will take the houses, horses, and the like; but it is not so noted in the text, *Mayukha.*

According to the *Smriti Chandrika*, But if there exist only one species of property out of the [above sources, as] concealed wealth, land, kine, and the rest, the uterine brother alone, even not re-united, takes it. The proof of this must be considered. Among uterine brothers, if some of them are re-united, but other brothers not; nevertheless, those re-united alone will take the wealth, because community of womb and re-union exists as a double cause [of

* *Dig.* 9, note. In logic, *Amya* and *Vyatireka*: the first is the relation of events, of which whenever one occurs the other also occurs; the second is the connection of circumstances, of which, when one occurs not, the other also does not occur, *Mayukha.*

succession.] Even so *Goutama*, "When a re-united [parcener] dies, his re-united co-heir shares his estate;" and *Brihaspati*, "Two brothers, who became re-united through affection, [after being separated], share mutually," *Mayukha*.

The son succeeds in all cases.—A son, whether re-united with his father or not re-united, shall obtain the entire paternal share, since the power of intercepting the right to take a share lies in the filial relation. Among several sons also, when one is re-united and the other is not, the re-united one alone succeeds by the text, "Of a re-united [co-heir] the re-united [co-heir], so of the uterine brother the uterine brother," *Mayukha*.

The son of one re-united succeeds before other re-united persons.—In a case of re-union between a father, son, and any other not being his son, the son alone succeeds, because the same has already been declared by the terms, "shall either give up or shall retain," &c., *Mayukha*.

In other cases, the parents, and first the mother.—In an assemblage of father, brothers, paternal uncles, and others not being sons re-united, the parents alone [take it]. Of them, again, the mother is first, and then the father, according to *Madana*, *Mayukha*.

Then the brother, paternal uncle, &c., equally.—But [after them] the brother, paternal uncle, and the rest, shall even take and share it [equally], for among them all the state of union exists, as the cause whence their right of taking [shares] is derived, *Mayukha*.

The brothers not re-united share with re-united uncles.—So likewise in an assemblage of un-re-united brothers, re-united paternal uncles, half-brothers, and others, they even share it [in common] by reason of the two phrases—"If not re-united, but [a whole brother if] re-united obtains the property, and not [exclusively] the son of a different mother;" the other, "As of a re-united [co-heir] the re-united [co-heir], so of the uterine brother the uterine brother," *Mayukha*.

The wife, if alone re-united.—In case of the re-union of the wife alone, she alone takes it, from the same text of a re-united [co-heir], the re-united [co-heir].

If others re-united, she does not succeed, but must be maintained.—In the assemblage of the other persons re-united together, with her also re-united, they alone succeed; she does not, moreover, in commencing the topic of re-union. Both *Sankha* and *Narada* have declared, "Among brothers, if any one die without issue, or enter a religious order, let the rest of the brethren divide his wealth, except the wife's separate property. Let them allow a maintenance to his women for life, provided they preserve unsullied the bed of their lord; but if they behave otherwise, the brethren may resume that allowance." "The maintenance of the daughter of such a one is enjoined to be made out of her father's share; if still un-initiated, she will take a share [for the purpose]; if he die after that, her husband shall support her," *Mayukha*, *Mitacshara Jim. Vahana.*

Among un-re-united persons succeeding to one re-united with other members of the family, the mother is first, then the father, the eldest wife.—As for what *Sankha*, in proceeding to expound re-union, says, "Of those also departed for heaven without male issue, the property goes to the brothers; in default of them, both parents will take it, or the eldest wife,"—it, according to *Madana*, is intended to fix the order of the un-re-united brothers, and the other upon the death of one dying re-united subsequent to the death of his paternal uncle, brother's son, or half-brother, with whom he had previously made a re-union; and, according to the same authority, in this case also first the mother, and next the father, *the eldest wife*, *i.e.*, she who [best] preserves her duty, *Mayukha*, *Mitac.*, *Jim. Vahana.*

END OF BOOK I.

BOOK II.

THE LAW OF CONTRACT.

THE British charters having reserved to the natives, as well with regard to matters of contract as of inheritance and succession, the native laws, we must now discuss some of the leading principles which distinguish the Hindu law of contracts. It will not be necessary to dwell at any length upon this subject, as there has been a substantive law of contract prepared for submission to the Legislative Council of India, which it is expected will very shortly become law, and by that code the subject of contracts will be governed. It is, however, very seldom that questions on the Hindu law of contract, purely unmixed with principles of English law, come before our courts. The law and usages of Hindus must regulate all matters of contract between Hindus. Marriage is a contract; but as amongst the Hindus it more properly forms a portion of the subject of inheritance, we have discussed it in the First Book. There is therefore no necessity to do more than refer to it here.

Menu, ch. viii. s. 4–7, classifies matters of legal proceedings under eighteen heads :—1. Contraction of debt. 2. Deposit, pledge. 3. Sale without owner. 4. Joint performance of work or concerns among partners. 5. Resumption or retraction of gifts. 6. Non-payment of wages or hire. 7. Non-performance of agreement, breach of contract. 8. Recession of sale or purchase. 9. Disputes between master and servant. 10. Boundary disputes. 11. Defamation, slander. 12. Personal injury. 13. Theft. 14. Violent seizure of property, robbery. 15. Adultery. 16. Duties of man and wife. 17. Partition of inheritance. 18. Gambling, playing with animate and inanimate materials. The above titles are sometimes differently classified and arranged, and a few more topics are introduced. Thus legal procedure in general, oral evidence, written testimony, ordeal, contracted service, miscellaneous matters, and forensic duties. These subjects are again subdivided and greatly multiplied by diversity of claims. As *Narada* has observed, "Of these, also, the distinctions are one hundred and eight fold : from the diversity of men's claims, there are one hundred ramifications," *Mitac.* ch. i. s. 2, § 6. *Jagannatha* treats only of the law of contracts and succession, omitting the law of evidence, the rules of pleading, the rights of landlord and tenant.

Intention and consent are essential to every contract.—The mind of the parties must be in a condition to contract. Therefore, a minor, which includes one of decrepit old age, an idiot, and a lunatic, except during a lucid interval, are incapable of contracting; so one intoxicated or suffering from extreme disease. *Menu* declares contracts entered into by them to be null and void, the party being considered *non sui juris;* so a contract entered into whilst the mind is under the influence of passion, as of fear, anger, lust, or grief, would be considered null. *Sir Thomas Strange* says, "A distinction is to be attended to between those disqualifications which operate as a bar, such as idiotcy or lunacy, and those in which an account may be taken of concurrent circumstances towards assisting to determine how far the imputed disqualification is to be sustained in order to justify the nullity contended for. The case of an agreement, for instance, under the circumstance of inebriation, is one in which the English and Hindu law will alike balance in coming to a conclusion." In such a case there can be no intention and consent. "The remark may apply to more of the questionable ones that have been specified, so as to afford ground to discriminate between contracts so circumstanced, as not to be capable of standing inquiry for a moment, and such as only require to be subjected to a very strict one before they are allowed," *ib.* Upon the same principle that men are protected against their own acts, occasioned through fear, force constraining the will, or fraud, will never be permitted to succeed, so advantage cannot be taken of what was not previously meant. *Mr Colebrooke*, in his work on Obligations, says, "A true assent implies a serious and perfectly free use of power, both physical and moral. This essential is wanting in promises made in jest or compliment, or made in earnest, but under mistake, or under deception or delusion, or in consequence of compulsion. Therefore, consent not seriously given, or conceded through error, extorted by force, or procured by fraud, is unavailable." *Jagannatha* says, "Where an owner, discriminating what may and what may not be done, and guided solely by his own will, declares, as is actually intended by him, his own property divested, and dominion vested in a person capable of receiving and designed by the donor over the thing meant to be given, such volition vests property in the donee. In cases of fear and compulsion, the man is not guided solely by his own will, but solely by that of another. In case of a man agitated by anger, or the like, he is not a person who discriminates between what may and what may not be done. If, terrified by another, he gives his whole estate to any person for relieving him from apprehensions, his mind is not in its natural state; but after recovering tranquillity, if he give anything in the form of recompense, the donation is valid. What is given as a bribe, or in jest, is a mere delivery or a gift in words only; there is no volition vesting property in another. As for what is given by mistake, as gold instead of silver, which should have been given, or anything delivered to a Sudra instead of a Brahmin, the gold and the Brahmin are not the *thing* and the *person* really intended, namely, silver and a Brahmin. Though it be ascertained that ten suvernas (*swernas*) (gold) should be paid, if, anyhow, through inattention, or the like, fifteen suvernas be delivered, the gift is not valid; for they are not what was really intended to be given; or the donation is in this case void, because the giver did not discriminate what should or should not be done," 3 *Dig.* 183, 2 *ib.* 3 *Ed. Mad.* 1864, p. 454.

There is little if any difference in this respect between the Hindu and the English law of contract. *Dr Broom*, in his commentaries on *Common Law*, says that a contract is founded on consent on the *aggregatio mentim* or union of minds in regard to some particular matter. It is of the essence of every contract or agreement that the parties to be bound thereby should consent expressly or impliedly to whatever is stipulated therein, for otherwise no obligation or reciprocal right can be created between them. To this effect the civil law lays down that *in omnibus rebus quœ dominium transferunt concurrat oportet affectus ex utrâque parte contrahentium nam sive ea venditio sive donatio, sive conductio, sive quœlibet alia causa contrahendi fuit, nisi animus utriusque consentit perduci ad affectum id quod inchoatur non potest.* The law of contracts accordingly will be found to fall under the first of the three sub-divisions of the *jus privatum* of the Romans. The *jus privatum* was that particular part of the Roman law which concerned the rights of individuals. *Jus privatum est quod singulorum utilitatem spectat*; and, as we read in the *Dig.*, *omne jus aut consensus fecit aut necessitas constituit aut firmavit consuetudo.* Now, a contract or agreement may with the most perfect accuracy be said to be synonymous with *jus quod consensus fecit*, to be a law which the parties have formed and voluntarily prescribed to themselves for their own guidance. Consent obviously implies acquiescence of the mind in something proposed or affirmed. The term involves, in contemplation of law, the existence of a physical and moral power, as well as a deliberate and free exercise of such power. Hence the absence of any of these capacities in either of these parties to a contract renders the person labouring under it incapable of binding himself thereby.

The English law upon the subject of contracts by infants, lunatics, idiots, and persons under the influence of intoxication and duress, will be found collected in *Broom's Common Law*.

The subject-matter of the contract must also be legal.—For a contract to tempt a man to violate the law, or to do that which is injurious to the community, is void.

With regard to a bribe for giving evidence, or procuring a man to give false testimony, which is denominated given on an illegal consideration, *Katyayana* says, it shall by no means be given although the consideration be performed. But if it had at first been actually given it shall be restored by forcible means—no doubt, as *Sir Thomas Strange* says, on the same principle as that recognised in English law, viz., that it is more consistent with sound policy and justice that money paid on an illegal consideration shall be recovered back by the party who improperly paid it, than by denying the remedy, to give effect to the illegal contract.*

A certain amount of money had been paid by one Hindu to another, in consideration of a promise by the latter that he would give his sister in marriage to the former. The girl's mother was alive. In a suit for recovery of the amount, on the ground that the latter had failed to fulfil his promise, held that the suit would lie, *Jogeswar Chakrabatti* v. *Panch Kauri Chakrabatti* 5 *Beng. L. R.* 395.

Contracts by wife.—The wife's power of contracting is commensurate with her right of property, as consisting of her stridhana, with the exception of land. This applying in Bengal only to such as may have been given her by her husband, of which she cannot dispose, and with regard to which it follows that she cannot contract, *Stra. H. L.* 276.

Debts contracted by a wife for necessaries in support of a family, including herself, will bind her husband. Amongst necessaries are included the nuptials of a daughter and disbursements for funeral rites. This power is said to be usually exercised in the absence of the husband from home. But absence is said to be illustrative only ; therefore *Katyayana* includes a disability in the husband, arising from whatever cause—for instance, from incurable disease. See *Grady's Hindu Law of Inheritance, tit.* "Charges on Inheritance."

The law does not require the contract to be in writing—the Hindu law in no instance making that ceremony obligatory. Oral evidence of the discharge of an obligation by writing is admissible. Act xiv. of 1840 does not apply to contracts between Hindus. The Act is not part of the *lex fori.* It affects the contract itself, and not merely the remedy. It makes the contract itself void, 1 *Mad. H. C. R.* 9. As an excessive or illegal gift may be resumed, so contracts may be rescinded. But this must be done within a reasonable time, and only where both parties can be placed in their original position, *caveat emptor.* *Narada* ordains, "A buyer ought at first to inspect the commodity, and ascertain what is good and what is bad in it ; and after such inspection he shall not be permitted to return the goods to the seller, unless it has a concealed blemish.

Hindu jurists classify the law of contracts under four heads—viz., 1. Bailment ; 2. Loans ; 3. Sale or exchange ; 4. Debt. We shall proceed to review the law in outline under these heads.

1st, Bailment.—This is a contract to return to the bailee at a specified time the property which the owner confided to the bailee, under a responsibility suited to its specific nature. In this class of bailments, a certain degree of care is impliedly stipulated,

* See *Collins* v. *Blantern*, 1 *Smith's Leading Cases*, pages 325 to 355.

the amount varying with the object of the bailment, and which forms the main subject of adjustment in every case in which a question arises. It will depend upon whether the benefit resulting from the bailment be reciprocal between the parties; and if not, to which of them it attaches. *Sir Thomas Strange* says, Familiar as the subject must be in every system of law, provisions regarding it abound in *Menu* and other Hindu text-writers; and admitting them to be consonant to the principles established elsewhere on the same subject, the agreement can scarcely be classed with that *identity* of conclusions, which, in proportion as the subject is not of technical institution, pure, unbiased reason in all ages and nations seldom fails to draw. With regard to our own juridical system, confessedly the most material, if not the whole, most of the principles alluded to, have been imported into it through Bracton from the Romans. With us, therefore, there has been in this instance no such identity of conclusion drawn—all has been derivation; nor can it reasonably be doubted, that with the Hindu law have originated (as far as we can see) those provisions applicable to the subject in question which the wisdom of ages and nations the most civilised have since been content to adopt. Of these, the standard founded on the care that every prudent man takes of his own property, remarkable as it is, is as old, at least, as *Brihaspati*, who charges with the value, adding interest, the bailee that suffers a thing bailed to be destroyed by his negligence, while he keeps his own goods with very different care. On the other hand, if a thing deposited be lost, together with the goods of the bailee, it is declared by various authorities to be lost to the bailor; and numerous texts on the subject of responsibility contain the equally remarkably exception, not of inevitable necessity, but in identical terms, of the act of God and of the king.

Bailments are classed by some Hindu law writers under four divisions, by others under six.—*Sir W. Jones* enumerates five in his Law of Bailments. But, he adds, not to multiply them inconveniently, by extending inquiry into every possible case in which a man possesses for a time the goods of another, the most important ones, as they occur in the Hindu law (from whence, it is plain, they have been derived from other codes), may be distributed according to the principle that governs their responsibility. This depends upon the object and benefit involved, which may be on the side of the bailor or on that of the bailee, or it may be mutual; for example, the *simple deposit*, together with the *commission without reward*, are for the sake and inure to the sole benefit of the bailor; whilst in that of *loans for use*, it is the bailee or borrower who is benefited; and in cases of mutual trusts, pledges, and the various kinds of *hiring*, both parties are interested.

Where the bailment is for the benefit of the bailor, as in the case of deposits and mandates, or commissions without reward.

(a.) **Of deposits**, by which he who accepts one is charged with the property of another without any consideration on the part of the owner, while on that of the bailee all is trouble and care. In this case the law exacts from the bailee no greater responsibility than the absence of such gross negligence as is inconsistent with any kind of engagement. *Menu* says, "As the bailment was, so should be the re-delivery, according to a rule in the Veda." So *Brihaspati* says, "The very thing bailed must be restored to the very man who bailed it, in the very manner in which it was bailed." *Sir Thomas Strange* says, "A delivery substantially good would be valid under a system that gives effect upon all occasions to the *reason* of the law, as opposed to the *letter*, if not carried to excess." The law requires the bailee to keep the deposit with care, restoring it on a single demand. The law also exacts on the part of the bailee the most perfect fidelity; the alienation of a deposit without permission, the using it without consent, or neglecting to preserve it, are denounced as criminal. If, however, with the goods bailed to him, his own be lost, he is exempt from responsibility, and the loss is the bailor's, even though it should not have happened by any act (as it is called) of God, of the king, or of robbers,—the presumption being, in all these cases, against anything like fault; while the rule is, that he is to make good the deposit "if in fault, and not unless he be in fault." But if the deposit have been kept with care, and yet have been lost, the bailee will not be responsible, though none of his own property have been lost, unless, indeed, it can be shown that he kept his own property with very different care, or that he appropriated some part of the deposit; so, in the absence of special stipulation, he is exempt from responsibility in case of robbery, which implies violence, unless, indeed, collusion is imputable to him. But the exemption does not extend to a loss occasioned by theft, if such a want of due care can be shown as must be taken to have led to spoliation. If the depository selected by the owner of the goods be confessedly an exposed one, of which he has notice, it is his own fault for trusting it, if they are lost or injured by the peril to which they are exposed. In the case of a sealed deposit, *Menu* declares "that the bailee shall incur no censure on the re-delivery, unless he have altered the seal and taken out something." Inevitable necessity will not excuse if the deposit has been used by the bailee contrary to the faith of the bailment, or if, having been previously demanded, it was not restored in time.

A curious anomaly exists in denouncing the heaviest punishment against him who by false pretences gets into his hands the goods of another, yet justifying such a proceeding in the case of a creditor who cannot by ordinary means obtain payment of his debts, or retaining under similar circumstances what has been regularly deposited —a proceeding that is called *legal deceit*. But the Hindus allow not only deceit, but force, to be practised for the purpose of securing rights or discovering truth.

(b.) **Mandates.**—A mandatory is one who, without expectation of reward, engages to execute for another a commission of any kind. Between the mandatory and the depositary the difference consists in the diligence added to the care for which, to a certain extent, the former is pledged, according to the subject-matter of the mandate. The Hindu law recognises the same responsibility in both cases, as far as regards care, with the contingencies to which things so bailed may be liable,—the benefit in both being exclusively his who is the owner of the article.

(c.) **Loans for use**, in contradistinction to loans of money or other things for consumption, which are contracts of a different nature, being for the sole benefit of the bailee, he is bound to use extraordinary care, and is answerable for slight negligence, though not for inevitable accident or irresistible force, unless the accident might have been avoided by reasonable care, or the force fairly resisted, especially if he had exposed the property to loss by his improvidence; so, if it have been lost after the expiration of the period for which it was borrowed, the lender cannot determine the loan at will unless some pressing and indispensable purpose of his own would be in danger of failing, if he did not get back at the moment desired the thing lent. In this, as in other bailments, the purest good faith must be observed, so that, where special use is contemplated, the intention of the borrowers should be disclosed.

(d.) **Mutual trusts, pledges, and hiring.**—These are cases where the benefit is reciprocal.

(a.) Mutual trusts are cases where reciprocal deposits, loans, &c., are made between two or more parties, which, whether they be partners in trade, co-parceners, or persons only connected by the transaction in question, are governed by the same rules, with, however, a reciprocal instance of a single application.

(b.) A pledge is an accessory contract, being a bailment of something to a creditor on a loan of money, which by Hindu law may be for security only, or for security joined with use, and in this respect it may be compared with the *vivum vadium* and the *mortuum vadium*, the living and the dead mortgage in ours. *Sir Thomas Strange* says, That though this be in general so, and though, to insure the efficiency of a pledge or mortgage, the Hindu law inculcates the necessity of possession, the authorities to this purpose are not applicable to a sort of mortgage much in use in Hindustan and the provinces subject to Bombay, termed *Drishta bandhaca* (*hypothecation of visible property*), by which (according to the usual course of mortgages with us) the pledge is assigned to the creditor as a security without possession or intention of possession till the stipulated time arrive; so that it may be doubted whether this mode of pledging be not originally Hindu instead of Attick, as has been supposed.

A creditor suing under a contract of hypothecation must prove that there was an actual pledge, and that the land was part of the debtor's estate at the time of pledge.

An instrument of hypothecation is a mortgage instrument, and may as such be registered under the Act xvii. of 1802.

A *drishtabandhaca*, fixing a time of payment, and stipulating that the mortgagee shall, on default, be put into possession and enjoyment of the property, is not strictly a conditional sale, although it expressly provides that in default it shall be deemed an outright sale, and in a suit for possession by the mortgagee the court will give the mortgagor a day for redeeming.

In England, at common law, the mortgagee had not only the possession, but the absolute property of the land on the debtor's failing to perform the condition, and the equity courts regarded a mortgage as redeemable till foreclosure, and in enforcing a lien, equity gives the debtor an opportunity of barring the mortgage or sale of the property to which the lien extends, by paying the amount due with interest on a day named by the court. This principle is acted on by the courts with reference to mortgages, and the mortgagor does not lose his equity of redemption, though the stipulated time for payment has been allowed to pass by, and though there may be a contemporaneous agreement clogging that right.

The mortgagee, however, has the right of foreclosure where the mortgagor entirely fails to redeem. There exists no reason whatever why the mortgagee should be deprived of the remedy given by his contract.

Re-purchase.—The parties may sell with a condition for re-purchase at a particular time. Then, in case of non-payment, at the time there is no equity to relieve against the sale. It is the intention of the parties which governs, and that may be shown by the deed itself, or by other instrument, or even by oral evidence. It is incorrect to suppose that the condition for re-purchase with a stipulation for absolute sale in case of failure to pay at the time is a penalty which cannot be enforced.

If a *bona fide* sale is accompanied by a power to re-purchase, this will not make the transaction a mortgage ; if it does not appear that such was the intention of the parties, the best general test of such intention is the existence or non-existence of a power in the original purchaser to recover the sum named as the price for such re-purchase. If there is no such power, there is no mortgage.

Waiver of right.—Where the mortgage provided that the mortgagee should be entitled to purchase the land if it were not redeemed by a specified time. After this date the mortgagee accepted from the mortgagor a small sum in part payment of the mortgage money. This is no waiver by the mortgagee of his right to purchase.

Where a mortgage contained an agreement to repay the money with interest by a certain day, and stipulated that if the mortgagor failed to pay the amount the mortgagee should be put into possession of the land, and he might enjoy it, and that when the mortgagor had the means he would redeem the land, and pay the debt with interest, and take back the deed. On the mortgagor's default, the mortgagee might sue for the money, and he is not bound to accept the land and forego his right of action.

Mortgages in Canara.—There are two species of mortgage known to the Canara law, upon which some cases have been decided by the High Court at Madras. The one is called a kanam* mortgage, the other an otti mortgage. An otti differs from a kanam mortgage,—first, in respect of the right of pre-emption which the otti holder possesses; secondly, in being for so large a sum, that practically the janmi's (proprietor's) right is merely to receive a peppercorn rent. A kanam mortgage cannot be redeemed before the lapse of twelve years from the date of its execution. A kanamdar's (mortgagee's) right to hold for twelve years depends upon his acting conformably to usage and the janmi's (proprietor's) interest, and is lost if he repudiates the janmi's title (a rule that applies in the English law of landlord and tenant). It can make no difference that this is done for the first time by the kanamdar in his answer to the suit, or that on appeal he takes the point as to non-redemption within twelve years. A kanam mortgagee does not forfeit his right to hold for twelve years from the date of the kanam by allowing the purappad (net rent) to fall into arrear. As the land cannot be reclaimed before the expiration of twelve years, it seems conformable with justice that the money should not be reclaimable until that period has elapsed. If the mortgagor is unable to give possession, it is reasonable that the mortgagee should be allowed to repudiate the contract and recover the amount advanced. Where the first kanam holder, in his answer to a redemption suit by the second kanam holder, for the first time denied his own kanam, and alleged an independent junma right, he does not thereby forfeit his right to rely upon the option to make a further advance to which, as kanam holder, he was entitled, though the denial and allegation were false, and though his documents in support of such allegation were forged. A melkanamdar cannot eject a kanamdar or his assignee before the expiration of twelve years from the date of the kanam.

Otti.—A karanavan, singly, may make an otti mortgage. An otti, like a kanam mortgage, cannot be redeemed before the expiration of twelve years from its date. During the continuance of the first otti mortgage, the janmi is in the same position as regards his right to make a second otti mortgage to a stranger after, as he was before the lapse of twelve years from the date of the first mortgage. An otti mortgagee has the option to make a further advance, if required, by the mortgagor. Where a janmi made an otti mort-

* Kanam and otti are both described as a species of mortgage.

gage, and more than twelve months after he made a second otti mortgage to a stranger, without having given notice to the first mortgagee, so as to admit of the exercise of their option to advance the further sum required by the janmi, the second mortgagee cannot redeem the lands comprised in the first mortgage. An otti holder, like a kanamdar, forfeits his right to hold for twelve years by denying the janmi's title. There is a species of mortgage which occurs in Canara, termed iladarawara mortgage, the mortgagee being in possession, and taking the rents and profits in lieu of interest, and the security carrying a right to redeem, but none to foreclose. This mortgagee pays the government revenue.

In the case of a pledge for use, the debt and interest being extinguished by the use or otherwise, it reverts to him who made it. If any part of it remain after the expiration of the time for payment, the pledgee or creditor may continue to use it, making a demand for payment, and giving notice of his intention to the debtor or his representative; or if it be a pledge for security only, he may, under the like circumstances, begin to use it if capable of use without injury to the substance, giving like notice; while an unjustifiable use of one being a violation of an implied agreement, works a forfeiture of interest, *Sir Thomas Strange.* In either case he may, by proper application, attach the article and have it sold for payment, an account of what is due upon it having been previously taken, the excess being paid into court for the benefit of the owner, *ib.* On this ground Hindu lawyers recommend that a pledge should be taken when a loan is made to a kinsman or a friend, against whom compulsory payment cannot be so conveniently enforced. So in the absence of the creditor or a representative, the debtor may redeem his pledge by paying into court what is due upon it.

Assignment.—By usage rather than the express letter of the law, a pledge is assignable, but the assignment, which can only be for an equal or less sum than that advanced upon it, should correspond with the original contract, from which any variation might embarrass the redemption on the part of the first pledgee. But the same thing cannot at the same time be pledged to two different persons for the full value for each on the ground of fraud.

Between different pledgees the first is preferred, subject to priority of possession, or there may be an equitable adjustment of the right according to circumstances, neither the bailor nor the bailee can alien the property pledged, the former particularly, where the interest of the latter continues. *Sir Thomas Strange* says, "It is agreed that a purchaser, being privy to an article being in mortgage at the time, the transfer would not avail him. It is further admitted that it may be restrained by injunction, by timely application to the Court, and in order to render it valid in favour of the alienee, he should see the thing for which he treats, and not only have reason to be satisfied that it is unencumbered, but obtain immediate possession, and he adds that a clandestine disposal by the owner to a third person of a thing already pledged to another for an existing debt, can scarcely take effect, unless contrary to the general policy of Hindu law. The creditor hence improvidently allowed the pledge to remain in the hands of his debtor. *Yajnavalchya* having declared that in other contested matters the latest act shall prevail, but that in the case of a pledge, a gift, or a sale, the prior contract has the greater force; and *Jagannatha* says, were it otherwise no man would make a loan, apprehending that the debtor would sell to another what he had already pledged." Thus distinguishing between a pledge and a deposit for safe custody, which latter, as he adds, has little comparative force, and may be at any time recalled by the owner.

Property in a pledge is never lost to the owner by any lapse of time, while it remains as such out of possession, although in other cases titles may be gained by long possession, and lost by silent neglect; for we have seen that it is the duty of the bailee faithfully to preserve the property for restitution to his creditor, who will be bound to indemnify his debtor for any damage it may sustain in his hands for want of due care, the debtor in the event of loss being obliged to replace it or make it good, the debt for which it was given, with the interest running upon it, remaining payable notwithstanding.

Hiring.—This is also a bailment which is productive of mutual benefit. It corresponds with other kinds of bailment when the benefit is on one side only; for as there may be a loan, so there may be a hiring for use, and as a man may agree to execute a commission gratuitously, so may the like service be undertaken for a reward or adequate compensation, which is always implied in hiring. The difference between this species of bailment and those already discussed, and that now under consideration, is, that in the latter it is reciprocal, the owner of the thing hired or the hirer of himself, for whatever purpose, being paid in the one case for the use of his property, and in the other for that of himself, while he who contracts for the particular thing or service derives a corresponding benefit from the temporary use if he so hires, and upon this reciprocity turns the responsibility which the bailment in question stipulates.

To this species of bailment the rules applicable to deposits are, as *Jagannatha* declares, equally applicable. Therefore the law of bailments, he adds, applies to a carriage, &c., received on hire, and so in the case of a person delivered by the king, &c., into the hands of a guardian, the meaning of which must be construed to be. *Sir Thomas Strange* adds, that it applies *a fortiori* to the case of hire, which, as it is for the benefit of both parties, cannot but be taken to impose a greater responsibility on the bailee than where the bailment is altogether for the sake and on account of him by whom it was made. The degree of responsibility is to be estimated by the peculiar nature of the bailment, *Narada* declaring that whatever (of things hired for a time, at a settled price) be broken or lost, he (the hirer) shall make good, except in the case of inevitable accident or irresistible force.*

It is a common practice in India to entrust materials to skilled workmen to make into manufactured articles for hire, whether they contract by the piece or by time. If they fail in performance, they forfeit their hire, though the work want but little of being completed, or the time of being expired, and as he is bound to be diligent in the execution of what he has undertaken, so is he answerable for reasonable care—that is, for any injury to or loss of what has been entrusted to him that can be traced to his fault; so a common carrier is answerable for loss not happening by what is called the act of God, or of the king, or robbers, he not having contributed to it by any act of his own. In all these cases of bailment, the bailor retains in the thing bailed a reversionary interest, to take effect when the purpose of the bailment shall have been answered.

Of loans or borrowing for consumption, whether of money or other thing answering the description. It differs from loan for use, which is a bailment, because the property of the money or article lent for consumption vests in the borrower, to be replaced by him with an equivalent, together with the stipulated compensation which is usually interest, where the loan is for money and the borrower guarantees the performance of the contract on his part usually by security, consisting of pledges, or sureties, or both.

Interest.—Interest upon loans has always been allowed by Hindu law, although it has been prohibited as a means of acquisition to the two higher classes, viz., Brahmins and Shatryas. Thus *Menu* declares, "That neither a priest nor a military man must receive interest on loans, though each of them may pay the small interest permitted by law in borrowing for some pious use to the sinful man who demands it."

It is expressly permitted to the mercantile class (vysya) as an unexceptional mode of subsistence. *Menu* says that interest ought to be reserved from day to day, though in practice it is payable by the month. *Sir Thomas Strange* says the longer or shorter period by which interest is reckoned concerns the option of repayment and the avoiding of fractions. A short period being in the debtor's favour, the creditor is not to stipulate for reckoning it by a longer one. Interest has in general been high in India. It is ruled by the risk even, and is high in the direct order of the classes. A higher

* If a man build a house on ground of which he is the lessee, he has a right on the expiration of his lease to take with him the thatch, the wood, and the bricks of which it is constructed.

rate is demandable as the class of the borrower or lender is inferior; the lower the class, the higher the interest. It varies also according to the existence or non-existence of a pledge. *Sir Thomas Strange* says, Though the law has prescribed certain rates as respectively applicable to the different classes, and serving as they do to govern cases in which interest becomes payable without previous agreement, it is to be recollected that the rules on the subject leave the parties at liberty to disregard them, substituting other terms where they think proper. The Hindu law contemplates cases where the risk being greater than the specified rate, will compensate a higher rate, which may be bargained for according to the nature of it, whether by sea or by land. The consideration in these cases being not only the increased risk of non-payment, but the superior profit accruing to the borrower by the danger to which he and his property are exposed. In all such cases the adjustment of the interest is to be settled between the parties "by men well acquainted with sea voyages or journeys by land, with times and with places."

But compound interest cannot be contracted for.—But where the interest cannot be paid at the time appointed, there is nothing to prevent renewing the contract after having come to an account, and adding the interest to the principal; from which date it will carry interest, provided the interest has not been allowed to accumulate so as to exceed the principal, for on arriving at that amount it must stop as it does upon a tender. But this rule does not extend to grain or other things, of which loans may be made not involving the notion of usury. In such cases the amount of interest running on is not limited to the principal. The provision in sect. 4 of *Reg.* xxiv. of 1802, against an award of interest in excess of the principal, refers only to the amount claimed for interest at the time the suit is brought. It has been held at Madras by the High Court, that in absence of a demand in writing interest up to the date of suit cannot be awarded upon sums not payable under a written instrument, of which the payment has been illegally delayed, and where a party has offered to pay interest, he should be relieved from interest from the date of such offer.

Where part payments were made on a bond, and credited in discharge of the principal, and an action was brought for the balance of the principal and the interest, and the lower Court allowed a sum for interest as due at the date of the plaint, which was greater than the principal, the High Court disallowed this excess, *Kakarlapudi Sitaramaraj* v. *Uppalapadi Janakayya*, 1 *Mad. H. C. R.* 5 *sec.* 1 *Bomb. H. C. R.* 47, where *Sausse C.J.* citing *Menu*, ch. viii. s. 151; *Mayukha*, ch. v. s. 1; *Steele's Sum of the Laws and Customs of the Hindu Castes*, p. 78; *Vachespathi Misra*, 1 *Colb. Dig.* 63; and *Stra. H. L. supra*, observed: Thus the rule of Hindu law is simply this, that no greater arrear of interest can be recovered at any one time than what will amount to the principal sum, but if the principal remain outstanding, and the interest be paid in smaller sums than the amount of the principal money, there is no limit to the amount of interest which may be thus received from time to time, 1 *Mad. H. C. R. addenda X.*

By Hindu law interest exceeding in amount the principal sum cannot be recovered at any one time, and Act xxviii. of 1865 has not, by repealing sect. 12 of *Reg. V.* of 1827, or otherwise, altered this rule of law, *Khushalchand Lalchand* v. *Ichparam Fakir* v. *Vithobaben. Malhari* 3 *Bom. H. C. R.* 23, *Ap. Civ. Jur.*

According to the usage of native bankers at Moorshedabad, interest is claimable on Hondees, drawn at 111 days' sight, *Dhunput Singh Doogur* v. *Maharajah Jugut Indur Bunwaree Gobind Deb.* 4, *H. W. R. Cal. ci. Rul.* 85.

A debt contracted at play, a sum due on account of suretyship, an unliquidated demand, do not bear interest in the absence of a special agreement.

Sureties.—A variety of persons are enumerated by Hindu jurists who should never be accepted as sureties, but more on the ground of prudence and caution than of legal disqualification. The rejection of one undivided brother as a surety for another would, however, be consonant to the strictest law.

Sir Thomas Strange says, That sureties are for appearance, for the honesty of the debtor, or for payment. Bail in an action may be taken from a plaintiff, as well as from a defendant, where the suretyship is for appearance generally. The production of the debtor at the time and place agreed, subject to insuperable impediments, must be *boná fide*, so that he may be amenable, if living, to payment, the law being indulgent, as to the time of production, where he has absconded, so with regard to the obligation of payment. The surety for honesty is answerable, if by his representations the creditor has been misled. Between surety for payment, and for appearance and honesty, there is this difference, that in the latter two cases the surety dying, and the principal neglecting to pay, the sons of the surety are not answerable, unless their father was himself indemnified, and then the son is liable, as he is in all cases where there are assets; and without interest, when the undertaking was for payment, where sureties are jointly liable, each is answerable for his proportion only of the debt, unless otherwise agreed.

The principal must in all cases be first sued.—If the surety is compelled to pay, he has his remedy over against his principal for repayment. Where a judgment has been obtained against several defendants, jointly and severally, and some of them paid the whole of the payment debt, they might sue the others for contribution; but one tort feasor cannot recover contribution against another. It is not necessary that the agreement for the loan, or the acknowledgment of the surety, should be in writing, although it is advisable to adopt that precaution. Trade and money-lending, although the proper business of the mercantile class, are permitted to the Brahmin and the Shatrya, if unable to subsist by more appropriate means.

Of purchase and sale, or of exchange.—Barter is in effect a sale, and subject to the same rules; the difference consists only in the distinction between a *price*, which is applicable to a *sale*, and an *equivalent*, which is applicable to exchange.

Sale then consists in the payment of the price and delivery of the article, according to agreement. On goods sold and delivered, but not paid for on demand, interest accrues after six months from the sale, so interest accrues on the price paid where the article has not been delivered. This, of course, applies only where there is no special agreement as to the times of delivery and payment. In the absence of any special agreement, and of the delivery of the goods, they are at the risk of the vendor. Therefore if their value falls whilst they remain in his hands, he must make it good with attention to the eventual profit, if it was purchased for exportation. If there has been no stipulation as to the price, the law will imply a reasonable one; *quantum valebat* to be settled, in case of dispute, by merchants.

Damages.—The price of *paddy*, contracted to be delivered at a season of the year, must be estimated at the market rates of the time agreed upon for delivery, if there be no stipulation to the contrary, *Gora Chund Mundle and others* v. *Lal. Chund Baboo, S. D. A., Decis. Beng.* 193.

Where the vendee refuses to accept the article purchased, the owner may dispose of the article as he pleases, the vendee being responsible for loss resulting from his not completing his purchase. If instead of paying down the price, *earnest** be paid, and the buyer afterwards break the agreement, the earnest is forfeited.

A contract was entered into by two persons for the sale and purchase of a house. The purchaser paid the *bayanch*, or earnest money, and the balance was to be made good on the execution and registry of a final deed of sale, within one month from the date of the contract. In the meantime, part of the house fell down, and the purchaser refused to complete the purchase. It was held, according to the *Vyavashta* of the law officers, that the contract might be annulled, if it so pleased the purchaser, as the buyers' ownership had not commenced, the term not having expired, and the price not having been paid, so that the seller's right to the property remained untouched. The earnest, however, was declared to be forfeited. *Nursing Bhana* v. *Sunkerdas Mukundas*, 1 *Borr.* 403, *Prendergast.* And if in such case the seller break it, he is liable to repay the earnest twofold, and not only the earnest money, but damages for the non-delivery.

By Hindu law a purchaser may recover in an action for breach of contract to deliver goods, not only double the earnest money,

* A sum paid to bind the contract.

but also damages for the non-delivery, *Alwar Chetti* v. *Vaidelinga Chetti*, 1 *H. C. R. Mad.* 9.

In action for damages for non-delivery of goods, before the purchaser can recover he must show that he paid or tendered the price, and that the vendor's right under the contract cannot be controlled by the course of dealing between the parties. Where the contract is to deliver goods within a reasonable time, and payment is to be made on delivery. If, before the expiration of that time, the vendor merely expresses an intention not to perform the contract, the vendee cannot at once bring his action, unless he exercise his option to treat the contract as rescinded.

In every contract of sale there is an implied warranty of title, and that the article is what it was represented to be according to the fair understanding of the buyer. With regard to the former, *Sir Thomas Strange* says, The general principle is, that a sale without ownership in the vendor, being void, there is no safety for a purchaser but in *market overt.*

Market overt.—Market overt, as opposed to all traffic with suspicious characters in secret places, at improper times, and for unfair prices, circumstances indicating fraud, is in strictness that which is carried on before the king's officers,* where, by means of proper entry, the seller may be known and got at. But it is said that market is mentioned as an instance only, and that the requisition of the law is satisfied by a purchase made openly in the presence of respectable persons. If the purchase is questioned, the purchaser must produce the seller, when the owner recovers his property, and the buyer receives back his price.* If the seller cannot be found, the owner is entitled to get back his property, paying the buyer one half what he paid for it, presuming the purchase on his part to have been fair. If the purchase have not been made in *market overt,* and the buyer cannot produce the seller, he is liable to relinquish the goods so bought, to the owner, on proof by the latter of his property, such a sale being regarded as void.

Sir Thomas Strange says, The equity of the Hindu rule, where the loss is divided, consists in the assumption that the owner was in some fault, as, on any other supposition he could not, it is imagined, have so lost his property, and the law draws the same inference even where he had been robbed of it. On this ground he forfeits half his value, as the price of getting it back under the special circumstances ; while the purchaser loses half what he gave for it, as a punishment for buying from one whom he cannot afterwards produce. Such is the difference by the Hindu law between a public and a private sale in respect to the title of the vendor.

Possession.—Possession of the subject of an agreement is not

* The establishment of *markets* and *fairs,* with the regulation of *weights* and *measures,* as well as the rights of pre-emption and embargo, belonged to the prerogative in India, ever since the time of *Menu.*

necessary by the Hindu law, as current in Mithila, to give validity to such agreement. *Srunarain Rai* v. *Bhya Jha*, 2 *S. D. A*.

A sale of property may be valid according to Hindu law, although not accompanied by actual delivery of possession, *Nagoobaee* v. *Moteegeer Gooroo*, 1 *Bom. H. C. R.* 5. Possession is not essentially necessary to give validity to a transfer by sale of immovable property, *Bhookan Bhaeebawa* v. *Bhagee Prag*, 1 *Bom. H. C. R.* 19.

Rescission of purchase and sale.—This is one of the eighteen titles of Hindu law enumerated by *Menu*, and results from that principle which requires the integrity of the article purchased—the law requiring that a thing shall be what it is represented to be. *Jagannatha* says, It is the buyer's own fault if he examine not the commodity, and it is his duty to know what may be the loss on each article, and what the gain; consequently the contract cannot be rescinded merely because the price of the article was light—it must have been excessive.

If a commodity be contracted for in gross, to be of certain specified quality, the person contracting to receive such commodity is not bound to take any part of the quantity agreed for, if the larger residue were not of the quality and denomination specified in the agreement, *Mohon Lall Jagore* v. *Norooju Cahooju*, *East's Notes*, case 16.

Where a person claimed possession of certain villages under an *Ikrárnámah*, or written acknowledgment from the conditional purchaser, alleged to have been executed nine years after the sale had become absolute, his claim was rejected, the agreement not being proved, or though proved, being either without a consideration, or the condition violated by the claimant, *Gopal Lal* v. *Raja Jorulnarain Singh*, 4 *S. D. A. Rep.* 182.

Brokers.—Brokers' bargains do not bind unless both principals are truly made acquainted with the terms of the bargain struck, *Mohon Lall. Jagore* v. *Roojee Cahoojee*, *East's Notes*, case 16.

Exact copies of brokers' memoranda of a contract must be given to both principals to make such contract binding, *Mohon Lall Jagore* v. *Roojee Cahoojee*, *East's Notes*, case 16.

Of marketable things the prices are as they have been settled by authority for the market, a combination to defeat which is punishable with the highest amercement, one thousand panas. On the discovery of a defect or blemish in the article, unknown to both parties at the same time, the contract may be rescinded, and the article returned within the period limited for the purpose, different periods being allowed for examination or trial, according to its nature, as it is more or less perishable. When fraudulently sold with a concealed blemish, it may be returned at any time.

Frauds by cheating in weights or measures are punishable by fines.

If there be a fraud in the original contract of sale, the sale will be vitiated, and the delivery afterwards will not pass the property; but if the contract of sale be complete, no fraud in obtaining possession of the goods will invalidate such contract, but possession so obtained is a transfer of the property. And where A. made a bargain for the purchase of certain goods from B., and A. sent his clerk to a partner of B.'s with a cheque, and the latter delivered the goods to the clerk, and the cheque turned out to be a forgery, and in the meantime A. had obtained an advance of money on the goods from C., and then absconded, it was held that C. was a *bona fide* purchaser, and was entitled to retain possession of the property (*Cassimbhoy Nathabhoy* v. *Junrai Balloo*, *Perry's Notes*, case 17.

So also for adulterating drugs or other things, or for disguising one thing for another, as the skin of a tiger by colouring the skin of a cat, or a ruby by tinging a glass bead, for which the penalty is eight times the amount of the original sale.

Debt.—*Sir Thomas Strange* says, That debt, for the most part, is the result of other contracts rather than a substantive and independent one, most of the principal rules respecting which have been already anticipated in the chapter on "Charges on the Inheritance," and in the other subjects of contract which we have already discussed in this book, both with regard to the particular circumstances under which particular persons are or are not capable of contracting debt, as well as the consideration upon which contracts are founded. The Act xiv. of 1840 does not apply to contracts between Hindus. The Act is not part of the *lex fori*. It affects the contract itself, and not merely the remedy. It enacts that no contract shall be allowed to be good. The contract itself is made void.

Penalty—Liquidated damages.—Where it is agreed that, in case of a breach of contract, a sum shall be paid, the amount will be regarded as liquidated damages, which the courts will enforce, and not as a penalty. Act xxviii. of 1855 shows that the intention of the Legislature is, that parties shall be left to make, and be compelled to stand by, their own agreements. The use of the terms "penalty," "liquidated damages," does not determine the intention of the parties to a written instrument; but it is to be determined, like other questions of distinction, by the nature of the provisions and the language of the whole instrument. But if the instrument contain many stipulations of varying importance, or relating to objects of small value, calculable in money, there is the strongest ground for supposing that a stipulation, applying generally to a breach of all or any of them, was intended to be a penalty, and not as liquidated damages.

The rule of construction, therefore, is, that although the stipulation may be held to be a penalty, and therefore not payable upon a breach of any particular stipulation, the resulting damages from which is strictly measurable in money, still the penalty might properly be taken as the amount of damages, measured by the parties themselves, in case of an entire non-performance.

Specific performance.—In decreeing specific performance of a contract, the Court will consider whether it can enforce the whole of the agreement, and if it cannot do so, it will refuse relief. The ascertainment of the amount of damages is a necessary preliminary, under sec. 192 of Act. viii. of 1859, for a specific performance of a contract, and payment of damages as an alternative in case of non-performance. The doctrine of specific performance, as applicable to partnership, is governed by the same rules as those which govern the doctrine in other cases.

Maintenance and Champerty.—Maintenance is the stirring up of improper litigation with a bad motive or purpose, contrary to public policy and justice. Champerty is a species of maintenance, and of the same character, with the feature of a condition or bargain providing for a participation in the subject-matter of the litigation superadded, *Patcha Kutti Chetti* v. *Kamala Nayakkan*, 1 *Mad. H. C. R.* 153. The law in England as to these offences does not apply to the natives of India. In dealing with their contracts on the ground of these offences, the Court must look to the general principles regarding public policy and the administration of justice, upon which that law at present rests. Specific performance has been decreed of a lease, though the lease formed part of an arrangement whereby, as a consideration for the lease, the petitioner was to lend the defendant money to enable him, *inter alia,* to commence legal proceedings against the then tenants of the subject-matter of the intended lease.

The purchase of a suit is not champerty, and there are many cases in the Sudder Court, and one in the High Court, to show that champerty is not illegal in the Mofussil, *Jug Mohun Lall* v. *Muss. Buddun Koer*, 9 *W. R. Civ. Rul.* 243.

A deed of sale of property for a specific consideration, although with the avowed object of enabling the seller to prosecute a claim at law, was held to be invalid on the ground of champerty, to constitute which the consideration must be indefinite, and the stipulation the transfer of a portion of the property sued for, on the transferee advancing money for the payment of costs, *Mt. Shurfun* v. *Sheikh Gholam Mohummud*, 7 *S. D. A. Rep.* 495.

One or two plaintiffs having engaged to defray the expenses of a suit, in consideration of a share of the property in litigation sold by the others to him, the plaintiffs were non-suited, and ordered to pay all costs, *Lootfonissa* v. *Weheronissa Khanum*, *S. D. A. Decis. Beng.* 289.

The plaintiffs in a suit having sold a portion of the lands in dispute to raise funds for carrying on the suit, the transaction was held to come within the law of champerty, and their suit was accordingly dismissed with costs, *Syud Keramut Ali* v. *Sumbhoonath Mitr, S. D. A. Decis. Beng.* 423.

R. entered into an agreement with G., that if a suit, which was then about to be brought by G. for the recovery of certain lands, should be decided in favour of G., R. was to pay G. 85 rupees, and G. was to make over to R. half the land recovered. R. was to pay G. 50 rupees in certain proportions, which R. was to lose if the suit was not decided in favour of G. G. recovered the land, and R. then sued him upon the above agreement. No issue was taken in the courts of first instance on the question whether the agreement was void for champerty. An issue was raised on this question by the Appellate Court, and (no evidence being taken) was decided in favour of defendant.

Held, in special appeal, that as it was not manifestly apparent on the face of the proceedings that the agreement was against morality or public policy, the Appellate Court ought not to have held it void. *Semble*, that the above agreement was not void on the ground of champerty; at any rate, that it was capable of explanation by a consideration of the surrounding circumstances, which the plaintiff should have had an opportunity of giving in evidence, *Kámráv Khanderáv* v. *Govind Pándshat et al., A. C. J. Bombay H. C. R.* 63.

A plaintiff having been admitted as proprietor of a moiety of an estate sued for, for the avowed purpose of bringing and maintaining the action, the suit was dismissed, *Muha Rajah Muheshur Bukhsh Singh* v. *Government, S. D. A. Decis. Beng.* 659.

An agreement to give up a part of the property claimed to a person, on condition of his advancing the funds required for the cost of suit, was held to be illegal, *Baboo Brijnerain Singh* v. *Rajah Teknerain Singh*, 6 *S. D. A. Rep.* 131; *Barwell & Stockwell, Mt. Zuhooroonnissa Khanum* v. *Rasuk Lal Mitta*, 6 *S. D. A. Rep.* 298.

A claim to ancestral property having been dismissed by the Provincial Court under the Hindu law of inheritance, an appeal was instituted from this decision; and it appearing that the appellant had entered into an agreement with a person to give him up one half of the estate claimed by him, if a decree should be passed in his favour, on consideration of that person advancing the money for the cost of the suit, it was held that the transaction was illegal, as savouring strongly of gambling, and the agreement was ordered to be cancelled before the appeal could be admitted, *Ram Gholam Sing.* v. *Keerut Sing and others*, 4 *S. D. A. Rep.* 12.

The substitution *pendente liti* of a legal bond for one rendered illegal by conditions of champerty, and which had been cancelled, will render a suit admissible, *Ali Awalfurah* v. *Kunazuk Joynub Bibi, S. D. A. Decis. Beng.* 483.

The courts will not enforce any *stipulations* of an agreement between parties, if other reciprocal stipulations in it involve illegal conditions, *Omeis Chunder Pal Chowdhree* v. *Bajpaie Muharajah Damoodur Chundur Deb, S. D. A. Decis. Beng.* 1850.

Bonds.—The obligor's consent is not necessary to the assignment of a common money bond.

Choses in action are assignable in India as well as in England, although in law the assignee cannot sue in his own name, *Jug Mohun Lall* v. *Muss. Buddun Koer*, 9 *W. R. Civ. Rul. Cal.* 243. By Hindu law the assignee of a debt can sue the debtor in his own name, *Kadeerbacha Sahib* v. *Rangasvamy Nayak*, 1 *Mad. H. C. R.* 150 ; 1 *M. H. C. R.*, special case, No. 61 ; *Vembakum Soma Yagee Janakee Ummall* v. *P. Moonoosamy Chetty.* This case decides that, according to Hindu law, not only is the beneficial interest in the subject-matter of the contract, but the contract itself, is assignable. The assignee, therefore, may sue in his or her own name. This doctrine is applicable to suits brought in the Madras Small Cause Court.

Promissory notes.—The making of a promissory note is altogether the act of the maker, and delivery to the promisee is required to make it complete.

Bill of exchange.—The omission by the holder to give notice of dishonour discharges the drawer of a hoondee from liability, *Jeetun Lall* v. *Sheo Churn*, 2 *W. R. Cal. Civ. Rul.* 214.

The law of British India, as enforced in the Mofussil, recognises no distinction between specialties and other contracts.

We have observed that a suit at law is not the only mode of enforcing a debt, *Menu* authorising the recovery of a man's property by the aid of laws divine and human, by stratagem, by the practice of *acharytum*,* and even by force.

Where a debtor has no effects to satisfy the judgment, the creditor being of equal or superior class with his debtor, an arrangement may be made for working out the debt, the work stipulated being consonant to the class of the debtor, and not excessive ; if it be, he will be entitled to his release. Should he be incapable of labour, time should be given him for payment. In such an arrangement, a Brahmin can only be compelled to pay according to his income, little by little. *Sir Thomas Strange* says, In every case of exemption in favour of a Brahmin, one of the sacerdotal class is intended ; all being born capable of that class, but few, comparatively speaking, belonging to it, the rest being secular Brahmins, pursuing various worldly callings permitted to them by the law.

It will be unnecessary here to dwell upon the procedure adopted by the courts to enforce the law of contract, or the pleadings and

* That is, setting *dherna* at the door of the debtor, abstaining from food till, by the fear of the debtor dying at his door, compliance on the part of the debtor is exacted.

evidence necessary to raise and prove the various issues in such suits, for they are, for the most part, now regulated by British legislation, and will be found in the various statutes relating to such subjects, and the different works devoted to their practical elucidation,—in *Mr Broughton's Civil Procedure Code*, and *Dr Field's Law of Evidence*, the latter being a valuable little work which may be safely commended to students as containing a clear and concise exposition of the principles of the law of evidence, a branch of legal training which is sadly neglected by students, and which ought, in consequence of its vast importance, to form a leading feature in legal education, but which is often neglected to give prominence to other subjects of less practical utility.

This outline of the law of contract would be still more imperfect than it is, if I were to omit to transcribe the high commendation which that distinguished jurist, *Sir Thomas Strange*, has bestowed upon Hindu pleading, and the Hindu law of evidence. He says, That Hindu Pleading was noticed with commendation by *Sir W. Jones*, and that, with some trifling exceptions, the Hindu law of evidence is, for the most part, distinguished nearly as much as our own by the excellent sense that determines the competency and designates the choice of witnesses, with the manner of examining, and the credit to be given them, as well as by the solemn earnestness with which the obligation of truth is urged and inculcated, insomuch that less cannot be said of this part than that it will be read by every English lawyer with a mixture of admiration and delight, as it may be studied by him to advantage. This high compliment is not in the least overstrained; and our admiration for the Hindu code of evidence may be raised to a high pitch when we recollect that it was in operation at least 1280 years before the birth of Christ,—a reflection that places the English code in an inferior point of view to the Hindu, the one being original, the other derived from other peoples and codes.

THE END.

APPENDIX.

THE LAW OF LIMITATION.

ACT No. XI. OF 1861,

PASSED BY THE LEGISLATIVE COUNCIL OF INDIA

(*Received the assent of the Governor-General on the* 1*st May* 1861).

LIMITATION OF ACTIONS.

ACT NO. XI. OF 1860.

An Act to amend Act XIV. of 1859 (*to provide for the Limitation of Suits*).

I. Suits now pending or instituted before the 1st day of January 1862 to be tried as if Act XIV. of 1859 had not been passed.—All suits now pending, or which shall be instituted before the 1st day of January 1862, shall be tried and determined as if Act XIV. of 1859 (*to provide for the limitation of suits*) had not been passed.

II. Sections XIX., XX., XXI., XXII., and XXIII., not to take effect till 1st January 1862.—Sections XIX., XX., XXI., XXII., and XXIII. of the said Act, shall not take effect or have any operation before the said 1st day of January 1862.

The following is the Act the operation of which is suspended by the foregoing Act :—

ACT NO. XIV. OF 1859.

(*Received the assent of the Governor-General on the* 5*th May* 1859.)

An Act to provide for the Limitation of Suits.

Preamble.—Whereas it is expedient to amend and consolidate the laws relating to the limitation of suits ; It is enacted as follows :—

I. Limitation of suits.—No suit shall be maintained in any court of judicature within any part of the British territories in India in which this Act shall be in force, unless the same is instituted within the period of limitation hereinafter made applicable to a suit of that nature, any law or regulation to the contrary notwithstanding; and the periods of limitation, and the suits to which the same respectively shall be applicable, shall be the following, that is to say :—

1. **Limitation of one year—Pre-emption suits.**—To suits to enforce the right of pre-emption, whether the same is founded on law or general usage, or on special contract, the period of one year to be computed from the time at which the purchaser shall have taken possession under the sale impeached.

2. **Limitation of one year—Suits for damages, summary suits, &c.**—To suits for pecuniary penalties or forfeitures for the breach of any law or regulation; to suits for damages, for injury to the person and personal property, or to the reputation; to suits for damages for the infringement of copyright or of any exclusive privilege; to suits to recover the wages of servants, artisans, or labourers, the amount of tavern bills or bills for board and lodging, or lodging only; and to summary suits before the revenue authorities under Regulation V. 1822 of the Madras Code—the period of one year from the time the cause of action arose.

3. **Limitation of one year—Suits to set aside sales under decrees or for arrears of Government revenue, &c.**—To suits to set aside the sale of any property, movable or immovable, sold under an execution of a decree of any civil court not established by royal charter, when such suit is maintainable; to suits to set aside the sale of any property, movable or immovable, for arrears of Government revenue, or other demand recoverable in like manner; to suits by a putneedar, or the proprietor of any other intermediate tenure saleable for current arrears of rent, or other person claiming under him, to set aside the sale of any putnee talook, or such other tenure sold for current arrears of rent; to suit to set aside the sale of any property, movable or immovable, sold in pursuance of any decree or order of a collector or other officer of revenue—the period of one year from the date at which such sale was confirmed or would otherwise have become final and conclusive if no such suit had been brought.

4. **Limitation of one year—Suits to set aside attachments, &c., by revenue authorities for arrears of Government revenue.**—To suits to set aside any attachment, lease, or transfer of any land or interest in land by the revenue authorities for arrears of Government revenue, or to recover any money paid under protest in satisfaction of any claim made by the revenue authorities on account of arrears of revenue or demands recoverable as arrears of revenue—one year from the date of such attachment, lease, or transfer, or of such payment, as the case may be.

5. **Limitation of one year—Suits to set aside summary decisions, &c.**—To suits to alter or set aside summary decisions and orders of any of the civil courts not established by royal charter, when such suit is maintainable—the period of one year from the date of the final decision, award, or order in the case.

6. **Limitation of three years—Suits to contest certain awards.**—To suits brought by any person to contest the justice of an award which shall have been made under Regulation VII. 1822, Regulation IX. 1825, and Regulation IX. 1833 of the Bengal code, or to recover

any property comprised in such award—the period of three years from the date of the final award or order in the case.

7. Limitation of three years—Suits to recover property comprised in an order made under clause 2, section 1, Act XVI. of 1838 or Act IV. of 1840.—To suits by any party bound by any order respecting the possession of property made under clause 2, section 1, Act XVI. of 1838, or Act IV. of 1840, or any person claiming under such party, for the recovery of the property comprised in such order—the period of three years from the date of the final order in the case.

8. Limitation of three years—Suits for goods sold by retail, suits for rent of buildings or lands, &c.—To suits to recover the hire of animals, vehicles, boats, or household furniture, or the amount of bills for any articles sold by retail; and to all suits for the rents of any buildings or lands (other than summary suits before the revenue authorities under Regulation V. 1822 of the Madras code)—the period of three years from the time the cause of action arose.

9. Limitation of three years—Suits for money lent, or interest, or for breach of contract where no written contract exists.—To suits brought to recover money lent, or interest, or for the breach of any contract, the period of three years from the time when the debt became due, or when the breach of contract in respect of which the suit is brought first took place, unless there is a written engagement to pay the money lent, or interest, or a contract in writing signed by the party to be bound thereby or by his duly authorised agent.

10. Limitation of three years—Suits for the same where there is a written contract which has not been registered within six months.—To suits brought to recover money lent or interest, or for the breach of any contract in cases in which there is a written engagement or contract, and in which such engagement or contract could have been registered by virtue of any law or regulation in force at the time and place of the execution thereof—the period of three years from the time when the debt became due, or when the breach of contract in respect of which the action is brought first took place, unless such engagement or contract shall have been registered within six months from the date thereof.

11. Limitation of twelve years—Suits for specialty debts and legacies.—To suits in cases governed by English law upon all debts and obligations of record and specialties; and to suits for the recovery of any legacy—the period of twelve years from the time the cause of action arose.

12. Limitation of twelve years—Suits for immovable property.—To suits for the recovery of immovable property or of any interest in immovable property to which no other provision of this Act applies—the period of twelve years from the time the cause of action arose.

13. Limitation of twelve years—Suits for shares in joint family property and for maintenance.—To suits to enforce the right to share in any property, movable or immovable, on the ground that it is joint family property; and to suits for the recovery of maintenance, where the right to receive such maintenance is a charge on the inheritance of any estate—the period of twelve years from the death of the persons from whom the property alleged to be joint is said to have descended, or on whose estate the maintenance is alleged to be a charge, or from the date of the last payment to the plaintiff, or any person through whom he claims, by the person in the possession or management of such property or estate on account of such alleged share, or on account of such maintenance, as the case may be.

14. Limitation of twelve years—Suits by proprietor of land to resume or assess lakhehraj or rent-free land—Proviso if the land has been held rent-free from the time of the permanent settlement. —To suits by the proprietor of any land, or by any person claiming under him, for the resumption or assessment of any *lakheraj* or rent-free land—the period of twelve years from the time when the title of the person claiming the right to resume and assess such lands, or of some person under whom he claims, first accrued: Provided that in estates permanently settled, no such suit, although brought within twelve years from the time when the title of such person first accrued, shall be maintained if it is shown that the land has been held *lakheraj* or rent-free from the period of the permanent settlement.

15. Limitation of thirty and sixty years—Suits against depositaries, pawnees, or mortgagees.—To suits against a depositary, pawnee or mortgagee of any property, movable or immovable, for the recovery of the same—a period of thirty years, if the property be movable, and sixty years if it be immovable, from the time of the deposit, pawn, or mortgage; or if in the meantime an acknowledgment of the title of the depositor, pawnor, or mortgagor, or of his right of redemption, shall have been given in writing, signed by the depositary, pawnee, or mortgagee, or some person claiming under him, from the date of such acknowledgment in writing.

16. Limitation of six years applicable to all suits not especially provided for.—To all suits for which no other limitation is hereby expressly provided—the period of six years from the time the cause of action arose.

II. Suits against trustees and their representatives for breach of trust, &c.—Proviso.—No suit against a trustee in his lifetime, and no suits against his representatives for the purpose of following in their hands the specific property which is the subject of the trust, shall be barred by any length of time; but no suit to make good the loss occasioned by a breach of trust out of the general estate of a deceased trustee shall be maintained in any of the said courts, unless the same is instituted within the proper period of limitation according to the last preceding section, to be computed from the decease of such trustee: Provided that nothing herein contained shall prevent a co-trustee from enforcing, against the estate of a deceased trustee, any claim for contribution, if he shall institute a suit for that purpose within six years after such right of contribution shall have arisen.

III. Shorter periods of limitation, if prescribed by particular Acts, to prevail.—When, by any law now or hereafter to be in force, a shorter period of limitation than that prescribed by this Act is specially prescribed for the institution of a particular suit, such shorter limitation shall be applied, notwithstanding this Act.

IV. Revival of right to sue by admission in writing—Proviso.—If in respect of any legacy or debt, the person who, but for the law of limitation, would be liable to pay the same, shall have admitted that such debt or legacy, or any part thereof, is due, by an acknowledgment in writing signed by him, a new period of limitation, according to the nature of the original liability, shall be computed from the date of such admission: Provided that if more than one person be liable, none of them shall become chargeable by reason only of a written acknowledgment signed by another of them.

V. Computation of period of limitation in suits to recover property purchased from depositaries, pawnees, or mortgagees—Proviso.—In suits for the recovery from the purchaser, or any person claiming under him, of any property purchased *bona fide* and for valuable consideration from a trustee, depositary, pawnee, or mortgagee, the cause of action shall be deemed to have arisen at the date of the purchase: Provided that, in the case of purchase from a depositary, pawnee, or mortgagee, no such suit shall be maintained unless brought within the time limited by Clause 15, Section 1.

VI. Computation of period of limitation in suits in Supreme Courts by mortgagee to recover immovable property mortgaged.—In suits in the courts established by royal charter by a mortgagee to recover from the mortgagor the possession of the immovable property mortgaged, the cause of action shall be deemed to have arisen from the latest date at which any portion of principal money or interest was paid on account of such mortgage debt.

VII. Computation of period of limitation in suits to avoid incumbrances or under-tenures in estates sold for arrears of Government revenue.—In suits to avoid incumbrances or under-tenures in an estate sold for arrears of Government revenue due from such estate, or in a putnee talook, or other saleable tenure, sold for arrears of rent, which by virtue of such sale becomes freed from incumbrances and under-tenures, the cause of action shall be deemed to have arisen at the time when the sale of the estate, talook, or tenure became final and conclusive.

VIII. Computation of period of limitation in suits between merchants for balances of accounts current.—In suits for balances of accounts current between merchants and traders who have had mutual dealings, the cause of action shall be deemed to have arisen at, and the period of limitation shall be computed from, the close of the year in the accounts of which there is the last item admitted or proved indicating the continuance of mutual dealings, such year to be reckoned as the same is reckoned in the accounts.

IX. Computation of period of limitation in case of concealed fraud.—If any person entitled to a right of action shall by means of fraud have been kept from the knowledge of his having such right or of the title upon which it is founded, or if any document necessary for establishing such right shall have been fraudulently concealed, the time limited for commencing the action against the person guilty of the fraud or accessory thereto, or against any person claiming through him otherwise than in good faith, and for a valuable consideration, shall be reckoned from the time when the fraud first became known to the person injuriously affected by it, or when he first had the means of producing or compelling the production of the concealed document.

X. Computation of period of limitation in suits where the cause of action is founded on fraud.—In suits in which the cause of action is founded on fraud, the cause of action shall be deemed to have first arisen at the time at which such fraud shall have been first known by the party wronged.

XI. Computation of period of limitation in case of legal disability.—If at the time when the right to bring an action first accrues, the person to whom the right accrues is under a legal disability, the action may be brought by such person or his representative within the same time after the disability shall have ceased, as would otherwise have been allowed from the time when the cause of action accrued, unless such time shall exceed the period of three years, in which case the suit shall be commenced within three years from the time when the disability ceased; but if, at the time when the cause of action accrues to any person, he is not under a legal disability, no time shall be allowed on account of any subsequent disability of such person or of the legal disability of any person claiming through him.

XII. What persons to be deemed to be under legal disability.—The following persons shall be deemed to be under legal disability within the meaning of the last preceding section:—Married women in cases to be decided by English law, minors, idiots, and lunatics.

XIII. Computation of period of limitation in case of absence of defendant.—In computing any period of limitation prescribed by this Act, the time during which the defendant shall have been absent out of the British territories in India shall be excluded from such computation, unless service of a summons to appear and answer in the suit can, during the absence of such defendant, be made in any mode prescribed by law.

XIV. Computation of period of limitation in case of suit prosecuted *bona fide*, but in wrong court.—In computing any period of limitation prescribed by this Act, the time during which the claimant, or any person under whom he claims, shall have been engaged in prosecuting a suit upon the same cause of action against the same defendant or some person whom he represents, *bona fide* and with due diligence, in any court of judicature which, from defect of jurisdiction or other cause, shall have been unable to decide upon it, or shall have passed a decision which, on appeal, shall have been annulled for any such cause, including the time during which such appeal, if any, has been pending, shall be excluded from such computation.

XV. Person dispossessed of immovable property otherwise than by due course of law, may recover possession notwithstanding any title that may be set up—Suits for dispossession to be brought within six months—Suit to establish title not to be affected.—If any person shall, without his consent, have been dispossessed of any immovable property otherwise than by due course of law, such person, or any person claiming through him, shall, in a suit brought to recover possession of such property, be entitled to recover possession thereof notwithstanding any other title that may be set up in such suit, provided that the suit be commenced within six months from the time of such dispossession. But nothing in this section shall bar the person from whom such possession shall have been so recovered, or any other person, instituting a suit to establish his title to such property and to recover possession thereof within the period limited by this Act.

XVI. Act not to interfere with equitable jurisdiction of Supreme Courts.—Nothing in this Act contained shall be deemed to interfere with any rule or jurisdiction of any court established by royal charter in refusing equitable relief, on the ground of acquiescence or otherwise, to any person whose right to bring a suit may not be barred by virtue of this Act.

XVII. Act not to extend to public property, nor to suits for the recovery of public claims.—This Act shall not extend to any public property or right, nor to any suits for the recovery of the public revenue, or for any public claim whatever, but such suits shall continue to be governed by the laws or rules of limitation now in force.

XVIII. Act not to apply to suits now pending, or to suits instituted within two years.—Suits afterwards instituted to be governed by this Act.—All suits that may be now pending, or that shall be instituted within the period of two years from the date of the passing of this Act, shall be tried and determined as if this Act had not been passed; but all suits to which the provisions of this Act are applicable that shall be instituted after the expiration of the said period shall be governed by this Act, and no other law of limitation, any Statute, Act, or Regulation now in force notwithstanding.

XIX. Proceedings for enforcing judgments, &c., of Supreme Courts to be taken within twelve years.—Proviso as to judgments now in force.—No proceeding shall be taken to enforce any judgment, decree, or order of any court established by royal charter, but within twelve years next after a present right to enforce the same shall have accrued to some persons capable of releasing the same, unless in the meantime such judgment, decree, or order shall have been duly revived, or some part of the principal money secured by such judgment, decree, or order, or some interest thereon shall have been paid, or some acknowledgment of the right thereto shall have been given in writing, signed by the person by whom the same shall be payable or his agent, to the person entitled thereto or his agent; and in any such case no proceeding shall be brought to enforce the said judgment, decree, or order, but within twelve years after such revivor, payment, or acknowledgment, or the latest of such revivors, payments, or acknowledgments as the case may be: Provided that for three years next after the passing of this Act, every judgment, decree, and order which may be in force at the date of the passing of this Act shall be governed by the law now in force, anything therein contained notwithstanding.

XX. Time for enforcing execution of judgment, &c., of a Civil Court not established by royal charter.—No process of execution shall issue from any court not established by royal charter to enforce any judgment, decree, or order of such court, unless some proceeding shall have been taken to enforce such judgment, decree, or order, or to keep the same in force within three years next preceding the application for such execution.

XXI. Preceding section not to apply to judgment, &c., in force at the time of the passing of this Act.—Nothing in the preceding section shall apply to any judgment, decree, or order in force at the time of the passing of this Act, but process of execution may be issued either within the time now limited by law for issuing process of execution thereon, or within three years next after the passing of this Act whichever shall first expire.

XXII. Time for execution of a summary award of Civil Court or revenue authority.—No process of execution shall issue to enforce any summary decision or award of any of the Civil Courts not established by royal charter, or of any revenue authority, unless some proceeding shall have been taken to enforce such decision, or award, or to keep the same in force within one year next preceding the application for such execution.

XXIII. Preceding section not to apply to summary awards in force at the passing of this Act.—Nothing in the preceding section shall apply to any summary decision or award in force at the time of the passing of this Act, but process of execution may be issued either within the time now limited by law for issuing process of execution thereon or within two years next after the passing of this Act, whichever shall first expire.

XXIV. Operation of Act—Trial of pending suits, &c., in any non-regulation Province or place to which the Act is extended.—This Act shall take effect throughout the Presidencies of Bengal, Madras, and Bombay, including the Presidency towns, and the Straits' Settlement; but shall not take effect in any non-regulation province or place until the same shall be extended thereto by public notification by the Governor-General in Council, or by the Local Government to which such province or place is subordinate. Whenever this Act shall be extended to any non-regulation province or place by the Governor-General in Council, or by the Local Government to which such province or place is subordinate, all suits which, within such province or place, shall be pending at the date of such notification, or shall be instituted within the period of two years from the date thereof, shall be tried and determined as if this Act had not been passed; but all suits to which the provisions of this Act are applicable, that shall be instituted within such province or place after the expiration of the said period, shall be governed by this Act and by no other law of limitation, any Statute, Act, or Regulation, now in force notwithstanding.

INDEX.

C

E.

N.

O.